C000178743

THE
BRITISH
FIELD MARSHALS

"... humbly beseeching all noble lords and ladies, with all other estates, of what estate or degree they be of, that shall see and read in this said book, that they take the good and honest acts in their remembrance and follow the same. Wherein they shall find many joyous and pleasant histories, and noble and renowned acts of humanity, gentleness and chivalries. For herein may be seen noble chivalry, courtesy, humanity, friendliness, hardiness, love, friendship, cowardice, murder, hate, virtue and sin . . . with many wonderful histories and adventures"

William Caxton's Preface to LE MORTE D'ARTHUR, by Sir Thomas Malory, Kt.

THE BRITISH FIELD MARSHALS 1736-1997

A BIOGRAPHICAL DICTIONARY

by

T. A. HEATHCOTE

With a Foreword by

GENERAL THE LORD GUTHRIE OF CRAIGIEBANK
GCB LVO OBE DL

CHIEF OF THE DEFENCE STAFF 1997–2001

Pen & Sword
MILITARY

First published in Great Britain in 1999
Reprinted in 2012 in this format by
Pen & Sword Military
an imprint of
Pen & Sword Books Ltd
47 Church Street
Barnsley
South Yorkshire
S70 2AS

Copyright © T. A Heathcote 1999 and 2012

ISBN 978 1 84884 881 8

The right of T. A Heathcote to be identified as Author of this Work has been asserted by him
in accordance with the Copyright, Designs and Patents Act 1988.

A CIP catalogue record for this book is
available from the British Library

All rights reserved. No part of this book may be reproduced or transmitted in any form or by
any means, electronic or mechanical including photocopying, recording or by any information
storage and retrieval system, without permission from the Publisher in writing.

Typeset in Plantin by
Phoenix Typesetting, Auldgirth, Dumfriesshire

Printed and bound in England by
CPI Group (UK) Ltd, Croydon, CR0 4YY

Pen & Sword Books Ltd incorporates the Imprints of Pen & Sword Aviation, Pen & Sword
Family History, Pen & Sword Maritime, Pen & Sword Military, Pen & Sword Discovery,
Wharncliffe Local History, Wharncliffe True Crime, Wharncliffe Transport, Pen & Sword Select,
Pen & Sword Military Classics, Leo Cooper, The Praetorian Press, Remember When, Seaforth
Publishing and Frontline Publishing

For a complete list of Pen & Sword titles please contact
PEN & SWORD BOOKS LIMITED
47 Church Street, Barnsley, South Yorkshire, S70 2AS, England
E-mail: enquiries@pen-and-sword.co.uk
Website: www.pen-and-sword.co.uk

Dedicated, by permission of the Pageantmaster, to the officers of the Royal Naval Reserve, the Royal Marine Reserve, the Territorial Army, the Royal Auxiliary Air Force and the Royal Air Force Volunteer Reserve who act as marshals at the Lord Mayor of London's Show.

CONTENTS

Tables:

Bibliography   343

Index   356

FOREWORD
by
GENERAL THE LORD GUTHRIE OF CRAIGIEBANK
GCB LVO OBE DL
CHIEF OF THE DEFENCE STAFF 1997–2001

I was intrigued for several good reasons when I learnt that Dr Tony Heathcote was compiling a biographical dictionary of the men who have been appointed Field Marshal in the British Army. No one who has pursued a military career, as I have for over forty years, can have failed to be fascinated by those who reached "the top of the tree". There has always been an aura of magic surrounding those who actually found the baton in their knapsack. It immediately struck me as an inspired idea to bring all the holders of this coveted rank together in one book. The timing had to be entirely appropriate, as, given the suspension of the rank under what might euphemistically be termed "normal circumstances", there was a good chance that the work would not only be definitive but might well remain so.

I have always strongly believed that the study of military history is an essential aid to any soldier's career. Did not Napoleon urge his officers to "study the great captains"? A work covering the careers of the great – and, equally important, the not so great – captains of our military past would be of considerable value. As I read the draft, it came to me that here was the complete history of the British Army over the last 250 years.

Two other points struck me at the same time. First, any fears that one might have that this was a dry reference work were quickly dispelled. The author writes with a sharply observant pen and, while there is a mass of detail, his text is greatly enlivened by anecdotes. Secondly, what diverse characters have held this rank! It is natural that initially the reader will be tempted to turn to the household names such as Wellington, Haig and Montgomery. But there is much to be gained by delving into the entries covering such colourful characters as King Ernest of Hanover, Sir Hugh Gough, Charles Earl of Lucan and many others, according to individual taste!

I can only add my sincere admiration for Tony Heathcote's achievement in compiling this fascinating and invaluable book. He was certainly well qualified for the task, having served at the Royal Military Academy, Sandhurst, as Curator for many years. It is worth recording here the superb contribution that he and other members of the Academic Staff at Sandhurst have made over the years.

I am delighted and honoured to be associated to such a worthwhile literary and historical project.

PREFACE AND
ACKNOWLEDGEMENTS

The aim of these biographies is to give an outline of the military careers of the field marshals of the British Army, with (so as to put the flesh of humanity on the dry bones of chronology) as much detail as space permits of their personal and private lives. Entries generally contain information relating to the dates and places of their subjects' birth and death; their family background and the number of their siblings; their marriages and children; their education; the dates of their first commissions and subsequent promotions; their regimental and staff appointments; their campaigns and battles; their commands and their other public appointments. Regiments are recorded at length because, to a soldier, his regiment is his family writ large. The dates of peerages, baronetcies or knighthoods are given when their award resulted in a change of style or title. Other honours and awards, including degrees, civil distinctions, county lieutenancies or appointments of an honorary or largely ceremonial nature, are omitted, following the principle set out by W.S.Gilbert (himself a deputy lieutenant for Middlesex) in *The Gondoliers*. ("On ev'ry side field marshals gleamed, small beer were Lords Lieutenant deemed.")

The presence of an officer in person in a battle, siege or other combat is indicated by the word "at" before the name or place of the engagement, the date of which is given in brackets. Numerals in **bold** within square brackets **[nn]** indicate the place of a field marshal in the seniority list (Table 1) which also gives the date when each field marshal was promoted to that rank. I have assumed a general knowledge on the part of the reader of the outcome and relative importance of battles and campaigns, of the organization of the army, and of the social, political and military history of the times in which the field marshals lived. To do otherwise would make this work not a set of biographies, but a history of the British Army and the British State in the story of which so many of the field marshals played an important part.

I take this opportunity of acknowledging my debt to everyone on whose help I have depended in writing this book, beginning with my much valued former colleague Matthew Midlane, Director of Studies at the Royal Military Academy Sandhurst, for his kind sponsorship of my continued access to the RMAS Central Library. My thanks are also due to Diane Hiller and Sarah Oliver, of the RMAS Central Library, for their efficiency in supplying many of the publications on which I have relied in this work, and for their invariable helpfulness to all their readers. I also wish to express my gratitude to all those who have contributed their time or scholarship to my research or who have otherwise encouraged me by their interest in this project, including especially His Grace the Duke of Argyll; Professor Robert O'Neal, Chichele Professor of Military History, Oxford; Professor I.F.W. Beckett of the Department of History at Luton University; Dr Paul Harris of the Department of War Studies at the RMAS; Dr John Sweetman, late Head of Political and Social Studies, RMAS; Alastair Campbell of Airds, Unicorn Pursuivant at Inveraray Castle; the Reverend Canon Tim Sedgeley, Vicar of St Mary's Church, Walton on Thames; Marjory Szurko, Librarian of Keble College, Oxford; Randolph Vine Esq, of the Huguenot Society, University College, London; Martine de Lee, Curator of the Staff College Collections, Camberley; Anne Ferguson, Media Resources Librarian at the RMAS; Tina Pittock, Curator of the Airborne Forces Museum, Aldershot; Angela Bolger, Curator of the Taplow Court Collection; G E Hughes Esq, Assistant Curator for Audley End, English Heritage; John A Flower Esq, of Penshurst; Colonel Gordon Spate, formerly TA Colonel for London and South East Districts, and to all those field marshals now on the retired or half-pay lists who were kind enough to comment on the relevant entries in this book while it was in preparation. I am especially grateful to Dr Gary Sheffield, Senior Lecturer in War Studies at the Joint Service Command and Staff College, Bracknell, for reading the work in draft and for making many valuable suggestions. All errors of fact or interpretation, however, are entirely those of the writer.

T.A.Heathcote.
Camberley, September, 1999

INTRODUCTION

In March 1995 the British Ministry of Defence received the report of an Independent Review of the Armed Forces' Manpower, Career and Remuneration, headed by an eminent businessman, Sir Michael Betts. The Betts Report made a number of far-reaching recommendations, of which only one was implemented immediately. This was the proposal that the "five-star" ranks of field marshal and its equivalent in the other Armed Services should disappear, on the grounds that they were unnecessary in relation to the size of these forces and that none of the close allies of the United Kingdom used such ranks. In adopting this recommendation, the Ministry of Defence added the gloss that this rank was appropriate only for those who had commanded large armies in successful operations or who had been at the head of the British Army in a major war. The rank was not formally abolished, but officers were no longer to be promoted to it except in the event of a major war or other special circumstances.

Nevertheless, a study of the history of this rank in the British Army reveals that, in former times, neither the number nor even the existence of British field marshals depended upon the Army's size. Likewise, high command in war (still less victory in battle) was not previously considered an essential qualification for promotion to this rank. In 1736, when the first two British field marshals were appointed, the British Army numbered some 60,000 regular soldiers. In 1995, it numbered about 112,000. The roll of the 138 British field marshals includes four British sovereigns, two British royal consorts, thirteen foreign monarchs (including six emperors, two of Japan, and one each of Germany, Austria-Hungary, Russia and Ethiopia, and seven kings, two each of the Belgians and of Nepal, and one each of Hanover, the Netherlands and Spain) and one marshal of France. One, Jan Smuts, was Prime Minister of the Union of South Africa and an officer of the South Africa Defence Force. Another, Sir Thomas Blamey, was a field marshal in the Australian Military Forces. Of the remaining 118, only thirty-eight held independent commands of any size in the field and only twelve were

1

either Commanders-in-Chief of the British Army or Chiefs of the Imperial General Staff during a major war.

The word "marshal" is derived from the Germanic roots *marho*, "horse" (cf. mare) and *skalko*, "servant". Like its Latin-derived cousin "constable" (*comes stabuli*, companion of the stable), its meaning has changed over the years and the title is now given to a variety of offices, ranging from those of distinguished military commanders at one extreme to police officers or stewards at the other. The first officer to be styled field marshal, in the sense of a general of the highest grade, was Count Johann Tilly von Tserclas, commander of the armies of the Catholic League and the Holy Roman Empire during the Thirty Years War, who was appointed to this rank in 1607. The rank was introduced into the Swedish Army by Gustavus Adolphus in 1621, into the army of Brandenburg-Prussia by Frederick William, the Great Elector, in 1658 and into the Russian Army by Peter the Great in 1716. The rank of marshal or field marshal has been awarded at various times in the armies of Australia, Austria-Hungary, Bavaria, China, Finland, France, Germany, India, Italy, Japan, the Netherlands, New Zealand, Pakistan, the Philippines, Poland, Portugal, Prussia, Russia, the Soviet Union, Sweden, Turkey, Uganda, the Ukraine, the United Kingdom and Yugoslavia. Each army had its own standards for appointment to this rank, unrelated to the size of their forces, or to its existence in the armies of their close allies. The highest rank in the United States Army, General of the Army (analogous with Admiral of the Fleet) was not created until the Second World War. Like that of Marshal of France, the rank of General of the Army is reserved for generals who have commanded great armies with success in a major war.

The rank of field marshal was introduced into the British Army by King George II in January 1736, as a means of rewarding the services of his two most senior generals, the Earl of Orkney and the Duke of Argyll. In principle, the rank of field marshal was one bestowed by the monarch without regard to seniority, but in practice it was rare for this not to be taken into account. Of the first two British field marshals, Orkney, as the senior ranking general, was promoted two days ahead of Argyll, so ensuring that their relative positions in the Army List remained unchanged. It is conceivable that the introduction of this rank owed something to a desire on the part of the monarch to conciliate Argyll, a great Scottish nobleman whose support was of value to his government, and that Orkney was promoted so that Argyll could be given this new rank. Two more field marshals were created in July 1739, bringing the total in post to three, as Orkney had died in 1737. Viscount Cobham, the last survivor of these three, died in 1749. There were no field marshals in the British Army from then until November 1757, when the three most senior generals in the Amy were promoted to this rank, with the aim of recognizing the position of the third, Sir John Ligonier, as Commander-in-Chief. In 1763, when only one field marshal (Ligonier himself) was still alive, George III promoted the senior ranking general, Lord Tyrawley. He made no other such promotions in the first thirty years of his reign, so that after Tyrawley died in 1773 the rank of field marshal in the British Army was again left vacant. It was revived shortly after the beginning of the French Revolutionary War, when the three senior generals of the Army (of whom the second was the King's brother, the Duke of Gloucester) were made field marshals in October 1793. None of these was expected to go on campaign, but the existence of the rank allowed the King's second son, the Duke of York, to be promoted field marshal in 1795. Another seven generals were promoted in July 1796, bringing the number actually in post to nine (two of the three promoted in 1793 having by this time died). The number of field marshals then gradually declined until, in 1807, there were only two (the Duke of York and the Duke of Kent). This figure rose to three in June 1813, when Wellington received his baton. Wellington was the first to be awarded a baton of the modern pattern (designed by the Prince Regent himself) covered with red velvet and surmounted by a gold figure of St George slaying a dragon. Previously field marshals and other commanding generals, if they did so at all, had carried a plain baton of polished wood with yellow metal ferrules. George IV promoted the two senior generals in the Army to mark his accession in 1821, bringing the total in post to eight, of whom only three were not royal personages. William IV followed this precedent on his own accession in 1830, by which time both of those promoted by his predecessor in 1821 had died. In November 1846 the three senior generals in the Army were promoted to field marshal to celebrate the fifth birthday of the Prince of Wales (the future Edward VII). As two of those promoted in 1830 had died, the number of "non-royal" field marshals in post then amounted to three. Of these three, Sir George Nugent died in 1849, the Duke of Wellington died in 1852 and the Marquess of Anglesey died in April 1854. Until the promotion of Lord Raglan in November 1854, in recognition of his command in the Crimea, there were for a period of seven months only two field marshals in the British Army, neither of them professional soldiers (one was the Prince Consort and the other the King of the Netherlands). This was once more the case from Raglan's death in July 1855 until October 1855, when the three senior generals in the Army were promoted to field marshal.

3

Thereafter the number of field marshals rose gradually, with four being created in January 1868 to mark the thirtieth anniversary of Victoria's accession and three in June 1877 to mark her Golden Jubilee. The accessions of Edward VII and George V were also marked by the promotion on each occasion of their two senior generals. George V, Edward VIII and George VI all assumed the rank of field marshal on their respective accessions, though no previous British sovereigns (including George II, who appointed the first British field marshals and was himself a capable general) had thought it necessary to add to their royal dignities in this way. In August 1914 the British Army List contained twelve field marshals, including King George V, the Duke of Connaught and the Emperors of Germany and Austria-Hungary. Four field marshals received their promotion in 1919, in recognition of their services in the First World War, though three pre-war field marshals had died in the meantime. Between 1894 and 1925 the senior retired officer of the Indian Army was appointed a field marshal on the British half-pay list. In 1925 one field marshal's post was created on the Indian establishment, in recognition of the Indian Army's contribution to British victory in the First World War.

In September 1939 there were twelve British field marshals, comprising nine professional soldiers (including the Duke of Connaught) and four reigning or former monarchs (King George VI, the Duke of Windsor, the exiled King of Spain and the Emperor of Japan). In 1946, after the end of the Second World War, there were sixteen, made up of thirteen professional soldiers, King George VI, the Duke of Windsor and the Prime Minister of South Africa. The practice that thereafter developed of awarding (or at least offering) a baton to every officer who served as Chief of the Imperial General Staff (later Chief of the General Staff) resulted in one new field marshal being appointed, on average, every three years. In 1995, when it was decided that this practice would be discontinued, the total stood at eleven, made up of one regular officer in post and seven on retired or half-pay, two royal dukes and the King of Nepal (the first and only honorary British field marshal).

An analysis of the 138 brief lives that make up this book shows that the qualities and attributes that gained an officer promotion to the rank of field marshal in the British Army varied significantly over a period of two centuries. Napoleon, who declared that every soldier carried a marshal's baton in his knapsack, would ask *"Est-il heureux?"* (Is he lucky?) when any general was recommended to him. It is a truism that life is a lottery and that, in any profession, being in the right place at the right time is essential for success. Likewise, being in the wrong place at the wrong time means that an individual never has the chance to demonstrate his or her talent. In any walk of life it is often a matter of luck that an opportunity for promotion occurs. The occasion might arise either through some personal event, such as the misfortune of another, whose death or departure creates an unexpected vacancy, or through great impersonal developments, particularly, for the military, those resulting in war. At the personal level, luck might place an individual of proven worth and efficiency under a vindictive or unsympathetic senior at a critical time, so that the chance of a well-deserved promotion is lost. With equal caprice, it will allow others (sometimes of far lesser merit) to prosper through the operation of cronyism or similar vested interests. At the impersonal level, a soldier is more likely to rise in his profession if his star allows him to serve at a time when there are wars in which he may demonstrate his military virtues. Apart from luck, the innate qualities essential for success in a military career demonstrably include a robust constitution, energy and, above all, ambition, for, as Francis Bacon wrote, "to take a soldier without ambition is to pull off his spurs". The evidence of these biographies suggests that, for men whose living lies in their swords, the prospect of the high pay and high offices that accompany high rank is a powerful incentive to ambition. This is not to say that the prospect of pecuniary benefit is the only spur to promotion. Every society offers a range of rewards to those who reach the peak of their profession. Even academics have been known to aspire to some recognition of their achievements. Military men have the added prospect of glory. In most countries there are significantly more statues of soldiers than of civilians.

To become a British field marshal an officer had, for the most part, to be lucky more in his battlefield survival than in his battlefield success. Of the 118 who served as regular officers in the British military, 107 stood up in battle to be shot at, most of them more than once, some of them many times. The palm for the greatest number of combats must go to Sir Henry Norman, who recorded his presence at some eighty engagements, ranging from pitched battles and sieges to skirmishes and affairs of outposts. The first field marshal to be appointed in the British Army, the Earl of Orkney, took part in his first active operations in Ireland in 1690. It is a reflection on the intractability of the Irish Question that the latest field marshal to be appointed in the British Army, Lord Inge, took part in his last active operations in Ireland in 1976. In the intervening period of almost three centuries British field marshals took part in some 320 recorded engagements in almost every campaign in which the British Army was involved and some in which it was not. The future King George VI served in the Royal Navy at the battle of Jutland and the future Duke of Edinburgh served at the battle of Cape Matapan. The Emperor Francis Joseph of Austria commanded in person at the battle of St Lucia (Verona) in 1848, as did the Emperor Haile Selassie of Ethiopia at Amba Aradam in 1936. Jan Smuts, a future Prime Minister of the Union of South Africa, fought against the British forces in the South African War. Six future field marshals fought under Marlborough at Malplaquet. Eleven were present at the storming of Badajoz and fifteen at Vittoria, where Wellington earned his baton. Ten served under Wellington at Waterloo. Sixteen served in the Crimea. A total of fifty-seven future field marshals received battlefield wounds, some losing a limb or the sight of an eye. Twenty-four were wounded on two or more occasions. Another eight became prisoners of war. At least three fought in duels.

In any of these encounters, the slightest deviation in the path of a blow or a missile could have ensured that the future field marshal never lived to gain his baton. Not only the violence of the enemy could bring a career to an early close; a soldier had also to contend with extremes of climate and with disease. A microbe could kill as surely as a musket and did not need a war in order to do so. Finally, in the period when promotion was determined by seniority and there was no fixed retirement age, a British general needed not only luck, but also longevity. Unless he was one of the few who were promoted regardless of seniority, in direct recognition of victory in battle, he had only to outlive his contemporaries in order to reach field marshal's rank. Thus Sir George Howard, first commissioned at the age of five, finally became a field marshal at the age of 73. Twenty-three field marshals were promoted while in their eighties. The youngest non-royal field marshal was the Duke of Wellington, promoted at the age of 44 for his victories in the Peninsular War. The oldest was the Marquess of Drogheda, promoted at the age of 91 for his seniority in the Army List. Nevertheless, even after achieving his high rank, a field marshal did not become immune to the hazards of his profession. Lord Raglan died from the rigours of campaign while commanding his army before Sevastopol. Lord Kitchener was lost at sea with HMS *Hampshire* off the Hebrides. Sir Henry Wilson was shot dead by Irish extremists outside his own house in London.

Some of the sociological information revealed in these biographies merely confirms previous studies of officers of the British Army. Most were younger sons. Many came from the landed gentry, especially from families belonging to the Anglo-Irish Protestant Ascendancy, and several from the nobility. A high proportion were the sons of military officers, but two were the sons of bank managers, one of a saddler, one of a solicitor's clerk and one of a village tailor. The details of regimental commissions show the extent to which officers moved between regiments to improve their career prospects. Other commissions show how officers could obtain extra-regimental promotion by brevet (to a titular but unpaid rank above that authorized by unit establishment) or by gaining a staff appointment (which carried extra pay). Many future field marshals obtained early promotion in these ways. These biographies also confirm the perception that an officer who serves with some kind of élite is more likely to be promoted than one who, while equally brave and efficient, remains in a less dashing branch. No officer reached the rank of field marshal other than from the cavalry, the Royal Armoured Corps, the Royal Artillery, the Royal Engineers or the infantry.

Students of social history will note that a good number of field marshals were married to women described as being of strong character or as contributing to their husbands' official duties through their personal influence or contacts. In a number of cases these ladies married to disoblige their parents. It may also be noted that most field marshals married and many produced large families. Some field marshals had children from more than one marriage. Before the advent of modern anaesthetics and antiseptics most wives endured in childbed a greater certainty of pain and as great a risk of death as did their husbands in the battlefield. In the same way that many officers never lived to reach high rank, many officers' wives, spirited or otherwise, never survived their last pregnancy to see their husbands achieve the honours to which they might have contributed. A noticeably high percentage of field marshals had mothers who were forceful characters, either married to weak husbands or widowed and left to bring up a young family single-handed. In respect of their own families, the lives of field marshals, like those of other men, demonstrate the truth of Bacon's assertion that "He that hath wife and children hath given hostages to fortune".

Other aspects of the field marshals' lives may be less well known. Eighteen members of the British Royal Family became field marshals, either as sovereigns, consorts, princes or royal dukes. Four field marshals (Conway, Hardinge, Kitchener and Alexander) sat in Cabinet as Secretaries of State for departments normally headed by civilian politicians. One (the Duke of Wellington) was Prime Minister. Twenty-one field marshals were members of the House of Commons at Westminster. Thirty-three held office as governor-generals, governors or high commissioners of self-governing dominions or other territories under British rule. Two field marshals (Jan Smuts and Sir Evelyn Wood) were qualified as barristers-at-law. Two more (Sir Thomas Blamey and Lord Byng) became policemen. Another (Chamberlain) was the inventor of snooker. Sir Evelyn Wood was injured by a giraffe and Sir Gerald Templer was wounded by a piano.

This dictionary of the British field marshals seeks to serve several readerships. To historians, it is presented as a work of synthesis rather than analysis, intended as a convenient reference book for use in further research. For cataloguers in museums, libraries, archives and art collections, it summarizes the field marshals' careers and services. To those who simply enjoy military history, these brief biographies are offered to supplement an existing level of knowledge and to indicate further fields of study for exploration. Other writers or researchers may find, in the lives of these field marshals, ideas for fuller biographies, documentaries, screenplays or historical fiction, in which, indeed, many of them have already appeared. To soldiers of all kinds, past, present and future, regular or volunteer, it is meant as a roll call of those officers who reached the highest rank that the British Army had to offer.

THE FIELD MARSHALS' BIOGRAPHIES

ADOLPHUS FREDERICK
HRH 1st Duke of Cambridge KG, GCB, GCMG, GCH
(1774–1850) **[26]**

Prince Adolphus Frederick, the tenth child and seventh son of King George III, was born in Buckingham Palace, London, on 24 February 1774 and was educated in England and Hanover, including a period at the University of Göttingen in 1786. During the French Revolutionary War he served under the command of his brother, the Duke of York **[15]**, in the Flanders campaigns of 1793 and 1794, first as a volunteer and then as a colonel of the Hanoverian Guards. Adolphus Frederick became a lieutenant general on 24 August 1798 and was created Duke of Cambridge on 24 November 1801. He was appointed colonel-in-chief of the King's German Legion in November 1803. The Duke of Cambridge was given command of the London Military District in 1804 and became colonel of the Coldstream Guards on 5 September 1805. He was promoted to general on 25 September 1803 and to field marshal (superseding forty generals senior to him) on 26 November 1813. Cambridge returned to Hanover in 1814 and, after the Electorate was raised to the status of a kingdom, was appointed Viceroy in November 1816. Despite his eccentric ways (among them the habit of speaking loudly and incessantly in conversation and repeating every comment three times) Cambridge proved himself to be a prudent ruler and conceded sufficient constitutional reforms to prevent Hanover being much affected by the revolutionary year of 1830. In June 1818, following the death of Princess Charlotte of Wales, Cambridge married Princess Augusta, third daughter of the Landgrave of Hesse-Cassel. They produced three daughters and a son, George, **[45]** who was for a time George III's only living legitimate grandchild. Cambridge was appointed colonel-in-chief of the 60th Rifles in January 1827. He remained Viceroy of Hanover until 1837, when his eldest surviving brother, the Duke of Cumberland **[25]**, succeeded to

9

the Hanoverian throne on the death of William IV. Cambridge and his family then returned to London. He died on 8 July 1850 and was buried at Kew.

ALBERT I
ALBERT LEOPOLD CLEMENT MARIE MEINRAD, HM
King of the Belgians, KG, GCB (1875–1934) **[94]**

Prince Albert, the second son of Phillipe, Count of Flanders and his countess, Marie of Hohenzollern-Sigmaringen, was born at Brussels on 8 April 1875. Count Phillipe was the younger brother of King Leopold II of the Belgians and had became heir to the throne on the death of the King's only son, Leopold, Duke of Brabant, in 1869. When the Count's elder son, Baudouin, died of influenza in 1891, Albert took his place in the line of succession. Albert attended the Ecole Royale Militaire at Brussels in 1891–92 and was commissioned as a lieutenant in the Belgian Grenadiers in December 1892. Like many other princes, he relished his military service and the comradeship of his brother-officers. He reached the rank of major in 1896. Belgian public opinion had turned against Leopold II, partly because of misgovernment in the Congo Free State (of which he was the personal ruler before its transfer to the Belgian government in 1908) and partly because of his scandalous private life and consequent estrangement from his wife and daughters. The Count of Flanders having died in 1905, Leopold II was succeeded by Albert on 17 December 1909. Happily married with a wife and a young family, Albert was welcomed as a contrast from his unpopular uncle. He sought to reconcile the different social classes and language groups among his subjects, but opposed demands for an extension of the franchise, arguing that a wider spread of literacy should come first. In foreign policy he was primarily concerned to preserve Belgian neutrality in any war between Germany and France and continually urged on his ministers the need to improve the state of the nation's defences. Albert refused to give up his constitutional position as commander-in-chief so as to allow this post to be held by a professional soldier, but supported a reorganization of the Army's command system and the creation, in 1910, of a general staff.

With the outbreak of the First World War Albert responded to the German demand for free passage through Belgium by ordering general mobilization on 31 July 1914. He assumed personal command of the Belgian Army, but was unable to resist the overwhelming German advance. By mid–October 1914 the Belgian government controlled only a small corner of his kingdom around Nieuport, together with the area held by the British around Ypres. He established his military HQ on the Belgian coast at La Panne and gradually rebuilt the Belgian Army from an effective strength of 53,000 at the end of 1914 to 170.000 by early 1918. Albert remained on the Western Front throughout the war and made frequent visits to his troops in the trenches. He made ascents in observation balloons and flew in aeroplanes over the German lines, where he was the only C-in-C of the war to come under enemy fire. In August 1918 Albert told Marshal Foch [88], the Allied Supreme Commander, that the time was ripe for a limited Belgian offensive in West Flanders. Foch then offered him command of Army Group Flanders, to be made up of the 4th Belgian Division, three French divisions and the British Second Army. Previously Albert had kept his army as a single command and had refused to accept any kind of Allied control over his forces. In consequence, he was not invited to attend meetings of the Allied War Council at Versailles. Nevertheless, on 11 September 1918, he accepted Foch's offer and, after joining the general Allied offensive two weeks later, reached Bruges late in October 1918.

In the post-war Treaty of Versailles Belgium's interests tended to be overlooked by her larger allies. Throughout the war Albert took the position that he was fighting in response to his international obligation under the 1839 Treaty of London, which not only guaranteed Belgian neutrality but also required Belgium to defend it. He hoped to obtain some reward for this at German expense, but apart from a priority in the queue for reparations, gained nothing in Europe except for a small area of Wallonia that had been ceded to Prussia in 1815. Overseas, the German Central African colonies of Ruanda and Burundi, captured during the war by troops from the Belgian Congo, were awarded to Belgium as mandates from the League of Nations. In the post-war settlement Belgium was freed from the previous obligation of neutrality imposed by the Treaty of London. At home Albert was faced with the problems of rebuilding the Belgian economy and restoring the devastated battle zones. On his return to Brussels he proclaimed a new constitution with a democratic franchise. He denied that this was due to fear of popular revolution and declared that it reflected the wartime aspirations of his soldiers and people. He accepted the long-standing demand for a Flemish university, but tension continued between the Flemings and the French-speaking Walloons. The Depression of the 1930s caused much hardship, with the rise of National Socialism in Germany adding further uncertainty to the political scene.

In August 1915 King Albert became colonel-in-chief of the 5th

(Princess Charlotte of Wales's) Dragoon Guards, so renewing a family connection with this regiment established by his great-uncle, King Leopold I of the Belgians [28]. On 4 July 1921 he was appointed a British field marshal and thus became the second Belgian monarch to hold this rank. After the 5th Dragoon Guards were amalgamated with the 6th (Inniskilling) Dragoons in 1922 to form the 5th /6th Dragoons (later the 5th Royal Inniskilling Dragoon Guards), Albert remained in post as colonel-in-chief of the new regiment until his death. Always a keen sportsman, he sought relaxation from his official duties in outdoor pursuits, especially in rock-climbing. On 17 February 1934, climbing alone on the riverside cliffs at Marche-les-Dames, King Albert was killed in a fall. He was buried in the royal mausoleum at Laeken and was succeeded by his son, Leopold III.

ALBERT
FRANCIS ALBERT CHARLES AUGUSTUS EMMANUEL, HRH Prince Consort, HSH Prince of Saxe-Coburg-Gotha, Duke of Saxony, KG, KT, KP, GCB, GCMG, KSI (1819–1861) [33]

Prince Albert, the second son of Ernest, Duke of Saxe-Coburg-Gotha, was born at Schloss Rosenau, Coburg, on 26 August 1819. Following his parents' separation and divorce amid allegations by the duchess that her husband abused her and by the duke that his wife was an adulteress, Albert spent much of his infancy in the custody of his paternal grandmother, the dowager duchess. This lady, together with her younger son, Leopold, future King of the Belgians [28], brought up Albert from an early age as a potential husband for Princess Victoria of Kent (heiress to the British throne), after the dynastic ambitions of their house were thwarted by the death of Leopold's first wife, Princess Charlotte of Wales. Albert attended Bonn University in 1837–39 and, by King Leopold's arrangement, visited Windsor in 1839. The young Victoria, Queen since 1837, fell in love with Albert, whose handsome appearance and charming manner made him an attractive match, and they were married on 10 February 1840. He went on to play an important part in the life of his adopted country, guiding the Queen's political decisions, promoting science and industry (especially through the Great Exhibition of 1851) and taking an interest in social problems. He had to contend with the anti-foreign prejudices of his wife's subjects and the opposition of her ministers, who resisted the Queen's wish for him to be given the title Prince Consort until she eventually granted it by the use of her Royal Prerogative. His last act of statesmanship was to modify a draft despatch from London to Washington that might have brought the United Kingdom into the American Civil War on the Confederate side.

Albert was made a field marshal on 8 February 1840, two days before his wedding. At the end of April 1840 he was appointed colonel of the 11th Hussars, the regiment that had escorted him on his arrival at Dover and was then given the title "Prince Albert's Own". In 1843 Albert became colonel and captain general of the Honourable Artillery Company of London. At first he took little part in army affairs, other than by discouraging the practice of duelling among officers, though he took an interest in military uniform and helped design a more functional head-dress, the 1844 pattern shako (commonly dubbed the "Albert pot"). In 1850 the Duke of Wellington [24] urged Albert to take over from him as Commander-in-Chief. Albert felt unable to agree for constitutional reasons. He nevertheless thereafter made a serious study of the British Army and echoed Wellington's opinion that it was not really an army at all, but a collection of regiments. During the Crimean War he advocated the use of the latest technology to improve the lot of the troops in the field and was responsible for the concept and design of the Victoria Cross. Albert was colonel of the Scots Fusilier Guards (later the Scots Guards) from 25 April 1842 and of the Grenadier Guards from 23 September 1842. He was also colonel-in-chief of the 60th Rifles from 15 August 1850 and of the Rifle Brigade from 23 September 1842. After his death the latter corps was given the additional title "the Prince Consort's Own". Prince Albert died at Windsor Castle, of a gastro-enteric affliction, on 14 December 1861 and was buried at Frogmore mausoleum.

ALEXANDER
The Honourable Sir HAROLD LEOFRIC GEORGE, Earl Alexander of Tunis, KG, GCB, OM, GCMG, CSI, DSO, MC (1891–1969) [113]

The Honourable Harold Alexander, third son of an Irish peer, the 4th Earl of Caledon, was born in Mayfair, London, on 10 December 1891. He was educated at Harrow School, where he joined the school's unit of the Volunteer Force and rose to the rank of corporal. At school, Alexander was given the nickname "Fat Boy", but, after joining the Army, was generally known to his contemporaries as "Alex". He entered the Royal Military College, Sandhurst, in 1910. Alexander became a cadet colour sergeant and passed out eighty-fifth in his batch of 172. He was commissioned on 23 September 1911 as a second lieutenant in the 1st Battalion, Irish Guards, and then served in London at regimental duty, with promotion to lieutenant on 5 December 1912. At the beginning of the First World War in August 1914 Alexander served as a platoon commander in the 1st Battalion, Irish Guards, during the retreat from Mons and at the first battle of Ypres, where he was wounded (1 November 1914). Invalided home, he was promoted to captain (temporary on 15 November 1914, substantive on 7 February 1915) in the newly-raised 2nd (Reserve) Battalion, Irish Guards. Alexander returned to the Western Front with this unit in August 1915 and was at Loos (25–30 September 1915), where he was awarded the MC. He was acting major and commanding officer of the 1st Battalion, Irish Guards, as a battle casualty replacement, for ten days at the end of October 1915, before returning to the 2nd Battalion as a company officer.

During the battle of the Somme Alexander was awarded the DSO for his conduct on 15 September 1916. He was promoted to acting major on 10 December 1916, when he rejoined the 1st Battalion, Irish Guards, as second-in-command. During May 1917 Alexander was once more this battalion's acting CO. He became a substantive major on 1 August 1917 and was promoted to acting lieutenant colonel on appointment as commanding officer of the 2nd Battalion, Irish Guards, on 15 October 1917. Alexander was slightly wounded in the third battle of Ypres (Passchendaele, 31 July–6 November 1917) and was at Bourlon Wood (27 November 1917) in the battle of Cambrai, where 320 of his 400-strong battalion became casualties. During the German offensive of Spring 1918 Alexander assumed acting command of the 4th Guards Brigade (23–30 March 1918). He commanded the 2nd Battalion, Irish Guards, at Hazebrouck (12–14 April 1918), where it suffered such heavy casualties that it undertook no further combat operations before hostilities ended on 11 November 1918.

After a period in London Alexander found employment in March 1919 with the Allied Relief Commission in a newly independent Poland. In May 1919 he moved on to the Allied Mission supervising the emergence of an independent Latvia. There he was given command of a force of ethnic Germans, whose communities had lived in Latvia for generations and who believed that they had the same right as the Latvian Balts to self-determination. Alexander became involved in a complicated series of operations in which troops of the German government, White Russians, Soviets and Baltic nationalists all took part. He was wounded by one of his own sentries on 9 October 1919, but recovered in time to wage a local campaign during the winter of 1919–1920. Alexander returned to the UK to become a substantive major and second-in-command of the 1st Battalion, Irish Guards, at Aldershot in May 1920. He was given command of the battalion, with promotion to substantive lieutenant colonel, on 14 May 1922. Alexander took this unit overseas to join the Army of Occupation at Constantinople, from where it went to Gibraltar in October 1922 and London in April 1923. He commanded it until 1926, when he entered the Staff College, Camberley. After qualifying as a trained staff officer, Alexander was given promotion to colonel, back-dated to 14 May 1926. In March 1928 he became Officer Commanding the Irish Guards Regimental District and 140th (4th London) Infantry Brigade in the Territorial Army. Alexander spent 1930 as a student at the Imperial Defence College, London, and in January 1931 obtained a temporary appointment as General Staff Officer, Grade 2, in the Directorate of Military Training at the War Office. On 14 October 1931 he married the twenty-six-year old Lady Margaret Bingham, younger daughter of the 5th Earl of Lucan and great-granddaughter of the 3rd Earl of Lucan [63] who had commanded the Cavalry Division at Balaklava. They later had a family of two sons and two daughters.

Between 1932 and 1934 Alexander served as GSO 1 at HQ Northern Command, York. He was then appointed to command the Nowshera Brigade on the North-West Frontier of India, with promotion to tempo-rary brigadier on 13 October 1934. During February–April 1935 Alexander commanded a punitive expedition against the Pathans in Malakand. In September 1935 he commanded his brigade in divisional-sized operations under Brigadier Claude Auchinleck [116], against the Mohmand Pathans. During this campaign, as in his previous wars, Alexander gained a reputation for always sharing the hardships and dangers of his men. He was noted as invariably reaching the mountain crests either with his troops or ahead of them. In a rare distinction for a middle-ranking officer of the British Army, Alexander was in 1935 appointed colonel of the 3rd Battalion, 2nd Punjab Regiment, in the Indian Army. He returned to England to be GOC-in-C Aldershot Command, with promotion to major general on 16 October 1937.

On mobilization for the Second World War in September 1939 Alexander became GOC 1st Division in the British Expeditionary Force sent to France. When the German offensive began on 10 May 1940 Alexander led his division in the advance into Belgium and the subse-quent retreat to Dunkirk, where he took over command of I Corps during the evacuation of the BEF and left, in the last destroyer, on 3 June 1940. On returning to the UK, he remained in command of

I Corps, deployed along the coasts of Yorkshire and Lincolnshire, until 13 July 1940 when he became GOC-in-C Southern Command. Alexander was promoted to lieutenant general (acting from 13 July 1940, substantive from December 1940) and remained in Southern Command until February 1942. He was promoted to general on 17 January 1942, with the award of the KCB. Sir Harold Alexander was then ordered to take command of the British land forces in Burma, where the Japanese were pressing on with a successful offensive. Sir Archibald Wavell [111], C-in-C, India, ordered Alexander to hold Rangoon. Alexander was unable to do so and abandoned the city on 6–7 March 1942. During the British retreat he took personal control of parties of troops in various local engagements and narrowly escaped capture. In mid-March he handed over his command to Lieutenant General W. J. Slim [117], prior to becoming C-in-C of all Allied forces in Burma on 27 March 1942. Alexander decided that he could not hold Mandalay and ordered Slim to retreat to India.

Alexander was one of the few defeated British generals to retain the confidence of the Prime Minister, Winston Churchill (a fellow Harrovian). He was recalled to the UK in July 1942 as commander-designate of the First Army in the Anglo-American invasion of French North Africa but, before this could take place, was appointed C-in-C Middle East. There his subordinates included General Sir Bernard Montgomery, the victor of El Alamein and commander of the Eighth Army. Alexander supported Montgomery and allowed him to claim sole credit for the subsequent British victories in North Africa. In February 1943 Alexander became commander of 18 Army Group and Deputy Supreme Allied Commander, Mediterranean. His capture of Tunis in May 1943 ended the Axis presence in Africa and was a victory of major strategic importance. He commanded the Allied invasions of Sicily in July 1943 and the Italian mainland in September 1943, where, at the end of 1943, he became commander of the Allied Group of Armies in Italy. Alexander made slow progress in the face of determined German resistance, difficult terrain, bad weather and the weakening of his forces in August 1944 by the diversion of French and American troops to southern France. Allied success was finally achieved on 29 April 1945 when he accepted the surrender of all enemy forces in northern Italy and the Tyrol. He was promoted to field marshal on 4 June 1944, handed over command in October 1945 and was raised to the peerage, becoming Viscount Alexander of Tunis, of Errigal, in January 1946.

Lord Alexander was appointed Governor-General of Canada in April 1946. He proved a popular and uncontroversial figure and fulfilled his duties with characteristic charm, establishing so successful a rapport with the Canadian people and government that his period of office, due to end in 1951, was extended by a further year. In 1952 Alexander was rewarded with the customary advancement of one rank in the peerage and became Earl Alexander of Tunis. On his return to the UK, he accepted the post of Minister of Defence in Churchill's second ministry. This ministry was at this time a co-ordinating body, working alongside three separate service departments, each headed by a separate cabinet minister. Churchill, who had been Minister of Defence in his wartime Cabinet as well as Prime Minister, kept control of all important defence matters in his own hands, so that Alexander (who only accepted the portfolio out of a sense of loyalty to Churchill) was left with little real power. Alexander, who disliked the shifts and intrigues associated with the conduct of political business, was glad to spend much of his time on overseas tours. He left the Cabinet in October 1954 and retired to his home at Winkfield Lodge, Berkshire, where he devoted himself to various good causes and supplemented his half-pay with a number of company directorships.

Alexander became colonel of the Irish Guards in August 1946 and retained this appointment until his death. He became honorary colonel of the London Irish Rifles in the Territorial Army in November 1949. Earl Alexander of Tunis died on 16 June 1969 at Wexham Park Hospital, near Slough, during an operation for a perforated aorta. He was buried in St Margaret's churchyard at Ridge, near his family home at Tytenhanger, near South Mimms, Hertfordshire. His eldest son, Shane, succeeded him as 2nd Earl.

ALFONSO XIII
HM King of Spain and the Indies, KG, GCVO
(1886–1941) **[98]**

King Alfonso XIII was born in Madrid on 17 May 1886, the posthumous and only son of Alfonso XII (a former gentleman cadet of the Royal Military College, Sandhurst) who died of tuberculosis at the age of 27. Alfonso XIII was therefore a king from the moment of his birth and his mother, Queen Maria Christina, acted as Regent until he came of age on 17 May 1902. On his assumption of regal power, Spain was poor and in decline, having lost almost all the remnants of its colonial empire as the result of defeat in the Spanish-American War of 1898. The domestic constitution was almost unworkable, but the frequent intervals between successive ministries gave the young king opportunities to implement his own policies. He re-established friendly relations with the USA and was generally supported by the British, whose resident ministers exercised powerful influence at his Court.

Alfonso determined to find a bride from the British Royal Family. His first choice was Princess Patricia, daughter of the Duke of Connaught [73], but that lady declined his suit. The exiled Empress Eugenie of the French, herself of Spanish birth, introduced him to her god-daughter, Victoria Eugenia ("Ena"), daughter of Queen Victoria's youngest child, the widowed Princess Beatrice of Battenberg. Each of the two young people found the other attractive and they were married at Madrid on 31 May 1906. A bomb, the third of several attempts on Alfonso's life, disrupted the wedding procession. Public opinion in the UK was shocked at the danger to which the incompetence of the Spanish police had exposed a British princess. Her uncle, King Edward VII [54], thereafter declined repeated invitations from Alfonso to make a state visit to Spain. Spanish public opinion, on the other hand, came to feel that the British Royal Family had taken advantage of Alfonso in encouraging him to marry a princess who inherited from her grandmother the genes of haemophilia. Her first child, Don Alfonso, was a haemophiliac (although he lived until 1933, when he was killed in a motoring accident in Florida), and her second, Don Jaime, was born profoundly deaf. During the First World War, in which Spain remained neutral, the King and Queen (who each had relatives fighting on opposing sides) took part in humanitarian activities and supported the activities of the International Red Cross.

Alfonso was closely identified with the Spanish Army, seeing it as one of the few unifying institutions in a nation where regional separatism remained strong. His political opponents argued that he was excessively influenced by his generals, especially in his support for their campaigns to extend Spanish control in Morocco. In 1921 a revolt of the Rif tribes was followed by the ambush of a Spanish force at Anual (22 July 1921). The survivors retreated to their base and eventually surrendered with the loss of nearly 15,000 men and 129 guns. Alfonso's personal prestige was much weakened by this humiliation of the generals to whom he had given personal encouragement. Recurrent political crises in Spain, with intimidation and assassination becoming the norm, led to the emergence in September 1923 of a quasi-fascist regime, the Military Directory, led by General Primo de Rivera. Alfonso maintained a distance from the Directory, while giving tacit approval to totalitarian measures that had the effect of restoring public order. The Army, however, remained top-heavy, with one officer to every seven men.

When Primo de Rivera attempted army reform, the military turned against him. In 1930 Alfonso dismissed the Directory and revived the former constitution. The elected ministers proved unable to cope with the resulting disorders and, early in 1931, municipal elections gave an overwhelming success to the republicans. Although there was still support for the monarchy in rural areas, where the influence of the church and the landlords was strong, Alfonso decided that his personal position was untenable and that an appeal to the monarchists would lead to civil war. He accordingly simply abandoned his capital and left Spain on 14 April 1931. Queen Ena deplored this decision and the royal couple remained estranged until shortly before Alfonso's death in Rome on 28 February 1941. Alfonso played no part in the Spanish Civil War of 1936–1938, in which his people suffered all the miseries that he hoped his abdication would prevent. The victorious Falangists, though insisting that Spain was once more a monarchy, made no move to restore him. On 15 January 1941 Alfonso, suffering from the angina which would soon kill him, abdicated in favour of his third son, Don Juan, Prince of the Asturias, whose eldest son eventually succeeded to the Spanish throne as HM King Juan Carlos in July 1975.

In his military capacity, Alfonso was colonel-in-chief of eighteen regiments in the Spanish Army and of the 5th Artillery Regiment in the Royal Bavarian Army. He was given the rank of general in the British Army on 17 May 1905 and became a British field marshal on 3 June 1928. Alfonso was appointed colonel-in-chief of the 16th (the Queen's) Lancers in June 1905 and of its successor unit, the 16th/5th the Queen's Royal Lancers, when this was formed in 1922. He retained this appointment and his rank as a field marshal in the British Army until his death in 1941.

ALANBROOKE
VISCOUNT, see **BROOKE,** Sir ALAN, **[112]**

ALLENBY
Sir Edmund Henry Hynman, 1st Viscount Allenby, GCB, GCMG, GCVO (1861–1936) **[90]**

Edmund Allenby, the eldest son of a country gentleman of modest means, was born at Brackenhurst, Nottinghamshire, on 23 April 1861 and grew up in East Anglia. Between 1875 and 1880 he attended Haileybury College, hoping to join the Indian Civil Service. He failed the competitive entrance examination for the ICS, but passed that for the Royal Military College, where he accordingly became a gentleman cadet in February 1881. Allenby passed in 5th in order of merit and passed out 12th, having become under officer of his cadet division. He was commissioned as a lieutenant in the 6th (Inniskilling) Dragoons on 10 May 1882 and joined this regiment in Natal. After a tour at the cavalry depot, Canterbury, between 1886 and 1888, he was promoted captain on 10 January 1888 and rejoined his regiment in South Africa. Allenby returned to the UK in 1890 and remained at regimental duty while studying for the Staff College entrance examination. He passed in, at his second attempt, in the same intake as Douglas Haig [85] who seems to have identified him as a potential long-term rival. Allenby was the more popular with their fellow-students, who elected him Master of the Staff College Draghounds, though the affluent Haig was better mounted and a more skilful rider. Allenby, as a cavalry officer, was also a keen polo player, though he eventually gave up this sport because of the difficulty of finding a pony to carry his weight. At the end of 1896, after a very short acquaintance, he made an impetuous offer of marriage to Adelaide Chapman, the third daughter of a Wiltshire landowner. She accepted despite the disapproval of her father, who felt that Allenby had limited prospects.

After passing out of the Staff College, Allenby was promoted to major on 19 May 1897 and was posted to Ireland, where he became brigade major of the 3rd Cavalry Brigade at the Curragh in March 1898. He rejoined his regiment (ordered to South Africa in October 1899 on the approach of war with the Boer republics) and reached South Africa after narrowly escaping shipwreck off the Cape Verde islands. Allenby had little enthusiasm for the war in which he found himself. He admired and liked the Afrikaners whom he met and was homesick for his young wife and baby son, to both of whom he was devoted. Nor did he relish the discomforts of campaigning, especially after twice breaking his false teeth on army biscuits. Nevertheless, Allenby emerged from the war with credit, having been in combat at Colesberg (11 January 1900); Klip Drift (15 February 1900); Dronfield Ridge (16 February 1900); Zand River (10 May 1900); Kalkheuval Pass (3 June 1900); Barberton (12 September 1900) and Tevreden (16 October 1900), where the British were defeated by a Boer force led by Jan Smuts [108]. Allenby was promoted to lieutenant colonel on 29 November 1900, but was not confirmed in his acting appointment as commanding officer of his regiment. Instead, he was given command of a mobile column in the guerrilla stage of the war. Allenby's column avoided the ambushes and traps to which others fell prey, but he was criticized for being over-cautious. War-weary and convinced of the futility of continuing the campaign, Allenby began to suffer from fever. His wife decided to join him in Durban, but arrived in March 1902, shortly before the war ended, to find him back on operations.

Allenby became a colonel on 22 August 1902 and transferred to command the 5th (Royal Irish) Lancers at Colchester. In 1906 he was given command of the 4th Cavalry Brigade, with promotion to major general on 10 September 1909. The following year he became Inspector General of Cavalry. There were those who felt his promotion changed him for the worse. He gained the nickname of "Apple-pie" from his insistence that the regulations governing uniform and equipment were observed to the letter. Like most cavalry officers of his day, he continued to stress the importance of the *arme blanche*. He soon became known as "the Bull", from his increasingly stormy temper and his burly physique. From this time onwards he became more impatient with those whose views differed from his own. His response to reasoned argument was often so violent that his staff trembled in his presence. Some were even reduced to a state of collapse, to the astonishment of Allenby himself, who in personal life was the kindest of men.

On the outbreak of the First World War in August 1914 Allenby went to France in command of the British Expeditionary Force's Cavalry Division. He was unpopular with his colleagues and was blamed for losing touch with half his force while covering the retreat from Mons, so that he could not aid the 4th Division at Le Cateau. Nevertheless, he was given command of the newly-formed Cavalry Corps when the BEF moved to Flanders in October 1914. In the first battle of Ypres (19 October–21 November 1914), he fed his units into the combat piecemeal, to fight on foot alongside the infantry. On 6 May 1915, during the second battle of Ypres (22 April– 24 May 1915), Allenby was given command of V Corps. Subsequent operations gave him a reputation for seeking to gain his objectives regardless of casualties. In October 1915 he was awarded the KCB and given command of the Third Army, with promotion to lieutenant general (substantive from 1 January 1916). At the second battle of Arras (9 April–16 May 1917) Sir Edmund Allenby achieved an initial success, but his final offensive failed with heavy losses. Allenby was blamed by Sir Douglas Haig [85], C-in-C of the British Expeditionary Force, for persisting with a faulty plan.

Allenby at this time was as convinced as were most British generals that the Western Front was the only important theatre. He therefore regarded his appointment as C-in-C of the Egyptian Expeditionary Force on 5 June 1917, even though it was accompanied by substantive promotion to general, as the end of his career. He only became enthusiastic when David Lloyd George, the Prime Minister, promised him the men, artillery and aircraft that previously had been denied to this theatre. Allenby arrived in Cairo at the end of June 1917 and immediately set out to infuse a new spirit into his army. His own private world was shattered when his son, serving as an artillery officer on the Western Front, was killed on 29 July 1917.

After the arrival of the reinforcements promised by Lloyd George, Allenby took the offensive with a careful deception plan. In one of the decisive actions of the war, the Desert Mounted Corps took Beersheba on 31 October 1917. Gaza was outflanked and fell to the British soon afterwards. Jerusalem was taken on 9 December 1917. Allenby, who entered the Holy City on foot, was said to have fulfilled the prophecy that it would fall only to "the prophet of God" (from the similarity of his name to the Arabic words *Allah* and *Nebi*). He issued a proclamation guaranteeing freedom of worship to all and the protection of the Holy places. He also settled long-standing disputes over what flags should fly over them by decreeing that only the British flag could be allowed in a city under British occupation. He foresaw the unsettling effect of the Balfour declaration of 9 November 1917 (promising the creation of a Jewish national home in Palestine) and forbade its publication in the areas under his control. Lloyd George saw in Allenby's victories a vindication of his own disposition to fight the enemy in the Middle East, rather than on the Western Front, where Haig's costly failure at the third battle of Ypres had once more proved the strength of the German defences. He therefore pressed Allenby to make Aleppo his next objective. In February 1918 the appointment of Sir Henry Wilson [91] as Chief of the Imperial General Staff helped Allenby's cause. Wilson, though regarding the Western Front as the decisive theatre, was prepared to humour Lloyd George and sent troops to Palestine from Mesopotamia. Much of the British infantry, however, had to be sent to the Western Front to meet the German offensive of Spring, 1918. In July and August 1918, Allenby crossed the Jordan in the direction of Amman, but had to fall back on both occasions. He launched a major offensive at Megiddo (Armageddon) on 19 September 1918, leading to the capture of Damascus on 2 October and Aleppo on 26 October 1918, four days before the Turkish Government sued for an armistice.

In the immediate post-war period Allenby was responsible for the military government of Palestine and Syria. He acknowledged the growing strength of Arab nationalism and advised against Syria becoming a French mandate. In March 1919 Allenby was appointed British High Commissioner in Egypt. He returned to the UK in the summer of 1919 to be fêted as a hero and raised to the peerage as Viscount

Allenby, of Megiddo and of Felixstowe, with a special remainder in favour of his nephew. He was promoted to field marshal on 31 July 1919. In 1921 the collapse of negotiations with Egyptian politicians was followed by anti-British riots. Allenby threatened to resign if the Cabinet did not make concessions to the Egyptians. These were made, though the ministers let it appear that Allenby had opposed rather than advocated them. British troops still remained in Egypt after the end of the British protectorate in 1922 and acts of terrorism by nationalist extremists continued to occur. Allenby tolerated these until November 1924, when Sir Lee Stack, Governor-General of the Anglo-Egyptian Sudan, was assassinated by an Arab nationalist. Allenby reacted with an angry note, delivered in person, in uniform at the head of a British cavalry regiment, demanding full compensation from the Egyptian government and the withdrawal of Egyptian troops from the Sudan. These demands were eventually met, but Allenby was manoeuvred by the new Conservative foreign secretary, Austen Chamberlain. into resigning in June 1925.

Allenby was colonel of the 5th (Royal Irish) Lancers from 1912 to 1922 and of its successor, the 16th/ 5th the Queen's Royal Lancers, from 1922 onwards. He became colonel of the 1st Life Guards in February 1920. In the Territorial Army, Allenby became honorary colonel of the 5th (Glamorganshire) battalion, the Welch Regiment, in August 1928 and of the Warwickshire Yeomanry in June 1932. He died in London from a sudden stroke on 14 May 1936 and his ashes were interred in Westminster Abbey. Allenby, with his victories in the Palestine campaign of 1917–1918, was the British Army's last and greatest captain of horse.

AMHERST
Sir JEFFERY, 1st Baron Amherst KB (1717–1797) [17]

Jeffery Amherst, the second son of a barrister, was born on 29 January 1717 at Riverhead, on the outskirts of Sevenoaks, Kent. His father obtained a place for him at the nearby Knole House as a page in the service of the 7th Earl (later 1st Duke) of Dorset, a great Whig magnate of the time. Amherst was commissioned as a cornet in Ligonier's regiment of Horse (later the 7th Dragoon Guards) on 10 July 1735 and served in the War of the Austrian Succession as an aide-de-camp to Sir John Ligonier [10] at Dettingen (27 June 1743) and Fontenoy (11 May 1745). After becoming a captain in the 1st Foot Guards and lieutenant colonel in the Army on 25 Dec 1745, he fought at Rocoux

(Rocourt, 11 Oct 1746) and Laffeldt (La Val, 2 July 1747). Amherst was promoted to major general on 22 May 1756 and at the same time became colonel of the 15th Foot. During the Seven Years War he served in Germany at Hastenbeck (15 July 1757) before being given command of an expedition against the French at Ile Royale (Cape Breton Island) in the Gulf of St Lawrence. After the capture of Louisbourg on 26 July 1758, Amherst became C-in-C of the British forces in North America, with appointment as colonel-in-chief of the 60th Royal American Regiment in September 1758. He then launched a three-pronged offensive against Canada. One army, under his personal command, took Ticonderoga (July 1759) and Crown Point (August 1759), while another, led by Sir William Johnson, captured Niagara (July 1759) and the third, under Major General James Wolfe, defeated the French at Quebec (13 September 1759). Montreal, the last major French garrison in Canada, capitulated on 8 September 1760. Amherst, an able tactician, trained his infantry to form a firing line two-deep rather than the conventional three-deep and justified this decision on the grounds that they would only be opposed by French Canadian militia and Indians, not by European regulars. His strategic success derived from his grasp of logistics and his arrangements for the transport and supply of his troops across a trackless wilderness, while co-ordinating the movement of forces separated by great distances. His conquest of Canada was a major victory, with lasting political consequences.

Amherst was made Governor-General of British North America in September 1760 and was promoted to lieutenant general on 19 January 1761, with the accolade of a Knight of the Bath later in the year. In 1763 the British had to face a major Indian war against a combination of tribes led by Pontiac, chief of the Ottawas. Sir Jeffery Amherst had previously taken the view that colonial Militia or locally raised Special Forces could defeat bands of marauding savages without the Regular Army becoming involved. When Pontiac destroyed isolated farms and tricked or starved British forts into surrender, Amherst was at first inclined to blame their redcoat garrisons for incompetence. Although he had underestimated both the strength and skill of his Native American enemies, he had little time for the concept of the noble red man and responded to Indian atrocities by distributing smallpox-infected blankets among the offending tribes. This war was still going on when Amherst returned to England in 1765. He was made Governor of Virginia, but resigned in 1768 when required to reside there. The post had not previously been a residential one and the new requirement was imposed by King George III to induce Amherst to resign, so freeing this office for a royal favourite. Amherst ceased to be colonel-in-chief of the 60th Royal American Regiment in September 1768, but in the following November, when the King realized the value of his services, he was reinstated in this post and moved from the 15th Foot to become colonel of the 3rd Foot, the Buffs. He remained colonel of the Buffs until April 1779, when he became colonel of the 2nd Troop of Horse Grenadier Guards, from which he moved to be colonel of the 2nd Troop of Horse Guards (later 2nd Life Guards) in March 1782.

Amherst became Lieutenant General of the Ordnance in 1772. In May 1776 he was raised to the peerage as Baron Amherst, of Holmesdale. He was promoted to general on 19 March 1778 and was appointed general on the staff (in effect, commander-in-chief) with a seat in the Cabinet, in the following month. His tenure of this office included the period of a major international conflict, the American War of Independence. In the Gordon Riots of June 1780 the military under his command were called out to restore order on the streets of London. Lord Amherst resigned in March 1782 and was succeeded by the Honourable Henry Conway [12]. After Conway's resignation in April 1783, Amherst again became the Cabinet's chief military adviser. He clung to office with great tenacity and in 1787 was granted a second peerage, as Baron Amherst, of Montreal, created with a special remainder in favour of his nephew. On the approach of war with Revolutionary France, he was reappointed as general on the staff in January 1793. In peace, Amherst had been criticized for promoting wealthy officers over those with greater experience. With the return of war, he was blamed for many of the shortcomings revealed by the opening campaigns and was succeeded as C-in-C by the Duke of York [15] in February 1795. He became field marshal on 30 July 1796. Amherst died on 3 August 1797, at his residence, Montreal Park, Riverhead. He married twice, firstly to Jane Dalison, the daughter of a Kent squire, and secondly to Elizabeth, eldest daughter of General the Hon George Carry. He had no children and his peerage, by special remainder, was inherited by his nephew, William Pitt Amherst.

ANGLESEY, MARQUESS OF
see **PAGET**, Lord HENRY, [37]

ARGYLL
2th DUKE OF, see **CAMPBELL**, JOHN, [2]

ARGYLL

5th DUKE OF, see **CAMPBELL, JOHN, [16]**

ARTHUR WILLIAM PATRICK ALBERT

HRH Duke of Connaught and Strathearn, KG, KT, KP, GCB, GCSI, GCMG, GCIE, GCVO, GBE, VD, TD (1850–1942) **[73]**

Prince Arthur, the third son and seventh child of Queen Victoria and her Consort, Prince Albert **[33]**, was born on 1 May 1850 at Buckingham Palace, London. His first two baptismal names were those respectively of the great Duke of Wellington **[24]** and of another Napoleonic veteran, William, Crown Prince of Prussia, later the German Emperor William I. Marked out for a military career from an early age, Prince Arthur attended the Royal Military Academy, Woolwich, from where he was commissioned as a lieutenant in the Royal Engineers on 19 June 1868. He subsequently transferred to the Royal Artillery on 2 November 1868 and to the Rifle Brigade (the Prince Consort's Own) on 3 August 1869. Prince Arthur served with this corps in Canada in 1870, at the time of the Fenian raids. He was promoted to captain on 1 May 1871 and transferred to the 7th Hussars in April 1874. Prince Arthur was created Duke of Connaught and Strathearn on 24 May 1874 and was promoted to major on 7 August 1875. After holding staff posts at Aldershot and Gibraltar, Connaught returned to the Rifle Brigade on 27 September 1876 on promotion to lieutenant colonel and commanded its 1st Battalion until 1880. In 1878, he went to Berlin to attend the wedding of the daughter of his eldest sister, Princess Victoria (mother of the future German Emperor William II **[71]**). There he fell in love with the bride's younger sister (his own niece) Louise Margaret Victoria, whom he married in March 1879. Connaught was promoted to colonel in the Rifle Brigade, with appointment as its colonel-in-chief, on 29 May 1880.

Connaught served in the 1882 expedition to Egypt, where he commanded the Guards Brigade at Tel-el-Kebir (13 September 1882). He was promoted to major general on 28 March 1883 and became colonel of the Scots Guards in June 1883. Between 1886 and 1890 Connaught was C-in-C, Bombay, with promotion to lieutenant general on 1 April 1889. His ambition to become C-in-C, India, was thwarted by the influence of those who saw this as a step towards him succeeding the Duke of Cambridge **[45]** as C-in-C of the British Army. The plan for Connaught eventually to succeed Cambridge was as strongly supported by the Queen (and by Cambridge himself) as it was opposed by Sir Garnet Wolseley [67] and others who wanted no more Royal commanders-in-chief to stand in the way of their own promotion. Sir Frederick Roberts [68] was therefore given an extension of his tour as C-in-C, India, and Connaught was appointed GOC-in-C Southern Command in 1890. He became GOC-in-C Aldershot Command, with promotion to general on 1 April 1893. Connaught was not given a field command in the South African War, but instead was made C-in-C, Ireland, when Roberts left this post to take command in South Africa in January 1900.

Connaught became heir presumptive to the duchy of Saxe-Coburg-Gotha when his childless elder brother, Alfred, Duke of Edinburgh, succeeded to this title in 1899. He immediately renounced his claims in favour of his nephew, the Duke of Albany. Connaught was promoted to field marshal on 26 June 1902 and became Inspector General of the Forces in 1904. He was also appointed a field marshal in the Prussian Army by his cousin, the Emperor William II [71]. Connaught was appointed in 1907 to the newly-created post of C-in-C, Mediterranean, but formed the view that it served no useful purpose and resigned at short notice in 1909. He became Governor-General of Canada in 1911. As the representative of the Crown in Canada, he played his part in encouraging the Dominion's contribution to the First World War, although he found himself at odds with the controversial Canadian Minister for Militia, Sir Sam Hughes. On the completion of his period of office in 1916 he returned to Europe, but was not again actively employed.

The Duke of Connaught was colonel-in chief of the 6th Inniskilling Dragoons from June 1897; the Highland Light Infantry from September 1902; the Royal Dublin Fusiliers from February 1904; the Royal Army Medical Corps from February 1919 and the Royal Army Service Corps from December 1932. He had been appointed colonel of the Grenadier Guards in May 1904 and of the Army Service Corps in September 1902. In the Indian Army, he was appointed colonel-in-chief of 129th (Duke of Connaught's Own) Baluchis in May 1904, while his duchess gave her name to the 124th (Duchess of Connaught's Own) Baluchistan Infantry, both of which became battalions of the 10th Baluch Regiment in 1922. In the auxiliary forces he was at various times honorary colonel of the South Irish Horse (Special Reserve); the Sligo Artillery Militia (Duke of Connaught's Own); the Hampshire and Isle of Wight Artillery Militia (Duke of Connaught's Own); the Royal East Kent Yeomanry (Duke of Connaught's Own, Mounted Rifles) and its successor unit, the 97th (Kent Yeomanry) Army Field Brigade, Royal Artillery; the

4th Battalion (Cambridge Militia), the Suffolk Regiment; the 3rd (Militia) Battalion, the Queen's Own (Royal West Kent) Regiment; the 3rd (Militia) Battalion, the Highland Light Infantry; the 3rd (Duke of Connaught's Own) Volunteer Battalion, the Hampshire Regiment and of the London Irish Rifles (28th Middlesex Rifle Volunteer Corps) and its successor, the 18th (County of London) Battalion, the London Regiment. He was also colonel-in-chief of the Volunteer Force raised for home defence during the First World War. In the New Zealand Army he was colonel-in-chief of the New Zealand Rifle Brigade, (Earl of Liverpool's Own).

The Duke of Connaught's later years were saddened by the deaths of his elder daughter, Crown Princess Margaret of Sweden, in 1920 and of his only son, Prince Arthur of Connaught, in 1938. Connaught's younger daughter, Princess Patricia, (whose name was given to a regiment of Canadian Light Infantry) renounced her royal status after eloping with a naval officer, the Honourable Alexander Ramsay (later a distinguished admiral), a younger son of the 13th Earl of Dalhousie. After the First World War Connaught spent much of his time on the south coast of France, where he freely entertained officers of the British Mediterranean Fleet at his villa. Formerly a colonel of the von Zeithen Hussars in the Imperial German Army, he expressed much satisfaction at being made an honorary corporal in the Chasseurs Alpins. He died on 16 January 1942 at his Surrey residence, Bagshot Park, (later occupied by the Royal Army Chaplains' Department and, after his marriage in 1999, by HRH Prince Edward, Earl of Wessex) and was buried at Frogmore Mausoleum, Windsor. His titles became extinct on the death without issue of his grandson in 1943.

AUCHINLECK
Sir CLAUDE JOHN EYRE, GCB, GCIE, CSI, DSO, OBE (1884–1981) [116]

Claude (originally Claud) Auchinleck was born in Aldershot on 21 June 1884, the eldest of the two sons and four children of Colonel John Claudius Auchinleck, of the Royal Artillery, and his wife Mary (May) Eyre, both of whom came from families belonging to the Anglo-Irish Protestant Ascendancy. They were married in 1875, when the colonel was aged 40 and his bride was 25. Colonel Auchinleck retired in 1890 and died two years later, probably from a tropical illness contracted in 1888 during his service in the Third Burma War. His widow, a practical woman, brought up her young family on the Continent, where she was able to live at lower cost than in the UK and found employment to supplement her pension from the military. Claude Auchinleck attended a preparatory school, Eagle House, at Crowthorne, Berkshire from 1894 to 1896, when he entered the nearby Wellington College with a foundation scholarship awarded to the sons of deceased officers. He decided on a military career and rose to be a corporal in the school's detachment of the local Rifle Volunteers. At Wellington Auchinleck acquired an indifference to personal comfort which remained with him for the rest of his life. A weakness in mathematics prevented him from following his father into the Royal Artillery and he therefore decided to join the Indian Army, where life was easier for officers without a private income. Auchinleck passed into the Royal Military College, Sandhurst, in January 1902 and was commissioned on 21 January 1903 as a second lieutenant on the Unattached List, prior to joining the Indian Army. His obligatory period in a British unit was spent with the 2nd Battalion, the King's (Shropshire Light Infantry), from which he went to the 62nd Punjabis in April 1904. Auchinleck was promoted to lieutenant on 21 April 1905 and spent the next two years on frontier duty in Tibet and Sikkim. At the end of 1907 he moved with his regiment to Benares (Varanasi) on the Gangetic plain, where he contracted diphtheria. He returned to the UK to convalesce, but, having few friends of his own age, soon became homesick for India and his regiment. During his stay in England he attached himself to his cousin's regiment, the Royal Inniskilling Fusiliers, at Aldershot. He returned to Benares in the summer of 1909 and became adjutant of the 62nd Punjabis, with promotion to captain on 21 January 1912.

After the beginning of the First World War in August 1914, the 62nd Punjabis joined the British forces defending the Suez Canal. Auchinleck became machine-gun officer of his battalion and took part in operations against the Turks at Ismailia (3 and 4 February 1915). In July 1915 the battalion was moved to Aden to counter a Turkish threat and from there went to Mesopotamia (Iraq) to join the attempted relief of Kut-al-Amara. Auchinleck took part in a series of costly and fruitless frontal attacks at Hanna, on the Tigris, (21–22 January 1916 and 8 March 1916) and was one of the few British officers of his battalion to survive these engagements. His unit was again in combat at the beginning of February 1917 and once more suffered heavy casualties. Auchinleck became its acting commanding officer on 8 February and led it in the crossing of the Tigris at Shumran (23 February 1917). He was promoted to acting lieutenant colonel on 24 February 1917 and remained in command of the 62nd Punjabis during the recapture of Kut (25 February 1917) and the British entry into Baghdad (11 March

1917). Auchinleck reverted to the rank of temporary major and battalion second-in-command on 12 March 1917 and was later awarded the DSO and mentioned in despatches for his services as acting CO. He was appointed brigade major of the 52nd Indian Infantry Brigade in September 1917, with substantive promotion to major on 21 January 1918. He remained in this post until the end of hostilities with Turkey on 2 November 1918. From November 1918 to May 1919, Auchinleck was a General Staff officer, grade 2, at Divisional HQ, Mosul, Kurdistan. He then became GSO 1, with promotion to brevet lieutenant colonel on 15 November 1919.

Auchinleck attended the Indian Staff College, Quetta, in 1920–1921. He then went on leave to Europe. While staying with his mother in a French hotel he met and was captivated by Jessie Stewart, the vivacious twenty-one year-old daughter of a Scots civil engineer. They were married in London in September 1921. On returning to India, Auchinleck became a temporary deputy assistant quartermaster general at Army HQ on 1 February 1923. In the post-war reorganization of the Indian Army, the 62nd Punjabis became the 1st Battalion, 1st Punjab Regiment. Auchinleck became second-in-command of this unit in September 1925, though as a trained staff officer he was mostly employed as an extra GSO 2 at the headquarters of Peshawar District, where his battalion was stationed. In 1927 he attended the newly-formed Imperial Defence College, London. Auchinleck returned to regimental duty in India in 1928, becoming commanding officer of the 1st Battalion, 1st Punjab Regiment, with promotion to substantive lieutenant colonel on 21 January 1929. In February 1930 he joined the Staff College at Quetta as GSO 1 and chief instructor of the Junior Division and was, with nineteen others, given promotion to substantive colonel, back-dated by virtue of his earlier brevet to 15 November 1923. Auchinleck ended his tour at Quetta in the autumn of 1932. After a period of leave in the UK, he was promoted to temporary brigadier on 1 July 1933, in command of the Peshawar Brigade. He led this in a brief punitive expedition against the Mohmand tribesmen in August 1933, for which he was mentioned in despatches. In August 1935 he commanded another punitive expedition, until superseded by the return of his divisional commander from leave at the end of September 1935. Auchinleck was again mentioned in despatches and was promoted to major general on 30 November 1935.

Auchinleck was appointed Deputy Chief of the General Staff, India, at the end of 1937. As such he was chairman of the Committee of the Army in India Modernisation Committee. This reported in October 1938, with far-reaching proposals for a re-armament programme scheduled for completion within the next five years. The British government in London, faced with a deteriorating international situation, set up its own committee, headed by Admiral of the Fleet Lord Chatfield, to examine the question of re-arming and reorganizing the Army in India. He was told to take account of the cost of modern weapons and the Government of India's limited financial resources. Chatfield incorporated all the recommendations of Auchinleck's report into the findings of his own committee, though few had been implemented by the time that the Second World War began in September 1939.

Auchinleck returned to India from a further period of leave in the UK to become GOC 3rd Indian Infantry Division. Late in 1939 Sir Edmund Ironside [107] (then Chief of the Imperial General Staff) casually mentioned to Lord Chatfield that he had difficulty in finding generals capable of holding high command. Chatfield recommended Auchinleck, who had impressed him in India. Auchinleck was given command of IV Corps in the UK in January 1940, with promotion to lieutenant general in the Indian Army on 16 March 1940. This move was resented by many British officers, who regarded the Indian Army as a local force, with limited experience of real war, and objected to their own promotion prospects in their own country being sacrificed to those of a high-flyer from a different Army. When the Allied campaign in Norway began to falter, Auchinleck, with a reputation for expertise in mountain warfare, was sent to take over command of the Anglo-French land forces. He arrived on 13 May 1940 but, lacking the artillery and air reinforcements for which he asked, was soon facing defeat. The Cabinet decided to abandon Norway and Auchinleck completed the evacuation of his army on 7 June 1940. In his despatches he criticized his British troops as soft and callow, comparing them unfavourably with the French Chasseurs Alpins. He also stressed the importance of air cover in modern war. The British military establishment took the view that Auchinleck had spent too long a time in India and too short a time in Norway for his opinions to be of value.

On 14 June 1940 Auchinleck was given command of the newly-formed V Corps, responsible for the defence of Dorset and Hampshire against an anticipated German invasion. On 19 July 1940 he succeeded Sir Alan Brooke [112] as GOC-in-C Southern Command, with Lieutenant General B. L. Montgomery [114] taking Auchinleck's place in V Corps. These two generals, "Monty" and "the Auk", so alike in their approach to hard living and tough training, agreed on little else. Montgomery reversed Auchinleck's policy of holding the shoreline in favour of building up a mobile reserve. He also visited the War Office to secure the retention of staff officers whom Auchinleck wished to use elsewhere. At the end of 1940 Auchinleck was nominated as C-in-C, India, in succession to his old friend and patron, Sir Robert Cassels, under whom he had served on the staff in India. Auchinleck was promoted to general and awarded the KCIE on 26 December 1940, prior to assuming his new command on 27 January 1941.

Auchinleck extended the base of recruiting for the Indian Army to include communities previously deemed by the British to be unsuitable for military service. He nevertheless maintained the existing prejudice against the Western-educated urban classes (at least in respect of the combat arms) and converted the battalions of the Indian Territorial Force, in which these groups were well represented, into regular units, recruited from the traditional "martial classes". At the same time he insisted on equality of treatment in all respects between British and Indian commissioned officers. Aware that Indian self-government could not be delayed for much longer, he told his Indian officers that they should all consider themselves nationalists. When Winston Churchill, the British Prime Minister, decided to move against the pro-Axis Regent of Iraq, he was impressed by Auchinleck's readiness to despatch troops from India. Although a force sent by Sir Archibald Wavell [111], C-in-C Middle East, occupied Baghdad before the Indian contingent arrived, Churchill compared Wavell's cautious approach unfavourably with Auchinleck's boldness and decided that the two should change places.

Auchinleck became C-in-C, Middle East, on 30 June 1941. On the advice of the cautious Sir John Dill [109] (Ironside's successor as CIGS), he resisted pressure from Churchill for an early offensive. With a view to instilling a more warlike spirit into GHQ Middle East, Auchinleck ordered that it should vacate its Cairo base and live in tents in the desert. Defeated by the impracticability of this scheme, he confined it to himself and his immediate entourage, so that he should not live in greater comfort than the commanders in the field. He found himself in dispute with his Deputy C-in-C, Sir Thomas Blamey [118], who considered that the Australians in Tobruk, who had stood a long siege, should be withdrawn and replaced by British troops. Auchinleck objected to this proposal, but was forced to give way when the Australian Government intervened in Blamey's support. Blamey took the view that Auchinleck was a bully, who viewed the army of a self-governing dominion in the same light as the Indian Army.

The long-awaited British offensive in the Western Desert began on 18 November 1941, but by February 1942 the British had been driven back to Gazala. Churchill began to have doubts about Auchinleck's fighting spirit and, supported by the Chiefs of Staff in London, ordered him to renew the offensive by 1 June 1942. This was pre-empted by an

Axis attack which, beginning at the end of May, captured Tobruk and drove the British back almost to the Egyptian border. On 25 June 1942 Auchinleck (who had gained a reputation for poor judgement in choosing his subordinates) took personal command of the Eighth Army. While preparations were made for the evacuation of Cairo, he established a firm defence line and halted the Axis advance at El Alamein (1–3 August 1942). Churchill visited Egypt, where he was entertained by the RAF in a comfortable station officers' mess and by Auchinleck in his desert tentage. He decided that Auchinleck should be relieved and that the post of C-in-C Middle East should be given to Sir Harold Alexander [113]. Auchinleck was offered command of the British forces in the Levant, Iraq and Iran, but declined, on the grounds that it would be a slight to the Indian Army for its former C-in-C to be relegated to a backwater. He returned to India late in August 1942 and went onto the Unemployed List on full pay.

Auchinleck was re-appointed as C-in-C, India, (in succession to Lord Wavell) on 18 June 1943. As such, he held overall responsibility for the British operations in Burma until South East Asia Command was established, under Lord Louis Mountbatten, on 15 November 1943. Thereafter, Auchinleck's main military task was the training, logistic support and administration of troops within India, together with those sent from India to various other theatres, ranging from the Mediterranean to the Pacific. As C-in-C, India, he was also War Member of the Governor-General's Council and took part in its policy-making decisions. In March 1945 he began to plan for the post-war reorganization of the Indian Army and raised the question of whether either British or Gurkha troops could remain in the Army of a self-governing dominion. An immediate problem was the fate of the 25,000 Indian soldiers who had joined the Indian National Army after having been captured by the Japanese. A number of officers were tried and convicted on various charges, but their cause was taken up by Indian politicians who argued that they had been fighting for India's freedom. Auchinleck upheld the convictions, considering that not to do so would not only insult the majority of the Indian Army, who had remained loyal to their oath of allegiance, but also weaken the constitutional reliability of the Army once self-government had been achieved. To avoid making martyrs, he remitted the more severe punishments and confirmed only those of dismissal with loss of pay. At the beginning of 1946 Auchinleck had to deal with refusals to do duty by Royal Air Force and Royal Indian Air Force personnel, together with an armed mutiny in the Royal Indian Navy. He was promoted to field marshal on 31 May 1946.

In February 1947 Mountbatten succeeded Wavell as Viceroy and Governor-General of India. Faced with the breakdown of law and order across much of northern India, the British Cabinet accepted Mountbatten's advice to bring forward the date of independence, with the partition of the Indian Empire into two independent successor states, to 15 August 1947. Auchinleck spent his last three months in office in dividing the Indian Army between the future Republic of India and the new Muslim state of Pakistan. On independence, he became Supreme Commander of the forces of both countries, but with no operational control over either. He was unable to ameliorate the post-partition massacres, but intervened in the fighting between India and Pakistan in Kashmir by ordering the British officers remaining with either army to play no part in the conflict. The British CIGS, Field Marshal Montgomery, had previously complained that Auchinleck was entirely wrapped up in the problems of the Indian Army, to the detriment of the British troops in India. He now told Mountbatten that Auchinleck was too old to accept the new order of things in India and should be removed, without the award of a peerage. At the end of September 1947 Mountbatten asked Auchinleck to propose the abolition of the Supreme Commander post and step down, on the grounds that his very eminence overshadowed the emergence of the new defence establishments and that politicians of each side believed that he was more sympathetic to the other. Auchinleck, contemptuous of Mountbatten and his political friends, did as he was asked. He refused the offer of a peerage that Mountbatten had obtained for him and left India on 1 December 1947.

Auchinleck was colonel of the Royal Inniskilling Fusiliers from April 1941 to September 1947 and of the 1st Punjab Regiment and the 4th Bombay Grenadiers from his first appointment as C-in-C, India. He retained his Indian Army colonelcies and for several years made regular visits to the regimental depots, showing special interest in the boys' battalions from which future recruits were drawn. His private life was unhappy from as early as 1937, when his wife was diagnosed as infertile. Feeling neglected by her husband during his war service, she consoled herself by an open *affaire* in India with Air Chief Marshal Sir Richard Peirse, whom she eventually married after being divorced by Auchinleck in 1946. After another twenty years of activity, including directorships of several commercial undertakings and charitable work for his old school and ex-service organizations, Auchinleck settled in Morocco, where he found the climate and way of life agreeable. By 1977 his friends became concerned for his welfare and the British Ambassador persuaded the Ministry of Defence to provide a batman for him, as the senior field marshal of the British Army. Sir Claude Auchinleck died in his sleep on 23 March 1981 and was buried in the British Military Cemetery, Casablanca.

BAGNALL
Sir NIGEL THOMAS, GCB, CVO, MC (1927-2002) **[134]**

Nigel Bagnall, the son of an officer in the Green Howards (Alexandra, Princess of Wales's Own Yorkshire Regiment) who later transferred to the Indian Army, was born on 10 February 1927. He was educated at Wellington College and joined the Army on 22 February 1945. After service in the ranks and as an officer cadet, Bagnall was granted a Regular Army Emergency Commission as a second lieutenant in the Green Howards on 4 January 1946. He transferred to the Parachute Regiment on 13 February 1946 and became a war substantive lieutenant on 5 July 1946. Bagnall served with the 8th Battalion, the Parachute Regiment, as part of the 6th Airborne Division in Palestine during the final period of the British mandate. He was then posted to the Army Emergency Reserve as a lieutenant in the Parachute Regiment, from which he transferred to the 1st Battalion, the Duke of Wellington's Regiment. Bagnall was granted a Regular Army commission as a lieutenant in the 1st Battalion, the Green Howards, on 24 September 1949. He then took part with this battalion in the counter-insurgency campaign against Communist terrorists in Malaya, where he served as a platoon commander, battalion intelligence officer and, finally, as a company commander. During his three years in Malaya he was several times engaged in personal combat and was awarded the Military Cross in 1950. He was promoted to temporary captain on 1 August 1951 and was subsequently awarded a bar to his MC, gazetted in May 1953, by which time he had become an instructor at the Officer Cadet Training Unit, Eaton Hall. In the summer of 1954 Bagnall returned to regimental duty to serve with the 2nd Battalion, the Green Howards, in the evacuation of the British garrison from the Suez Canal Zone and the establishment of a new Middle East base in Cyprus. Bagnall became a substantive captain on 21 November 1954. His battalion took part in the counter-insurgency campaign against EOKA (the Greek Cypriot terrorist organization seeking to bring about Enosis, the union of Cyprus with Greece), until the end of 1955, when it returned to the UK. Bagnall transferred to the 4th/7th Royal Dragoon Guards on 25 April 1956, prior to the disbandment of his battalion on 1 May 1956. He became a temporary major on 28 August 1956 and then attended the Staff College, Camberley, from which he passed out in 1958. In 1959 he married Anna Caroline Church, with whom he later had two daughters.

Between January 1960 and September 1961 Bagnall was a General Staff officer, grade 2, in the Directorate of Military Operations at the War Office. He was promoted to substantive major on 10 February 1961 and qualified at the Joint Services Staff College in the same year. After a period of regimental duty with the 4th/7th Royal Dragoon Guards, he served from May 1964 to March 1966 as military assistant to the Vice-Chief of Defence Staff and was promoted brevet lieutenant colonel on 1 July 1965. He then became GSO 1 (Intelligence) at the Directorate of Borneo Operations until January 1967, with substantive promotion to lieutenant colonel on 31 December 1966. From March to October 1967 Bagnall was GSO 1 at HQ Far Eastern Command, as military assistant to the Commander-in-Chief, Sir Michael Carver [129]. In November 1967 he was given command of his regiment, then stationed at Omagh, Northern Ireland. After preparing for conversion from its previous role as an armoured reconnaissance regiment, the 4th/7th Royal Dragoon Guards moved to Sennelager, Germany, where it was re-equipped with main battle tanks. Bagnall handed over command in April 1969 and was promoted to colonel on 30 June 1969. Between November 1969 and December 1970 he was a member of the directing staff at the Joint Services Staff College, with promotion to brigadier on 30 July 1970. Bagnall was appointed Commander, Royal Armoured Corps, in I (British) Corps in the British Army of the Rhine in December 1970 and remained in this post until August 1972, when he was given a Defence Fellowship at Balliol College, Oxford. From September 1973 to September 1975 he was secretary of the Chiefs of Staff Committee at the Ministry of Defence, with promotion to major general on 3 June 1974.

Between September 1975 and October 1977 Bagnall was GOC 4th Division. He returned to the Ministry of Defence in January 1978 as Assistant Chief of Defence Staff (Policy) and remained there, with promotion to lieutenant general on 1 November 1979, until March 1980. In November 1980 he was given command of I (British) Corps, followed by the award of the KCB in the following year. Sir Nigel Bagnall was promoted to general on appointment as C-in-C, British Army of the Rhine, on 1 January 1982, and retained this post until March 1983. Between August 1983 and June 1985 he was Commander of the NATO Northern Army Group and, as such, introduced important changes in the way his armoured formations planned to counter the forces of the Warsaw Pact. Sir Nigel Bagnall became

Chief of the General Staff in August 1985 and introduced the Higher Command and Staff Course at the Staff College, an important innovation in the training of the Army's senior officers. He was promoted to field marshal on 9 September 1988, when he retired from active duty. He was colonel commandant of the Royal Armoured Corps from August 1985 to 1988 and of the Army Physical Training Corps from February 1981 to September 1988. His history of the conflicts between Rome and Carthage, *The Punic Wars*, was published in 1990.

BAKER
Sir GEOFFREY HARDING, GCB, CMG, CBE, MC
(1912–1980) [128]

Geoffrey Baker, the only son and youngest of five children of a major (later lieutenant colonel) who had joined the Indian Military Accounts Department from the 2nd Bengal Infantry, was born on 20 June 1912, at Murree, on the North-West Frontier of British India. He was educated at Wellington College and the Royal Military Academy, Woolwich, where he became an under officer and won the Sword of Honour before being commissioned as a second lieutenant in the Royal Artillery on 28 January 1932. From his fair colouring and height, Baker was nicknamed "George the Swede" and was thereafter known as "George" by his familiars. He joined the 11th Field Brigade, Royal Artillery, at Aldershot and was promoted to lieutenant on 28 January 1935. After qualifying on the Long Survey Course at the School of Artillery, Larkhill, Baker went with his battery in 1935 to Meerut (Mirath), near Delhi. From there, he joined F Battery, Royal Horse Artillery, at Peshawar in 1937. Baker went with this battery to Egypt in June 1939, where it was equipped with 25-pdr field guns and became part of the newly-formed 4th Regiment, Royal Horse Artillery, in the 4th Indian Division. Baker was promoted to captain on 28 January 1940 and, in May 1940, was appointed as a General Staff officer, grade 3, on the staff of the C-in-C, Middle East. He became an acting major and GSO 2 on 13 July 1940. After attending the Middle East Staff School at Haifa, Palestine, he was appointed Brigade Major, Royal Artillery, of the 4th Indian Division in October 1940 and subsequently took part in the campaign in Italian East Africa (Ethiopia and Eritrea), where he was wounded three times and received a mention in despatches. Baker was awarded the Military Cross for his conduct at Keren (3 February –26 March 1941). He was posted to the Middle East Staff

School as an instructor, with promotion to local lieutenant colonel, on 29 January 1942. From December 1942 to July 1943, Baker was GSO 1 (Staff Duties) at HQ, Eighth Army, in the Western Desert campaign, with promotion to acting lieutenant colonel on 14 January 1943. He became commanding officer of 127 Field Regiment, Royal Artillery, part of the 51st (Highland) Division, in July 1943 and led this unit in the invasion of Sicily.

From March 1944 to April 1945 Baker was Colonel, General Staff (Staff Duties) in 21 Army Group. He landed in Normandy in June 1944 and served in the campaign in North West Europe until the end of hostilities. He was promoted to acting colonel on 23 March 1944, war substantive lieutenant colonel and temporary colonel on 23 September 1944 and acting brigadier on 19 April 1945, when he was appointed Brigadier co-ordinating Administrative Services, in the Control Commission for Germany. In July 1945 he became Brigadier, General Staff (Staff Duties) in 21 Army Group, returning to the Control Commission in February 1946. He was promoted to substantive major on 1 July 1946. Baker married in 1946 Valerie ("Tim") Lockhart, the daughter of a major in the Royal Hampshire Regiment. They later had a daughter (who became a talented military artist) and two sons. From January 1947 to August 1949 he was a deputy director of Staff Duties at the War Office. He subsequently became assistant quartermaster general in a divisional headquarters. Baker was promoted to substantive lieutenant colonel on 31 December 1951, when he became commanding officer of the 3rd Regiment, Royal Horse Artillery, at Munsterlager. He returned to the War Office in December 1952, with promotion to temporary brigadier, and became a substantive colonel on 29 June 1953. Baker attended the Imperial Defence College during 1955 before being appointed Chief of Staff and Director of Operations in the counter-insurgency campaign in Cyprus, a post that he held from November 1955 to January 1957.

Baker then became Commander, Royal Artillery, in the 7th (later renumbered as 5th and then as 1st) Armoured Division in the British Army of the Rhine, followed by appointment as Assistant Chief of Staff (Operations) of NATO's Northern Army Group in February 1959. He was promoted to major general on 3 February 1960, on appointment as Chief of Staff, Southern Command. In November 1961 he became COS, Contingencies Planning, at Supreme Headquarters Allied Powers in Europe (a post newly created in consequence of increased international tension, at the time of the construction of the Berlin Wall by the German Democratic Republic). His main task here was to plan for the "Liveoak" project, which envisaged the NATO Allies using armed force to maintain road links between the Federal Republic of Germany and the Western sectors of Berlin. Baker again returned to the War Office on 2 September 1963, with promotion to lieutenant general and appointment as Vice Chief of the Imperial General Staff. He retained this post (after April 1964 as Vice Chief of the General Staff at the Ministry of Defence) until July 1966, with the award of the KBE in 1964. Between October 1966 and February 1968, Sir Geoffrey Baker was GOC-in-C Southern Command, with promotion to general on 7 May 1967. He became Chief of the General Staff in October 1968. His period in this office coincided with the beginning of the British Army's prolonged deployment in aid of the civil power in Northern Ireland, coupled with continuing reductions in defence expenditure and the withdrawal of troops from more attractive stations east of Suez. Sir Geoffrey Baker was promoted to field marshal on 31 March 1971, on completing his period in office as CGS. He became a colonel commandant of the Royal Artillery in July 1964 and was colonel commandant of the Royal Horse Artillery from November 1970 to March 1971, as well as of the Royal Military Police from March 1968 to March 1971. After retiring from active duty, Sir Geoffrey Baker held various City directorships and lent his support to a number of worthy causes, including in particular those associated with the Royal Artillery. In 1970, he was appointed Master Gunner, St James's Park. He became seriously ill in 1976 and died on 8 May 1980.

BARRETT
Sir ARTHUR ARNOLD, GCB, GCSI, KCVO
(1857–1926) [93]

Arthur Barrett, the third son of a clerk in holy orders, was born at Carshalton, Surrey, on 3 June 1857. He was commissioned as a sub-lieutenant (probationary lieutenant) in the 44th Foot on 10 September 1875 and joined this regiment in India. Barrett transferred to the Bengal Staff Corps in January 1879 and was posted to the 3rd Sikhs, Punjab Frontier Force. He served in the Second Afghan War with this unit, at Shutargardan (2 October 1879); Sherpur (23 December 1879) and Kandahar (1 September 1880). Barrett transferred to the 5th Gurkhas, Punjab Frontier Force, in 1882. He was promoted to captain on 10 September 1886 and served with the 5th Gurkhas in various minor expeditions on the North-West Frontier in 1888 and 1891. He became a major on 10 September 1895 and was on the staff, first as deputy assistant and then as assistant quartermaster general, in the Tirah expedition of 1897–1898. Barrett was present at Sampagha Pass (29 October 1897) and Arhanga Pass (31 October 1897) and then in the Bazar Valley expedition (25–30 December 1897), for which he was mentioned in despatches and promoted to brevet lieutenant colonel (substantive from 20 May 1898). He became assistant adjutant general of the Punjab Frontier Force, after which he commanded the 1st Battalion, the 5th Gurkha Rifles, from 1899 to 1905, with promotion to colonel on 11 October 1902.

Barrett served at Army Headquarters as Deputy Adjutant General (India), before returning to the Punjab to take command of a brigade, with promotion to major general on 1 December 1906. He commanded this formation in operations during 1908 against the Zakka Khel Pathans in the Bazar Valley and the Mohmands at Mazrina and Koda Khel. Barrett was twice mentioned in despatches for this campaign and, in 1909, was awarded the KCB. Sir Arthur Barrett became Adjutant General (India) in 1909, with promotion to lieutenant general on 3 October 1911. He was appointed GOC 6th (Poona) Division in 1912.

During the First World War Barrett was given command of the Indian Army's expedition to Mesopotamia ("Force D"). He defeated a Turkish force at Saihan (19 November 1914), entered Basra three days later and quickly moved inland to take Kurna on 8 December 1914. These early successes created great hopes in the Government of India for a rapid advance that would end with the capture of Baghdad. Barrett felt that he had neither the numbers nor logistic resources to attempt this and dispersed his troops so as to protect his gains against the local Arabs. In March 1915 Force D was reinforced to Corps strength, under General Sir John Nixon, previously the commander of India's Southern Army. Nixon had a reputation as a thrusting field commander, whereas Barrett was considered to have shown himself as over-cautious. Barrett, seeing his supersession as a slight, immediately obtained the opinion of a medical board that he was unfit for duty in the Mesopotamian climate and left the theatre within twenty-four hours. On returning to India, Barrett took up the vacant post of GOC Northern Army and commanded its frontier operations against the Mohmands in 1915 and 1917. He was promoted to general on 1 August 1917 and commanded the British field forces in the Third Afghan War (May-August 1919).

Barrett retired in May 1920 and was promoted to field marshal on 12 April 1921 (succeeding to the Indian Army vacancy created by the death of Sir Charles Egerton [86]). Unusually for an officer of his time and service, Barrett was a radical in political and social questions, disliked sport, played few games and rode no more than his duties required. His main off-duty interests were botany and gardening. His domestic life was marked by personal affliction. His first wife died in 1897, three years after their marriage, leaving a daughter who married in 1918, but predeceased her father in 1921. In 1907 Barrett married Ella Lafone, the daughter of a gentleman living in South Kensington. She died without issue in 1917. Sir Arthur Barrett died at his home in Sharnbrook, Bedfordshire, on 20 October 1926.

BINGHAM
GEORGE CHARLES, 3rd Earl of Lucan, GCB
(1800–1888) [63]

George, by courtesy Lord Bingham, the eldest son of the 2nd Earl of Lucan and his countess, *née* Lady Elizabeth Belasyse, was born in London on 16 April 1800. The Binghams were an Anglo-Irish family that had held lands at Castlebar, County Mayo, since Elizabethan times. George Bingham's parents had fallen in love when they first met, but Lady Elizabeth had been forced by her father to marry Bernard Howard, later the 15th Duke of Norfolk. She subsequently eloped with Lucan and married him, after being divorced by Howard. Lucan's family disapproved of her and the couple separated in 1804. George Bingham was educated at Westminster School, before being commissioned as an ensign in the 6th Foot on 29 August 1816. He exchanged to the 3rd Foot Guards, becoming a lieutenant in the Army and going onto the half-pay list on 24 December 1818. Bingham became a lieutenant in the 8th Foot on 20 January 1820, a captain on the half-pay in the 74th Foot on 16 May 1822, a captain in the 1st Life Guards on 20 June 1822 and a major, unattached, on 23 June 1825. He transferred to the 17th Lancers on 1 December 1825 and took command of this regiment with promotion to lieutenant colonel on 9 November 1826. As a commanding officer he proved a ruthless martinet, demanding perfection in every aspect of training and turn-out. He lavished his own money on his regiment's horses and uniforms, so that the regiment became known as "Bingham's Dandies". He worked himself as hard as his men, but his quarrelsome and arrogant nature made him generally unpopular. Bingham took his profession seriously and, in the Russo-Turkish War of 1828–29, served as an observer with the Russian Army in the Balkans campaign.

In 1826 Bingham was elected MP for Mayo, partly with votes controlled by a local proprietor, Major Fitzgerald. When Fitzgerald did not receive the reward he expected, he challenged Bingham to a duel. Bingham immediately accepted, but Fitzgerald, who had hoped to be bought off, withdrew. In 1829, Bingham married Lady Anne Brudenell, seventh and youngest daughter of the 6th Earl of Cardigan. In 1830 he succeeded as 3rd Earl of Lucan and took his seat in the House of Lords as a representative Irish peer. Lucan returned to the half-pay list in April 1837, in order to concentrate on his Irish estates. He dismissed his land agent, after accusing him of misappropriation. After a court-room brawl, both Lucan and his agent were removed from their position as local magistrates. Lucan's energy and determination, coupled with his disregard for sentiment and public opinion, made him one of the most hated landlords in Ireland. He argued that the Irish population was too large for the land to support, a view that he considered to be proved correct by the potato famine of 1847. His apparent callousness earned him the name of "The Exterminator", though he genuinely believed himself much misunderstood. Much of Lucan's energy and income was spent in lawsuits against his neighbours. His countess, a lady of imperious ways who rarely left London society, complained of Lucan's neglect and parsimony. Her brother, the 7th Earl of Cardigan, took her part. He and Lucan, so alike in age, background and character, had never liked each other. By 1854 they had become irreconcilable.

Lucan was promoted to colonel on 23 November 1841 and to major general on 11 November 1851. When an army was assembled in 1854 for the Crimean War, he applied for command of a cavalry brigade. He was given command of the Cavalry Division, in which the Light Brigade was to be commanded by Cardigan. Lucan was promoted to local lieutenant general on 6 September 1854 and was at the Alma (20 September 1854), where in obedience to the orders of the army commander, Lord Raglan [38], he held the cavalry in reserve, for which he was dubbed "Lord Look-on". He played a prominent part in the battle of Balaklava (25 October 1854), where he was wounded. After publicly dissenting from Raglan's Balaklava despatches, in which Lucan was blamed for the ill-fated charge of the Light Brigade, he was relieved of his command in February 1855. Lucan was refused the court martial for which he asked, but continued to argue his case in Parliament and in public correspondence. He never again held a command, though he was made colonel of the 8th Hussars in November 1855 and was promoted lieutenant general on 24 December 1858. Lucan became colonel of the 1st Life Guards on 27 February 1865 and was promoted to general on 21 June 1865. During the next twenty years, he was superseded in promotion to the rank of field marshal by six other generals junior to him, of whom only two (Napier [58] and Grant [59]) could claim to have been successful field commanders. Lucan finally protested in 1886, when Paulet [62], who was ten years junior to him as a general and had been one of his own staff officers in the Crimea, was promoted to field marshal. It was rumoured that the War Office was surprised to find Lucan still alive, although, as his name had continued to appear in the Army Lists, this seems unlikely. A more probable reason was that he had not been forgiven for publicly challenging Raglan's Balaklava despatches. He was promoted to field marshal on 21 June 1887, on the occasion of Queen Victoria's Golden Jubilee. He died on 10 November 1888, in South Street, Mayfair, and was buried near his estate at Laleham, Middlesex.

BIRDWOOD
Sir WILLIAM RIDDELL, 1st Baron Birdwood, GCB, GCSI, GCMG, GCVO, CIE, DSO (1865–1951) [95]

William Birdwood, the second son of a member of the Bombay Civil Service, was born at Kirkee, Maharashtra, on 13 September 1865. Between 1877 and 1882 William Birdwood attended Clifton College, where he joined the school cadet corps, attached to the 2nd Gloucester Engineer Volunteers. In 1883 he obtained a Militia commission in the 4th Battalion, the Royal Scots Fusiliers, with the intention of transferring directly to the Regular Army, but instead entered the Royal Military College, Sandhurst, where he reached the rank of under officer. Birdwood was gazetted as a lieutenant in the 12th (Prince of Wales's Royal) Lancers on 9 May 1885 and joined this regiment in India. After the obligatory period of one year's probation with a British unit in India, he transferred to the Bengal Staff Corps and served with the 11th Bengal Lancers on the North-West Frontier in 1891. In 1893 he became adjutant of the Governor-General's Bodyguard and married Janetta (Jenny), daughter of a baronet, Sir Benjamin Bromhead. Their marriage proved a long and happy one, producing a son and two daughters. Birdwood was promoted to captain on 9 May 1896 and served in the Tirah campaign of 1897–1898, at Chagru Kotal, Dargai, (18 October 1897); Sampagha Pass (29 October 1897); Arhanga Pass (31 October 1897); Saran Sar (9 November 1897); the Warran Valley (16 November 1897) and Dwatoi (24 November 1897). He was mentioned in despatches for this campaign and went on leave to England in 1899.

On the outbreak of the South African War Birdwood asked for an attachment to the British Army and obtained a post on the staff of a mounted brigade in Natal. He was at Colenso (15 December 1899); Spion Kop (24 January 1900); Vaal Kranz, (5–7 February 1900);

Pieter's Hill (19–27 February 1900); Laing's Nek (6–9 June 1900); Machadodorp (28 July 1900) and Lydenberg (5–8 September 1900), before joining the personal staff of Lord Kitchener [79] at Army HQ, Pretoria, in October 1900. Birdwood was promoted to major on 29 November 1900 and to temporary lieutenant colonel in December 1901 (substantive on 26 June 1902). When Kitchener became C-in-C, India, at the end of 1902, Birdwood went with him as assistant military secretary and played an important part in devising a new system of regimental names and numbers to suit Kitchener's reorganization of the Indian Army. Birdwood became military secretary, with promotion to colonel, on 26 June 1905. He held this post until Kitchener returned to England in 1909, except for a brief spell as Chief of Staff with the punitive expedition to Mohmandistan, where he was at Karga (24 May 1908). After a period of leave in the UK, Birdwood was given command of a brigade at Kohat, with promotion to major general on 3 October 1911. In 1912 he was appointed Quartermaster General, India and defended Kitchener's reforms against the Army in India Commission, headed by Lord Nicholson [82]. In 1913 Birdwood became Secretary to the Government of India in the Army Department.

On 18 November 1914, Kitchener, who had become Secretary of State for War, asked for Birdwood to go to Egypt to train and command the Australian and New Zealand troops assembling there. On being released by the Government of India, Birdwood arrived in Egypt at the end of November 1914, with the rank of temporary lieutenant general and the status of a corps commander. On Kitchener's orders, he subsequently examined the approaches to the Dardanelles, where he formed the view that warships could not pass the straits unless a major force was landed to support them. At the Gallipoli landings Birdwood went ashore in command of the Australian and New Zealand Army Corps (ANZAC) at Ari Burnu (later named Anzac Cove) on 25 April 1915. He became a substantive lieutenant general on 28 October 1915 and was in executive command of the evacuation of Gallipoli (December 1915-January 1916). In March 1916 Birdwood went to the Western Front in command of I ANZAC Corps (remustered as the Australian Corps in November 1917) to form part of the British Second Army under Plumer [89]. Birdwood commanded the Second Army from December 1917 to March 1918, during Plumer's absence in Italy. He was promoted to general on 23 October 1917 and was awarded the KCB. Sir William Birdwood's Australian Corps held the German attacks of March-April 1918, after which he was given command of a new Fifth Army in May 1918. He led this formation throughout the final Allied offensive, liberating Lille on 17 October 1918 and reaching the Belgian city of Tournai on 10 November 1918. In the post-war honours Birdwood was awarded a baronetcy.

From May 1915 Birdwood had been directly responsible to the Australian government for the administration of its troops in Europe. He made a tour of Australia and New Zealand in 1919–1920 and was given an enthusiastic reception by his ANZAC veterans. In 1920 Sir William Birdwood returned to India, where he succeeded Sir Arthur Barrett [93] in command of the Northern Army (reorganized as Northern Command in 1921). Birdwood was promoted to field marshal on 20 March 1925 and served as C-in-C, India, from August 1925 until May 1930. During this period Indian public opinion pressed for an increase in the number of full military commissions granted to Indian cadets. Birdwood, like many British officers of the Indian Army, resisted this. Rather than allowing Indian commissioned officers to serve throughout the whole Indian Army, he concentrated them in a small number of segregated units and thus worsened their prospects of promotion compared with those of British officers joining the Indian Army.

Birdwood had hopes of becoming Governor-General of Australia, but when no offer was made, he accepted instead the post of Master of Peterhouse, Cambridge. In March 1933 he became colonel of the Royal Horse Guards. In 1937, as the senior field marshal after the Duke of Connaught [73], who was too ill to be present, Birdwood presented George VI [106] with his baton in the ceremony first devised for George V [80] in 1910. Birdwood retired from Peterhouse in 1938. He was created Baron Birdwood, of Anzac and of Totnes, and became honorary colonel of 75 (Cinque Ports) (Home Counties) Anti-Aircraft Regiment, Royal Artillery, in the Territorial Army. Two years later, during the Battle of Britain, he was able to observe their shooting in the skies over his official residence, Deal Castle, of which he had become the Captain in 1935. Lord Birdwood died at Hampton Court Palace on 17 May 1951. He was the first C-in-C, India, to serve in that appointment while holding the rank of field marshal, and was the first officer of the Indian Army to be a field marshal while in active employment.

BIRENDA BIR BIKRAM SHAH DEVA
HM King of Nepal (1945-2001) [131]

King Birenda, born in 1945, succeeded to the throne of Nepal on the death of his father, King Mahendra [124] in 1972. Having received a modern Western education, he liberalized the system under which Nepal was governed at local level by elected non-political councils (*panchayats*) while central government remained in the hands of ministers directly appointed by the King. He introduced a number of constitutional reforms between 1975 and 1977, but growing political unrest, accompanied by student demonstrations, led to serious disturbances in 1979. The King called for a national referendum on the question of whether political parties should again be allowed in Nepal. The result was declared to be in favour of retaining government through the *panchayats*, but further constitutional changes resulted in the establishment of an elected national parliament. Ministers were still chosen by the King, but became subject to dismissal if they were unable to command a majority in parliament. King Birenda's government maintained the policy of permitting his Gurkha subjects to enlist in the British and Indian armies, for economic rather than political reasons, as the pay and pensions of Gurkha soldiers contributed greatly to the wealth of the country. King Birenda became an honorary general in the British Army in 1973 and an honorary field marshal (the only one ever appointed) on 18 November 1980. On 31 May 2001, together with his Queen, he was murdered by his son, Crown Prince Dipendra, who then killed himself.

BLAKENEY
Sir EDWARD, GCB, GCH (1778–1868) [43]

Edward Blakeney was the fourth son of Colonel William Blakeney of Newcastle-on-Tyne, who came from an Anglo-Irish family and sat for a Galway constituency in the Irish parliament from 1776 to 1783. Early in the French Revolutionary War the young Blakeney was commissioned as a cornet in the 8th Light Dragoons on 28 February 1794. He became a lieutenant in the 121st Foot on 4 September 1794 and a captain in the 99th Foot (later disbanded) on 24 December 1794. Blakeney served in 1796 in the expedition that captured the Dutch colonies in Guiana. In this campaign he was taken prisoner three times and experienced much hardship. He exchanged to the 17th Foot in March 1798, after which he took part in the Helder campaign where he was at Krabbendam (11 September 1799); Alkmaar (19 September 1799); Egmont (2 October 1799) and Kastrikum (6 October 1799). Blakeney became a major on 17 September 1801. He went on the half-pay list in 1802, but after the renewal of war with France joined the 47th Foot on 9 July 1803. He exchanged into the 7th Royal Fusiliers on 24 March 1804, served with this regiment in the descent on Copenhagen (August 1807) and at Martinique (February 1809) and was promoted to lieutenant colonel in the Army on 28 April 1808.

Following garrison duty in Nova Scotia, Blakeney and his fusiliers joined the Peninsular War in June 1810. He fought at Busaco (27 September 1810) and at Albuera (16 May 1811), where he was wounded while commanding his regiment's 2nd Battalion during the advance of the Fusilier Brigade. Blakeney became a regimental lieutenant colonel in the place of the commanding officer of the 1st Battalion, the 7th Royal Fusiliers, who fell at Albuera. He was at Aldea de Ponte (27 September 1811); Ciudad Rodrigo (stormed 19 January 1812); Badajoz (6 April 1812), where he was severely wounded; Vittoria (21 June 1813); Pamplona (June-July 1813); the Pyrenees (27 July 1813) and the Nivelle (10 November 1813). Blakeney then returned to England on leave, where he married Maria Gardiner, daughter of a general in the East India Company's service, and was promoted colonel on 4 June 1814. He resumed command of his battalion late in 1814 and sailed with it to the war in America, where he fought at New Orleans (8 January 1815). He was awarded the KCB in January 1815.

Sir Edward Blakeney returned to Europe too late to fight at Waterloo, but remained in France with the Army of Occupation until 1819. He continued in command of the 7th Royal Fusiliers until he was promoted to major general on 27 May 1825. He served in Portugal in 1826, as a brigade commander in the British mercenary force supporting the constitutional government against Dom Miguel, the absolutist claimant to the Portuguese throne. Blakeney became colonel of the 7th Royal Fusiliers on 20 September 1832 and was promoted to lieutenant general on 28 June 1838. Between 1838 and 1855 he commanded the forces in Ireland. He became a general on 20 June 1854 and colonel of the 1st Foot (the Royal Scots) on 21 December 1854. In September 1856 Blakeney was appointed Governor of the Royal Hospital, Chelsea. He was promoted to field marshal on 9 November 1862 and was appointed colonel-in-chief of the Rifle Brigade (the Prince Consort's Own) on 28 August 1865. He died on 2 August 1868, at the Royal Hospital, and was buried at Twickenham.

BLAMEY
Sir THOMAS, GBE, KCB, CMG, DSO (1884–1951) [118]

Thomas Blamey was born at Lake Albert, near Wagga Wagga, New South Wales, on 24 January 1884. He was the fourth son and seventh child of a cattle drover and farmer of modest means, who had migrated to Australia from Cornwall in 1862. Blamey was educated at Wagga Wagga Public School, where he was a keen member of the cadet corps.

He joined the New South Wales education service as a pupil teacher in 1899, and moved to Fremantle Boy's School, Western Australia, in 1903, where he continued to be an enthusiastic instructor in the school cadet movement. In 1906 Blamey came third in the competitive examination for commissions in the regular Australian Staff Corps. The available vacancies were nevertheless allotted to candidates from other states and it was only after an appeal (hinting at legal action) that Blamey was commissioned as a lieutenant in November 1906, as a staff officer (cadets) based at Melbourne, Victoria. In November 1909 he married the thirty-four year-old Minnie Millard, daughter of a prosperous Melbourne stockbroker. They later had two sons, the elder of whom became an officer of the Royal Australian Air Force and was killed in 1932 in a flying accident. Blamey was promoted to captain on 1 December 1910. After passing the Staff College entrance examination, he attended the Indian Staff College, Quetta, between January 1912 and December 1913. After qualifying there, Blamey was sent to the UK for experience of staff duty with the British Army and arrived in London in June 1914. Before taking up his staff post (with the Wessex Division of the Territorial Force), he toured the battlefields of the Franco-Prussian War and was deported from Germany after displaying an interest in the defences of Metz.

On the outbreak of the First World War in August 1914 Blamey was assigned to the War Office for intelligence duties. Early in December 1914 he joined the 1st Division, Australian Imperial Forces, in Egypt as a General Staff officer, grade 3, with promotion to acting major. He was one of the few Australian officers trained in staff duties and proved himself exceptionally able in this field. He landed with his division at Anzac Cove, Gallipoli, on 25 April 1915 and was in personal combat during a night patrol on 13 May 1915. After three months in Gallipoli, Blamey was appointed assistant adjutant and quartermaster general of the 2nd Division, AIF. He landed in France in the spring of 1916 and returned to the 1st Division, AIF, as GSO 1 in July 1916. Blamey took command of the 2nd Battalion, AIF, in January 1917. At the end of June 1917 he commanded the 1st Infantry Brigade, AIF, before returning to his previous post as GSO 1 at divisional headquarters. Blamey was promoted to brigadier general in May 1918, when he became Chief of Staff of the Australian Corps. Its successes at Hamel (4 July 1918) and Amiens (8 August 1918) owed much to Blamey's careful planning. After the end of hostilities in November 1918 he was involved in organizing the repatriation of the AIF, before going home himself in 1919.

Blamey reverted to his substantive rank of colonel and served at Army HQ, Melbourne, first as Director of Military Operations and later as

Deputy Chief of the General Staff. From August 1922 to the beginning of 1925, he was the Australian representative on the Imperial General Staff in London. He was appointed Second Chief of the General Staff in Australia, as a substantive brigadier general, in 1925. At this time, the Chief Commissioner of the Victoria Police resigned following a bitterly-fought strike among his policemen. Sir Harry Chauvel, famous as the commander of the Australian Light Horse in the recent war and, at this time, Inspector General of the Australian Military Forces, suggested Blamey as a suitable replacement. Blamey, who saw no further career prospects as a soldier, was happy to accept. He resigned from the permanent forces and took charge of the Victoria Police on 1 September 1925. His new career began amid controversy when a police raid on a disorderly house found an individual who claimed to be Blamey and produced a key-ring, with Blamey's police badge, as identification. Blamey subsequently declared that he had lent his keys to a wartime comrade, who happened to be visiting Melbourne, to allow him to help himself to drinks from Blamey's police locker. Nevertheless, his attempts to suppress details of the incident were widely regarded as an abuse of authority. He survived this affair and went on to introduce many reforms into his police force. Those who opposed him were posted to remote districts. The Police Association, the policemen's trade union, was crushed. Blamey was equally autocratic in his approach to the Victoria government and refused to accept any interference by politicians in his command decisions. At the end of his first five-year term, the Labour-controlled administration reappointed him, but reduced his salary by a half. His original salary was restored in 1932 when the conservative Country Party came to power. He was awarded a knighthood in 1935. In May 1936, Sir Thomas Blamey tried to suppress details of an incident in which the chief of his Criminal Investigation Branch was shot and wounded in highly questionable circumstances. This led to a public scandal followed by a judicial investigation. Blamey's evidence was found to be "unacceptable" and on 9 July 1936 he was forced to resign as the alternative to being dismissed.

On leaving the permanent forces in 1925 Blamey had joined the Militia, the citizen force on which Australia relied for national defence in time of war. Between 1931 and 1937 he commanded the 3rd Division as a major general of Militia. When his tenure of command expired, he became a radio journalist in Melbourne, broadcasting to his listeners on the dangers of the growing international tension in Europe. In 1939 Blamey was appointed first as the Chairman of the Australian Manpower Committee and then as Controller General of Recruiting.

Blamey's first wife had died, after a long illness, in 1932. He married again, in April 1939, this time to Olga Farnswood, a Melbourne fashion artist who was several years younger than her new husband, but equally forceful and even more colourful in her ways. On 28 September 1939, after the beginning of the Second World War, Blamey became GOC 6th Division, Australian Imperial Forces. In April 1940 he was promoted to lieutenant general and given command of the Australian Corps. He joined his HQ and the 6th Australian Division in Palestine on 20 June 1940.

Blamey made it one of his prime concerns to ensure that British generals understood that Australian troops remained under the control of the Australian government. He reluctantly accepted the decision of Sir Archibald Wavell [111], C-in-C Middle East, to commit the 6th Australian Division to battle in Libya before it had received its full scale of equipment, though the success of the Australians at Bardia (3 January 1941) justified Wavell's optimism. Yielding to pressure from the Australian government, Wavell carried out his promise to place the British forces in Libya under command of Blamey's Australian Corps early in February 1941. Blamey reached Libya, but was almost at once recalled to Cairo to prepare for the British expedition to Greece under Sir Henry "Jumbo" Wilson [115]. Blamey landed in Greece on 19 March 1941, where he commanded a corps made up of Australian and New Zealand formations in a brief revival of the famous ANZACs of the First World War and survived numerous German air attacks on his HQ. When the campaign was lost, Blamey and a small group of key personnel escaped in a RAF flying boat on 25 April 1941. He was much criticized for giving the last available seat to his remaining son, a major on his staff. He was also criticized because Lady Blamey had arrived in the Middle East in January 1941, contrary to the policy of the Australian government that no dependants of the AIF should join their menfolk there. Lady Blamey refused to return home, pointing out that the wives of several senior officers of the British Army were in Egypt, where they supported their husbands' social duties. Blamey declared that he could not force his wife to leave and sent all communications on the subject to her solicitors.

On returning from Greece, Blamey was made Deputy Commander-in-Chief, Middle East. This office had little real function, as it had been created by the British only as a means of retaining all the field commands for British or Indian Army generals while meeting Australian pressure for a share of senior appointments. Blamey continued to be directly responsible to his own government as commander of the Australian Imperial Force. He clashed with Wavell's successor, Sir

Claude Auchinleck [116] over the question of replacing the Australian troops who had stood a long siege in Tobruk. When Blamey insisted that they should be relieved by British troops, Auchinleck threatened to demand his dismissal, but the Australian government supported Blamey and Auchinleck (whom Blamey regarded as a bully) was forced to give way. Blamey was promoted to general on September 1941. After a brief visit to Australia in November 1941, he arrived back at Cairo shortly after the Japanese attack on Pearl Harbor (7 December 1941).

With the decision of the Australian government to recall its forces from the Middle East, Blamey returned to Australia on 23 March 1942 to be appointed C-in-C, Australian Military Forces, and Commander Allied Land Forces, South West Pacific. He also took over the financial and administrative powers previously held by the Australian Military Board. Between September 1942 and January 1943 he exercised personal command of the operations in New Guinea, where he defeated the Japanese in a hard-fought jungle campaign ending with the re-capture of Buna (9 December 1942). Thereafter, the Allied Supreme Commander in this theatre, General Douglas MacArthur, conducted operations through task forces of United States personnel, under his immediate control. MacArthur wished to minimize the role played by Australian troops and used his influence over the Australian Prime Minister, John Curtin, to weaken Blamey's position. Nevertheless, Blamey was able to remain in post as C-in-C and, in the closing stages of the war, persuaded Curtin to allow him to undertake an offensive campaign in Papua and the Solomon Islands. The aim of the campaign was to establish Australian military and political prestige in the area, but he was criticized by ministers who were facing popular demands for demobilization and who suspected Blamey of seeking personal glory.

Blamey retired on 31 January 1946. His business investments had prospered, so that he was able to live in comfort, but he resumed his role as a journalist and urged Australia to keep up her defences and to care for her ex-servicemen. A suggestion that he should be promoted to field marshal in the post-war distribution of honours was ignored by the Australian Labour Prime Minister of the day. It was taken up again by Sir Robert Menzies, Blamey's old ally, when he returned to power as Liberal Prime Minister in December 1949. The British military establishment declared (quite untruthfully) that retired generals could not be promoted to this rank. Menzies defeated this objection by restoring Blamey to the active list and promoting him to the rank of field marshal in the Australian Military Forces on 8 June 1950, back-dated to 1 January 1950. A few weeks later, Blamey was stricken with a paralysis of his legs. He rallied and hoped to go to London to receive his baton from King George VI [106], but never recovered his mobility. Sir Thomas Blamey was the only Australian officer to become a field marshal. He died of a stroke at the Repatriation General Hospital, Melbourne, on 27 May 1951.

BOYLE
RICHARD, 2nd Viscount Shannon (1674–1740) [3]

Richard Boyle, born in 1674, began his military career as a volunteer serving with James Butler, Duke of Ormonde, at the Boyne (1 July 1690) and later in the Low Countries, in the Nine Years War. After succeeding his grandfather, Francis Boyle (fourth son of the 1st Earl of Cork) as 2nd Viscount Shannon, he served at Landen (29 July 1693), where he was wounded and taken prisoner. He obtained his first commission on 16 February 1694, as a sub-brigadier in Ormonde's Troop of Horse Guards and cornet in the Army. Shannon remained in this campaign until the end of the Nine Years War, with promotion to cornet in his troop and major in the Army in 1697. He left the Horse Guards in February 1702 on appointment as colonel of a newly-raised unit, Prince George of Denmark's Regiment of Marines. During Ormonde's expedition to Cadiz (September-October 1702) Shannon commanded a brigade of grenadiers at the storming of Vigo, after which he was sent home with the despatches as a reward for bravery. He became a major general in 1706 and a lieutenant general in 1709. Shannon was appointed to command a planned expedition to Spain, but the project was cancelled in July 1710. He then became a member for the Commission for the inspection and regulation of Army clothing. After the disbandment of his marines, he became colonel of the Edinburgh Regiment (later the 25th Foot) in January 1715.

Shannon was appointed commander-in-chief in Ireland in 1720. He remained in this post for the next twenty years (by far the longest tenure in its history) until his death in December 1740. Shannon became colonel of the King's Carabiniers (later the 6th Dragoon Guards) in June 1721. He retained this appointment until March 1727, when he became colonel of the 4th or Scots Troop of Horse Guards. He was promoted to general in 1735 and to field marshal on 2 June 1739. Viscount Shannon sat as Member of Parliament successively for Arundel (1707–1710), Hythe (1710–1711) and East Grinstead (1715–1734). He married Grace, daughter and co-heiress of John Senhouse, a country gentleman, of Nether Hall, Cumberland, and had one child, a daughter. Shannon died on 20 December 1740, at his residence, Ashley Park, Walton-on-Thames. His title, for lack of a male heir, became extinct. His viscountess died in 1755. In accordance with her will, their only daughter, Grace, Countess of Middlesex, erected a magnificent monument to his memory, in the parish church of St Mary, Walton-on-Thames.

BRAMALL
Sir EDWIN NOEL WESTBY, Baron Bramall, KG, GCB, OBE, MC (1923-) [132]

Edwin (Dwin) Bramall, whose father had served in the First World War as an officer in the Royal Field Artillery, was born on 18 December 1923. He was educated at Eton College and entered the Army on 12 August 1942. After serving in the ranks and as an officer cadet, he was granted a Regular Army emergency commission as a second lieutenant in the King's Royal Rifle Corps on 22 May 1943. Bramall was promoted to war substantive lieutenant on 22 November 1943 and joined the 2nd Battalion, the King's Royal Rifle Corps, a motorized infantry battalion. He landed in Normandy on 7 June 1944, in advance of the main body of his battalion and served with it, first as a platoon commander and later as battalion intelligence officer, throughout the campaign in North West Europe. Bramall took part in various actions in France, the Low Countries, the Reichswald and north-western Germany until hostilities ended on 6 May 1945. After being wounded on 16 July 1944 at Fontaine Etoupafour, south-west of Caen, he subsequently rejoined his battalion at Falaise. On 27 October 1944, while going to help a wounded corporal in a minefield, he trod on a landmine, which did not detonate. Bramall was awarded the Military Cross (announced in December 1944 and gazetted in March 1945) for his conduct in a patrol action in southern Holland. He survived another landmine incident, unhurt, on 30 March 1945.

In September 1945, when his battalion went to Libya, Bramall was appointed staff captain at a divisional HQ in India. Between June and December 1946 he was a divisional deputy assistant adjutant general in the occupation of Japan. He was granted a permanent commission in the Regular Army as a lieutenant with effect from 18 June 1946 and became a war substantive captain on 29 September 1946. He became a General Staff officer, grade 3, in the Directorate of Military operations at the War Office in March 1947, remaining in this post until August 1948. In 1949, Bramall married Dorothy Avril Wentworth of Stoke Bruerne Park, Northamptonshire, the only daughter of a retired brigadier general. They later had a son and a daughter. Bramall was an instructor at the School of Infantry from August 1949 to September 1951, with promotion to substantive captain on 18 December 1950. After qualifying at the Staff College, Camberley, he was promoted to temporary major on 2 February 1953. He served as GSO 2 (Operations) of an infantry division in the Middle East from then until January 1955, when he returned to the UK to become a training company commander at the Rifle Depot, Winchester. In September 1956 Bramall joined the 1st Battalion, the King's Royal Rifle Corps, in Libya, as a company commander, and became a substantive major on 18 December 1957. He was made a local lieutenant colonel on 10 May 1958, when he returned to the Staff College as an instructor in the grade of GSO 2. Bramall was promoted to brevet lieutenant colonel on 1 July 1961 and returned to regimental duty on 2 February 1962 as second-in-command of the 1st Battalion, the 2nd Green Jackets (the King's Royal Rifle Corps) in Berlin and later at Colchester. He became a temporary lieutenant colonel on 29 April 1963, with appointment as GSO 1 (Defence Re-organisation) on the staff of Earl Mountbatten of Burma, Chief of Defence Staff at the Ministry of Defence.

Bramall returned to regimental duty as commanding officer of the 2nd Green Jackets (KRRC) on 25 January 1965, with promotion to substantive lieutenant colonel. He commanded this unit (later the 2nd Battalion, the Royal Green Jackets) in Malaysia during the confrontation with Indonesia (1965–1966) and was mentioned in despatches. He then became colonel and GSO 1 at the Staff College, where he served from March to November 1967 with promotion to brigadier on 30 June 1967. Bramall commanded the 5th (Airportable) Infantry Brigade from November 1967 to December 1969. During 1970, he attended the Imperial Defence College. Bramall became a major general on 28 July 1971 and was GOC 1st Division, in the British Army of the Rhine, from January 1972 to November 1973. He was appointed commander of the troops in Hong Kong in December 1973, was promoted to lieutenant general on 12 December 1973 and was created KBE in January 1974. On 15 May 1976 Sir Edwin Bramall became C-in-C, United Kingdom Land Forces, and was promoted to general.

He returned to the Ministry of Defence as Vice Chief of the Defence Staff (Personnel and Logistics) in May 1978. He faced a crisis resulting from the decision of the Labour Government of the day to impose pay restraint on government employees. The Treasury insisted that recommendations for an increase in military salaries, to take account of inflation, could not be fully implemented. Fearing an exodus of trained personnel and even the possibility of calls for military trade unions, the

Chiefs of Staff instructed Bramall to give the media an "off-the-record" briefing with factually accurate, but politically embarrassing, material. Despite ministerial anger, the Cabinet subsequently agreed almost all the proposed pay award. The government was defeated in the General Election of 1979, largely because of its refusal to allow fair pay for public employees, but its Conservative successor soon adopted even more severe counter-inflationary measures. Bramall became Chief of the General Staff in July 1979 and had to meet demands by the Secretary of State for Defence, John Nott, for further cuts in defence spending. Bramall's offer to reduce the number of troops in BAOR was found to be politically and internationally unacceptable and was rejected, as he had expected. Nevertheless, it had reduced the pressure for reductions in the Army vote and the burden of defence cuts fell mostly on the Royal Navy. During the South Atlantic campaign of 1982 (arising partly from Nott's decision to reduce the Royal Navy's presence in this area), Bramall supported the plan to land British troops at San Carlos Water. Mindful of Gallipoli in 1915 and Anzio in 1944, where initially successful landings had not been immediately exploited, he gave strong support to the rapid advance that led to the defeat of the Argentinian ground forces. As CGS, Bramall also had the responsibility for setting up the British Peace Monitoring and Training Team in Zimbabwe (formerly Rhodesia) at the time of transition to majority rule after a prolonged armed struggle. In the continuing emergency in Northern Ireland, he was able to make significant reductions in the number of infantry battalions deployed there, while making increased use of Intelligence resources and Special Forces.

Bramall was promoted to field marshal on 1 August 1982, when he completed his period in office as CGS. He became Chief of the Defence Staff in October 1982 at a time when, as a result of British success in the South Atlantic war, the constant Treasury-led pressure for defence cuts was slightly eased. Nevertheless, the new Defence Secretary, Michael Heseltine, demanded "efficiency savings" (meaning not savings *in* efficiency, but *through* efficiency). These were achieved by further centralization within the Ministry of Defence (a process Bramall himself had generally supported since his time on Mountbatten's staff) and by combining various support functions into single tri-service organizations. As CDS, Bramall developed the concept of the "Fifth Pillar" that he had first devised when CGS, pulling together the minor "out-of-area" activities such as the work of defence attachés and various forms of assistance to small friendly countries. He left this office in November 1985 and was granted a life peerage as Baron Bramall of Bushfield in 1987. He was colonel commandant of the 3rd Battalion, the Royal Green Jackets, from December 1973 to June 1984 and of the Special Air Service Regiment from 1984 to 1992, and colonel of the 2nd King Edward VII's Own Gurkha Rifles (the Sirmoor Rifles) from September 1976 to September 1986.

BROOKE
Sir ALAN FRANCIS, 1st Viscount Alanbrooke, KG, GCB, OM, GCVO, DSO (1883–1963) [112]

Alan Brooke, the sixth son and ninth and youngest child of a Fermanagh baronet, Sir Victor Brooke, was born at Baneres-de-Bigorre, near Pau, Gascony, on 23 July 1883. He was educated at Pau, in a school for the children of British families, though he spoke French as his native language and his French birth made it necessary for him to be naturalised as a British subject when he later decided to make his career in the British Army. After three months' study in England, Brooke passed into the Royal Military Academy, Woolwich, from which he was commissioned as a second lieutenant in the Royal Field Artillery on 24 December 1902. He joined the 48th Battery at Fethard, in southern Ireland. He was promoted to lieutenant on 24 December 1905 and was subsequently posted to the 30th Battery, stationed in the Punjab, where he arrived in December 1906. Brooke's hearing was found to have been damaged by the firing of his own guns, a common affliction of artillery officers. After returning to England for a specialist medical examination, he was advised to leave regimental duty and make his career on the staff. Brooke therefore studied for the Staff College entrance examination, though without success. While in the UK he became engaged to Jane Richardson, the daughter of a retired colonel whose estate lay near that of Brooke's own family in County Fermanagh. He returned to India to take up a post in N Battery, Royal Horse Artillery, and later became officer commanding H Ammunition Column in IX Brigade, Royal Horse Artillery. Brooke was married on 28 July 1914 while on leave in the UK. Six days later, when the First World War began, he was ordered back to India to rejoin his command. He reached Egypt, where fortuitously he met his ammunition column on its way to France. He resumed command and rejoined his brigade in the closing stages of the first battle of Ypres.

Brooke was promoted to captain on 30 October 1914 and became adjutant of his Royal Horse Artillery brigade in February 1915. He served in this post during the battles of Neuve Chapelle (10–13 March 1915) and Festubert (15–25 May 1915) and subsequently was appointed Brigade Major, Royal Artillery, 18th (Eastern) Division, on 21 November 1915, with substantive promotion to major on 24 April 1916. He served in this post during the battle of the Somme (1 July –18 November 1916) and was credited with introducing the concept of the "creeping barrage", though Brooke himself maintained that he took the idea from the French. In recognition of his services on the Somme, Brooke was gazetted DSO on 1 January 1917. He was posted to the Canadian Corps as deputy assistant adjutant general, Royal Artillery, on 13 February 1917 and was responsible for the artillery plan in the attack on Vimy Ridge (9 April 1917). He became a General Staff officer, grade 2, in the Canadian Corps on 28 August 1917 and served in this appointment throughout the third battle of Ypres (31 July–6 November 1917). Brooke joined the staff of the First Army in June 1918, and became GSO 1, with promotion to acting lieutenant colonel, on 20 September 1918.He remained in this post until the end of hostilities in November 1918. During the course of the First World War he was mentioned in despatches six times. He became a brevet lieutenant colonel on 1 January 1919 and was nominated for a place in the first post-war course at the Staff College, Camberley, later that year.

After passing out of the Staff College, Brooke served from February 1920 to January 1923 as GSO 2 in the 50th (Northumbrian) Division of the Territorial Army. He was then appointed an instructor at the Staff College, Camberley, where he became friendly with another instructor, Bernard Montgomery [114], to whom he later gave much support. While at Camberley, Brooke was in a road accident, while driving a fast, open car. He was badly hurt and his wife was fatally injured, leaving him with two young children. In January 1927 Brooke joined the first batch of students at the newly-opened Imperial Defence College, London. He returned to regimental duty in 1928 and became Commandant of the School of Artillery, Larkhill, with the rank of temporary brigadier, on 4 February 1929. He was given promotion to substantive colonel, back-dated to 1 January 1923. In 1929 Brooke married Benita, widow of Captain Sir Thomas Lees, a baronet who had been killed serving with the Dorset Yeomanry in the Dardanelles. They had a long and happy marriage, with one daughter, who was killed in a riding accident in 1961, and a son who in due course succeeded his half-brother as 3rd Viscount Alanbrooke. Brooke returned to the Imperial Defence College in 1932, as an instructor. In April 1934 he became brigadier of 8th Infantry Brigade at Plymouth. He was promoted to major general on 8 November 1935, when he was appointed Inspector, Royal Artillery, in the Directorate of Military Training at the War Office. He became Director of Military Training in August 1936. At the end of 1937,

Brooke was given command of the new Mobile Division. On 27 June 1938 he was promoted to lieutenant general and was appointed GOC Anti-Aircraft Corps, consisting of five Territorial anti-aircraft divisions. This became Anti-Aircraft Command in March 1939, with Brooke as its GOC-in-C. He was made a colonel commandant of the Royal Artillery in May 1939, was awarded the KCB and became GOC-in-C, Southern Command in July 1939.

With the outbreak of the Second World War on 3 September 1939 Sir Alan Brooke's command became II Corps in the British Expeditionary Force sent to France under Lord Gort [110]. Brooke soon came to have doubts about the morale of the French Army and also about Gort's intellectual capacity to cope with the role of a C-in-C. Gort, younger than Brooke (and promoted over his head in 1937), in turn regarded Brooke as a faint-hearted defeatist. In the campaign of May 1940, Brooke gained credit for his cool and efficient conduct of operations during the BEF's retreat to Dunkirk. After returning to the UK, he was sent back to France with orders from Winston Churchill, the British Prime Minister, to organize a new BEF with a view to holding Normandy and Brittany. Brooke persuaded Churchill that such a scheme was unrealistic and succeeded in evacuating three combat divisions and large numbers of logistic units from the rear areas. He resumed his role as GOC-in-C Southern Command on 19 June 1940, with responsibility for the defence of the coastline between Sussex and Wales. He was critical of the counter-invasion strategy, based on a series of static defence lines, adopted by Sir Edmund Ironside [107], C-in-C Home Forces. On 19 July 1940 Churchill removed Ironside from office and appointed Brooke in his place. Brooke reversed Ironside's plan and built up a strong mobile reserve. In December 1941 Churchill, irritated by the continued opposition of Sir John Dill [109], Chief of the Imperial General Staff, replaced him with Brooke, who was then given promotion to general, back-dated to 7 May 1941.

As CIGS, Brooke controlled British military policy, under the direction of the Prime Minister, for the rest of the Second World War. He was on terms of mutual admiration and exasperation with Churchill and felt that a vital part of his duty was to dissuade the Prime Minister from adopting strategies that the professional soldiers considered unsound. Brooke was also responsible for the selection of generals for senior command appointments. He refused to give Gort another field command, was ambivalent about Sir Harold Alexander [113], encouraged and protected Sir Bernard Montgomery [114] (to whom he had handed over command of II Corps at Dunkirk) and ensured that Sir William Slim [117] remained in command of the Fourteenth Army in Burma. Brooke attended the major Allied conferences at Casablanca, Washington, Quebec, Moscow, Cairo and Teheran. Realizing the importance of maintaining good Anglo-American relations, he kept on cordial terms with most American leaders, with the notable exception of his opposite number, General George C. Marshall. Brooke was promoted to field marshal on 1 January 1944.

At the end of the war Brooke was ready to leave office, but was persuaded to remain in post while the new Labour ministers at the War Office gained experience of subjects unfamiliar to them. He was created Baron Alanbrooke, of Brookeborough, in September 1945 and Viscount Alanbrooke in January 1946. Alanbrooke was appointed Master Gunner, St James's Park, in succession to Lord Milne [97] in 1946. He was colonel commandant of the Glider Pilot Regiment from November 1942 to July 1945 and a colonel commandant of the Royal Horse Artillery, from 1946 to 1954. In June 1946 he was succeeded as CIGS by Viscount Montgomery. Disappointed in his hope of becoming Governor-General of Canada when this post was awarded to Lord Alexander of Tunis [113], Alanbrooke entered the commercial world as a director of a number of banks and large corporations. In semi-retirement, he continued his long-standing interest in ornithology. He died of a heart attack on 17 June 1963, at his home in Hartley Witney, Hampshire, and was buried in the nearby cemetery of St Mary's Church.

BROWNLOW
Sir CHARLES HENRY, GCB (1831–1916) [78]

Charles Brownlow, born on 12 December 1831, came from a long-established Anglo-Irish family. He obtained a cadetship in the East India Company's service and was commissioned as an ensign in the Bengal Army on 20 December 1847. In 1851 he was appointed as adjutant of the 1st Sikh Infantry, a regiment raised for the local defence of the North-West Frontier. He was promoted to lieutenant on 10 September 1852 and took part in the Hazara campaign of 1852–53, where he was mentioned in despatches. Brownlow was again mentioned in despatches in August 1854, after a combat in Mohmandistan, where he was shot through both lungs.

On the outbreak of the Indian Mutiny in 1857, Brownlow, still serving on the North-West Frontier, was ordered to raise a new regiment, the 8th Punjab Infantry. During the Mutiny campaign he remained on the frontier in command of this unit and took part in an expedition against the Yusufzai Pathan tribesmen in 1858. Like all officers of the Company's service, Brownlow was transferred to that of the Crown in India in August 1858. He was promoted to captain on 3 November 1858. In 1860 he served with the Indian contingent in the Second China War and was at the attack on the Taku Forts (21 August 1860) and the subsequent occupation of Peking (Beijing). He joined the Bengal Staff Corps (established in January 1861 to replace the previous system of regimental cadres) and was promoted to brevet major on 13 February 1861. In the post-Mutiny reconstruction of the Bengal Army, the 8th Punjab Infantry was brought on to the permanent establishment and re-numbered as the 20th (Punjab) Bengal Native Infantry. It took part, under Brownlow's command, in the Ambala campaign of 1863 and was involved in fierce fighting against the Pathan tribesmen at Eagle's Picquet (22 and 26 October 1863) and Crag Picquet (12 November 1863). Brownlow was promoted to lieutenant colonel on 5 August 1864 and commanded his regiment in the large-scale Hazara campaign of 1868. He became a colonel on 11 August 1869. His last involvement in active operations was on India's North-Eastern border, as brigadier general commanding a column in the 1871 Lushai campaign, after which he was awarded the KCB.

Sir Charles Brownlow then commanded a brigade at Rawalpindi until 1877, when he returned to England. Between 1879 and 1889 he served on the staff of the Duke of Cambridge, C-in-C of the British Army, as assistant military secretary for India. He was promoted to major general on 1 July 1881, to lieutenant general on 7 September 1884 and to general on 22 January 1889. In 1890 he retired and married Georgina King, eldest daughter of the owner of Warfield Hall, Berkshire. After several changes in designation, his old regiment became the 20th Duke of Cambridge's Own Infantry (Brownlow's Punjabis) in 1904. Brownlow was appointed colonel of this regiment in May 1904 and, as the senior retired officer of the Indian Army, was promoted to field marshal on 20 June 1908. He died on 5 April 1916 and was buried in the churchyard of St Michael the Archangel, Warfield.

BURGOYNE
Sir JOHN FOX, 1st Baronet, GCB (1782–1871) [50]

John Fox Burgoyne was the illegitimate son of Lieutenant General John Burgoyne, soldier, politician and dramatist, best known as the "Gentleman Johnny" whose surrender at Saratoga was one of the decisive episodes in the American War of Independence. Earlier in his life, General Burgoyne had eloped with and married Lady Charlotte Stanley, daughter of the 11th Earl of Derby. They had no children and, after his wife's death, Burgoyne set up house with a popular singer, Susan Caulfield. His position in society prevented them from marrying, though they had four children together. The eldest of these, John Fox Burgoyne, took his second name from his baptismal sponsor, Charles James Fox, a friend and political ally of his father. After General Burgoyne died in 1792, his children were brought up by his late wife's nephew, the 12th Earl of Derby. John Fox Burgoyne was educated at Eton and the Royal Military Academy, Woolwich. He was commissioned as a second lieutenant in the Royal Engineers on 28 August 1798 and was later sent to join the British force besieging Valetta, where the French were finally starved into surrender in September 1800. Burgoyne was promoted to lieutenant on 1 July 1800. He continued in the Mediterranean theatre and served as aide-de-camp to General Henry Fox (Charles James Fox's elder brother) until receiving promotion to second captain on 6 March 1805. Burgoyne took part in the British expedition to Egypt at the end of 1806 and was at the capture of Alexandria in February 1807, the subsequent siege of Rosetta and the withdrawal to Alexandria in April 1807. After returning to Sicily, he joined the staff of Sir John Moore and went with his army to Sweden in May 1808 and Portugal in September 1808. As the engineer officer of the Light Division, he was with the rearguard in the early part of the retreat to Corunna and blew up the bridges at Benavente and Castro Gonzala (29 December 1808) as the French approached. Burgoyne returned to Portugal in April 1809, in the army under Sir Arthur Wellesley [24].

Burgoyne was at the passage of the Douro (Oporto, 12 May 1809) and, when Wellesley decided in October 1809 to fall back and hold Lisbon, joined with his fellow engineers in the construction of the lines of Torres Vedras. He was commended for his demolition of Fort Concepcion (20 July 1810) and for his command of the Portuguese troops serving with the British at El Bodon (25 September 1811), where he was thanked by Wellington in the field and was noticed by the French Marshal Marmont. As engineer officer of the 3rd Division, he served at Busaco (27 September 1810); the second siege of Badajoz (1–10 June 1811) and Ciudad Rodrigo (stormed 19 January 1812). For his services in leading the assault there, he was promoted to major on 6 February 1812. Burgoyne's next siege was again at Badajoz (17 March–6 April 1812) where he once more led the 3rd Division's storming parties. He was rewarded with promotion to lieutenant colonel on 27 April 1812. He subsequently served at Salamanca (22 June 1812);

the siege of Burgos (16 September–21 October 1812); Vittoria (21 June 1813); the siege of San Sebastian (stormed 31 August 1813); the passage of the Adour (23–26 February 1814) and the siege of Bayonne (27 February–13 April 1814). His next campaign was in the war against the United States, where he was the chief engineer at New Orleans (8 January 1815) and Fort Bowyer (Mobile Bay, 8–12 February 1815). Burgoyne returned to Europe too late for the battle of Waterloo, but served as chief engineer in the Army of Occupation until 1818.

From 1821 until 1826 Burgoyne was at the Royal Engineers Depot, Chatham. He then returned to Portugal in the force of British mercenaries sent to support the constitutional government against Dom Miguel, the absolutist claimant to the Portuguese throne. He was garrison engineer at Portsmouth between 1828 and 1831, with promotion to colonel on 22 July 1830, after which he became chairman of the Board of Public Works in Ireland. He held this post until 1845, during which time he was promoted to major general on 28 June 1838 and was awarded the KCB. Sir John Burgoyne was appointed Inspector General of Fortifications in 1845. He became involved in relief works during the Irish famine of 1846–1847 and sat as a member of various official commissions, including those to decide on the postal system, and the site of Waterloo Bridge. He became a lieutenant general on 11 November 1851.

In 1853 Burgoyne was sent by the British government, at his own suggestion, to inspect the Turkish fortifications on the lower Danube. On the outbreak of the Crimean War in 1854, he joined the British army under Lord Raglan [38] at Varna as an official adviser. When the Allies invaded the Crimea, Burgoyne played an important part in the selection of Kalamita Bay as the site for the army's disembarkation. He was also influential in the Allied decision not to attempt a *coup de main* against Sevastopol but to march round the city and conduct a regular siege from its south side. This resulted in the Allied forces spending the winter of 1854–55 in the field, for which Burgoyne was much blamed. He was recalled by the Cabinet in February 1855, after continual disagreements with his French allies. Burgoyne's popularity revived at the end of the war and he received various honours, including a baronetcy in 1856. He became a colonel commandant of the Royal Engineers on 22 November 1854, followed by promotion to general on 5 September 1855 and to field marshal on 1 January 1868. Burgoyne was married and had a daughter, who married an officer in the Army, and a son, Hugh, who joined the Royal Navy and was among the first recipients of the Victoria Cross. Captain Hugh Burgoyne was lost, with many of his crew, when the experimental warship HMS *Captain* was swamped in the Bay of Biscay in September 1870. Burgoyne never recovered from the loss of the son who had been the focus of his love and hopes. He died from the effects of grief on 7 October 1871, at Pembroke Gardens, London, and his baronetcy became extinct. Sir John Fox Burgoyne was the first field marshal to come from the Corps of Royal Engineers.

BYNG
Sir JOHN, 1st Earl of Strafford, GCB, GCH (1772–1860) [40]

John Byng, the third son of Major George Byng of Wrotham Park, Barnet, and the grandson of George Byng, 1st Viscount Torrington, was born in 1772. He joined the 33rd Foot as an ensign on 30 September 1793 and was promoted to lieutenant on 1 December 1793. He became a captain on 24 May 1794 and served with the 33rd in the Flanders campaign of 1794–5, and was at Geldermalsen (4 Jan 1795), where he was wounded. During the winter retreat into Germany his foot was affected by frostbite, after which he was known in his family as "Old Toes". In 1796 Byng became an aide-de-camp in the Southern District of Ireland, where he was wounded during the suppression of the insurgency of 1798. He became a major in the 60th Royal American Regiment on 1 January 1800 and lieutenant colonel of the 29th Foot on 14 March 1800. He transferred to the 3rd Foot Guards in 1804. In June 1804 he married Mary Stevens, eldest daughter of Peter Mackenzie of Grove House, Bushey, Hertfordshire. She later died, soon after the birth of her only child. Byng served with his regiment in the fruitless expedition to Hanover in 1805, in the more successful campaign around Copenhagen (August-September 1807) and in the disastrous invasion of Walcheren (August-December 1809). In 1809 he married Marianne, the second daughter of a baronet, Sir Walter James. He was promoted to colonel on 25 July 1810 and joined the army in the Peninsula in September 1811, where he was given command of a brigade in the 2nd Division. Byng was promoted to major general on 4 June 1813 and was at Vittoria (21 June 1813); the Pyrenees (27–30 July 1813); the Nivelle (10 October 1813); the Nive (10–18 December 1813), where he was wounded; Orthez (27 February 1814) and Toulouse (10 April 1814). After being made a KCB in the victory honours of 1814, Sir John Byng served in the Hundred Days campaign in command of the 2nd Guards Brigade. He was at Quatre Bras (16 June 1815) and Waterloo (18 June 1815), where he played an important part in the defence of Hougoumont.

63

Byng remained with the Army of Occupation until 1819 when he was appointed to command Northern District in England. He became a lieutenant general on 27 May 1825. He was colonel of the 4th West India Regiment from December 1816 until its disbandment in April 1819 and colonel of the 2nd West India Regiment from July 1822 to January 1828. He then became colonel of the 29th Foot. Between 1828 and 1831 Byng commanded the forces in Ireland. He then became MP for Poole and represented this borough until 1835, when he was created Baron Strafford as a reward for having supported the Reform Bill. His family's services to Peel's ministry were further recognized in 1843 when he was made Earl of Strafford (reviving an extinct title connected with his grandmother's family) and Viscount Enfield. He was promoted to general on 23 November 1841, became colonel of the Coldstream Guards on 15 August 1850 and a field marshal on 2 October 1855. By his second wife, who had died in 1843, Strafford had a son and three daughters. He died in London on 3 June 1860 and was succeeded as 2nd Earl by his eldest son, George Stevens Byng.

BYNG
Sir JULIAN HEDWORTH GEORGE BYNG, 1st Viscount Byng, GCB, GCMG, MVO (1862–1935) **[100]**

The Honourable Julian Byng was born at his family seat, Wrotham Park, Barnet, on 11 September 1862. He was the last of the seven children of George, 2nd Earl of Strafford (son of Sir John Byng, 1st Earl **[40]**), and his second wife, Harriet, younger daughter of Charles Cavendish, 1st Lord Chesham. The 2nd Earl had an earlier family of six children by his first wife, Lady Agnes Paget (daughter of the 1st Marquess of Anglesey **[37]**), who died in 1845. As the youngest of a large brood, Julian Byng was generally dressed in his brothers' cast-offs and became accustomed to a frugal and unpretentious way of life that he maintained throughout his life. Between 1874 and 1878 he was educated at Eton College, where he was given the nickname "Bungo" to distinguish him from his two elder brothers, who were known respectively as "Bingo" and "Bongo". He then entered the Army via the Militia, obtaining his first commission on 27 August 1879 as a lieutenant in the 2nd (Edmonton) Royal Middlesex Rifles. The Prince of Wales (the future Edward VII **[54]**), learning from the Earl of Strafford at a social gathering that Julian Byng remained unprovided for, offered him a vacancy in the 10th (Prince of Wales's Own Royal) Hussars. This gracious gesture was not altogether welcome to the Earl, as the officers of the 10th Hussars were expected to have a private income three times that which he was able to give his youngest son. Nevertheless, as the offer could not be refused, Byng became a lieutenant in this regiment on 27 January 1883.

In March 1883 Byng joined this regiment in India, where the low cost of living enabled him to live within his means. The 10th Hussars embarked for England on 6 February 1884, but were diverted to Suakin on the Red Sea, to take part in operations against the Mahdists. Byng was at El Teb (29 February 1884) and Tamai (13 March 1884), where he was mentioned in despatches. He returned to the UK with his regiment in April 1884. He became adjutant of the 10th Hussars in October 1886, shortly before he inherited a substantial legacy on his father's death. He was promoted to captain on 4 January 1890 and entered the Staff College, Camberley, in January 1893. Byng passed out of the Staff College in December 1894 and rejoined his regiment, where he served as a squadron commander until 1897, when the 10th Hussars were posted to Aldershot. He joined the staff there as a deputy assistant adjutant general, with promotion to major on 4 May 1898. At a garrison dinner party he met the 27-year old Evelyn Moreton, daughter of the tenant of Crookham Hall, Fleet. This lady, the granddaughter of a Greek millionaire, was both well-connected and unconventional. As wilful as she was determined, she fell in love with Byng. He was about to propose marriage when mobilization for the South African War led him to say nothing, so that she should not feel bound to him if he were wounded and disabled.

Byng was ordered to Natal as a deputy assistant provost marshal. When he arrived there early in November 1899 he was promoted to temporary lieutenant colonel and given command of a newly-raised colonial regiment, the South African Light Horse. By a combination of physical and moral force, he established military discipline in a unit made up of mostly South Africans and Canadians, plus a group of Texans who had arrived with a consignment of mules bought from the USA and had decided to stay for the fighting. Byng led his light horsemen at Hlangwhane Hill (14 December 1899); Bastion Hill (19 January 1900) and in other actions around Ladysmith, followed by operations in Cape Colony (December 1900-April 1901) and in the Orange River area (April 1901-March 1902). He was mentioned in despatches five times and gained a reputation for personal courage and coolness under fire. He became a substantive lieutenant colonel on 29 November 1900 and brevet colonel on 15 February 1902. After his last combat in this war, at Langewacht (23 February 1902) he wrote to Evelyn Moreton, with whom he remained in correspondence, asking her to marry him and to cable her reply. She responded by accepting, and telling him to return at once. He did so and horrified his future mother-in-law by arriving at Fleet with a North American accent and table manners acquired from two years in the veldt. After a honeymoon in Paris, the couple went to South Africa and then to India, where Byng took command of the 10th Hussars at Mhow. Their time there was one of personal unhappiness. Evelyn Byng suffered several miscarriages, ending with medical mistreatment after which she was unable to bear children. Byng himself was badly injured in a polo accident that, leaving him with a shortened arm, required him to leave his regiment and return to England early in 1904 for medical treatment.

Byng was appointed commandant of the newly-formed Cavalry School in 1905 and moved with it from Netheravon to Bordon, Hampshire. He then became brigadier general of the 2nd Cavalry Brigade at Canterbury. In June 1906 he took over command of the 1st Cavalry Brigade at Aldershot, under Sir John French [83]. Byng wished to train his units primarily to fight on foot, like light horse, but was frustrated by French's insistence on the importance of the *arme blanche*. He was promoted to major general on 1 April 1909, when he was given command of the East Anglian Division of the new Territorial Force. In October 1912 Byng went to Egypt as commander of the British forces there. He established cordial relations with Lord Kitchener [79], the British Consul General and, as Kitchener was a bachelor, Evelyn Byng, the senior Army wife in Cairo, became the leading British hostess there. When the First World War began, Kitchener was on leave in England. He became Secretary of State for War and recalled Byng from Egypt to command a new 3rd Cavalry Division.

Byng landed with his division at Ostend on 8 October 1914. During the first battle of Ypres (19 October- 21 November 1914) he operated in support of I Corps and was personally in the presence of the enemy at Sanctuary Wood (31 October 1914). On 4 May 1915 he was given command of the Cavalry Corps in succession to Sir Edmund Allenby [90], with promotion to temporary lieutenant general, (substantive on 3 June 1916) and the award of the KCMG. In August 1915 Sir Julian Byng was ordered to Gallipoli to command IX Corps. He soon formed the view that the British position was untenable and that the campaign should be abandoned. His role in the successful evacuation of his corps, at the end of 1915, gained Byng much credit and he returned to the Western Front in February 1916 to command XVII Corps. In May 1916 he was given command of the Canadian Corps, whose soldiers then began to call themselves "the Byng Boys", from a popular musical comedy of the day. He established a good rapport with his troops,

encouraging them to observe conventional standards of dress and discipline, while at the same time he gained their respect by frequent visits
to the front-line trenches. Byng commanded the Canadians in the battle
of the Somme, including the operations at Courcelette (15–16
September 1916) and Thiepval Ridge (26–30 September 1916). In the
battle of Arras (9–14 April 1917) Byng and the Canadian Corps
achieved a major success at Vimy Ridge.

Byng left the Canadian Corps on 9 June 1917, when he was given
command of the Third Army. He commanded this formation in the
battle of Cambrai (20 November–7 December 1917), with promotion
to general on 23 November 1917. The German offensives of March-
April 1918 fell heavily on the Third Army, but Byng was able to retreat
without his line being broken. When the tide turned in favour of the
Allies, Byng's army took the offensive on 21 August 1918. It broke
through the Hindenburg Line on 27 September and pressed on to reach
Maubeuge on 10 November 1918. Byng went home on leave, to find
that his wife had decided to go to Brussels as a lady-in-waiting with the
Royal party taking part in the re-entry to Brussels of King Albert I of
the Belgians **[94]**.

Byng was sent to Calais in January 1919, to deal with a mutiny arising
mostly from delays in demobilization. Combining a humanitarian
approach with a clear readiness to use force if necessary, he rapidly
restored order, with only a few irreconcilables brought to punishment.
Byng was offered the post of GOC-in-C Southern Command, but
declined so as not to harm the promotion prospects of his juniors. He
agreed to become chairman of the United Service Fund, a charity that
had accumulated millions of pounds from the proceeds of canteens and
messes during the war. When the Treasury was slow to hand over the
money, Byng forced it to disgorge by threatening to resign and so cause
a public scandal. In August 1919 he was raised to the peerage as Baron
Byng of Vimy, of Thorpe-le-Soken, and retired from the Army on
7 November 1919, at his own insistence, to ensure that the United
Service Fund was seen to be separate from the government.

Lord Byng, who had previously become an honorary general in the
Canadian Militia, was appointed Governor-General of Canada in
August 1920. He proved a generally popular figure, especially among
ex-servicemen, though his readiness to speak out on questions such as
the condition of the inner cities or animal welfare (a particular concern
of his wife) ruffled feathers among the Canadian establishment. Lady
Byng proved a tempestuous vicereine, noted as much for the lavish-
ness of her hospitality as for the violence of her language when vexed.
As Byng's tenure of office approached its end, he found himself in a

constitutional crisis. The Canadian Liberal prime minister, Mackenzie King, facing the certainty of losing a vote of censure over rum-running by his customs officers, sought a dissolution of Parliament. Byng refused until the Conservative opposition had a chance to form a government. After various parliamentary manoeuvres, King was re-elected on a platform of defending Canadian autonomy against British colonialism. Byng, who maintained throughout that he had acted with constitutional propriety, completed the normal term of his appoint-ment and returned to the UK in 1926, when he was raised to the rank of a viscount.

In June 1928 he was offered the post of Chief Commissioner of the Metropolitan Police. He declined on the grounds of age and ill-health, but eventually agreed, in response to pressure from his wife (whom he had not previously consulted), from the King and from the Cabinet. Byng's appointment was deplored by left-wing politicians, who saw him as an aristocrat who would use the police to crush the working class, but was welcomed by right-wing opinion for the same reason. In practice, he did much to improve the efficiency and morale of his force, by making sudden unannounced visits to stations and constables on the beat, improving welfare arrangements and acting against corruption. In Opposition, the Labour Party's Home Affairs spokesman had viewed him as yet another retired senior Army officer given a job that should have gone to a professionally qualified civilian. When a Labour Government came into office in 1928, Byng offered to resign, but was told that the new Cabinet had full confidence in him. He remained in post until September 1931, when he retired, suffering from a heart condition. Byng was made a field marshal on 17 July 1932 and died at his Essex home, Thorpe Hall, on 6 June 1935. He had become colonel of the 3rd (King's Own) Hussars in May 1912 and retained this post until January 1922, when he became colonel of the 10th (Prince of Wales's Own Royal) Hussars. In the Territorial Army, he was honorary colonel of the Suffolk Heavy Brigade, the Royal Artillery, and the 5th Battalion, the Essex Regiment.

CAMBRIDGE
HRH 1st DUKE OF, see **ADOLPHUS FREDERICK [26]**

CAMBRIDGE
HRH 2nd DUKE OF, see **GEORGE WILLIAM FREDERICK [45]**

CAMPBELL
Sir COLIN, 1st Baron Clyde, GCB, KSI (1792–1863) **[46]**

Colin Campbell was the eldest of four sons of a Glaswegian carpenter, Colin Macliver, and his wife, Agnes Campbell. His uncle, Colonel John Campbell, an officer of the 78th Highlanders, provided for his education and obtained him a commission, by nomination, as ensign in the 2nd Battalion, the 9th Foot, on 26 May 1808. Colin Campbell fought in this unit in the army under Wellesley **[24]** at Rolica (17 August 1808) and Vimiero (21 August 1808). He returned to the Peninsula later in 1808, in Sir John Moore's army, and took part in the retreat to Corunna (December 1808-January 1809). After joining the 1st Battalion, the 9th Foot, with promotion to lieutenant on 28 June 1809, Campbell took part in the Walcheren expedition (August-September 1809). There he contracted the malarial fever (from which he suffered for the rest of his life) that eventually forced the British to abandon the campaign. He served with the 1st Battalion, the 9th Foot, at Barossa (5 March 1811); Tarifa (October 1811-January 1812); Vittoria (21 June 1813) and San Sebastian, (25 July 1813), where he was wounded leading the forlorn hope in the first assault. Campbell was promoted without purchase to a captaincy in the 60th Royal American Regiment on 3 November 1813, but was still with the 9th at the passage of the Bidassoa (7 October 1813), where he was wounded for a second time. In 1814 he joined the 7th Battalion, the 60th Royal American Regiment, in Nova Scotia, and was subsequently with its 5th Battalion in Gibraltar, from 1816 until 1818, when this unit was disbanded.

Campbell then transferred to the 21st Royal North British Fusiliers and joined this regiment in Barbados in April 1819. Between 1821 and 1825, he held a staff appointment in British Guiana, after which he purchased his majority on 26 November 1825. He became a lieutenant colonel, unattached, on the half-pay list, on 26 October 1832, with the aid of Lord Fitzroy Somerset **[38]** and Sir Henry Hardinge **[41]**, fellow-veterans of the Peninsular War, who lent him the necessary purchase money. In 1835 Campbell obtained a lieutenant-colonelcy in the 9th Foot, from which he exchanged immediately to the 98th Foot to take command when the regiment returned to England from South Africa in 1837. He went with it to China in 1841, to reinforce Sir Hugh Gough **[44]** in the Opium War, and was at Chinkiang (21 July 1842). Campbell was promoted to colonel on 23 December 1842 and became garrison commander in the newly-acquired British colony of Hong Kong, an appointment that he retained until 1844. In February 1847 he was given command of a brigade in the British forces occupying the kingdom of Lahore, in the Punjab.

Campbell saw combat in the Second Sikh War at Ramnagar (21 November 1848); Chilianwala (13 November 1848) and Gujarat (21 February 1849). He was made a KCB in 1849. Despite declaring himself too old for active service, Sir Colin Campbell led successful expeditions against Pathan tribesmen on the North-West frontier between 1849 and 1852. His decision not to continue an offensive in Swat was followed by a public rebuke from the young Lord Dalhousie, the Governor-General of India, for having been excessively cautious. Campbell completed his campaign and then resigned in protest.

In February 1854, on the approach of the Crimean War, Campbell was selected to command a brigade of Highlanders. He was promoted to major general on 20 June 1854 and was at the battle of the Alma (20 September 1854), where his horse was shot under him. Campbell was appointed colonel of the 67th Foot on 24 October 1854. He remained in command of the Highland Brigade and took to wearing a Highlander's feathered bonnet in preference to the cocked hat of a general officer. At the battle of Balaklava (25 October 1854) he commanded the famous "thin red line" that drove off a threatened attack by Russian cavalry. When the Duke of Cambridge [45] returned to the UK, Campbell took his place in command of the 1st Division. After the death of the army commander, Lord Raglan [38], in June 1855, command in the Crimea passed to Sir James Simpson. A proposal was then made to offer Campbell a command in Malta as a way of removing him from the theatre of operations. When Simpson left the Crimea, Campbell (the next senior ranking officer) was passed over in favour of his immediate junior in the theatre, Major General William Codrington, a Guards officer who had not seen active service prior to landing in the Crimea. Ostensibly, this appointment was in response to popular agitation for the appointment of a younger officer, but it may possibly have reflected some social prejudice arising from Campbell's humble origins. Codrington had been promoted major general on the same date as Campbell but had been four years junior to him as a colonel and stood fifty-eight places junior to him in the major generals' list. Campbell took his supersession by Codrington as a slight and returned on leave to London, intending to resign. He was received graciously by the Queen and Prince Albert [33], after which he declared his readiness to return to duty, serving even as a corporal if the Queen so wished it. He was promoted to lieutenant general on 4 June 1856 and returned to the Crimea, having agreed to serve under Codrington as a corps commander. When Codrington decided not to divide his army into corps unless hostilities were renewed, Campbell went back to England, where he commanded South-East District from July to September 1856.

On 11 July 1857 Campbell was appointed C-in-C, India, in succession to the Hon George Anson, who had died of cholera soon after the beginning of the Indian Mutiny. He embarked the next day and arrived in Calcutta a month later. After waiting until his reinforcements arrived, he then marched into Oudh (Awadh), relieving and evacuating Lucknow (14–19 November 1857), fighting at Cawnpore (Kanpur, 6 December 1857) and re-taking Lucknow (11–19 March 1858). Though not present in the field at any other serious engagements, Campbell controlled the operations of several separate armies until the end of this war. He became colonel of the 93rd Highlanders in January 1858 and was promoted to general on 14 May 1858. Sir Colin Campbell was raised to the peerage as Baron Clyde in July 1858. He was faced with a mutiny by the East India Company's European troops, to whom a parsimonious government had denied the customary enlistment bounty when their service was transferred from the Company to that of the British crown. Clyde had some personal sympathy with these men, but used his British troops to enforce discipline while the Cabinet made a few grudging concessions. He left India in June 1860, to become colonel of the Coldstream Guards in July 1860 and a field marshal (passing over 24 generals senior to him) on 9 November 1862. Campbell, who never married, died at Chatham on 14 August 1863 and was buried in Westminster Abbey.

CAMPBELL
JOHN, 2nd Duke of Argyll and Duke of Greenwich (1678–1743) [2]

John Campbell, the eldest son of Archibald, 10th Earl (later 1st Duke) of Argyll, chief of the Clan Campbell and head of one of Scotland's most powerful and politically active noble families, was born on 10 October 1678. Known in his early years by the courtesy title Lord Lorne, he received his first commission on 7 April 1694, as colonel of a regiment of Foot, raised mostly from his father's clansmen. This regiment was disbanded in 1698, at the end of the Nine Years War. In the War of the Spanish Succession Lorne joined Marlborough's army in the Low Countries and served at Kaiserswerth (April-June 1702). On succeeding as 2nd Duke of Argyll in 1703, he returned to Scotland and began the political career appropriate to a great nobleman of his day.

Argyll played an important part in the achievement of the 1707 Act of Union and was rewarded by being created Earl of Greenwich, thus enabling him to sit in the House of Lords of the new United Kingdom in his own right. He became colonel of the 4th Troop of Horse Guards in September 1703, rejoined Marlborough's army in 1706 and fought as a major general and brigade commander at Ramillies (23 May 1706); the siege of Ostend (19 June–9 July 1706); Oudenarde (11 July 1708) and the siege of Lille (capitulated 8 December 1708). Argyll became colonel of a regiment of infantry (later the 3rd Foot, the Buffs), in February 1707 and was promoted to lieutenant general in April 1709. He took part in the siege of Tournai (27 June–3 September 1709) and was at Malplaquet, where several musket balls passed through his coat, hat and wig. By this time he had come to see himself as an equal in martial prowess to Marlborough himself. Though punctilious in obeying orders, Argyll openly corresponded with Marlborough's Tory enemies in London. He cast doubt on Marlborough's military ability (especially after the heavy casualties incurred at Malplaquet) and suggested that Marlborough was prolonging the war for the sake of his own personal ambitions.

In January 1711 Argyll was promoted to general and was given command of the British army in Spain, but as that campaign was about to be abandoned by the new Tory ministry in London, his main task proved to be the evacuation of his troops. He returned to the United Kingdom, considerably out of pocket, to be appointed commander of the forces in Scotland in 1712. He turned against the Tories over the question of the malt tax, an iniquitous measure that threatened the Scotch whisky interests. Argyll and many other Scots regarded the imposition of this tax as a breach of the Act of Union. In a reversal of his previous policy, he campaigned for dissolution of the Union (which had become just as unpopular with the English as with the Scots) and a parliamentary motion for repeal was lost by only four votes. On the death of Queen Anne in 1714 Argyll gave his support to the Hanoverian Succession and was rewarded by being appointed colonel of the Royal Horse Guards in June 1715. During the Jacobite Rising of 1715 he commanded the government forces in Scotland. After foiling an attempt to seize Edinburgh, he met and defeated the Earl of Mar's Jacobite army at the battle of Sheriffmuir (13 Nov 1715). Despite his victory, Argyll (who had become noted for changing his political views) fell under suspicion and was removed from his colonelcy of the Royal Horse Guards in 1717. By February 1719 he was back in favour and was created Duke of Greenwich in recognition of his services during the 1715 campaign. In 1725 he became Master General of the Ordnance.

Thereafter, together with his brother, the Earl of Islay (later 3rd Duke of Argyll) and the Earl of Stair [5], he was one the triumvirate that controlled government patronage in Scotland. He became colonel of a regiment of Horse (later the 2nd Dragoon Guards) in August 1726 and was re-appointed as colonel of the Royal Horse Guards in August 1733.

When the rank of field marshal was introduced into the British Army, Argyll, as the second senior ranking general, was promoted on 14 January 1736 (two days after the Earl of Orkney [1]). It is possible that the very creation of this rank, which had not been awarded even to Marlborough himself, may owe something to a desire on the part of George II to conciliate this great and influential Scottish nobleman. Nevertheless, in 1740, after he had again decided to oppose ministerial policies, Argyll was removed from his colonelcy and from all his official posts. After the fall of Walpole he regained his public offices and, in February 1742, his colonelcy of the Royal Horse Guards. He was appointed commander of the forces in the United Kingdom, but, to his chagrin, was not made Commander-in-Chief. After a few weeks, he resigned from this and all his public appointments. Argyll's health was now giving way and he played no further active part in public life.

Argyll was first married at the age of 16, to the daughter of a wealthy London merchant. This match was not a success and he fell in love with one of Queen Anne's maids of honour, Jane Warburton, the daughter of a Cheshire squire. She retained her rustic mannerisms, regarded by Argyll as a refreshing contrast to the affectation and immorality he saw in polite society, and they were married after his first wife died without issue. Their daughters received little education, as the Duke regarded learning as a threat to female virtue, while the Duchess, who had married well despite her own lack of schooling, considered it superfluous. They thus grew up to be the noisiest and most hoydenish girls in London and were given the sobriquet of "the Screaming Sisterhood". The undutiful conduct of his eldest daughter, abetted by the wife to whom Argyll was devoted, contributed to the stroke which affected him at the end of his life. He died on 4 October 1743. His English dukedom, for lack of a direct male heir, became extinct and his Scottish titles were inherited by his brother, the Earl of Islay.

CAMPBELL
JOHN, 5th Duke of Argyll (1723–1806) [16]

John Campbell, born in June 1723, was the eldest son of another John Campbell (Campbell of Mamore), a professional soldier who was a cousin of John, 2nd Duke of Argyll [2] and became the 4th Duke of Argyll in 1761. Campbell of Mamore became colonel of a regiment of Foot (later the 21st Royal Scots Fusiliers) on 1 November 1738. At the beginning of the Jacobite Rising of 1745, his son (the future field marshal and 5th Duke) was serving with this regiment in Flanders, having been granted his first commission as its lieutenant colonel, probably in the previous year. The young Campbell rejoined his father (at this time a major general) at their clan stronghold of Inveraray, where they were eventually authorized by the government to call out the Argyllshire Militia and to raise an emergency regiment from their clan followers. He had his first encounter with the Jacobites at Loch Fyne (10 November 1745) and later marched to join General Hawley, under whose command he was defeated at Falkirk (17 January 1746). He remained in the field and was at Culloden (12 April 1746), the final battle of this campaign. Campbell transferred to the 42nd Foot (the Black Watch) in 1749 and commanded this regiment in Ireland. He was promoted to colonel on 10 November 1755 and was appointed colonel of the newly raised 54th Foot on 27 December 1755. He became colonel of the 14th Dragoons in April 1757 and of the Argyllshire Fencibles, with promotion to major general, on 25 June 1759.

In March 1759 he married a twenty-five year old widow, Elizabeth, Duchess of Hamilton. This lady was the younger of the two beautiful Gunning sisters, daughters of an Anglo-Irish squire, with little in their favour but their good looks and charming manners, with which they took London society by storm. The elder sister married the Earl of Coventry, while Elizabeth married the 6th Duke of Hamilton in a clandestine wedding in Mayfair, with a ring taken from a bed-curtain. She bore him two sons, each of whom in turn later succeeded to his dukedom. When he died in January 1758, she was briefly engaged to the Duke of Bridgwater, before rejecting him in favour of Campbell. During her husband's absence at the time of the London riots of March 1768, she defied the demands of the mob that every householder should illuminate their property in honour of John Wilkes, champion of the cause of liberty. Despite being pregnant at the time, she directed her servants in resisting the subsequent three-hour siege. The offspring of her second marriage included three sons, of whom the two younger succeeded their father in turn. She was thus the wife of two dukes, the fiancée of a third and the mother of four more. She herself was created a baroness in the peerage of the United Kingdom in her own right in 1776 and died in 1790.

Campbell was promoted to lieutenant general on 19 January 1761 and assumed the courtesy title of Marquess of Lorne, when his father,

General John Campbell of Mamore, succeeded as 4th Duke of Argyll later that year. Lorne was appointed C-in-C, Scotland, in 1762 and was created Baron Sundridge in the peerage of the United Kingdom in 1766. He was colonel of the 1st Foot (the Royal Scots) from 1765 to 1782, when he became colonel of the 3rd Foot Guards. Lorne succeeded his father as 5th Duke in 1770. He became a general on 19 March 1778 and a field marshal on 30 July 1796. He died on 25 May 1806.

CARVER
Sir RICHARD MICHAEL POWER, Baron Carver, GCB, CBE, DSO, MC (1915-2001) [129]

Michael ("Mike") Carver was born on 24 April 1915 at Bletchingley, Surrey, the second of four sons of a businessman whose family firm had long-established links with the Egyptian cotton industry. His father, who served during the First World War as a transport officer with the army in Palestine, was distant but tolerant, while his mother, proud of her remote connections with the family of the Duke of Wellington [24], devoted herself to her children. Carver was educated at Winchester College and the Royal Military College, Sandhurst, where among other prizes he was awarded the King's Medal, presented to the gentleman cadet passing out highest in order of merit. He was commissioned as a second lieutenant in the Royal Tank Corps on 31 January 1935 and, after special-to-arm training at the Corps Depot, Bovington, joined the 2nd Battalion, Royal Tank Corps, at Farnborough, Hampshire, in October 1935. Carver then attended a six-month course at the Royal Military College of Science, Woolwich, before returning to his battalion. Shortly after being promoted to lieutenant on 31 January 1938, he sailed for Egypt with the 1st (Light) Battalion, Royal Tank Corps. On the formation of the Royal Armoured Corps in April 1939, the Royal Tank Corps became the Royal Tank Regiment, with Carver's battalion being remustered as the 1st Royal Tank Regiment. At the end of December 1939, he was appointed camp commandant of the head-quarters of the Mobile Division (Egypt), renamed the 7th Armoured Division in February 1940. On 7 May 1940 he became staff captain (Q) in this headquarters, as an acting captain, and remained in that post, organizing the division's logistic support, throughout the campaign against the Italians in the Western Desert that ended in February 1941. Carver was twice mentioned in despatches, gazetted in April and July 1941 respectively.

Between April and August 1941 Carver attended the Middle East Staff School at Haifa, Palestine, where he qualified as a staff officer. He then returned to the 7th Armoured Division as an acting major, first as deputy assistant quartermaster general and then as General Staff officer, grade 2. In September 1941 he was transferred to Cairo as GSO2 to help form a new armoured Corps (XXX Corps) HQ. He became a war substantive captain and temporary major on 7 November 1941. Carver took the field with XXX Corps as GSO2 at Corps HQ in October 1941 and remained with it throughout the active operations in the desert from November 1941 to August 1942. His performance in combat was recognized by the award of the Military Cross, gazetted in September 1942. He was promoted to acting lieutenant colonel on 21 August 1942, on appointment as GSO 1 of the 7th Armoured Division. He became a war substantive major and temporary lieutenant colonel on 6 January 1943. Carver was appointed commanding officer of the 1st Royal Tank Regiment on 14 April 1943. He led this unit in the operations that ended the North African campaign with the fall of Tunis in September 1943. The regiment reached the outskirts of Tunis on 7 May 1943, where he was awarded the DSO.

In the Italian campaign, Carver landed at Salerno with his regiment in mid-August 1943. He was at Afragula (2 October 1943) and the crossing of the Volturno Canal (29 October 1943), where he was awarded a bar to his DSO, before returning to the UK at the end of December 1943. He remained in command of the 1st Royal Tank Regiment in the Normandy campaign, in frequent combat in the *bocage* country until he became acting brigadier in command of the 4th Armoured Brigade on 27 June 1944, as a battle casualty replacement. He was promoted to temporary brigadier on 27 December 1944. Carver led this brigade in the operations around Caen (July 1944); Falaise and Argentan (14–18 August 1944); Audenarde (6–7 September 1944); the Reichswald (February 1945) and the crossing of the Rhine (24 March 1945). At Venlo (18 November 1944), his driver was wounded and his scout car damaged by a landmine. In the Reichswald a German shell splinter passed through Carver's jersey and shirt. After the end of the campaign in North West Europe, he remained in Germany in command of his brigade until February 1947. He then joined the Fighting Vehicle Directorate in the Ministry of Supply, London. Carver became an acting lieutenant colonel on 1 August 1947 and a substantive major on 31 January 1948. In November 1947 he married Edith Lowry-Corry, of Edwardstone Hall, Suffolk, with whom he later had two sons and two daughters.

During 1950 Carver attended the Joint Services Staff College at

Latimer, Buckinghamshire. Between May 1951 and November 1952 he was assistant quartermaster general (Plans) at the Nato HQ, Allied Forces Central Europe, Fontainebleau, with promotion to brevet lieutenant colonel on 1 July 1951. Carver then became head of the combined exercise planning staff under Field Marshal Viscount Montgomery [114] at Supreme Headquarters Allied Powers Europe, with promotion to temporary colonel on 11 December 1952. He was promoted to substantive lieutenant colonel on 27 March 1954 and substantive colonel on 17 June 1954. From June 1954 to November 1956 he served in East Africa, first as deputy chief of staff and then, from 22 October 1955, as chief of staff with promotion to temporary brigadier. He was mentioned in despatches for his part in the closing stages of the counter-insurgency campaign against the Mau Mau terrorists in Kenya. During 1957 he attended the Imperial Defence College. Between February 1958 and December 1959 Carver was Director of Plans at the War Office. Influenced by the theories of the military writer Basil Liddell Hart (of whom he became a friend and qualified admirer) and by his own war-time experience, he formed the view that the British Army should be composed predominantly of mobile armoured divisions, trained for major conventional operations in Europe. In January 1960 he was given command of the 6th Infantry Brigade at Münster in the British Army of the Rhine. Carver was promoted to major general on 4 September 1962, when he became GOC 3rd Division, stationed on Salisbury Plain. In February 1964 he was sent with most of this formation to Cyprus, to relieve the troops of the British garrison there in the Anglo-Greek-Turkish Truce Force (formed in consequence of the outbreak of inter-communal violence on the island in December 1963). At the end of March 1964 this force was replaced by a United Nations Force, of which Carver's troops formed the main part, with Carver himself becoming its deputy commander and chief of staff. He returned to the UK with most of his division in July 1964.

Carver became Director of Army Staff Duties at the Ministry of Defence in October 1964. Among the many problems of organization with which he was faced in this post was that of the structure of the Army's two part-time reserve forces (the locally-based, mostly combatant, Territorial Army and the centrally-organized, mostly logistic, Army Emergency Reserve). The TA was at this period organized as a combatant force of ten infantry divisions and an air defence artillery brigade, for use in a major conventional war. Carver considered that this concept was unrealistic in the nuclear age and that so large a force could not be adequately recruited, equipped or trained. He therefore recommended that it should be replaced by an Army Volunteer Reserve, which, like the AER, would provide individual or sub-unit reinforcements for the Regular Army. This proposal, involving the disbandment of many regiments with long-established roots in the communities from which they were recruited, was vehemently opposed by supporters of the TA. Nevertheless, in 1967, with the approval of the Army Board, the TA and AER were combined to form a new force, the Territorial and Army Volunteer Reserve, established largely as Carver had recommended. Armoured and artillery units, the most powerful and prestigious arms in the TA's order of battle, were reduced to one and six regiments respectively. Infantry battalions, many of which had just celebrated the centenary of their formation as Rifle Volunteers, were reduced by much the same extent.

Carver was created a KCB shortly before his promotion to lieutenant general on 28 June 1966, on appointment to command the Far East Land Forces, with headquarters in Singapore. Both in that post and as joint service C-in-C Far East, a post he assumed on 1 February 1967 with promotion to local general (made substantive on 29 March 1968), Sir Michael Carver had to deal with a number of problems. These mainly arose from the considerable reduction in British Forces in this theatre after the end of "confrontation" with Indonesia in Borneo, accelerated by a series of financial crises faced by the Labour government. This caused difficulties, not only for Malaysia and Singapore, but also for Australia and New Zealand, both of which countries had forces of all three services under Carver's command. A major reduction in the Brigade of Gurkhas was a further consequence of the changed situation. With the war in Vietnam then at its height, Carver found himself much involved with politico-military diplomacy, dealing with allies, both in the South East Asia Treaty Organization and outside it, as well as directly with representatives of the United States and other Commonwealth countries.

Between May 1969 and February 1971 he was GOC-in-C Southern Command, where he supported the proposal to combine all the Home Commands into the single UK Land Forces Command. Carver became Chief of the General Staff in April 1971 and remained in that post during the next two years, dealing with problems arising from the Army's heavy commitments in aid of the civil power in Northern Ireland and from the effect of continued budgetary reductions. He was promoted to field marshal on 18 July 1973 and became Chief of the Defence Staff in October 1973. After the return to office of a Labour administration in February 1974, Carver found himself having to handle a major defence review aimed at containing and, if possible,

reducing defence expenditure. He also had to deal with the reper-
cussions of the Turkish invasion of Cyprus in July 1974. The defence
review, completed in November 1974, led to further reductions in
British forces east of Suez and in the Mediterranean.

Carver retired from active duty on ceasing to be CDS in October
1976 and was granted a life peerage as Baron Carver, of Shackleford in
June 1977. In August 1977 the Cabinet appointed Lord Carver as
Resident Commissioner (designate) in Rhodesia, with the intention that
he should act as governor during a period of transition to majority rule.
He visited the country, but it proved impossible at this time to achieve
agreement between various political parties and, when it became clear
that he would no longer be required, he resigned his appointment in
November 1977. Lord Carver remained at his home near Fareham,
Hampshire, speaking and writing on defence issues and continuing to
publish military historical works, (by 1999, totalling sixteen) including
his own autobiography and a biography of Lord Harding [120]. In
retirement, he became a critic of NATO's nuclear weapons policy and
of British retention of a nuclear deterrent (which he regarded as superfluous to that of the USA), though he favoured a strengthening of
NATO's conventional strength. From 1984 to 1992, he was an active
member of the House of Lords' Select Committee on Science and
Technology

Lord Carver was colonel commandant of the Royal Electrical and
Mechanical Engineers from February 1966 to February 1976, of the
Royal Tank Regiment from January 1968 to January 1973 and of
the Royal Armoured Corps from April 1974 to April 1977. In the
Territorial and Army Volunteer Reserve, he was honorary colonel of
the Bristol University Contingent, Officers Training Corps, from
March 1972 to March 1977. He died on 9 December 2001.

CASSELS
Sir ARCHIBALD JAMES HALKETT, GCB, KBE, DSO
(1907–1996) [127]

James ("Jim") Cassels, the only son of an Indian Army officer (the future
General Sir Robert Archibald Cassels, then a captain in the 32nd
Lancers), was born in Quetta, British Baluchistan, on 28 February
1907. He was educated at Rugby School and the Royal Military College,
Sandhurst, where he won the Sword of Honour. He was commissioned
on 30 August 1926 as a second lieutenant in the Seaforth Highlanders
(Ross-shire Buffs, Duke of Albany's Own) and joined the 2nd Battalion

of this regiment in Central India in 1928, with promotion to lieutenant on 20 August 1929. Cassels was ADC to his father (at this time, GOC Northern Command, India) from May 1930 to December 1931 and took part in operations against the Afridis on the North-West Frontier between October 1930 and January 1931. The 2nd Battalion, the Seaforth Highlanders, moved to Palestine in 1932 and to the UK in 1934, with Cassels becoming adjutant in March 1934. In 1935 he married Joyce Kirk, the daughter of a former brigadier general, with whom he later had a son. Cassels was again ADC to his father (who had become C-in-C, India) between November 1935 and November 1938. He was promoted to captain on 22 March 1938. At the outbreak of the Second World War in September 1939 Cassels was at his regimental depot, Fort George, Inverness. On 1 May 1940 he was appointed brigade major of 157 (Highland Light Infantry) Brigade, a formation in the Territorial 52nd (Lowland) Division sent to France in June 1940, after the evacuation of the BEF from Dunkirk. His brigade was withdrawn through Cherbourg, after a fighting retreat in which he was mentioned in despatches.

After attending a War Course at the Staff College, Camberley, Cassels was appointed a General Staff officer, grade 2, in the 52nd (Lowland) Division in September 1940. He was promoted to temporary major on 31 October 1940 and spent a year with this division, training for mountain warfare, until going to the War Office as Deputy Director (Plans). He became an acting lieutenant colonel on 5 October 1941, followed by promotion to war substantive major and temporary lieutenant colonel on 5 January 1942. Cassels returned to his division as GSO 1 in July 1942 and remained in this post until June 1943. He was promoted to substantive major on 30 August 1943. From January to June 1944 Cassels served as Brigadier, General Staff, involved in preparations for the Allied landings in Normandy. On 10 July 1944 he became a war substantive lieutenant colonel and temporary brigadier, after which he commanded the 152nd Infantry Brigade in the Territorial 51st (Highland) Division during the Normandy campaign. He survived a rocket attack on his HQ by RAF Typhoons and was later awarded the DSO for his leadership as a brigade commander. Cassels served throughout the North-West Europe campaign until the end of hostilities in May 1945 and took part in operations around Le Havre, the Ardennes, the Reichswald, the crossing of the Rhine and the advance into northern Germany. On 28 May 1945 he was promoted to acting major general on appointment as GOC 51st (Highland) Division in the Rhineland. He became a temporary major general and war substantive colonel on 28 May 1946.

From March to December 1946 Cassels commanded the 6th Airborne Division in counter-insurgency operations in Palestine, where he was again mentioned in despatches. During 1947 he attended the Imperial Defence College, after which he was, between January 1948 and December 1949, Director, Land/Air Warfare, at the War Office. He became a substantive major general on 26 February 1948. He was appointed Chief Liaison Officer, United Kingdom Services staff, at Melbourne, Australia, in December 1949. During the Korean War Cassels became the first GOC Commonwealth Division when this was formed in June 1951. His relations with Lieutenant General John W. "Iron Mike" O'Daniel and his successor, Lieutenant General Paul W. Kendal, commanding the United States I Corps to which the Commonwealth Division was assigned, were often frosty, due largely to different ways of planning and operating. The failure of the War Office to keep his British units up to strength obliged Cassels to rely heavily on his Canadian and Australian troops and to dilute his combat units with Korean personnel, despite protests from the Treasury that this caused balance-of-payment problems. He ended his tour in Korea in September 1952 and was awarded the KBE on his return to the UK.

Sir James Cassels became a temporary lieutenant general on appointment to command I Corps in Germany on 4 January 1953, with promotion to substantive lieutenant general on 2 February 1954. From November 1954 to August 1957 he was Director General of Military Training, at the War Office. He served in Malaya as Director of Emergency Operations until January 1959, with promotion to general on 29 November 1958. He then became the first Chief of Staff of the Federation of Malaya's Armed Forces, in the period prior to the achievement of independence in 1959. Cassels was GOC-in-C Eastern Command from June 1959 to January 1960, after which he became C-in-C, British Army of the Rhine and Commander of NATO's Northern Army Group. Between June 1963 and October 1964 he was Adjutant General, in a post that enabled him to make several improvements in the conditions of service in the Army. He became Chief of the General Staff in February 1965 but found himself ill-suited to the Whitehall environment. Cassels displayed little enthusiasm for the scheme devised by his Director of Staff Duties (the future Lord Carver [129]) for replacing the combat formations of the Territorial Army by an Army Volunteer Reserve, intended mostly to provide individual reinforcements for the logistic or supporting services. Although this plan was carried into effect in 1967, most of the consequent unpopularity fell on Carver and the Labour government of the day. Accepting the arguments of those who stressed the value of part-time citizen soldiers as a military thread in their local societies, he authorized the formation of the Territorials, a new category of the reserves, armed with obsolete rifles, primarily for duties in aid of the civil power in the event of a nuclear strike on the UK. This allowed the retention of many keen, well-trained individuals, whose services would otherwise have no longer been required, and also preserved the time-honoured name as the first element in the title of the new Territorial and Army Volunteer Reserve. Cassels was promoted to field marshal on 29 February 1968, one day after ending his service as CGS. He was colonel of the Seaforth Highlanders from March 1957 to February 1961 and of its successor, the Queen's Own Highlanders, from then until February 1966. He was also colonel commandant of the Royal Military Police from May 1957 to February 1968 and of the Army Physical Training Corps from January 1961 to December 1965. Sir James Cassels retired to his Highland home in Alves, Moray, and married Joy, Mrs Kenneth Dickson, after the death of the first Lady Cassels in 1978. He died in December 1996.

CAVAN
EARL OF, see **LAMBART,** Sir FREDERICK, **[101]**

CAVENDISH
Lord FREDERICK (1729–1803) **[21]**

Lord Frederick Cavendish, third son of the 3rd Duke of Devonshire, was born in August 1729. He was first commissioned on 29 April 1749 as an ensign in the Coldstream Guards and was promoted to lieutenant in the regiment and a captain in the Army on 22 April 1752. He entered Parliament in 1751 and represented various constituencies in Derbyshire during the next twenty-nine years. At the beginning of the Seven Years War, Cavendish became a captain in the 1st Foot Guards and lieutenant colonel in the Army on 1 June 1756. Between April and September 1757 he served under the Duke of Cumberland in Germany. He became a colonel on 17 May 1758 and joined the staff of Charles, 3rd Duke of Marlborough for the descent on St Malo (June 1758). He took part in a smaller raid on French shipping and naval stores at Cherbourg in early August and was in a second attack on St Malo in September 1758. Cavendish was wounded in street fighting during the retreat to the sea and commanded the rear-guard covering the re-embarkation of the British troops, before he was obliged to surrender. The French commander, the Duc d'Aiguillon, Governor of Brittany, offered to release him on parole. Cavendish gallantly declined on the grounds that, as an MP, he would have to vote for the supplies that supported the war. Not to be outdone in gallantry, d'Aiguillon declared that this was no more an obstacle than the contingency that Cavendish (who had in fact entered a pact not to marry until the war was over) might sire children who would fight against France in some future war. Cavendish therefore returned to England and was regularly exchanged for a French officer of equal rank. In 1760 he rejoined the Allied army in Germany and commanded a brigade there, until the war ended in 1763. Cavendish was colonel of the 67th Foot from October 1759 to October 1760, when he became colonel of the 34th. He was promoted to major general on 7 March 1761 and to lieutenant general on 30 April 1770. During the American War of Independence he sympathized with the colonial cause and did not seek active employment. He became a general on 20 November 1782 and a field marshal on 30 July 1796. Lord Frederick Cavendish died at his home in Twickenham on 21 October 1803, still unmarried and very rich.

CHAMBERLAIN
Sir NEVILLE BOWLES, GCB, GCSI (1820–1902) [70]

Neville Chamberlain was born in Rio de Janeiro on 10 January 1820, one of five sons of the second marriage of the British consul general. In 1833 Chamberlain became a gentleman cadet at the Royal Military Academy, Woolwich, but was withdrawn after a year and was commissioned as an ensign in the Bengal Native Infantry on 24 February 1837. He served in the First Afghan War, at the storming of Ghazni (23 June 1839) and in various engagements around Kandahar, where he was wounded on 12 January 1842 and again on 29 May 1842. Chamberlain transferred to the 1st Cavalry of Shah Shuja's Contingent with promotion to lieutenant on 16 July 1842 and was with this regiment in the hard-fought march from Kandahar to Kabul during August and September 1842. During the final British withdrawal from Kabul, he was again wounded, at Haft Kotal (16 October 1842) and Ali Masjid (6 November 1842). He joined the Governor-General's Bodyguard in January 1843 and was at Maharajpur (29 December 1843). He sailed for England in February 1845, on medical leave, and returned to India late in 1846 as military secretary to the Governor of Bombay. During the Second Sikh War Chamberlain served as brigade major with the Bengal Irregular Cavalry and was at Chilianwala (13 January 1849) and Gujarat (21 February 1849). He was promoted to captain in the 16th Bengal Native Infantry on 1 November 1849 and to brevet major on 2 November 1849.

Chamberlain became the commander of the Punjab Irregular Frontier Force, with promotion to brevet lieutenant colonel, on 28 November 1854 and led its troops in a number of expeditions against the Pathan tribes of the North-West Frontier between 1855 and the outbreak of the Indian Mutiny in May 1857. He was then given command of the troops sent from Peshawar to join the British force besieging Delhi. During the siege, Chamberlain served as adjutant general of the Bengal Army and was wounded on 14 July 1857. He resumed command of the Punjab Frontier Force as brevet colonel on 27 November 1857 and undertook a further series of minor operations to discourage the hill tribes from raiding British India. He was awarded the KCB for his services during the large-scale Ambela campaign, where he was wounded on 20 November 1863. Sir Neville Chamberlain then returned to the UK, with promotion to major general on 5 August 1864. He went back to India in 1869 to accompany an official visit by Alfred, Duke of Edinburgh, Queen Victoria's second son (later Duke of Saxe-Coburg and Gotha) and was promoted to lieutenant general on 1 May 1872. In 1873 Chamberlain married Charlotte Reid, the daughter of a major general. There were no children of the marriage.

In February 1876 Chamberlain succeeded Sir Frederick Haines [65] as C-in-C Madras, with promotion to general on 1 October 1877. He was then selected to head a mission to the Amir of Afghanistan, Sher Ali (whom Chamberlain had met during the First Afghan War). Frustrated by the Amir's continued reluctance to accept a British diplomatic presence at Kabul, Lord Lytton, the Viceroy and Governor-General of India, ordered Chamberlain to cross the border into Afghanistan unless he was opposed by force. Chamberlain, an experienced frontier officer with no faith in Lytton's policies, replied that he was as sure of armed resistance as if he had seen half his escort shot down in front of him. When a token party was turned back, Lytton declared war on Afghanistan. Chamberlain returned to Madras and left India in February 1881. He went on to the retired list in February 1886 and became a field marshal on 25 April 1900, the second officer to reach this rank directly from the Indian Army. Chamberlain died on 18 February 1902 at Lordswood, near Southampton, and was buried at the nearby village of Rownhams. He was generally credited as one of the originators of the billiard-table game to which he gave the name "snooker", the long-established term applied to new cadets at the Royal Military Academy, Woolwich.

CHAPPLE
Sir JOHN LYON, GCB, CBE (1931-) [136]

John Chapple was born on 27 May 1931 and was educated at Haileybury and Imperial Service College, Hertfordshire. He entered the Army on 20 October 1949 and served in the ranks first as a rifleman in the King's Royal Rifle Corps and then as an officer cadet until 3 June 1950, when he was granted a National Service commission as a second lieutenant in the Royal Artillery. After completing his period of obligatory full-time service in October 1951, Chapple went to Trinity College, Cambridge, from which he graduated three years later. During this time, he served in the Territorial Army as a National Service officer in 461(Middlesex) Heavy Anti-Aircraft Regiment, Royal Artillery (a successor of the same Territorial regiment, the Finsbury Rifles, in which Field Marshal Lord Harding [120] had held his first commission), before being transferred first to the 4th Battalion, the South Lancashire Regiment and then to the 5th Battalion, the King's Regiment. He did not actually join either of these infantry units, but was employed as the officer commanding the infantry sub-unit of the Cambridge University Contingent, University Training Corps. Chapple joined the Regular Army on 9 August 1954, when he was granted a commission in the 2nd King Edward VII's Own Gurkha Rifles (the Sirmoor Rifles), with seniority as a lieutenant from 9 February 1953. He became a temporary captain on 25 March 1956 and a substantive captain on 9 February 1957. During the course of his career, Chapple served with the 2nd Gurkhas in Singapore, Malaya, Hong Kong and Borneo. In 1959 he married Annabel Hill, with whom he later had a son and three daughters. Chapple became a temporary major on 9 February 1961 and subsequently attended the Staff College, Camberley. From February 1963 to April 1965 he was deputy assistant adjutant and quartermaster general in the 12th Infantry Brigade Group, with promotion to substantive major on 9 February 1964. After a further period of regimental duty he served for two years as brigade major of the Brigade of Gurkhas and then attended the Joint Services Staff College, Latimer, Buckinghamshire. He was promoted to lieutenant colonel on 30 June 1969 and served as commanding officer of the 1st Battalion, the 2nd Gurkha Rifles, from April 1970 to May 1972.

Between June 1972 and October 1973 Chapple was an instructor and

General Staff officer, grade 1, at the Staff College, with promotion to colonel on 30 June 1973. In late 1973 he was awarded the first Services Fellowship at Cambridge University. Chapple served in the Directorate of Staff Duties at the Ministry of Defence from December 1973 to March 1976 and was promoted to brigadier on 30 June 1975. He then commanded the Gurkha Field Force, later renamed the 48th (Gurkha) Infantry Brigade, until November 1977. He returned to the Ministry of Defence in February 1978 as Principal Staff Officer to the Chief of Defence Staff and remained in this post until June 1980, when he became commander of the British Forces in Hong Kong. Chapple was promoted to acting major general on 16 June 1980 and later became a substantive major general, with seniority from 1 April 1980. He was also major general of the Brigade of Gurkhas from June 1980 until October 1982, when he left Hong Kong to become Director of Military Operations in the Ministry of Defence. He was appointed Deputy Chief of the Defence Staff (Programmes and Personnel) in December 1984. He was created KCB and promoted to lieutenant general on 2 January 1985. Sir John Chapple was promoted to general on 29 June 1987, on appointment as C-in-C, United Kingdom Land Forces. He became Chief of the General Staff in September 1988 and was promoted to field marshal on 14 February 1992, after completing his tenure of this post. From 1993 to 1995 Sir John Chapple served as Governor and C-in-C, Gibraltar. He was colonel of the 2nd King Edward VII's Own Gurkha Rifles from 1986 to 1994, when it was amalgamated with the other Gurkha regiments of the British Army to form the Royal Gurkha Rifles. He was also honorary colonel of the Oxford University Contingent, Officers Training Corps, from 1987 to 1995. In retirement Sir John Chapple maintained his long-standing twin interests in ornithology and militaria. He continued to hold high office in many bodies associated with these fields and was elected President of the Zoological Society of London.

CHETWODE
Sir Philip Walhouse, 1st Baron Chetwode, 7th baronet, GCB, OM, GCSI, KCMG, DSO (1869–1950) [102]

Philip Chetwode was the elder son of George Chetwode, later 6th baronet, and his wife Alice Bass, sister of the 1st Lord Burton, a wealthy brewer and philanthropist. He was born in London on 21 September 1869 and was educated at Eton College. He obtained his first commission in the Militia, in the 3rd Battalion, the Oxfordshire Light

Infantry, from which he entered the Regular Army as a second lieutenant in the 19th Hussars on 20 November 1889. He served in this unit under Lieutenant Colonel John French [83] in the UK, with promotion to lieutenant on 6 August 1890, and went with it to India in 1891. Chetwode was detached from his regiment to take part in the Chin Hills expedition of 1892–93 and was promoted to captain on 7 February 1897. He was with the 19th Hussars in South Africa when war with the Boer republics began in 1899 and was at Reitfontein (24 October 1899); Ladysmith (7 December 1899); Laing's Nek (2–9 June 1900); Belfast (26–27 August 1900) and several other engagements in the Transvaal, the Orange River Colony and Cape Colony, up to the end of hostilities in 1902. Chetwode served in the Cavalry Division under French and was twice mentioned in despatches, with the award of the DSO. He became a major on 21 December 1902 and succeeded his father as 7th baronet in 1905.

French, who had become GOC 1st Division at Aldershot, then attempted to find Sir Philip Chetwode an appointment on his staff, but this plan failed, as Chetwode was not a qualified staff officer. Eventually, he was given a staff post as assistant military secretary at Aldershot in 1906. Chetwode was promoted to lieutenant colonel on 3 January 1908 on appointment as commanding officer of the 19th Hussars. He became a colonel on 4 October 1911 and was given command of the London Mounted Brigade in the newly-formed Territorial Force in April 1912. At the time of the Curragh Incident in March 1914 he agreed to accept command of the 3rd Cavalry Brigade when its brigadier general, Hubert Gough, offered to resign if he was ordered to lead it against the Ulster Unionists. This decision led to ill-feeling against Chetwode among the many Army officers who either came from the Anglo-Irish ascendancy or sympathized with it. In the event, Gough was allowed to retain his command at the Curragh and Chetwode remained in command of his brigade of Yeomanry until mobilization on the outbreak of the First World War in August 1914. He was then given command of the 5th Cavalry Brigade, with promotion to temporary brigadier general.

Chetwode went to France in the British Expeditionary Force and took part in its early actions, including Cerisy (29 August 1914) and the first battle of Ypres (19 October–21 November 1914). He became GOC 2nd Cavalry Division, with promotion to temporary major general, in July 1915, followed by promotion to substantive major general on 1 January 1916. Chetwode remained on the Western Front until November 1916, when he was given command of the Desert Mounted Corps in Palestine and was promoted to temporary lieutenant general. His first independent action was at Rafa (January 1917), where a charge by the New

Zealand Mounted Brigade enabled him to achieve a victory. At the 3rd battle of Gaza (26 March–19 April 1917), Chetwode, unable to find water for his men and horses, withdrew at a critical stage and so exposed the previously successful infantry to a Turkish counter-attack. Sir Archibald Murray, C-in-C of the Egyptian Expeditionary Force, blamed Chetwode's superior, Sir Charles Dobell, for this defeat and appointed Chetwode in his place. When Sir Edmund Allenby arrived in Egypt to succeed Murray at the end of June 1917, Chetwode submitted to him a detailed plan for a new offensive. Allenby adopted this and gave Chetwode command of a newly-formed XX Corps. Chetwode played an important part in the subsequent campaign, in which the Egyptian Expeditionary Force, after driving the Turks out of Jerusalem and Damascus, reached the borders of Turkey itself. During these operations he was wounded and received eight mentions in despatches. He became a substantive lieutenant general on 1 January 1919.

After the war Chetwode held a series of posts at the War Office, as Military Secretary, from 1919 to October 1920, as Deputy Chief of the General Staff, from October 1920 to September 1922, and as Adjutant General from then until early 1923, when he became GOC-in-C Aldershot Command. In this appointment he encouraged a return to training for mobile operations, rather than the static positional warfare of the Western Front. He was dubious about the value of tanks for this role and supported the retention of horsed cavalry. Chetwode was promoted to general on 1 June 1926. On the completion of his tenure of command at Aldershot, with no vacancies available for him in the UK, he accepted the post of Chief of the General Staff, India, normally a lieutenant general's appointment. In November 1930 he became C-in-C, India. Indian politicians, who saw this issue as an important test of British sincerity in the approach to self-government, were at this time pressing for an increase in the number of commissions granted to Indian cadets. Chetwode opened the Indian Military Academy at Dehra Dun, so that Indian cadets no longer had to go to England for their training, and increased the number of Indian units in which they could serve. At the same time, however, he changed the officer establishment of these units to conform to that in the British Army, so that the promotion prospects of these Indian cadets became less favourable than those of British cadets joining the Indian Army. He was promoted to field marshal on 13 February 1933 and left India at the expiry of his appointment in May 1934. Chetwode became colonel of the Royal Scots Greys (2nd Dragoons) September 1925 and of the 15th/19th, the King's Royal Hussars, February 1944 and retained both appointments until January 1947. He was also colonel of the 8th King George's Own Light Cavalry, in the Indian Army, and honorary colonel of the 2nd/10th Dragoons, in the Canadian Militia. In 1899, he married Alice Hester Stapleton-Cotton, a great-niece of the first Viscount Combermere [39]. They had a son (who died in 1940) and a daughter, who became a noted travel writer, Penelope Chetwode. Her marriage to a young poet of middle-class origins (the future Sir John Betjeman) was greeted by her father without enthusiasm. He was raised to the peerage as Baron Chetwode, of Chetwode, in 1945. Lord Chetwode died in London on 6 June 1950 and was succeeded as 2nd baron by his grandson, Philip.

CLARKE
Sir ALURED, GCB (1745–1832) [31]

Alured Clarke, the son of a minor country gentleman, was born in 1745 and was first commissioned in 1759 as an ensign in the 50th Foot. He served in Germany with this unit in the Seven Years War, with promotion to lieutenant in 1760. Clarke became a captain in the 5th Foot in 1767 and a major in the 54th Foot in 1771. He was promoted to lieutenant colonel in the 7th Royal Fusiliers on 20 September 1775. In the American War of Independence he went with his regiment to New York, where he transferred to the Hessian contingent as muster-master. Clarke was promoted to colonel on 16 May 1782, with appointment as lieutenant- governor of Jamaica, where he remained until 1791. He was promoted to major general on 28 April 1790 and was appointed colonel of the 1st Battalion, the 60th Royal American Regiment in July 1791. He retained this post until August 1794, after which he was successively colonel of the 68th Foot until October 1794, of the 5th Foot until August 1801 and thereafter of the 7th Royal Fusiliers. After leaving Jamaica, he served in Quebec before returning to England in June 1793. During 1795 Clarke commanded the British force that took over control of the Cape of Good Hope, where the local Dutch authorities surrendered without bloodshed. Clarke then sailed on to India, where throughout 1796 he served as C-in-C, Madras. He was given a knighthood and promotion to lieutenant general on 28 January 1797 and, in March 1797, became C-in-C, India. In the interregnum between Sir John Shore and the Earl of Mornington (later Marquess Wellesley), Sir Alured Clarke acted as Governor-General of Bengal (March-May 1798). He completed his tenure as C-in-C, India, in March 1801 and was promoted to general on 29 April 1802, but did not hold any further command. On 22 August 1830 he was one of the two senior ranking generals in the Army who were promoted to field marshal to celebrate the accession of William IV. He died on 16 September 1832, while visiting his niece, Mrs Eyton, wife of the vicar of Llangollen.

CLYDE
LORD, see **CAMPBELL**, Sir COLIN, **[46]**

COBHAM
VISCOUNT, see **TEMPLE**, Sir RICHARD, **[6]**

COLBORNE
Sir JOHN, 1st Baron Seaton, GCB, GCMG, GCH
(1778–1863) **[42]**

John Colborne, the only son of an unsuccessful salt works speculator, was born on 16 February 1778 at Lyndhurst, Hampshire. He was educated first at Christ's Hospital and then, after his father's death and his mother's remarriage, at Winchester College. Without the funds to buy a commission, Colborne obtained his first appointment by nomination, as an ensign in the 20th Foot, on 10 July 1794. All his subsequent promotions were obtained without purchase. He became a lieutenant on 4 September 1795 and captain-lieutenant on 11 August 1799. Colborne took part with his regiment in the expedition to the Helder (September-October 1799) and was at Alkmaar (4 September 1799), where he was wounded. He was promoted to brevet captain on 12 January 1800 and served in the British force sent to Egypt in August 1801. He became a captain in his regiment (succeeding to a vacancy created by a duel) on 9 December 1802 and moved with it to Malta, Sicily and Calabria, where he was at Maida (4 July 1806). He became a major and military secretary on the staff of Sir John Moore on 21 January 1808. Colborne served with Moore in Sweden in May 1808 and in Portugal in August 1808. He returned to the Peninsula in Moore's army later that year and fought at Benevente (29 December 1808), in the retreat to Corunna and in the final battle there (16 January 1809). He was one of the officers recommended for promotion by the dying Sir John Moore, mortally wounded in this battle.

Colborne became lieutenant colonel of a garrison battalion on 2 February 1809 and exchanged to the 66th Foot on 2 November 1809. He returned to the Peninsula in the army commanded by Sir Arthur

Wellesley [24] and was at Ocana (19 December 1809) attached to the Spanish army of La Mancha. Colborne formed a high opinion of the Spanish soldiers' fighting qualities and took the view that the defeats they suffered were the result of a bad system, not of bad material. He rejoined the 66th and was at Busaco (27 September 1810) and Albuera (16 May 1811), where he commanded a brigade. Colborne then joined 52nd Light Infantry. He commanded this regiment at Ciudad Rodrigo (19 January 1812), where he was badly wounded, and subsequently returned to England for surgery. There, in June 1813, he married Elizabeth Yonge, youngest daughter of the rector of Newton Ferrers, Devon. They later had three daughters and five sons. After a brief wartime honeymoon, Colborne returned to the Peninsula, where he made his reputation as a master of outpost duties. He led the 52nd Light Infantry at San Sebastian (9 August 1813) and the operations around Pamplona (October 1813) and commanded a brigade at the passage of the Bidassoa (7 October 1813); the Nivelle (10 November 1813) and the Nive (10 December 1813). Colborne then resumed command of the 52nd Light Infantry and was with it at Orthez (27 February 1814); Toulouse (10 April 1814) and the siege of Bayonne (27 February–13 April 1814). He was promoted to colonel on 4 June 1814, followed by the awarded of the KCB.

With the war apparently over, Sir John Colborne became military secretary to the Prince of Orange [34], at the head of the army of the new United Kingdom of the Netherlands. When Napoleon returned to France, Colborne played a valuable part in dissuading the Prince from launching an offensive before the Duke of Wellington could arrive to take command of the Allied armies. Colborne then rejoined the 52nd Light Infantry. He was at Waterloo (18 June 1815), where in the closing stage of the battle he led the 52nd forward on his own initiative, repulsing the Imperial Guard and beginning the general advance that drove the French from the field.

After the war Colborne was lieutenant-governor of Guernsey from 1821 to 1828, with promotion to major general on 27 May 1825. In 1828 he was appointed lieutenant-governor of Upper Canada, where he was faced with demands from local politicians for a more representative form of government. In 1837, believing that he no longer had the confidence of the ministers in London, he resigned, but before this could take effect, the outbreak of a rebellion in Lower Canada (Quebec) led to his appointment as Governor-General and C-in-C of all Canada. Colborne, who had already moved troops in anticipation of trouble, commanded in person at St Eustache (14 December 1837), the only armed clash of any significance. He became a lieutenant general on

28 June 1838, but again offered to resign because of his differences with the Earl of Durham, who had been sent to report on the Canadian problem. When Durham himself resigned, Colborne remained in office and was there when another revolt occurred in October 1838. Despite support from sympathizers from the United States, this was quickly suppressed by Colborne's troops. He then returned to the UK, where he was created Baron Seaton in December 1839.

Between 1843 and 1849 Seaton was High Commissioner of the Ionian Islands, at that time a British protectorate. He was promoted to general on 20 June 1854 and commanded the forces in Ireland from 1855 to1860. He was successively colonel of the 94th Foot from 12 December 1834, of the 26th Foot from 28 March 1838 and of the 2nd Life Guards from 24 March 1854. He became a field marshal on 1 April 1860 and retired to Torquay, where he died at on 17 April 1863. Lord Seaton was buried in the churchyard of Holy Cross, Newton Ferrers, where his father-in-law had been the rector.

COMBERMERE
VISCOUNT, see **COTTON**, Sir STAPLETON, **[39]**

CONNAUGHT
HRH DUKE OF, see **ARTHUR WILLIAM PATRICK ALBERT [73]**

CONWAY
The Honourable HENRY SEYMOUR (1721–1794) **[12]**

Henry Conway, born in 1721, was the second son of the 1st Baron Conway of Ragley and had family connections with Sir Robert Walpole, the great Whig Prime Minister. His first commission was dated 27 June 1737, as a lieutenant in Molesworth's **[9]** regiment of dragoons (later the 5th Royal Irish Dragoons), then stationed in Ireland. Conway entered the Irish parliament as MP for Antrim in October 1741. In the following December he became an MP at Westminster, where he sat for various constituencies in his family's gift for the next forty-three years, apart from a short break in 1774–1775. He became a lieutenant in the 1st Foot Guards and captain in the Army on 14 February 1741 and was promoted to captain in the regiment and lieutenant colonel in the Army on 10 May 1742. During the War of the Austrian Succession he was at

Dettingen (27 June 1743) and Fontenoy (11 May 1745), where he served on the staff of Field Marshal Wade [7] and of the Duke of Cumberland respectively. Conway returned to England with Cumberland at the time of the Jacobite Rising. He became colonel of a regiment of infantry (later the 48th Foot) on 6 April 1746, shortly before fighting in Cumberland's army at Culloden (16 April 1746). At Laffeldt (La Val, 2 July 1747) Conway was unhorsed and captured, but was subsequently released on parole in accordance with the civilized custom of the time. He became colonel of a more senior regiment (later the 34th Foot) in July 1749 and visited it in Minorca, where it formed part of the British garrison. In 1751 Conway became colonel of a regiment of dragoons (later the 13th Hussars) in Ireland. In 1754 he was appointed colonel of a regiment of Horse (later the 7th Dragoon Guards) on the Irish establishment. Conway was promoted to major general on 12 March 1755. In parliament he joined the Duke of Devonshire and served under him as Chief Secretary for Ireland from April 1755 to January 1757.

In the Seven Years War Conway was selected to lead the descent on Rochefort. King George II, who jealously guarded his control of military appointments, declared that Conway was too young and that the command should go to the sixty year-old General Sir John Mordaunt. After long delays, the expedition sailed in September 1757. Conway personally led an attack that carried one of the French forts. Mordaunt decided that the French defences further inland were too strong and decided to re-embark his troops. Conway urged Mordaunt to continue the expedition, but declined Mordaunt's offer to allow him to do so on his own responsibility. Neither general emerged with credit and when Ligonier [10], as Commander in Chief of the Army, suggested Conway for a command in North America, the King refused to hear of it. Conway was promoted to lieutenant general on 30 March 1759 and became colonel of the 1st Royal Dragoons six days later. He again took the field in March 1761, serving in Germany under Prince Ferdinand of Brunswick, and was at Kirch-Denken (15 June 1761) where he commanded the Allied centre. He later succeeded the Marquis of Granby in command of the British troops in Germany.

After the end of the war in 1763, Conway resumed his political career. He opposed the government over the question of John Wilkes and general warrants and was removed from his colonelcy as a result. When a new ministry came into power in July 1765, Conway was given office as Secretary of State for the Southern Department until May 1766 and for the Northern Department until January 1768. He served first under the Marquess of Rockingham and then, after his fall in July 1766, defected to the rival Grafton-Pitt alliance. Conway was colonel of the

4th Dragoons from January 1768 to October 1770, when he became colonel of the Royal Horse Guards. He was promoted to general on 25 May 1772. During the American War of Independence, he strongly opposed government policy and was not actively employed. Conway re-entered the Cabinet in March 1782, as Commander-in-Chief, and served in successive ministries until April 1783, when he was succeeded by Sir Jeffery Amherst [17]. In the general election of 1784, Conway became one of "Fox's Martyrs" and lost his seat in the Commons. He then withdrew from public life and devoted himself to his Thames-side villa, Park Place, near Henley. When the rank of field marshal was revived on 12 October 1793, Conway was the senior ranking general in the British Army and was promoted accordingly. He died at Park Place on 12 October 1795.

While on parole in December 1746, Conway married a young widow, Caroline, Countess of Aylesbury and sister of the future 5th Duke of Argyll [16]. Their only child, Anne (a cousin and goddaughter of Horace Walpole) made a brilliant marriage in 1769 with John Damer, son of the wealthy Lord Milton (later Earl of Dorchester). Conway settled his entire fortune of £10,000 on her, but within a few years Damer had run up debts of over £70, 000. When his father refused to pay his debts, Damer shot himself in Covent Garden. Anne Damer, a talented sculptress, supplemented her income with various commissions, including the two heads on the keystones of the central arch of Henley Bridge (rebuilt by her father) and the bust of Nelson in London's Guildhall.

COTTON
Sir STAPLETON, 6th Baronet, 1st Viscount Combermere, GCB, GCH, KSI (1773–1865) [39]

Stapleton Cotton, born at Llewenny Hall, Denbighshire on 14 November 1771, was the second son of a Shropshire baronet and MP, whose lavish hospitality and devotion to country sports eventually led him into severe financial difficulties. The young Cotton was educated at Westminster School and at a private military academy in Bayswater. He obtained a commission, without purchase, as a second lieutenant in the 23rd Royal Welsh Fusiliers on 26 February 1790 and was promoted to lieutenant on 16 March 1791. Following the outbreak of war with Revolutionary France, Cotton transferred to the 6th Dragoon Guards, with promotion to captain, on 28 February 1793. He served with this regiment in the Flanders campaign, where he took part in the retreat from Dunkirk in 1793 and was at Premont (17 April 1794); Beaumont (Le Cateau, 26 April 1794) and Willems (Tournai, 10 May 1794). He became a major in the 59th Foot on 28 April 1794, in a paper transaction enabling him to be appointed, on 9 May 1794, lieutenant colonel of the 25th Light Dragoons, a regiment newly-raised for service in India. This regiment disembarked at the Cape of Good Hope in July 1796 for a bloodless campaign against local Dutch settlers, who had risen against the British occupation established in 1795. The 25th Light Dragoons then sailed on to India, where it took part in the war against Tipu Sultan of Mysore, until the end of hostilities in May 1799.

On the death of his elder brother Cotton became heir to his father's baronetcy. At the end of 1800 he returned to the UK, having exchanged command of the 25th for that of the 16th Light Dragoons, then stationed at Brighton. He was promoted to colonel on 1 January 1800. Between 1802 and 1805 he commanded the 16th Light Dragoons in Ireland, where he was involved in the suppression of "Emmett's Rebellion" in and around Dublin in June 1803. Cotton was promoted to major general on 30 October 1805 and was given command of a cavalry brigade at Weymouth. At the same time he was elected MP for Newark and continued to represent this borough until he became a peer. In April 1809 he went to the Peninsular campaign, where he commanded a cavalry brigade in the army under Sir Arthur Wellesley [24]. Cotton was at the passage of the Douro (Oporto, 12 May 1809) and Talavera (28 July 1809). On succeeding his father as 6th baronet, Sir Stapleton Cotton returned to the UK at the end of 1809 to settle his affairs. He rejoined the army in the Peninsula in May 1810 and was given command of the cavalry, with local promotion to lieutenant general. He was at Busaco (27 September 1810) and then covered the British withdrawal to the Lines of Torres Vedras.

Cotton led his cavalry at Sabugal (3 April 1811) and Fuentes d'Onoro (3 and 5 May 1811) and was promoted to lieutenant general in the Army on 1 January 1812. He was at Salamanca (22 July 1812), where, on the night after the battle, he was shot in the arm by a Portuguese sentry, whose challenge he had failed to answer. Cotton went home for medical treatment and did not return to the Peninsular War until July 1813. He then took part in the battles of the Pyrenees (27–30 July 1813); Orthez (27 February 1814) and Toulouse (10 April 1814). His services were recognized with the award of a peerage, as Baron Combermere, in 1814.

During the Hundred Days campaign command of the British cavalry was given not to Lord Combermere but to a more senior general, the Earl of Uxbridge [37]. Combermere, who succeeded to the command after Uxbridge was wounded at Waterloo, remained in France with the

Army of Occupation until 1816. He served from 1817 to 1820 as Governor and C-in-C, Barbados. Combermere became colonel of the 3rd King's Own Hussars in January 1821 and was commander of the forces in Ireland from 1822 to 1825. He was then appointed C-in-C, India, with promotion to general on 27 May 1825. In 1826 he led the Bengal Army to victory over the Jat kingdom of Bhurtpoor (Bharatpur) and took its previously impregnable capital by storm. He was made a viscount in 1827 and colonel of the 1st Life Guards in September 1829, shortly before his return from India. Combermere became a field marshal on 2 October 1855, as one of the three senior ranking generals in the British Army promoted at that time. He married three times, first, in 1800, to the nineteen year-old Lady Anna Clinton, who died in 1807 and secondly, in 1814, to the twenty year-old Caroline Fulke Greville, the daughter of a captain in the Royal Navy. This lady, twenty years younger than her husband, gave him a son (who eventually succeeded him) and two daughters. She did not accompany him to India and, on his return to the UK, left him after fifteen years of marriage. Soon after her death in 1837, Combermere married Mary Woolley Gibbings, the only daughter of an Irish squire. He lived happily with his second viscountess, with whom he had three children. Lord Combermere died on 21 February 1865 and was buried at the parish church of Wrenbury, Shropshire.

CUMBERLAND
HRH DUKE OF, see **ERNEST AUGUSTUS,** King of Hanover [25]

DACRES
Sir RICHARD JAMES, GCB (1799–1886) [61]

Richard Dacres, the elder son of Vice Admiral Sir Richard Dacres, Royal Navy, was born in 1799. He entered the Royal Military Academy, Woolwich, in 1815 as a gentleman cadet and was commissioned as a second lieutenant in the Royal Artillery on 15 December 1817. Dacres did not become a lieutenant until 29 August 1825, a consequence of the Royal Artillery's system of promotion by regimental seniority, coupled with the high number of artillery officers commissioned during the Napoleonic wars. On 18 December 1837 he became captain of the 2nd Troop, Royal Horse Artillery. He commanded this unit during the next fourteen years, serving in various stations at home and overseas without seeing active service,. As the promotion block eased, Dacres was promoted to major on 11 November 1851 and lieutenant colonel on 23 February 1852. On the outbreak of the Crimean War in 1854 he was given command of the horse artillery brigade in the Cavalry Division under Lord Lucan [63]. Dacres was at the Alma (20 September 1854), Balaklava (25 October 1854) and Inkerman (5 November 1854), where he had his horse shot under him. On the death of Brigadier Fox Strangeways, Dacres succeeded him as Commander, Royal Artillery, in the army in the Crimea, with responsibility for the heavy batteries besieging Sevastopol as well as for the horse and field artillery. He was promoted to colonel on 23 February 1855 and to major general on 29 June 1855, with the award of the KCB. Sir Richard Dacres commanded the Woolwich garrison between 1859 and 1864. He became colonel commandant of the Royal Horse Artillery in July 1864 and was promoted to lieutenant general on 18 December 1864, to general on 2 February 1867 and to field marshal on 27 March 1882. He died at Brighton on 6 December 1886.

DALRYMPLE
JOHN, 2nd Earl of Stair (1673–1747) [5]

John Dalrymple, the second son of Sir John Dalrymple of Stair (later 2nd Viscount and 1st Earl of Stair), was born in Edinburgh on 2 July 1673. He first came to public notice in April 1682, at the age of nine, when he killed his elder brother in a shooting accident. In 1685 he was sent to the Netherlands, where he studied at Leyden University under the auspices of his grandfather, Sir James Dalrymple, an influential Scottish supporter of William of Orange. After the Glorious Revolution of 1688, Sir James was created 1st Viscount Stair. His eldest son, Sir John Dalrymple, the Master of Stair, became, in January 1691, William III's Secretary for Scotland. As such, he was responsible for the orders leading to the infamous Massacre of Glencoe (13 February 1692). Public outcry at this atrocity obliged the Master of Stair to give up office in July 1692, although he later resumed public life and succeeded his father as 2nd Viscount in November 1695. He was created 1st Earl of Stair in April 1703 and played a major part in the achievement of the Act of Union of 1707.

The young John Dalrymple joined William III's army in the Low Countries, where he served in the Nine Years War as a volunteer with the Earl of Angus's Regiment (the Cameronians) at Steenkerke (23 July 1692). In 1695, when his father succeeded to the Scottish peerage as

Viscount Stair, John Dalrymple became Master of Stair. The new Master of Stair was granted a commission in 1702 as captain in the 3rd Foot Guards and lieutenant colonel in the Army. He served in the War of the Spanish Succession with Marlborough's army in Flanders, where he led storming parties at Peer (7 August 1702) and Venlo (23 September 1702). In 1703, when his father became the 1st Earl of Stair, the Master of Stair assumed the courtesy title of Viscount Dalrymple. Lord Dalrymple briefly commanded a Scottish regiment in the Dutch service, before being appointed, in January 1706, colonel of the Cameronians (later the 26th Foot), the regiment with which he had served in the Nine Years War. Dalrymple was at Ramillies (23 May 1706) as major general commanding a brigade and became colonel of a regiment of dragoons (later the 2nd Dragoons, the Royal Scots Greys) on 24 August 1706. He succeeded his father as 2nd Earl of Stair in January 1707, but remained in the field with Marlborough's army and commanded a cavalry brigade at the battle of Oudenarde ((11 July 1708) and in the subsequent operations around Lille. Stair was at Malplaquet (11 September 1709) and the siege of Douai (23 April–25 June 1710), where he became a lieutenant general on 1 June 1710. He played his final part in this war by covering the siege of Bouchain (9 August–12 September 1711). He was given a temporary appointment as general on 1 January 1712, but was shortly afterwards recalled by the incoming Tory ministry and removed from his regimental colonelcy in 1714.

Back in London, Stair fell in love with Viscountess Primrose, a young widow who had been abused by her late husband and had vowed never to marry again. Stair managed to be seen at her bedroom window, thus obliging her to marry him for the sake of her reputation. After the accession of George I, Stair was once more in favour at court and, on 4 March 1715, was appointed colonel of a regiment of dragoons (later the 6th Inniskilling Dragoons). He was appointed head of the British diplomatic mission to Versailles, where he organized an efficient intelligence system that kept the British government in London fully aware of the plans of the Jacobite court in exile. As British ambassador, he became a popular figure in French society and lived in great state. To fund this, he invested heavily in John Law's Mississippi Company. When this collapsed in 1720, Stair, like many others in France, lost heavily. He returned to the United Kingdom, where he turned his energies to restoring his fortune, largely at the expense of the tenants of his Highland estates. In Scotland he worked closely with the 2nd Duke of Argyll [2] and Argyll's younger brother, the Earl of Islay (later 3rd Duke of Argyll) and formed with them the triumvirate that controlled government patronage there. He later broke with the ministry and, in 1734, was again deprived of his colonelcy. Stair was nevertheless promoted to the rank of general, by virtue of his seniority in the Army, on 27 October 1735.

After the fall of Sir Robert Walpole's ministry, Stair's position improved. As the senior ranking general in the British Army, he was promoted to field marshal on 18 March 1742 and was given command of the Pragmatic Army in Germany in the War of the Austrian Succession. He was also re-appointed as colonel of the Inniskilling Dragoons on 25 April 1743. Following the example of his old chief Marlborough, Stair marched his army deep into Germany, but was hampered by unreliable allies, conflicting orders from London and his own advancing years and made little headway against his capable French opponents. King George II arrived to take command in person and, at Dettingen (27 June 1743), led the Pragmatic Army to its first and only victory. Stair was present at the battle, displaying his old courage, though a combination of a broken rein and failing eyesight almost led to him being taken prisoner. After this battle, finding that George II was more disposed to listen to the advice of his German generals, Stair asked for permission to return to his estates. This was granted, to the relief of all parties, though he was made commander of the forces in England in 1744 and was re-appointed as colonel of the Scots Greys on 28 May 1745. Stair was not called on to take the field during the Jacobite Rising of 1745. He died at Queensferry House, Edinburgh, on 9 May 1747, and was buried at Kirkliston. Stair was the first British field marshal to lead an army on active service while holding that rank.

DE LA ROCHEFOUCAULD
FRANCIS (FRANCOIS), Marquis de Montandre
(1672–1739) **[4]**

Francois de la Rochefoucauld, a brother of Isaac Charles, 3rd Marquis de Montandre, was born in France in September 1672. He was brought up to be a canon in St Victor's Abbey, Paris, but became a Protestant and subsequently fled from France to avoid religious persecution. He joined one of the Huguenot regiments in the army of William III and served in his campaigns in Ireland, under his fellow-Huguenot, Henri Massu de Ruvigny (later Earl of Galway). On 15 February 1692, as Francis de Montandre, Esquire, he was commissioned as a captain and brevet lieutenant colonel, commanding Francis du Cambon's regiment of Foot. This unit had fought in Ireland and joined William III's army in the Low Countries in September 1692. Montandre returned with his regiment to Ireland in 1698 at the end of the Nine Years War and was still on the Irish establishment in 1702. After the death of his elder brother in 1702 he assumed the title of marquis. In 1703, at the beginning of the War of the Spanish Succession, Galway wrote to Marlborough asking him to find a place for Montandre with his army in the Low Countries. Marlborough replied that, despite holding Montandre in esteem, he had nothing to offer him.

Galway himself was given command of an army in the Peninsula in 1704 and was able to appoint Montandre to his own staff, with the local rank of brigadier general. Montandre served at the sieges of Badajoz (3–17 October 1705) and Alcantara (5–14 April 1706) and in the advance to Madrid in June 1706. He was then sent home with the despatches, as a reward for brave conduct. Montandre was promoted to major general, ante-dated to 1 June 1706, and became colonel of an infantry unit (previously Dungannon's Regiment) on 23 November 1706, as a battle casualty replacement. Shortly afterwards, this entire regiment was captured by a troop of Spanish dragoons, so that Montandre derived little benefit from his colonelcy. When the survivors were repatriated to Portsmouth in 1713, he was put to the expense of clothing both them and the recruits who were raised to bring the regiment back up to strength. In the meanwhile, Montandre continued to serve in the Peninsula under Galway and was given command of a brigade of four British regiments that landed in Portugal in June 1707. He commanded this brigade at the Caya (7 May 1709), where he was praised for his conduct covering the Allied retreat. In April 1709 he became colonel of a regiment of dragoons, under Huguenot officers, raised for the Portuguese service at British expense. He was again sent home with the despatches in September 1709 and gave up the colonelcy of his dragoon regiment at the end of that year.

In April 1710 Montandre married the twenty-seven year-old Mary Anne von Spanheim, the only surviving child of the Prussian Ambassador to London. This marriage had the approval of George I and retained Montandre in royal favour. He was promoted to lieutenant general on 9 May 1710. In 1713, with the post-war reductions, his British regiment was disbanded. Montandre was appointed colonel of a newly-raised regiment on the Irish establishment in 1715. This regiment was disbanded in 1718 and, despite many applications, Montandre was never again awarded a colonelcy. He nevertheless remained in favour at court under George II and become Master General of the Ordnance in Ireland on 16 January 1728. Montandre was promoted through seniority to general on 27 October 1735 and to field marshal on 2 July 1739. He died "of a complication of distempers" at his home in Grosvenor Square, London, on 11 August 1739 and was buried near the grave of his parents-in-law, in Westminster Abbey, leaving no children.

DEVERELL
Sir CYRIL JOHN, GCB, KBE (1874–1947) [105]

Cyril Deverell, the son of a subaltern (later major) in the 9th Foot, was born at St Peter Port, Guernsey, on 9 November 1874. He was educated at Bedford School and obtained his first commission on 6 March 1895 as a second lieutenant in the 2nd Battalion, the Prince of Wales's West Yorkshire Regiment. He served with this unit in the Gold Coast (later Ghana) and took part in the expedition that deposed King Prempeh of the Ashanti (Asante). He then joined the 1st Battalion of his regiment and accompanied it first to Hong Kong, then to Singapore and finally to India, where it remained during the South African War. Deverell was promoted to lieutenant on 3 August 1898. In 1902, despite the Army's disapproval of married subalterns, he married his commanding officer's daughter, Hilda Grant-Dalton, with whom he later had a son and a daughter. Deverell became a captain on 23 February 1904. He attended the Indian Staff College, Quetta, from 1906 to 1908, followed by appointment as a General Staff officer, grade 2, in the 4th (Quetta) Division.

When the First World War began in August 1914 Deverell was on leave in the United Kingdom. He was posted as brigade major of the 85th Infantry Brigade in the 28th Division and served in the British Expeditionary Force in France at the second battle of Ypres (April–May 1915). He was given promotion to substantive major on 3 June 1915. From July to October 1915 he commanded a Territorial Force unit, the 1st/4th Battalion, the East Yorkshire Regiment, in the then relatively quiet Armentières sector. Deverell was then promoted to temporary brigadier general and given command of the 20th Infantry Brigade, part of the 7th Division. He became a substantive lieutenant colonel on 26 August 1916 and remained in command of his brigade during the battle of the Somme (31 July–18 November 1916). On 1 January 1917 he was made a substantive colonel and temporary major general on becoming GOC 3rd Division. Deverell remained on the Western Front in command of this formation for the rest of the war and took part with it in the battles of the Ancre, the third battle of Ypres,

Cambrai, the German Spring offensive of 1918 and the final Allied advance leading to the Armistice of 11 November 1918.

Deverell became a substantive major general on 1 January 1919, on appointment as GOC 53rd (Welsh) Division, Territorial Army. From 1921 to 1925 he was GOC United Provinces District, part of Eastern Command, India. He was awarded the KBE in 1926. Sir Cyril Deverell became Quartermaster General, India, in 1927. He was promoted to lieutenant general on 13 March 1928 and became Chief of the General Staff, India, in 1930. He returned to the UK to serve as GOC-in-C Western Command from 1931 to 1933 and as GOC-in-C Eastern Command from 1933 to 1936. He became Chief of the Imperial General Staff in February 1936. Deverell believed that the British Army should be trained and equipped to provide an expeditionary force capable of conventional operations in the mainland of Europe, but Cabinet policy at this time was to avoid making any kind of preparation for a Continental war. Leslie Hore-Belisha, the Secretary of State for War (advised by the influential military theorist Basil Liddell Hart) decided that Deverell, identified as the leading proponent of a Continental strategy, should go. Sir Cyril Deverell was abruptly removed from office on 6 December 1937. He had become colonel of the Prince of Wales's West Yorkshire Regiment in 1934 and retained this post until his death, but otherwise played little further part in military affairs. He retired to his home at Court Lodge, Lymington, and died there on 12 May 1947.

DILL
Sir JOHN GREER, GCB, CMG, DSO (1881–1944) **[109]**

John Dill, the second child and only son of the local branch manager of the Ulster Bank, was born on 25 December 1881 at Lurgan, County Armagh. Dill's parents died within a short time of each other, when he was twelve, and their two children were brought up by an aunt and her husband, an Ulster clergyman. After attending Cheltenham College and the Royal Military College, Sandhurst, Dill was commissioned on 8 May 1901 as a second lieutenant in the 1st Battalion, the Prince of Wales's Leinster Regiment (Royal Canadians). He joined this unit on active service in the South African War and took part in various minor operations in Cape Colony, the Orange River Colony and the Transvaal between June 1901 and May 1902, before returning with his battalion to Ireland in October 1902. Dill was promoted to lieutenant on 27 May 1903 and served in various stations in southern England as battalion adjutant from 1906 to 1909. In 1907, despite the official disapproval of married subalterns, he married Ada Le Mottée, daughter of a colonel in the Royal Irish Regiment. During 1909 Dill was signals officer of his brigade. He was promoted to captain on 12 July 1911. He entered the Staff College, Camberley, in January 1913 and passed out in the following year.

After the beginning of the First World War Dill obtained his first staff appointment on 5 October 1914, as brigade major of the 25th Infantry Brigade. This formation joined the British Expeditionary Force in November 1914. Dill served with it at Neuve Chapelle (10–13 March 1915) and was awarded the DSO in June 1915. He was appointed a General Staff officer, Grade 2, in the Territorial 55th (West Lancashire) Division, on 3 January 1916, with promotion to substantive major on 8 May 1916. From July to November 1916 Dill served as GSO 2 in the Canadian Corps. He was promoted to brevet lieutenant colonel on 1 January 1917 and to temporary lieutenant colonel on 1 February 1917, when he became GSO 1 of the 37th Division. Dill joined the Operations branch of the BEF's General Headquarters in October 1917. He remained there, with appointment to Brigadier General, General Staff, on 27 March 1918, until he returned to England in February 1919, having been eight times mentioned in despatches. He then became one of the two chief instructors at the Staff College, as a temporary brigadier general and substantive colonel from 3 June 1919.

In September 1922, following several months on the half-pay list, Dill was appointed as colonel in command of the Welsh Border Brigade in the 53rd (Welsh) Division of the Territorial Army. In November 1923 he became temporary colonel commandant (an appointment that for a short time replaced that of brigadier general) of the 2nd Infantry Brigade at Aldershot. Dill joined the staff of the Imperial Defence College in November 1926 in the rank of colonel. On 19 January 1929 he became a temporary brigadier and was appointed chief of the General Staff in the Indian Army's Western Command. He was promoted to major general on 11 December 1931 and returned to England to become commandant of the Staff College in January 1932. In December 1932 he became colonel of the East Lancashire Regiment (his original corps, the Leinster Regiment, having been disbanded on the establishment of the Irish Free State in 1922).

Dill was appointed Director of Military Operations at the War Office in January 1934. He was promoted to lieutenant general on 13 April 1936 and became GOC British Troops in Palestine and Transjordan in September 1936. In 1937 Dill returned to the United Kingdom to become GOC-in-C Aldershot Command, with the award of the KCB.

He hoped to become Chief of the Imperial General Staff in succession to Sir Cyril Deverell [105] but the then Secretary of State for War, Leslie Hore-Belisha, advised by the influential military writer, Basil Liddell Hart, decided to reduce the age of officers on the Army Council. Sir John Dill was therefore passed over in favour of Lord Gort [110]. At the beginning of the Second World War in September 1939, when Gort became C-in-C of the British Expeditionary Force, Sir John Dill was again passed over as CIGS, this time in favour of Sir Edmund Ironside [107]. He was, instead, given command of I Corps in the BEF and was promoted to general on 1 October 1939, with an antedate to 5 December 1937 that had the effect of making him one day senior to Gort in that rank.

Dill was recalled to London in April 1940 to take up the newly-created post of Vice Chief of the Imperial General Staff and succeeded Ironside as Chief of the Imperial General Staff on 27 May 1940, after the British defeats in France. Dill's personal life was under great strain at this time, as his wife, who had long been in poor health, suffered a series of strokes that left her paralysed and unable to speak. Her death in December 1940 was a happy release and in October 1941 Dill married the widow of a brigadier who had formerly been on his staff, Nancy Furlong, a daughter of the brewer Henry Charrington. Dill's relations with the Prime Minister, Winston Churchill, were unhappy. He regarded Churchill's demands for aggressive operations as impractical and dangerous, though he gave support to the Prime Minister's concept of forming the Commandos, élite units used to raid the enemy coasts. Dill refused to contemplate taking the offensive before ample resources had been gathered. Churchill regarded this approach as unimaginative and obstructionist. He questioned Dill's fighting spirit and nicknamed him "Dilly-Dally". Early in 1941 Dill visited the Middle East and held talks with the Yugoslav and Turkish governments. His advice against sending troops to support Greece was seen to be justified when this expedition was defeated and was followed by British reverses in North Africa. Churchill became increasingly exasperated at what he saw as Dill's excessive caution and introduced a new rule that a CIGS should retire from this appointment on reaching the age of 60. This enabled him to ensure Dill's departure by 25 December 1941. Dill was given promotion to field marshal on 18 November 1941 and was nominated as Governor of Bombay. He was still CIGS on the outbreak of war with Japan on 7 December 1941 and went with Churchill to the Washington Conference later that month.

Dill was then appointed Head of the British Joint Staff Mission in Washington, where he established a great rapport both with President

Franklin D. Roosevelt and General George C. Marshall, Chief of Staff of the United States Army. He was present at all the major Allied conferences of 1943 and became a member of the Combined Policy Committee dealing with the development of the atomic bomb. Dill's frank and open dealings with Marshall did much to cement the Anglo-American alliance. He passed on to Marshall details of the various imaginative plans that Churchill propounded to Roosevelt, so that Marshall could immediately point out their impracticability if Roosevelt accepted them. He also encouraged Marshall in the policy of dealing with Germany first, to the great benefit of the British home front, rather than concentrating on the Pacific theatre, which the US Navy Chief of Staff would have preferred. Dill's role was as much diplomatic as military and he played a vital part in achieving the adoption of a common strategy by the Western Allies.

Dill's successor as CIGS, Sir Alan Brooke [112], sought a peerage for him, but Churchill refused to recommend it. The only further award Dill received was that of appointment in November 1942 as colonel commandant of the newly-raised Parachute Regiment. During 1944 his health began to deteriorate and he died of aplastic anaemia, in Washington DC, on 4 November 1944. He was given a State funeral, followed by the honour (normally accorded only to United States citizens) of burial in the Arlington National Cemetery. An equestrian statue, one of only two in that place, was erected in recognition of his contribution to the special relationship between the UK and the USA.

DROGHEDA
MARQUESS AND EARL OF, see **MOORE,** CHARLES, **[29]**

EDINBURGH
HRH DUKE OF, see **PHILIP [119]**

EDWARD VII
ALBERT EDWARD, HM King of Great Britain and Ireland, Emperor of India (1841–1910) **[54]**

Albert Edward, eldest son and second child of Queen Victoria and her consort Prince Albert [33], was born on 9 November 1841 and named respectively for his father and for his maternal grandfather, the Duke of Kent [23]. Created Prince of Wales and Earl of Chester soon after his birth, he was known as the Prince of Wales for most of his long life. Fearing that her son might copy the dissolute and improvident ways of her father and uncles, Victoria provided him with strict tuition and rules of behaviour. On 9 November 1858 he was commissioned as a colonel, unattached. He was also given a military governor, Colonel Robert Bruce, who in obedience to Royal instructions, kept him under close control until he reached the age of 21. The Prince of Wales attended Christ Church, Oxford, from 1859 to 1860 and Trinity College, Cambridge, from January to December 1861. During July and August 1861, he was attached to the Grenadier Guards at the Curragh, where he was taught company drill and passed an examination conducted by the Commander-in-Chief (his mother's cousin), the Duke of Cambridge [45]. This was the summit of Wales's military experience. The Queen denied him any part in her political duties and he instead became the leader of fashionable society, especially after Victoria herself withdrew into secluded widowhood. He was promoted to general on 9 November 1862. In March 1863 he married Princess Alexandra of Denmark. As Princess of Wales, she provided him with heirs and, accepting the conventions of her time, tolerated with resignation her husband's various mistresses and adulterous affairs. In April 1863 the Prince became colonel of the 10th Royal Hussars. He was colonel-in-chief of the Rifle Brigade (the Prince Consort's Own) from August 1868 to May 1880, when he was appointed colonel-in-chief of the three regiments of Household Cavalry.

The Prince of Wales became a field marshal on 29 May 1875. In 1882 he volunteered to serve in the campaign in Egypt, but the Cabinet decided that he could make no useful contribution. His offer was declined on the grounds that the precedents for an heir to the throne serving in war were of too early a date to be valid. In 1891 the Prince of Wales was a witness in a libel case, having been present at a game of baccarat when one player, a senior colonel, was accused of cheating. His playboy lifestyle then became a matter of public comment, so that he was obliged to issue a statement condemning intemperance and gambling. He kept up a keen interest in his racing stables and maintained his habit of attending lavish social events at home and abroad. Visiting Belgium in August 1900, he survived an attempted assassination by a sympathizer with the Boer cause in the South African War. He succeeded to the throne as Edward VII on 22 January 1901, though a serious illness led to the postponement of his coronation until August 1902.

As King, Edward VII became colonel-in-chief of the Royal Artillery; the Royal Engineers; the Grenadier, Coldstream, Scots and Irish regiments of Foot Guards; the King's Own (Royal Lancaster Regiment); the Norfolk Regiment and the Gordon Highlanders. As Emperor of India, he became colonel-in-chief of the 6th King Edward's Cavalry (previously connected with him as the 6th Prince of Wales' Bengal Cavalry); the 11th King Edward's Own Lancers, Probyn's Horse (previously the 11th Prince of Wales's Bengal Lancers); the 33rd Queen's Own Light Cavalry; the 2nd Queen's Own Sappers and Miners; the 2nd Queen's Own Rajput Light Infantry; the 102nd King Edward's Own Grenadiers (previously the 2nd Prince of Wales's Own Bombay Grenadiers); the 2nd King Edward's Own Gurkha Rifles (previously the 2nd Prince of Wales's Own Gurkha Rifles) and the Queen's Own Corps of Guides. In the auxiliary forces, variously as King or as Prince of Wales, he was colonel and captain general of the Honourable Artillery Company as well as colonel-in-chief of the Duke of Lancaster's Own Yeomanry; the Norfolk Yeomanry (King's Own Royal Regiment) and the Queen's Own Oxfordshire Hussars. He was honorary colonel of the Prince of Wales's Own Norfolk Artillery Militia; the 3rd (Militia) Battalion, the Duke of Cornwall's Light Infantry; the 3rd (Militia) Battalion, the Gordon Highlanders; the 5th (Sutherland and Caithness) Battalion, the Seaforth Highlanders (Ross-shire Buffs, the Duke of Albany's) and the 8th (Post Office Rifles) and 15th (Prince of Wales's Own Civil Service Rifles) County of London Battalions, the London Regiment, as well as most of their various successors or predecessors.

In domestic politics, Edward reigned as a constitutional sovereign and urged caution on the extreme Conservatives in the House of Lords when they rejected the Liberal budget of 1909. In foreign affairs, as "the uncle of Europe", his visits to other heads of state gained him a reputation as a diplomat and peacemaker, though he had little real influence on events. Edward's personal relations with the Emperor William II of Germany [71] were outwardly cordial, but privately cool. This was partly because of the differences between William and his mother, King Edward's elder sister Victoria, (widowed on the early death of her husband the Emperor Frederick) and partly because of William's open disapproval of his uncle's life-style. Edward held the appointment of colonel of the 1st Prussian Dragoon Guard Regiment and appointed William II a field marshal in the British Army. He was on more cordial terms with the Habsburgs and became colonel of the Austrian 12th Hussars in 1888. After his accession, in an exchange of courtesies with the Emperor Francis Joseph [76], he was appointed a field marshal in the Austro-Hungarian Army in 1903. Edward VII was the first British monarch to be a field marshal in his own Army and the only one to be appointed while Prince of Wales. His reign, though marked by turbulence in both domestic and foreign politics, came to be seen by its survivors as a golden twilight age before the cataclysm of the First World War. He died at Buckingham Palace on 6 May 1910 and was buried in St George's Chapel, Windsor.

EDWARD VIII
EDWARD ALBERT CHRISTIAN GEORGE ANDREW PATRICK DAVID, HM King of Great Britain and Ireland, Emperor of India, later HRH Duke of Windsor, KG, KT, KP, GCB, GCSI, GCMG, GCIE, GCVO, GBE, ISO, MC (1894–1972) [104]

Prince Edward (known in his family as David) was born on 23 June 1894 at White Lodge, Richmond Park, Surrey, the first in a family of five sons and one daughter of the then Duke and Duchess of York (later George V [80] and Queen Mary). Although in direct line of succession from his birth, Edward was initially given a naval education and was trained as a cadet at Osborne, Isle of Wight, from May 1907 until May 1909, when he moved to the Royal Naval College at Dartmouth. On the death of Edward VII [54] in May 1910, Prince Edward became heir apparent and assumed the titles of Duke of Cornwall and Earl of Chester. On his sixteenth birthday he was created Prince of Wales in a ceremony specially devised to appeal to Welsh national sentiment. The Prince found the event and the regalia rather fanciful and was glad to go to sea for three months, as a midshipman in the battleship *Hindustan*, later in 1911. He entered Magdalen College, Oxford, in 1912 and studied there for two years, during which he served as a cadet in the infantry sub-unit of the Oxford University Contingent, Officers Training Corps. In the summer of 1914 the Prince of Wales began what was planned to be a structured military education with a course in cavalry training, attached to the Household Cavalry. With the outbreak of the First World War, he was commissioned as a second lieutenant in the 1st Battalion, Grenadier Guards, on 6 August 1914. When this unit embarked for France on 8 September 1914, George V refused to allow him to go with it, or to perform on active service the only military duties for which he had any training, those of a platoon commander. Instead, the Prince of Wales was transferred to the 3rd Battalion, Grenadier Guards, in London.

After numerous requests, the Prince of Wales succeeded in obtaining the King's permission to go to France at the end of 1914. He was promoted to lieutenant on 19 November 1914 and was appointed staff lieutenant at the General Headquarters of the British Expeditionary Force. The King authorized him to go as far forward as his duties required, but forbade him to join in the fighting in the trenches. This prohibition remained a cause of dissatisfaction to the Prince of Wales who, like most young men of the time, wished to share the dangers of his friends and contemporaries. Instead, he was employed on the staff, where he was too junior in rank to be given important duties and too high in status to be used as an ADC. The Prince of Wales was allowed an attachment to the 2nd Division until May 1915, when he joined the headquarters of I Corps. In June 1915 he was allotted to the staff of the newly-formed Guards Division, commanded by Lord Cavan [101]. The Prince came under shell-fire on a number of occasions, on one of which his staff car was hit and his driver was killed. He was promoted to captain on 10 March 1916 and was awarded the Military Cross shortly afterwards, despite his representations that many more deserving officers had been overlooked. George V had previously had to order him to wear the decorations that he had been given by the French and Russian governments. The Prince himself, feeling he had done nothing to earn them, did so with reluctance. When it became clear that he would not be allowed into the line with the Guards Division, he asked to be allowed to leave the Western Front. In March 1916 the Prince of Wales went to Egypt, ostensibly to report on the defences of the Suez Canal, but in practice to boost the morale of the British troops. He then returned to France and rejoined Cavan, who by this time had assumed command of XIV Corps. Cavan felt that the future sovereign should study international affairs and reproved him for neglecting this subject in order to perform duties that any staff officer could do. An attempt to train Edward as an artillery officer proved a failure. He could not reach the required standard in mathematics, did not understand gun drill and thought that officers of the Royal Artillery compared unfavourably, in social terms, with his old comrades in the Foot Guards. In November 1917 the Prince went to Italy with the Allied reinforcements sent there after the victory of the Central Powers at Caporetto. He remained there until June 1918, when he returned to France until hostilities ended on 11 November 1918.

With the war over, the Prince of Wales began a series of tours of the British Empire, the Far East, and the United States. Everywhere he was greeted with acclaim. During the next eighteen years the Prince became popular at home and abroad, a leader of fashion and the world's most eligible bachelor. He had been demobilized from the Army in 1919, but returned to the active list with the rank of lieutenant general on 1 September 1932. On the death of his father on 20 January 1936, he succeeded to the throne as Edward VIII and, following the precedent set by George V, became a field marshal the next day. It soon became clear that the new King wished to bring an element of freshness and informality into the role of the monarchy. Influenced partly by his experience of military service in the First World War, he had developed vague humanitarian views on social matters and several times expressed sympathy for those whose lives were blighted by the consequences of mass unemployment. In November 1936 he gave hope to the distressed miners of South Wales and alarm to his Conservative ministers by saying that "something must be done" to find work for them.

By this time, however, Edward's reign was nearly over. He had fallen in love with an American lady of strong character and considerable charm, Mrs Wallis Simpson, whom he became determined to marry. Stanley Baldwin, the Conservative Prime Minister of the day, supported by the Labour Opposition and by the Dominion prime ministers, advised him that the King's marriage was a matter of state and that an insurmountable objection to Mrs Simpson becoming Queen was that the Church of England taught that marriage was for life. It was therefore unacceptable for Edward, as Supreme Governor of that Church, to marry a lady with not merely one, but two divorced husbands still living. Despite all the urging of his friends, family and ministers, Edward decided that, if he had to choose between his crown and Mrs Simpson, he would give up the former. He abdicated on 11 December 1936, telling his people that he could not carry out his duties in the way that *he* would wish to do, without the support and companionship of the woman he loved. He was succeeded by his younger brother, the Duke of York, who came to the throne as George VI **[106]**. Public opinion turned against Edward, who was seen by all classes as having put his personal feelings before his duty. Working class people in particular felt he had given Baldwin a way of removing someone who they imagined could have been "the people's king" and could not understand why he simply did not keep Mrs Simpson as a mistress, in the way that they expected kings to behave.

George VI granted his brother the title of HRH the Duke of Windsor. When the Duke married Mrs Simpson in France on 3 June 1937, she became Duchess of Windsor, but neither then nor later would George VI allow her the status of a Royal Highness. On the outbreak of the Second World War Windsor sought employment in the public service. After agreeing to waive his rank as field marshal, he was made a major general and was attached to the British Military Mission in Paris. Sir

Edmund Ironside [107], Chief of the Imperial General Staff, initially objected to this appointment, on the grounds that Windsor would gain access to secret plans and that he could not be trusted not to disclose them to his Duchess, who would in turn gossip about them to her society friends. Windsor was reluctant to accept subordination to the Head of Mission, Major General Sir Richard Howard-Vyse. He wished to visit British sectors of the front and, when he was refused permission to do so by Lord Gort [110], C-in-C of the British Expeditionary Force, appealed to George VI. The King refused to intervene and Windsor had to be content with visiting the French sectors in his role as a liaison officer. With the fall of France in June 1940, Howard-Vyse told Windsor that there were no duties left for him to perform. Windsor then decided that the safety of his Duchess must be his first concern and fled with her first to Spain and then to Portugal. He refused orders to return to the United Kingdom and, in August 1940, accepted the post of Governor of the Bahamas. This enabled him to support the war effort by promoting cordial relations with his American friends, including un-authorized private meetings with President Franklin D. Roosevelt. At the end of the war, Windsor was offered another West Indian post as Governor of Bermuda. He declined this and eventually returned to exile in France, where he died of cancer of the throat at his home in the Bois de Boulogne, Paris, on 28 May 1972. Before his death, the Duke of Windsor had come to a form of reconciliation with the British Royal Family. He was buried among his ancestors at Frogmore Mausoleum, Windsor.

As Prince of Wales, he was colonel-in-chief of the 12th (Prince of Wales's Royal) Lancers; the Royal Scots Fusiliers; the South Wales Borderers; the Duke of Cornwall's Light Infantry; the Prince of Wales's Volunteers (South Lancashire Regiment); the Middlesex Regiment (Duke of Cambridge's Own); the Seaforth Highlanders (Ross-shire Buffs, the Duke of Albany's); the Prince of Wales's Leinster Regiment (Royal Canadians) and the Royal Wiltshire Yeomanry (Prince of Wales's Own Royal Regiment). He was also colonel of the Welsh Guards and honorary colonel of the 5th (Prince of Wales's) Battalion, the Devonshire Regiment; the 4th/5th (Earl of Chester's) Battalion, the Cheshire Regiment and the 15th (County of London) Battalion (Prince of Wales's Own Civil Service Rifles), the London Regiment and its successor unit, the 16th London Regiment (Queen's Westminster Rifles). As King Edward VIII, he was colonel-in-chief of the Life Guards, the Royal Horse Guards, the Royal Artillery, the Royal Engineers, the Royal Tank Corps and the five regiments of Foot Guards, as well as captain general of the Honourable Artillery

Company. He relinquished all his regimental appointments at the time of his abdication, but remained a field marshal on the active list until his death.

EDWARD AUGUSTUS
HRH Duke of Kent and Strathearn, KG, KT, KP, GCB, GCH (1767–1820) [23]

Prince Edward Augustus, the fourth son of George III, was born at Buckingham House (later Palace), London, on 2 November 1767 and was brought up in England before being sent to Hanover at the age of 18 to complete his education. There he followed the example of his royal brothers and many other noblemen of the time by incurring debts that would only grow greater in the course of his career. He was appointed a colonel in the Hanoverian Guards and a brevet colonel in the British Army on 30 May 1786. Prince Edward Augustus became colonel of the 7th Royal Fusiliers on 9 August 1789 and later joined them, as their commanding officer, at Gibraltar. He went with his regiment (in which his German ideas of discipline made him extremely unpopular) to Canada in 1791. Prince Edward Augustus was promoted to major general on 2 October 1793. He then volunteered to join an expedition against the French West Indies, where he commanded a grenadier brigade at the capture of Martinique and St Lucia in March 1794. Edward Augustus was then given command of the British garrison in Nova Scotia, where he was promoted to lieutenant general on 12 January 1796. In October 1798, following a serious fall from his horse, he returned to England, where he was created Duke of Kent and Strathearn on 23 April 1799 and became a general on 10 May 1799. Kent went back to Canada as commander-in-chief in the autumn of 1800, but once more returned to England on health grounds. In 1801 he became colonel of the 1st Foot (the Royal Scots). In 1802 he was appointed Governor and C-in-C, Gibraltar, with orders to improve discipline there. He decided to close half of the ninety wine-shops in the colony and to place the remainder out of bounds to all NCOs and private soldiers. This led to an attempted mutiny on Christmas Eve 1802. Kent was widely held to have gone too far. He was recalled and his successor re-opened the wine-shops.

Kent was promoted to field marshal on 5 September 1805. He took no further part in active military affairs and, after the final defeat of Napoleon in 1815, went to live in Brussels where he could avoid his creditors. In 1817 Princess Charlotte of Wales, the Prince Regent's only legitimate offspring, died in childbirth. The Duke of York [15], who then became next in line to the throne, was childless. Kent, like his unmarried brothers, hastened to find a wife. His bride was Princess Mary Louise Victoria, aged thirty-two, widow of Prince Charles of Leiningen and sister of Princess Charlotte's bereaved husband, Leopold of Saxe-Coburg [28]. They married in 1818 and lived in Leiningen, before journeying to England for the birth of their only child, Princess Alexandrina Victoria of Kent, on 24 May 1819. This princess's first name reflected her father's gratitude to the Emperor Alexander I of Russia, who had supplied the funds for Kent's marriage into the pro-Russian Saxe-Coburg family. Kent died at Sidmouth on 23 January 1820 and was buried in St George's Chapel, Windsor Castle. None of his elder brothers were survived by legitimate offspring, with the consequence that his only child, Princess Victoria of Kent, succeeded to the British throne on the death of her uncle, William IV, in 1837.

EDWARD GEORGE NICHOLAS PAUL PATRICK,
HRH 2nd Duke of Kent, KG, GCMG, GCVO (1935-) [137]

Prince Edward of Kent was born in Belgrave Square, London, on 9 October 1935, the elder son of George, Duke of Kent (fourth son of HM King George V [80]) and his wife, Princess Marina of Greece and Denmark. Prince Edward succeeded as 2nd Duke of Kent on 25 August 1942, following the death of his father (then serving as an air commodore in the Royal Air Force) in a flying accident. He was educated at Eton College and the Royal Military Academy Sandhurst, where he was an officer cadet in Alamein Company, Victory College. The Duke of Kent was commissioned as a second lieutenant in the Royal Scots Greys (2nd Dragoons) on 29 July 1955 and was subsequently promoted to lieutenant on 29 July 1957 and to captain on 29 July 1961. After regimental duty in the UK, in the British Army of the Rhine and in Hong Kong, he qualified at the Staff College, Camberley, in 1966. He then served from February 1967 to May 1968 as a General Staff officer, grade 2, at HQ Eastern Command. The Duke of Kent was promoted to major on 31 December 1967. He then returned to the RMAS as an instructor in Rhine Company, Victory College, until 1970, when he rejoined his regiment to command "C" Squadron. Between June and December 1971, he was involved in peacekeeping duties with UNFICYP, the United Nations force in Cyprus. In July 1971, the Royal Scots Greys were amalgamated with the 3rd Carabiniers to form the

Royal Scots Dragoon Guards (Carabiniers and Greys). Between October 1971 and July 1972 the Duke was GSO 2 (Weapons) in charge of a team working on the development of a tracked combat reconnaissance vehicle. In October 1972 he became a military staff officer in the Procurement Executive at the Ministry of Defence. The Duke of Kent was promoted to lieutenant colonel on 30 June 1973, but political factors restricted his command opportunities and he retired from the Army on 15 April 1976.

The Duke of Kent was appointed colonel-in-chief of the Royal Regiment of Fusiliers in July 1969, and of the Devonshire and Dorset Regiment and the Lorne Scots Regiment of Canadian Militia in June 1977. He became colonel of the Scots Guards in September 1974 and was re-appointed to the active list as a supernumerary major general on 11 June 1983. In June 1961 the Duke of Kent married Katharine Worsley, the daughter of a Yorkshire baronet. They later had two sons and a daughter. He was promoted to field marshal on 11 June 1993 and continued to carry out a full programme of public, ceremonial and charitable duties across a wide field of interests, gaining the respect of all with whom he came into contact.

EDWARD
HRH Prince WILLIAM AUGUSTUS EDWARD of Saxe-Weimar, KP, GCB, GCVO (1823–1902) [69]

His Serene Highness Prince Edward of Saxe-Weimar was born on 11 October 1823 at Bushey Park, the home of the Duke of Clarence (later William VI). He was the eldest son of Duke Bernard of Saxe-Weimar-Eisenach and Princess Ida of Saxe-Meinengen, younger sister of the Duchess of Clarence (later Queen Adelaide). Prince Edward was brought up at Bushey Park, where he was a playfellow of his royal cousins, Princess (later Queen) Victoria and Prince George of Cambridge [45], with both of whom he remained on close terms in later life. Edward was naturalized as a British subject and, after training as a gentleman cadet at the Royal Military College, Sandhurst, was commissioned as an ensign in the 67th Foot on 1 June 1841. He became an ensign in the Grenadier Guards and a lieutenant in the Army on 8 June 1841, with promotion to lieutenant in the regiment and captain in the Army on 19 May 1846. Prince Edward was adjutant of his battalion from November 1850 to December 1851. In 1851 he married Lady Augusta Lennox, second daughter of the 5th Duke of Richmond. The Duke of Saxe-Weimar-Eisenach, Prince Edward's uncle, acting in his capacity as head of their ducal house, decreed that this marriage was to be considered as morganatic because Lady Augusta was not of princely birth.

Prince Edward was promoted to major in the 3rd Battalion, Grenadier Guards, on 20 June 1854. He served with this unit in the Crimean War and was at the Alma (20 September 1854); Sevastopol (19 October 1854), where he was wounded; Balaklava (25 October 1854) and Inkerman (5 November 1854). Prince Edward was promoted to lieutenant colonel on 12 December 1854 and to colonel on 5 October 1855. In 1866 Victoria granted him and his wife the style of Royal Highness. This settled the morganatic question, as Lady Augusta thereby became HRH Princess Edward of Saxe-Weimar, though the couple did not produce any children to inherit his title. Prince Edward was promoted to major general on 6 March 1868 and was GOC Home District from 1870 to 1876. He became a lieutenant general on 6 July 1877. Between October 1878 and April 1881 he was GOC Southern District, with promotion to general on 4 November 1879. Prince Edward became colonel of the 10th Foot in November 1878. His last active employment was as C-in-C, Ireland, from October 1885 to September 1890. He was appointed colonel of the 1st Life Guards in November 1888 and was promoted, from the retired list, to field marshal on 22 June 1897, on the occasion of Victoria's Diamond Jubilee. This gave rise to adverse comment in *The Times* on the grounds that his career had included no great military achievements. He died on 16 November 1902 in Portland Place, London, and was buried at Chichester, near Goodwood, the seat of his wife's family.

EGERTON
Sir CHARLES COMYN, GCB, DSO (1848–1921) [86]

Charles Egerton, the third son of a major general, was born on 10 November 1848. After attending the Royal Military College, Sandhurst, he was commissioned as an ensign in the 31st Foot on 9 June 1867. He immediately transferred to the 76th Foot in India and was promoted to lieutenant on 19 October 1869. Egerton joined the Bengal Staff Corps on 9 August 1871. In 1877 he married Anna Wellwood Hill, from Edinburgh, who later bore him three sons. Egerton became a captain on 8 June 1879 and was appointed a squadron officer in the 3rd Punjab Cavalry. During the Second Afghan War he was with his regiment at Kandahar (1 September 1881), where he was mentioned in despatches. He spent his regimental career on the North-West Frontier and took part in minor operations in various areas, including Baluchistan (1881); Hazara (1888); the Khyber (1891), where he was wounded, and Waziristan (1894–95). He was promoted to major on 8 June 1887, brevet lieutenant colonel on 1 September 1891 and colonel on 1 September 1895. In 1896 Egerton commanded the contingent of Indian troops sent to hold Suakin on the Red Sea coast of the Sudan, while its Egyptian garrison was withdrawn for service under Kitchener [79] on the Nile. He then served on the North-West Frontier as a senior staff officer in the Tochi expedition of 1897–98. He became GOC Frontier District and Punjab Frontier Force, with promotion to local major general on 1 April 1899 and substantive major general on 1 April 1902. After commanding an expedition into Waziristan, Egerton was promoted to lieutenant general on 28 October 1902. He was promoted to general on 11 July 1903 and was awarded the KCB.

During 1903–1904 Sir Charles Egerton commanded the troops in British Somaliland, where he conducted a campaign against a local warlord, Muhammad bin Abdullah (known to the British as "the Mad Mullah"). Three previous expeditions had failed, but Egerton, paying careful attention to the logistic requirements of desert operations and supported by the Royal Navy on the Red Sea coast, inflicted a significant defeat on the Somalis at Jidbali (10 January 1904). He was given command of the Secunderabad District and became colonel of his old regiment, by this time renumbered as the 23rd Cavalry (Frontier Force), in May 1904. On his retirement in 1907, Egerton was appointed a member of the Council of India, advising the Secretary of State for India, where he gave his support to the reforms introduced by Lord Kitchener as C-in-C, India. Thereafter he played a diminishing part in Indian affairs until he left the Council of India in 1917, on completion of his second five-year period of office. Sir Charles Egerton, as the senior retired general of the Indian Army, was made a field marshal on 16 March 1917, succeeding to the vacancy created by the death of Sir Charles Brownlow [78] in the previous year. He died at Christchurch, Hampshire, on 20 February 1921.

ERNEST (ERNST AUGUST) I
ERNEST AUGUSTUS, HM King of Hanover, HRH Duke of Cumberland, KG, KP, GCB, GCH (1771–1851) [25]

Prince Ernest Augustus, the fifth son of George III, was born at Kew on 5 June 1771. After reading classics and military studies at Göttingen University, he was given his first commission in 1790, as a lieutenant in the Hanoverian 9th Hussars. After the beginning of the war with Revolutionary France, he became a lieutenant colonel in 1793 and joined the Hanoverian contingent fighting in the Low Countries as part of the army commanded by his brother, the Duke of York [15]. Prince Ernest was promoted to major general in both the British and Hanoverian Armies in February 1794 and was at Willems (10 May 1794), where he was wounded in the right arm and lost an eye. After returning to England for medical treatment, he rejoined the army in the field and was at Nijmegen (10 December 1794), where he captured a French dragoon by lifting him bodily from his saddle and carrying him back to camp. During the British retreat into Germany in the winter of 1794–95 Prince Ernest commanded the Hanoverian cavalry. He was promoted to lieutenant general on 18 May 1798 and was created Duke of Cumberland in April 1799. On becoming a peer, he spoke in the House of Lords against the Adultery Bill of 1799, which sought to prohibit the guilty parties in a divorce from marrying each other. In what is said to have been the only liberal statement he ever made, Cumberland declared that few men were inclined to marry the females they had seduced and that it would be cruel to such women to deny them even the possibility of this. He became colonel of the 15th Light Dragoons on 28 March 1801, taking an interest in the regiment and occasionally commanding in person. He preferred German to British officers, regarding the latter as insufficiently deferential, and caused great offence by striking one of the Light Dragoon officers with a cane. In the Volunteer Force raised from patriotic citizens at the time of a threatened French invasion in 1803, Cumberland gave his name to a fashionable London corps of riflemen, the Duke of Cumberland's Sharpshooters. He became a general on 25 September 1803 and commanded a division of Hanoverian troops in northern Germany in the brief campaign of 1806.

On 31 May 1810 Cumberland was found in his London house, bleeding from a severe head wound, with the dead body of his valet nearby. An inquest declared that the valet had attacked his master while insane and had been killed by him in self-defence. Other explanations were freely offered in the scandal-sheets and one editor was imprisoned for seditious libel. Cumberland returned to Hanover, where he assumed the government in his father's name. He raised a new Hanoverian Army and led it in the German War of Liberation of 1813–1814. Cumberland was present at Leipzig (16–18 October 1813) and was promoted to field marshal on 26 November 1813. In May 1815 he married his cousin, the twice-widowed Princess Frederica of Mecklenburg-Strelitz. His mother, Queen Charlotte, disapproved of the new Duchess of

Cumberland and refused to receive her at court. Cumberland became colonel of the Royal Horse Guards in June 1827, but resigned in 1830 in protest at the Household Cavalry being placed directly under the C-in-C. He also protested when William IV approved a new constitution for Hanover, granted by the Viceroy (their brother, the Duke of Cambridge [26]) without consulting Cumberland as heir-apparent.

Notwithstanding the revolutions that affected much of Europe in the early 1830s, Cumberland opposed reform both at home and abroad. As the eldest surviving male heir of George III, he became King of Hanover on the death of William IV in June 1837 and immediately cancelled the constitution that had been granted by the Duke of Cambridge. Fear that King Ernest might succeed his young niece, Queen Victoria, to the throne of England, was one of the main reasons why her ministers pressed her to make an early marriage, with the hope that she soon would produce a new heir. He protested at Victoria's marriage to Prince Albert of Saxe-Coburg-Gotha [33] and refused to attend their wedding. Nevertheless, the people of Hanover seemed to like the down-to-earth ways of their new King and Queen, who, after generations of absentee monarchs, at least lived in their country. King Ernest was prevailed upon to grant a measure of reform in 1840, with the result that his regime survived the revolutionary year of 1848 virtually unscathed. He died at Herrenhausen Palace, Hanover, on 18 November 1851 and was succeeded by his son, the blind King George V (later deposed when the kingdom of Hanover was incorporated into Prussia).

FESTING
Sir FRANCIS WOGAN, GCB, KBE, DSO (1902–1976) [123]

Francis Festing, the only child of a captain (later a brigadier general) in the 4th Battalion, Northumberland Fusiliers, was born in Dublin on 28 August 1902. He was educated at Winchester College, where, through the influence of an eccentric aunt, he became a convert to the Church of Rome. After attending the Royal Military College, Sandhurst, Festing was commissioned as a second lieutenant in the 3rd Battalion, the Rifle Brigade (the Prince Consort's Own) on 23 December 1921. When this battalion was disbanded in the post-war reduction of the Army, he joined the 2nd Battalion, the Rifle Brigade, and served with this unit first at Chanak and then at Aldershot. Festing was promoted to lieutenant on 23 December 1923. Between 1926 and 1929 he was aide-de-camp to Major General Sir John Burnett-Stuart (late of the Rifle Brigade), GOC 3rd Division at Bulford, Salisbury Plain. Festing rejoined his battalion in 1929 and remained at regimental duty in southern England until 1934, when he went to the Staff College, Camberley. He obtained his first staff appointment in February 1936 as a General Staff officer, grade 3, at HQ Eastern Command, attached as air liaison officer to No. 2 (Army Co-operation) Squadron, Royal Air Force, Hawkinge. He was promoted to captain in his regiment on 1 September 1936. In 1937 Festing married Mary Riddell, a daughter of an old recusant family of Swinburne Castle, Hexham, Northumberland. They later had four sons. In February 1938 he returned to the Staff College, Camberley, as a GSO 2 and instructor. He was promoted to substantive major on 1 August 1938 and remained at the college until mobilization on the outbreak of the Second World War in September 1939.

Festing was promoted to temporary lieutenant colonel on 1 April 1940, when he was appointed GSO 1 (Air Liaison) for service in the expedition to Norway. After the Allies withdrew from Norway in May 1940, Festing went to the War Office as GSO 1 in the Military Operations Directorate. In September 1940 he was given command of the 2nd Battalion, the East Lancashire Regiment. This unit was deployed in a counter-invasion role in Surrey until February 1941, when it moved to the Highlands for training in amphibious warfare. On 13 April 1942 he was appointed to the command of the 29th Infantry Brigade and was promoted to war substantive lieutenant colonel, temporary colonel and acting brigadier. He led this formation in the descent on Madagascar in May 1942 and in the subsequent landing at Tamatava (September 1942), where he was awarded the DSO. From the manner in which he encouraged others towards the battle area as well as from his conspicuous presence there himself, he gained the nickname "front-line Frankie". Festing became a war substantive colonel and temporary major general on 28 November 1942, in command of a new formation, the 36th Division, then being formed in India. After training for jungle warfare, this division moved to Burma where it took part in the second battle of Arakan (24 February- 5 June 1944). Between August 1944 and May 1945 the 36th Division was involved in intensive operations in northern Burma, ending with the pursuit of the defeated Japanese to Rangoon. Festing became a substantive major general on 3 November 1944. He proved an inspiring leader, frequently appearing in the forefront of the battle, where on one occasion he nearly drove his jeep into a Japanese ambush and on another he took command of a platoon whose leader had been killed.

After the end of hostilities Festing was appointed GOC Land Forces, Hong Kong, in August 1945. He was Director of Weapons and

Development at the War Office from February 1947 to June 1949, when he returned to Hong Kong as Commander, British Forces and temporary lieutenant general. In October 1949 he became seriously ill with a blood clot on the brain. He was flown back to the UK, where he spent several months in treatment and convalescence. For much of 1950 Festing was President of the Regular Commissions Board, as a substantive major general. He was then posted to Supreme Headquarters Allied Powers Europe, as Assistant Chief of Staff (Organization and Training). He was promoted to lieutenant general on 6 February 1952, with the award of the KBE. Sir Francis Festing became GOC British Troops, Egypt, in April 1952, where he took strong measures in response to attacks on his men by Egyptian extremists. He was appointed GOC-in-C Eastern Command, based at Hounslow, in July 1954. Festing disliked this post and spent as much time as possible in his Northumbrian homeland. When he appeared at the end of one exercise, disgruntled Territorials of an inner London infantry battalion gave him a hostile reception.

In August 1956 Festing was appointed C-in-C Far East Land Forces, with promotion to general on 29 November 1956. He became Chief of the Imperial General Staff in September 1958 and was faced with the task of implementing the Cabinet decisions to end conscription and reduce the size of the Army. Festing was able to persuade the ministers that the manpower reduction should be to 180,000, rather than to 165,000 as had originally been planned, but still had to accept the loss of fifteen battalions from the order of battle, with many regiments being amalgamated and given new titles. He was promoted to field marshal on 1 September 1960 and was succeeded by Sir Richard Hull [126] in November 1961. As CIGS, Festing worked under both Labour and Conservative defence ministers. He declared a preference for the former, arguing (not entirely accurately on any count) that Labour ministers were very likely ex-lance-corporals who would defer to the professional advice of senior officers, whereas Tory ministers were probably ex-majors of "ineffectual Yeomanry regiments" who thereby considered themselves military experts. Despite his tall and imposing bearing, Festing's own appearance in uniform frequently invited criticism, as he was noted throughout his career for a scruffy and unkempt turn-out. He was honorary colonel of a Territorial battalion of the Royal Northumberland Fusiliers from February 1948 to March 1953, when he became colonel of the entire regiment (a post that he retained until October 1965). Festing was colonel commandant of the 3rd Green Jackets (the Rifle Brigade) from November 1958 to January 1966 and of its successor, the 3rd Battalion, Royal Green Jackets, until August

1968. On the half-pay, he continued to devote himself to his impressive collection of early firearms and Japanese swords. Sir Francis Festing died at his home near Hexham on 3 August 1976. He was buried in a specially consecrated plot in one of his own fields, next to the Anglican parish church of St Luke, Greystead. Sir Francis Festing, with all the zeal of a convert, was punctilious in his religious observances throughout his military career and took pleasure in being the first practising member of the Church of Rome to head the British Army since the Glorious Revolution of 1688.

FITZGERALD
Sir JOHN FORSTER, GCB (c.1785–1877) [52]

John Fitzgerald, whose date of birth is given variously as either 1784 or 1786, was the younger son of an Irish landowner who sat in the Irish Parliament as MP for County Clare. He was commissioned on 29 October 1793 as an ensign in an independent company of Foot in Ireland. In 1794 Fitzgerald became a captain on the Irish half-pay, from which he obtained a full-pay captaincy in the 46th Foot on 31 October 1800. He returned to the half-pay list in 1802, but rejoined the 46th, with promotion to major, on 25 September 1803. Between 1804 and 1809 he was on the rolls of the New Brunswick Fencibles, a corps raised for local defence in Canada. Fitzgerald became a lieutenant colonel in the 60th Royal American Regiment on 25 June 1810 and joined its 5th Battalion in the Peninsula early in 1812. He was at Badajoz (17 March–6 April 1812), where he was wounded commanding the battalion; Salamanca (22 July 1812); Vittoria (21 June 1813), where he took command of his brigade through battle casualty, and the Pyrenees (27 July 1813). Fitzgerald was wounded and captured in the Pyrenees, on 13 August 1813, and remained a prisoner of war until hostilities ended in April 1814. He was with his battalion in Ireland until 1816 and at Gibraltar until 1818, when its personnel were transferred to the 2nd Battalion of the 60th Royal American Regiment in Quebec. Fitzgerald was given command of this unit and was promoted to colonel on 12 August 1819. He then held various posts in Canada during the next five years and married Charlotte Hazen, daughter of a prominent member of local society in St John's, New Brunswick. She bore him two daughters and a son who was later killed in action serving as a captain in the 14th Light Dragoons during the Second Sikh War.

In 1824, when his regiment was remustered as the 60th Rifles and ceased to be a localized corps intended primarily for service in North

America, Fitzgerald exchanged to the 20th Foot, then stationed in Bombay. He became a major-general on 22 July 1830 and was awarded the KCB. After commanding a division of the Bombay Army, Sir John Fitzgerald returned to Europe and was promoted to lieutenant general on 23 November 1841. He was colonel of the 85th Light Infantry from April 1840 to November 1843 and of the 62nd from then until March 1850, when he became colonel of the 18th Foot (the Royal Irish Regiment). Between 1851 and 1857 he sat as a Liberal MP for County Clare. Fitzgerald was promoted to general on 20 June 1854 and to field marshal on 29 May 1875. After the death of his first wife, he married Jean Ogilvy, the daughter of a former colonel in the Madras Army. He raised a second family with her and, late in life, became a convert to the Church of Rome. He retired to Tours, in France, where he died on 24 March 1877. On the orders of the French Minister for War, Fitzgerald's funeral cortège was escorted by the local garrison and given the honours appropriate to a Marshal of France. At the time of his death he was the oldest officer in the British Army.

FOCH, FERDINAND
Marshal of France, GCB, OM (1851–1929) **[88]**

Ferdinand Foch, the third child and second son of a revenue official, was born at Tarbes, Gascony, on 2 October 1851. In 1870 he was a student at a Catholic school, the Collège de St. Clement, in Metz, Lorraine. When the Franco-Prussian War began, the school had broken up for the summer recess. Foch enlisted as a private soldier in the 4th Infantry Regiment, but saw no combat service. After the armistice he returned to school in Metz, which was by that time under German occupation. Soon afterwards, Lorraine was annexed by the new German Empire, for which Foch, like most Frenchmen of his generation, developed a deep hatred. He entered the Ecole Polytechnique in 1872 and transferred to the Ecole d'Application at Fontainebleau, for training as an artillery officer, in the following year. He passed out third in his class in 1874 and chose to join the 24th Artillery Regiment at his home town, Tarbes. Foch was promoted to captain in the 10th Artillery Regiment in September 1878. This unit was based at Rennes, Brittany, where he made his home and married Julie Bienvenue, daughter of a local lawyer. In 1880 he was posted to the Ministry of War in Paris, with the task of writing a new artillery training manual.

In 1885 Foch was selected for training at the Ecole Supérieur de Guerre (the French Army Staff College), Paris. After qualifying there, he joined the staff of the 31st Division at Montpellier. He returned to the Ministry of War in 1890, where he joined the Troisième Bureau (the operations and plans branch) of the French General Staff, with promotion to major in February 1891. He was appointed assistant professor of military history, strategy and tactics at the Ecole Supérieur de Guerre in October 1895. Foch was promoted to lieutenant colonel in 1896 and became professor of his department. He proved an inspiring lecturer, stressing the importance of leadership in war and teaching that victory was achieved by the commander, not by the army. At this time, in consequence of the Dreyfus case, there was a reaction against the influence of Catholicism and conservatism in the French Army. Foch, whose brother was a Jesuit, was removed from his professorship in October 1901 and was sent to command the 29th Artillery Regiment at Laon. He was denied the promotion that went with regimental command, until 1903, when he became colonel of the 35th Artillery Regiment at Vannes, Brittany. Foch was appointed chief of staff of V Corps at Orleans in 1905. Two years later, he was promoted to brigadier general and given command of the artillery of V Corps.

In October 1908 Foch became commandant of the Ecole Supérieur de Guerre. One of Foch's innovations was to establish a centre for advanced studies, to be "a school for future marshals". Exercises were conducted amid cries of *"Vite, vite"* and *"Allez, allez"*, to simulate the pressures of actual operations, of which neither Foch nor the majority of his students had at this time any personal experience. He was visited by Henry Wilson [91], commandant of the British Army Staff College. Wilson, overcoming his inclination to look down on French officers as being mostly of bourgeois origins, soon became one of Foch's greatest admirers. Foch began with equal reservations, but responded favourably to Wilson's evident respect for the French Army and his mastery of the French language, so that the two became close allies. In 1911 Foch became a major general commanding the 13th Infantry Division. He was promoted to lieutenant general in October 1912 and given command of VIII Army Corps. In September 1913 he was appointed to the command of XX Army Corps, at Nancy, the intended spearhead of the French attack when war came with Germany.

During the first weeks of the First World War in August 1914, Foch was involved in the battle of the frontiers and attacked the Germans with some success at Morhange (20 August 1914). He was then ordered by General Joffre, the French C-in-C, to take command of a new formation, later the 9th Army. Foch led this in the first battle of the Marne (6–9 September 1914), animating his Frenchmen with voice and gesture and constant cries of *"attaquez"*. In his own family, a son and a

123

son-in-law were both killed on 22 August 1914, fighting in Belgium. Foch was appointed C-in-C of the French armies of the North on 4 October 1914. During 1915 he launched several fruitless offensives in Artois, after which he abandoned his old theories of the irresistibility of the vigorous offensive, in favour of a policy of wearing down the enemy by successive assaults, each delivered in a different sector. Foch commanded the French forces that took part in the battle of the Somme (July -November 1916), fighting alongside their British allies who were by this time under Sir Douglas Haig [85].

Early in December 1916, Joffre, aware that General Robert Nivelle was about to take his place as C-in-C, created a new post for his protégé, Foch, as the head of an office to provide the government with advice on strategy. In May 1917, when General Pétain took the place of Nivelle, Foch was appointed Chief of the General Staff at Army HQ, partly because he was known to enjoy the confidence of Sir Henry Wilson (since January 1915 the principal British liaison officer in Paris). Pétain's frequent absence on visits to the armies in the field allowed Foch to establish a strong position for himself as the government's main military adviser. Following the victory of the Central Powers at Caporetto, late in October 1917, Foch rushed to the Italian army, much as he had rushed to the British and Belgian armies in Flanders in 1914. Despite his whirlwind Gascon manner, which caused some offence to the Italians, his ability to work with Allied armies gained general recognition.

The German offensive on the Western Front in the spring of 1918 forced the Allies to establish a supreme commander, with the authority to co-ordinate the actions of their armies in the field. The French Premier, Georges Clemenceau, suggested Foch. Wilson, by this time Chief of the Imperial General Staff in London, strongly supported the proposal. On 28 March 1918 the British Cabinet agreed to a unity of command and, on 14 April 1918, acknowledged Foch as C-in-C of the Allied armies. This title was accepted by the governments of France and the USA, followed (in June and September 1918 respectively) by those of Italy and Belgium. Foch had no combined Allied staff or headquarters and controlled operations mostly through his allocation of the reserves under his direct command. He used them first to stem the German offensives and then, from mid-July 1918, to support successful counter-attacks launched by the various Allied armies. Foch appreciated that the German army on the Western Front could still mount a formidable defence and his initial plan was to wait for the arrival of the tanks, now being produced in large numbers, and of the Americans. On 6 August 1918 he was appointed a Marshal of France, in recognition of the Allied victory at the 2nd battle of the Marne in July 1918. As the Allies continued their advance, he supported the impetus of the general offensive with the cry of *"tout le monde à la bataille"*. His role was essentially that of a co-ordinator rather than a commander and, in his own words, he was "a conductor who beat time well". When the Germans sued for an armistice in November 1918, Foch insisted on an Allied occupation of the Rhineland, hoping that this would be followed by a French annexation. The British reluctantly agreed to this in return for Foch's equally reluctant agreement to the internment of the German battle fleet under the guns of the Royal Navy. Foch headed the Allied commanders who received the German envoys at Compiègne on 8 November 1918. In rejecting any attempt at negotiation, he avenged the French humiliation at the hands of Germany that he had experienced in his youth.

After the war, Foch broke with Clemenceau, who saw that neither the British nor the Americans would accept the extension of French borders to the Rhine. He also broke with David Lloyd George, the British Prime Minister, over the same issue and declined Lloyd George's suggestion that he go to the aid of the Poles against the Red Army in July 1920. Foch was made a British field marshal on 19 July 1919. He died of a heart attack, in Paris, on 20 March 1929, and was buried beside the tomb of Napoleon at Les Invalides.

FRANCIS JOSEPH
FRANZ-JOSEPH, HIM Emperor (Kaiser) of Austria and King of Hungary, KG (1830–1916) **[76]**

Francis Joseph, the eldest son of the Archduke Francis Charles (younger brother of the Emperor Ferdinand I) was born on 18 August 1830 at the palace of Schönbrunn, Vienna. Ferdinand, childless, sickly and of weak intellect, had not been expected to outlive the previous Emperor, Francis II, and it was generally supposed that Archduke Francis Charles would succeed to the Habsburg throne. The Archduke and his forceful wife, the Archduchess Sophie, therefore brought up Francis Joseph as a future Emperor. In 1842 he went through a course of military training and in 1843 he was appointed colonel of a dragoon regiment. Like many other royal princes, Francis Joseph relished army life and became popular with the military.

In 1848, when the Habsburg Empire was torn by revolution, conservative generals gave their support to Francis Joseph. The Emperor Ferdinand abdicated in Francis Joseph's favour and Archduke Francis

Charles renounced his own claims to the succession. Francis Joseph took part in the campaign in Verona and was at Santa Lucia (6 May 1848). Military victories (achieved in Hungary with Russian aid) restored the old regime and Francis Joseph thereafter always regarded the Army as the major unifying force in his multi-ethnic empire. In the war of 1859 against France and Sardinia, he accompanied his armies in the field in northern Italy, and took personal command after their defeat at Magenta (4 June 1859). He was routed at Solferino (24 June 1859), after which he accepted that his military training had not prepared him to be a general. Nevertheless, Francis Joseph remained close to his Army. He always attended the autumn manoeuvres and, when working at his desk, wore the uniform of an infantry lieutenant. He lived in frugal style and became the first bureaucrat of his empire, spending ten hours a day in his cramped office. His first audience of the day was always given to the head of his military chancellery.

In his private life Francis Joseph suffered many misfortunes. His daughter Sophie died in infancy. His estranged brother, who became the Emperor Maximilian of Mexico, was defeated and executed after a national uprising. Maximilian's widow, the Empress Charlotte (Carlotta) lost her mind. Archduchess Sophie, though thwarted in her expectation of becoming Empress, dominated Francis Joseph. A devout Roman Catholic and upholder of the established order, she encouraged him in the reactionary policies from which he only reluctantly retreated as his reign wore on. She chose his wife, Elisabeth ("Sisi"), a young princess of the Wittelsbach dynasty of Bavaria, whom he married in 1854. Elisabeth never cared for the protocol-ridden Habsburg court and resented the dominance of her mother-in-law in every aspect of her family life. Bored by court life and neglected while her husband occupied himself with public business, she travelled to various spas and tried various cures for her depression. After her pregnancies, she took to a regime of physical exercises and restrictive diets, losing so much weight as to make her husband fear for her health. In 1865, at the peak of her beauty, she at last succeeded in forcing the Emperor, who remained devoted to her, to give her control of her children, previously kept by the Archduchess Sophie. Their only son, Crown Prince Rudolph, later contracted a social illness that he transmitted to his wife, so that she became infertile before she had produced a son to carry on the succession. Rudolph committed suicide in mysterious circumstances at Mayerling in January 1889. The Empress, having resumed her foreign travels, was assassinated by an Italian anarchist in Geneva in September 1898. Francis Joseph's next heir, his nephew, the Archduke Francis Ferdinand, defied the Emperor and contracted a morganatic marriage.

126

The Archduke and his wife were assassinated by Serb extremists on 28 June 1914 at Sarajevo, capital of the recently-annexed province of Bosnia. Francis Joseph and his ministers determined to use this tragedy as an opportunity to crush the growing threat of Serb nationalism once and for all. In a fatal miscalculation, they unleashed a war that destroyed the brilliant polyglot empire that they intended it to preserve and brought ruin on all the great powers of Europe. Francis Joseph's death during the First World War, after the third longest reign of any prince in European history, marked the end of an epoch. He died at the Schönbrunn Palace on 21 November 1916 and was buried in the Capuchin Church, Vienna.

Francis Joseph's connection with the British Army was entirely of a ceremonial nature. He became colonel-in-chief of the 1st (King's) Dragoon Guards in March 1896 and, in an exchange of courtesies with Edward VII [54], a field marshal on 1 September 1903.

FREDERICK AUGUSTUS
HRH Duke of York and Albany, KG, GCB, GCH
(1763–1827) [15]

Prince Frederick Augustus, born on 16 August 1763 at St James's Palace, London, was the second son of King George III. His first public office, to which he was elected soon after his birth, was that of Bishop of Osnaburg, a dependency of Hanover, with which it was later united. He was known by this title until November 1784, when he was created Duke of York and Albany. His first commission, as a colonel in the Army, was granted on 1 November 1780. He had displayed an interest in military matters from early childhood and completed his education with a series of visits to various German states, including Prussia, where he attended the last review to be held by his namesake, Frederick the Great. Prince Frederick became colonel of the 2nd Troop of Horse Grenadier Guards on 23 March 1782 and a major general on 20 November 1782. He was promoted to lieutenant general on 27 October 1784 and at the same time became colonel of the Coldstream Guards. His admiration for the Prussian system of discipline led him to find fault with the efficiency of his regiment and to consider his officers neglectful of their duty. One of them, Captain and Lieutenant Colonel Charles Lennox (later 4th Duke of Richmond) spoke insultingly, in York's presence, both of the Duke himself and of the Prince of Wales. When Lennox ignored a rebuke from a partisan of the royal brothers, York let it be known that he considered Lennox to have behaved in a way unworthy of a gentleman. This amounted to a challenge and, waiving both his military rank and social position, he offered to give Lennox (a noted marksman) satisfaction in a duel. At their meeting, on 26 May 1789, Lennox's bullet clipped a curl from his colonel's hair. York refused to return the fire, saying he had come out merely to satisfy Lennox, not to injure him and invited him to take a second shot if he wished (which Lennox could not, in honour, do, even though York declined to withdraw his critical remarks). In January 1791 the Duke of York married the eldest daughter of Frederick William II of Prussia. The new Duchess of York was at first very popular and set a new style in ladies' fashions, but the marriage did not prove a success and the couple separated. The Duchess set up her own home in Weybridge, where she lived surrounded by lapdogs.

In 1793 York led the British army sent to the Low Countries in the war against Revolutionary France. Despite his inexperience in war, his royal blood carried weight in the protocol-conscious camps of the Allied armies and York's headquarters became noted for its fine table and generous hospitality. York himself was promoted to general on 12 April 1793, shortly before the beginning of active operations. The Allied forces achieved some initial successes, but failed to follow them up and instead settled down to the old pattern of trench-warfare in Flanders that had cost the British Army so dear in the past, as it would do again in the future. York laid siege to Dunkirk, but, when the French counter-offensive came, was defeated at Hoondschoote (8 September 1793). He was forced to abandon his heavy guns and to retreat to Ostend. York then became the target of blame from British politicians whose own relentless search for reductions in defence expenditure had for years starved the Army of its needs. In the next year's campaign he achieved a victory at Willems (10 May 1794), but was overwhelmed at Tourcoing (18 May 1794), where York himself, conspicuous in his blue Garter sash and thanking God for the speed of his horse, only narrowly escaped capture. When their allies later abandoned the campaign, the British made a winter retreat into Germany and suffered greatly from lack of supplies and shelter, before being evacuated via Bremen in April 1795.

York remained in the field until December 1794. He was promoted to field marshal on 18 February 1795, a week after succeeding the aged Sir Jeffery Amherst [17] as the effective commander-in-chief of the Army, though he was not given this title until 1798. This appointment, at the relatively young age of 32, was made mostly in response to the wishes of King George III. York's promotion, by which he superseded eleven generals senior to him (seven of whom later became field marshals) was the first time that this rank had been awarded other than by strict seniority. Nevertheless, York proved to have found his *métier* as a military administrator rather than a field commander. While much of the credit for the reforms carried out under his authority must go to his principal staff officers, York was not a mere figurehead and always considered himself to be a professional soldier. It was with his active support that a Royal Military College (forerunner of both the Staff College and the Royal Military Academy Sandhurst) was set up, where officers could be trained in staff duties and gentlemen cadets could be trained for commissions in the Line. He also gave his support to an "Asylum" (later the Duke of York's School) for the sons of deserving old soldiers. When the RMC moved to its new home at Sandhurst in 1812, the settlement that grew up at its southern gate was named York Town in his honour.

York again took the field in September 1799, when he landed at the Helder with an army of 30,000 British troops and 12,000 Russians. His first engagement, at Bergen (19 September 1799), was inconclusive. He had more success at Egmont (3 October 1799), but the logistic weaknesses of his army were already apparent and, after achieving a victory at Kastrikum (7 October 1799), he ordered a retreat. On 18th October 1799, with only three days' rations left and the weather beginning to break, he signed an armistice allowing him an unopposed embarkation.

York always had an eye for good-looking women. He was also, like many great men of his time, careless about living beyond his means. These two factors led to his undoing in February 1809, when Radicals in the House of Commons attacked York, and thus the Cabinet in which he sat, for what a later age would describe as "sleaze". The duke's discarded mistress, Mrs Mary Anne Clarke, gave evidence that she had taken money from officers who wished for particular appointments and had given their names to York, who passed them on for his staff to implement. The government majority in the Commons ensured that York escaped parliamentary censure, but it was clear that he had derived at least some indirect benefit from these proceedings, while Mrs Clarke's spirited performance when questioned at the bar of the House gained her some sympathy at the ministry's expense. York had to resign before demands for his dismissal became too strong and was not reinstated until 25 May 1811. He became colonel-in-chief of the 60th Royal American Regiment in 1797 and colonel of the 1st Foot Guards in 1805. As Commander in Chief, he lent his name to a number of short-lived regiments raised for emergency service, including the York Rangers; the York Chasseurs; the York Light Infantry Volunteers (a corps of British and German sharpshooters) and the Duke of York's Greek Light

Infantry. Unhappily married himself, he encouraged his niece, Princess Charlotte of Wales, in her love-match with Leopold of Saxe-Coburg [28]. After her death in November 1817 York was once again next in succession to the Prince of Wales, but did not live to take his place on the throne. He died at Arlington House, the London home of his friend the Duke of Rutland, on 5 January 1827 and was buried at St George's Chapel, Windsor. His place in the folklore of the English-speaking world is secured by the nursery rhyme and contemporary march-tune, "The Grand Old Duke of York".

FRENCH, Sir JOHN DENTON PINKSTONE
1st Earl of Ypres, KP, GCB, OM, GCVO, KCMG
(1852–1925) [83]

John French, the only son and youngest of seven children of a retired naval officer, was born on 28 September 1852, near Deal, in Kent. Despite his English birth, French considered himself Anglo-Irish by descent, as his great-grandparents had held estates in Ireland. French joined the training ship *Britannia* at Dartmouth in August 1866 as a naval cadet. From there he went to sea as a midshipman in the new iron-clad *Warrior* and was present at the loss of HMS *Captain*, swamped in the Bay of Biscay. He resigned from the Royal Navy in 1870 and obtained a commission in the Suffolk Artillery Militia, from which he joined the Army as a lieutenant in the 8th (Queen's Royal Irish) Hussars on 28 February 1874. A few weeks later he transferred to the 19th Hussars and joined this regiment at Aldershot. In June 1874 he married Isabella Soundy, the attractive daughter of a tradesman. Their divorce in 1878, with Isabella named as a co-respondent (and said to have been paid off by the wealthy husband of one of French's sisters) would normally have ended an officer's career. Nevertheless, French rose above the scandal and continued at regimental duty in Ireland. He became a captain on 16 October 1880 and, in the same year, married Eleanora Selby-Lowndes, one of the seven daughters of a prosperous Buckinghamshire squire known collectively as "the Belles of Bletchley". French became adjutant of the Northumberland Hussars Yeomanry in 1881. He was promoted to major on 3 April 1883 and returned to the 19th Hussars in October 1884. In the Gordon Relief Expedition, he commanded a squadron of his regiment in the Sudan. He was at Abu Klea (16 January 1885) and gained the favourable notice of Sir Redvers Buller, himself a favourite of the expedition commander, Sir Garnet Wolseley [67]. French was promoted to lieutenant colonel on 7

February 1885 and was sent home with the despatches in recognition of his conduct in the campaign.

French remained at regimental duty with the 19th Hussars at various stations in southern England and was given command of the regiment in April 1888. He was promoted to brevet colonel on 7 February 1889 and sailed with his regiment to India in September 1891. With his wife and children left behind in England, French had ample opportunity to indulge in *affaires,* one of which led to his being cited by another officer as co-respondent in a divorce case. He returned to England in 1893 and was placed on the half-pay list. In 1895 Sir Redvers Buller found an appointment for him at the War Office, writing a new cavalry training manual. In 1897, French was given command of the newly-formed 2nd Cavalry Brigade, serving under Buller at Aldershot, and became a temporary major general. He was at this time harassed by debts and borrowed heavily from the wealthy Douglas Haig [85], an officer of lower rank than himself, with whom he had become friendly when at the War Office. French became a substantive major general on 23 September 1899.

On the approach of war with the Boer republics in South Africa, French was selected by Buller to command the newly-formed Cavalry Division. On reaching Cape Town (together with Haig, to whom he had allotted a senior post on his staff), he was sent to Natal as a subordinate to the British commander there, Sir George White [75]. French was at Elandslaagte (21 October 1899) and Lombard's Kop (30 October 1899), after which the British were driven back into Ladysmith. French and Haig escaped, under Boer fire, on the last train to leave the town. French commanded the Cavalry Division at Colesberg (1 January 1900) and was one of the few senior officers not to be removed by Lord Roberts [68] when he arrived to take over command in South Africa from Buller shortly afterwards. French had no high opinion of Roberts and was ambivalent in his relations with Roberts' Chief of Staff, Lord Kitchener [79], whose austere character was the opposite of French's own extrovert personality. French disliked Sir William Nicholson [82], under whom Roberts had decided that all the army's transport was to be centralized, and managed to retain the cavalry divisional transport under his own control. French commanded the Cavalry Division at Klip Drift (15 February 1900); Paardeberg (17–26 February 1900); Dreifontein (10 March 1900); Vet River (5–6 May 1900); Poplar Grove (7 March 1900); Zand River (10 May 1900) and Diamond Hill (11–12 June 1900). In July 1900, with the conventional phase of the war over, he was awarded the KCB.

Sir John French returned to the United Kingdom in 1902, having made his name as a successful commander of cavalry. He was promoted to lieutenant general on 15 September 1902 and was given command of I Army Corps at Aldershot, in succession to Buller, whom Roberts (by this time C-in-C) had decided to remove. Through the influence of Lord Esher, the enigmatic close friend and adviser of King Edward VII [54], French was appointed to succeed the Duke of Connaught [73] as Inspector General of the Forces, with promotion to general on 12 February 1907. In this appointment he resisted all suggestions that the cavalry should no longer rely on the *arme blanche* as its primary weapon, although at the same time he stressed that cavalrymen should be trained to dismount and use their rifles when necessary. He supported the reformers who had long pressed for a reorganization of British infantry battalions into four large companies instead of eight small ones.

In March 1912, French succeeded Nicholson as Chief of the Imperial General Staff. He forced through the re-organization of infantry battalions, but allowed a devaluation of the rank structure. Infantry majors (previously field officers on the regimental staff) became company commanders, while captains and sergeants (who had previously commanded their own companies and sections) became seconds-in-command respectively of the new large companies and platoons. Infantry subalterns (who had previously been the lieutenants of their companies' captains) were made commanders of the new platoons. While CIGS, French became friendly with his quick-witted and persuasive Director of Military Operations, Henry Wilson [91]. Under Wilson's influence he made numerous visits to northern France, touring the frontier districts by bicycle and encouraging the francophile Wilson in his aim of committing the British Army to fight on the Continent alongside France in any war with Germany.

French was made a field marshal on 3 June 1913. The suggestion came from King George V [80], though French himself gave the credit to the then Secretary of State for War, J. E. B. Seeley. At the time of the Curragh Incident in March 1914, when a number of Army officers indicated their readiness to resign rather than enforce the provisions of the Home Rule Bill upon Ulster, French appeared to agree to their demands. Fury among the government's supporters resulted in the agreement being disavowed and in Seeley being obliged to resign. French was not personally in sympathy with the behaviour of the Curragh officers and blamed Lord Roberts, himself a product of the Anglo-Irish Protestant ascendancy, for stirring up much of the trouble. Nevertheless, at the urging of Henry Wilson (another strong supporter of the Unionist cause), French resigned, on the grounds that a British officer could not go back on his word to suit the convenience of ministers.

Although out of office, French continued to be regarded as the future C-in-C of the British Expeditionary Force in the event of a major war. On the outbreak of the First World War in August 1914 he led the BEF (which the German Kaiser Wilhelm II [71] described to his own conscript citizen soldiers as "General French's contemptible little army of mercenaries") to the Continent. The BEF first encountered the Germans on 23 August 1914 at Mons. It was forced back to Le Cateau, where, after another battle on 26 August 1914, it resumed the retreat from Mons, an episode that, like various other retreats in the history of the British Army, entered British folklore as an example of endurance and determination. Shocked by the scale of his casualties French decided to preserve his army by withdrawing from active operations in order to refit. He was over-ruled by the Cabinet. The new Secretary of State for War, Lord Kitchener, met French in Paris and ordered him to remain in the line and to conform to the movements of the French armies. French himself resented both Kitchener's appearance (wearing his field marshal's uniform, in which rank he was senior to French) and the virtual subordination of the BEF to the French C-in-C, General Joffre, who was junior to French in rank and less experienced than him in war. The BEF was subsequently moved to Flanders, where it stood to meet the Germans at Ypres (12 October–11 November 1914).

With more than half of his original "Old Contemptibles" having become casualties, French remained on the defensive until the spring of 1915. Under pressure from Joffre, he then launched a series of offensives, all of which failed to break through the German line. French argued that his failures were due to lack of resources, in particular a shortage of artillery ammunition. This "shell scandal" had the effect of weakening Kitchener's prestige as Secretary of State for War and led to the creation of a new Ministry of Munitions headed by David Lloyd George. By August 1915 French had twenty-eight divisions under command, totalling 900,000 men. His final offensive, at Loos (25 September–13 October 1915), made inroads into the German position, but was repulsed with heavy casualties. French's former protégé, Sir Douglas Haig, had, from the beginning of the war, freely corresponded with Kitchener, George V [80] and the Prime Minister, Herbert Asquith, expressing to all of them the view that French lacked the intellectual and military ability to command a great army. Haig claimed that the failure at Loos was due to French having kept his reserves too far back. Sir William Robertson [92], French's Chief of Staff since January 1915, supported Haig. He reported that French was impossible to deal with, as his mind was never the same for two consecutive minutes. Asquith ordered French to hand over command of the BEF to Haig on 6 December 1915. Relations between Haig and French were thereafter marked by mutual dislike and contempt.

French was given the newly-created post of C-in-C, Home Forces, and was raised to the peerage as Viscount French of Ypres and High Lake in February 1916. He revised the existing plans for meeting a German invasion, a contingency he thought unlikely, but which was still taken seriously by the Cabinet. When in command of the BEF, French had complained that too many troops were being kept in England. Now he felt that too many were being sent to the Continent in support of fruitless offensives by Haig, whom he had come to consider incompetent and self-seeking. Lord French's tasks included the defence of the United Kingdom against German air raids. His experience of the wasteful and inefficient division of responsibility for air defence between the Royal Navy and the Army led him to support the establishment of a Royal Air Force. During this period French continued an *affaire* with Winifred Bennett, the neglected wife of a British diplomat and the former mistress of one of his own officers who had been killed in the opening stages of the war.

Lord French was appointed Lord Lieutenant of Ireland on 27 April 1918. The Cabinet decision (never carried into effect) to introduce conscription in that country had driven the Irish nationalists into the arms of the extreme republican party, Sinn Fein. This was followed by an intensification of the armed struggle against British rule, so that French was, in effect, the head of a military government. He organized a counter-insurgency campaign and urged the use of aircraft and armoured cars to make up for a shortage of troops on the ground. Regarding Sinn Fein as an unrepresentative minority, he failed to see that the old concept of Home Rule was no longer acceptable to the bulk of the Irish population. With the end of the war in Europe, French proposed various resettlement plans to foster the loyalty of Irish ex-servicemen, but was foiled by inter-departmental rivalry and by Treasury parsimony. As unrest grew, he reinforced the Royal Irish Constabulary by two special forces, the "Black and Tans" (recruited from demobilized soldiers) and the Auxiliaries (made up of ex-officers who were given the powers of police sergeants and the status of Temporary Cadets). None of these expedients could restore the power of the British government in the face of national opposition. French himself narrowly escaped assassination in December 1919. His struggle with Sinn Fein was made more personal by the public speeches made in favour of this party by his sister, Charlotte (Lottie, a rich widow who was also a socialist) and by one of his former mistresses, the beautiful Maud Gonne. In April 1920, when control over Irish affairs was handed back to a Cabinet minister, French became an executive rather than a policy-making figure. He ceased to be Lord Lieutenant in April 1921 and was created Earl of Ypres in June 1922. He died of cancer of the bladder, at his official residence, Deal Castle, on 22 May 1925. He was colonel of the 19th (Queen Alexandra's Own) Hussars from February 1902 to 1922 and of its successor the 15th/19th Hussars, as well as of the Irish Guards from June 1916 until his death. He was also colonel-in-chief of the Royal Irish Regiment from March 1913 until its disbandment in 1922 and honorary colonel of the Cambridgeshire Regiment in the Territorial Force (later the Territorial Army) from April 1909 until his death in 1925.

GEORGE V
GEORGE FREDERICK ERNEST ALBERT, HM King of Great Britain and Ireland, Emperor of India (1865–1936) [80]

Prince George, the second son of the then Prince and Princess of Wales (later King Edward VII [54] and Queen Alexandra) was born at Marlborough House, London, on 3 June 1865. He was intended for a career in the Royal Navy and joined the training ship *Britannia* at Dartmouth in September 1877. Together with his elder brother (Prince Albert Victor, later Duke of Clarence), Prince George went round the world between 1879 and 1882, doing duty as a midshipman in the cruiser *Bacchante*. In September 1884 he qualified for promotion to lieutenant. He was given command of a torpedo boat in 1889 and of the gunboat *Thrush* in 1890, followed by promotion to commander in August 1891.

On the death of the Duke of Clarence in January 1892, Prince George became the Prince of Wales's direct heir and was created Duke of York a few months later. He inherited not only his brother's place in succession to the throne, but also his fiancée, Princess May (only daughter of the Duke of Teck), whom he married in July 1893. York served in a number of ships and reached the rank of captain, but his royal duties brought his time as a naval officer to an end and his last command was of the cruiser *Crescent* in 1898. After the accession of his father as Edward VII on 22 January 1901 the Duke of York became Duke of Cornwall and York. He was known by this title until 9 November 1901, when he was created Prince of Wales. On 6 May 1910 he succeeded his father as King George V

During the First World War George V became a figure of national unity. He held numerous investitures and toured military establishments, hospitals and factories. He visited the Grand Fleet at Scapa Flow five times and his armies in France and Flanders seven times. On one visit to the Western Front he broke his pelvis when his horse, alarmed by cheering troops, reared and threw him. He admired and supported Lord Kitchener [79] as Secretary of State for War and was, throughout the war, the recipient of correspondence on military subjects from Sir Douglas Haig [85], a royal favourite. George V endorsed the appointment of Haig as C-in-C of the British Expeditionary Force in place of Sir John French [83] at the end of 1915 and later supported Haig against attempts by David Lloyd George, the Prime Minister of the day, to remove him from this command. George V also supported Haig's ally, Sir William Robertson [92] as Chief of the Imperial General Staff, but agreed to Robertson's removal in February 1918, when Lloyd George made this a question of confidence. During the war George V instituted three new decorations. These were the Military Cross (in December 1914) for acts of courage by captains, subalterns or sergeants, the Military Medal (in April 1916) for similar acts by the rank and file, and the Order of the British Empire (in June 1917) for public service by well-recommended individuals of any kind.

In 1915 George V was persuaded by Lloyd George to institute "the King's Pledge" of abstinence from alcohol throughout his household for the duration of the war, as an example to his subjects working in munitions factories. Apart from the naturally austere Kitchener, none of his ministers (least of all Lloyd George) and few others in the country followed this lead. In May 1917 the King, bowing to ministerial pressure for all British subjects possessing German titles to disclaim them, changed the name of his own family from Saxe-Coburg to Windsor. He declined to offer refuge to his friend and cousin, the Emperor Nicholas II of Russia [84] after the latter's abdication in March 1917, fearing that the arrival in England of an unpopular autocrat with a German-born wife would place his own throne in jeopardy. In the post-war period George V emerged as the model of a modern constitutional monarch. He insisted that the first Labour government be given a fair chance, exercised a moderating influence in the General Strike of 1926 and welcomed the formation of the National Government in 1931. He died at Sandringham, Norfolk, on 20 January 1936, and was buried at St George's Chapel, Windsor. He had a daughter and five sons, the eldest of whom succeeded him as Edward VIII [104].

George V was first commissioned in the Army on 26 June 1902, when, as Prince of Wales, he became a general. After succeeding to the throne, he was waited upon by his field marshals, who formally asked him to add himself to their number. He did so, with an antedate to 7 May 1910, and was thus the first British monarch to assume the rank of field marshal on his accession. Successively as Duke of York, Prince of Wales and King, he became at different times colonel-in-chief of many regiments, including the 1st and 2nd Life Guards and their successor, the Life Guards; the Royal Horse Guards; the 1st (Royal) Dragoons; the 10th Royal Hussars (Prince of Wales's Own); the Royal Artillery; the Royal Engineers; the five regiments of Foot Guards; the King's Own (Royal Lancaster Regiment); the Royal Fusiliers (City of London Regiment); the King's (Liverpool Regiment); the Norfolk Regiment; the Royal Welch Fusiliers; the Black Watch (Royal Highlanders); the King's Royal Rifle Corps; the Manchester Regiment; the Queen's Own Cameron Highlanders; Princess Victoria's (Royal Irish Fusiliers) and the Royal Tank Corps. In the Indian Army he was colonel-in-chief of the 1st Duke of York's Own Lancers (Skinner's Horse); the 18th Prince of Wales' Own Tirana Lancers; the 26th Prince of Wales's Light Cavalry; the Central India Horse; the 1st Prince of Wales's Sappers and Miners; the 14th Prince of Wales's Own Ferozepur Sikhs; the 61st Prince of Wales's Own Pioneers; the 130th Prince of Wales's Baluchis; the 4th Bombay Grenadiers and the 1st Prince of Wales's Gurkha Rifles. In the auxiliary forces, he became, after his accession, colonel and captain general of the Honourable Artillery Company and continued as honorary colonel of King Edward's Horse (The King's Colonials); the Duke of Lancaster's Own Yeomanry; the Norfolk Yeomanry (King's Own Royal Regiment); the Duke of York's Own Loyal Suffolk Hussars; the 5th London Brigade, Royal Artillery; the 3rd (Militia) Battalion, the Prince of Wales's West Yorkshire Regiment and the 8th Battalion, the Hampshire Regiment (Princess Beatrice's Isle of Wight Rifles).

GEORGE VI
ALBERT FREDERICK ARTHUR GEORGE, HM King of Great Britain and Ireland, Emperor of India (1895–1952) [106]

The future King George VI was born on 14 December 1895 at York Cottage, Sandringham, the second of five sons of the then Duke and Duchess of York (later King George V [80] and Queen Mary). He was a shy and nervous child, greatly in awe (like the rest of their children) of his royal parents, whose life-style inhibited any outward expression of affection. In early childhood Prince Albert ("Bertie" to his family) developed a speech impediment, which he strove to overcome with great determination and eventual success. Like his father, he was originally intended for a naval career and followed his example by attending the naval colleges at Osborne, in 1909, and Dartmouth, in 1911. Prince Albert joined the cruiser *Cumberland* as a cadet in January 1913 and was gazetted as a midshipman on 15 September 1913. He was appointed to the battleship *Collingwood* in October 1913 and served in this ship on deployment to the Mediterranean. Shortly after the outbreak of the First World War in August 1914 Prince Albert was sent ashore with the first of the several gastric problems that affected his naval career. In November 1914 he was posted to the War Staff at the Admiralty. He rejoined *Collingwood* at Portsmouth as her senior midshipman in February 1915. After promotion to acting sub-lieutenant on 15 September 1915, he was again sent ashore for medical treatment. George V, who refused to allow the more robust Prince of Wales [104] to serve in combat, was far less concerned with the health of his second son and, despite medical advice to the contrary, supported Prince Albert in his wish to rejoin the fleet. The Prince was therefore able to go back to *Collingwood* on 5 May 1916 and to serve in her at Jutland (31 May 1916). He was promoted to lieutenant on 15 June 1916, but at the end of August was once more sent ashore, suffering from a duodenal ulcer. After a period on the staff at Portsmouth, he joined the battleship *Malaya* in May 1917 and remained in this ship until August 1917, when a recurrence of gastric illness ended his time as a sea-going officer. On 1 January 1918, at his own suggestion, he was posted to HMS *Daedalus*, the Royal Naval Air Station at Cranwell. He served there as the officer commanding No 4 Squadron, Boy Wing. When the Royal Air Force was formed on 1 April 1918, Prince Albert transferred to the new service as a flight lieutenant. In August 1918, he was given command of a cadet training squadron at St Leonard's-on-Sea. He reached the Western Front just before the end of the war, where he joined the staff of the Independent Force, RAF, under Sir Hugh Trenchard. Prince Albert represented his father in the triumphal re-entry into Brussels of King Albert I of the Belgians [94]. He qualified as a Royal Air Force pilot on 31 July 1919 and was promoted to squadron leader on 1 August 1919.

In October 1919, Prince Albert entered Trinity College, Cambridge, where he spent the next three terms. He was created Duke of York and Earl of Inverness in June 1920. He then met and fell in love with Lady Elizabeth Bowes-Lyon, ninth of the ten children of the 14th Earl of Strathmore. York proposed to her the following year, but was refused, as Lady Elizabeth, brought up in a happy domestic life, had little desire to enter the restrictive circles of the Royal Family. York persevered in his suit and the couple married on 26 April 1923. Their marriage proved a happy one, with the Duke of York's health improving as his Duchess gave him a calm and loving home, with two daughters born in 1926 and 1930 respectively. He undertook his share of public duties, with a special interest in "the Duke of York's camps", where boys from public schools and the run-down industrial areas mixed together. He rose steadily through the ranks of the Royal Navy and Royal Air Force, to become a rear admiral on 3 June 1932 (on which date he also became a major general in the Army) and an air chief marshal on 21 January 1936.

The Abdication crisis of late 1936 was greeted by the Yorks with horror. Neither wished for the throne that Edward VIII [104] chose to vacate in order to marry the woman he loved. Nevertheless, with a characteristic regard for duty, York accepted the crown and took the regnal name of King George VI, to emphasize the continuity of the monarchy and to indicate that his model would be his late father. Following the precedent set by George V and Edward VIII, he became a field marshal from the date of his accession, on 11 December 1936. He set himself to restore the prestige of the British Crown and succeeded in gaining the respect and sympathy of his subjects. When the Second World War began in September 1939 George VI assumed a natural role as the symbol of his country. His modest and self-disciplined manner made it easier for ordinary people to identify with their King than with the war-time Prime Minister, Winston Churchill (viewed by many members of the working class as a war-monger and strike-breaker). During the war, in addition to his normal duties of state, George VI made frequent visits to units of the armed forces at home and abroad. He went to France before the German offensive in 1940, to North Africa after the Allied victories in 1943 and to Normandy ten days after the Allied landings in June 1944. He maintained a personal interest in senior military appointments and, at the end of 1939, supported Sir Edmund Ironside [107], the Chief of the Imperial General Staff, and Lord Gort [110], the C-in-C of the British Expeditionary Force in France, in their complaints against the Secretary of State for War, Leslie Hore-Belisha. In 1940, when invasion was expected, George VI refused the advice of his ministers to send the Queen and the princesses to safety in Canada. He installed a small-arms range in the grounds of Buckingham Palace where he practised with revolvers and sub-machine guns for personal defence in case of a German assault. Accompanied by Queen Elizabeth, he made visits to the East End of London, Coventry and other cities devastated by German air raids. He continued to work from Buckingham Palace during both the Blitz of 1940–1941 and the attacks by V-weapons in 1944–1945 and was at the palace when it was hit by a bomb on 11 September 1940. To mark courageous acts by civilians or service personnel when not in the physical presence of the enemy he instituted two new decorations, the George Cross and the George Medal.

Victory in Europe on 8 May 1945 was followed by a general election that gave the Labour party a landslide victory and a mandate to introduce far-reaching domestic reforms. The King, reigning as a constitutional monarch, retained his popularity with all classes, while his new ministers introduced an ambitious programme laying the foundations of a Welfare State. On 22 June 1947, as British rule over the Indian sub-continent came to its end, George VI disclaimed his title as Emperor of India. He continued with his public duties, but his health, never robust, began to decline. He was found to be suffering from cancer and, in September 1951, underwent an operation for the removal of his left lung. His medical advisers doubted his ability to survive further surgery. Not long after saying farewell to his heiress, Princess Elizabeth, on her departure for a visit to Kenya, King George VI died in his sleep at Sandringham, on 6 February 1952. He was buried at St George's Chapel, Windsor.

As Duke of York, he was colonel of the Scots Guards and colonel-in-chief of the 11th Hussars (Prince Albert's Own); the Somerset Light Infantry (Prince Albert's); the East Yorkshire Regiment (awarded the additional title "the Duke of York's Own" in 1935); the Royal Army Ordnance Corps and the Leicestershire Yeomanry. As King, he became colonel-in-chief of the Life Guards; the Royal Horse Guards; 1st the Royal Dragoons; the Royal Scots Greys (2nd Dragoons); the Royal Tank Corps (later the Royal Tank Regiment); the Royal Artillery; the Royal Malta Artillery; the Royal Engineers; the five regiments of Foot Guards; the Royal Norfolk Regiment; the Royal Welch Fusiliers; the Royal Berkshire Regiment (Princess Charlotte of Wales's); the King's Royal Rifle Corps; the Queen's Own Cameron Highlanders and the Duke of Lancaster's Own Yeomanry. He was captain general of the Royal Armoured Corps, of the Honourable Artillery Company and of the Royal Artillery from 1951, when this appointment replaced that of colonel-in-chief of the Royal Artillery. After the Second World War, he introduced the new designations of the King's Troop, Royal Horse Artillery (previously the Riding Troop) and the Sovereign's Company, Royal Military Academy Sandhurst (previously the Champion Company).

GEORGE WILLIAM FREDERICK CHARLES

HRH 2nd Duke of Cambridge KG, KT, KP, GCB, GCSI, GCMG, GCIE, GCVO (1819–1904) [45]

Prince George, the only son of Adolphus, 1st Duke of Cambridge [26], was born on 26 March 1819, at Cambridge House, Hanover. Until the birth of his cousin, Princess Victoria of Kent, later that year, he was King George III's only legitimate living grandchild. His early boyhood was spent in Hanover, where he survived both a serious attack of scarlet fever and an attempted assassination by his deranged tutor. Prince George was appointed a colonel in the Hanoverian Foot Guards in 1828. He was educated in England between 1830 and 1836 and then returned to Hanover, where his father was Viceroy. On the accession of the Duke of Cumberland [25] as King Ernest I of Hanover, the Cambridges returned to England, where Prince George was commissioned as brevet colonel in the British Army on 3 November 1837. After an attachment to the 33rd Foot at Gibraltar, from September 1838 to September 1839, he served in various stations in the UK with the 12th Lancers. While at Dublin, he met an Irish actress, Louisa Fairbrother, a lady three years older than himself, whom he later married in defiance of the Royal Marriages Act. Unable to share her husband's titles, she took the name Mrs FitzGeorge and lived with him and their three sons as respected members of London society. Though in many ways a model husband and father, Prince George for many years kept a mistress, Louisa Beauclerk. After her death, he fell in love with Eleanor Vyner and remained attached to her for the rest of his life. Gossip also had it that his annual visits to Hanover involved a long-established relationship with a lady there.

Prince George became a lieutenant colonel of the 8th Light Dragoons on 15 April 1842 and colonel of the 17th (later Duke of Cambridge's Own) Lancers ten days later. He commanded this regiment in Yorkshire (including duties in aid of the civil power at Leeds in August 1842) until April 1843, when he was appointed colonel on the staff of Lord Seaton [42], British High Commissioner of the Ionian Islands. After returning to the UK, Prince George was promoted to major general on 1 April 1845 and commanded at Dublin between 1847 and 1852. He succeeded to his father's dukedom on 8 July 1850 and was appointed Inspector General of Cavalry on 1 April 1852. He became colonel of the Scots Fusilier Guards (later the Scots Guards) in September 1852 and was promoted to lieutenant general on 19 June 1854.

On the approach of the Crimean War, Cambridge used his influence with the Queen to obtain an appointment in the expedition to the Crimea, arguing, with great emotion, that he would be disgraced if he did not go. He was given command of the 1st Division, consisting of the Guards and Highland Brigades and was at the Alma (20 September 1854) and Inkerman (5 November 1854) where his horse was shot under him. He subsequently suffered some kind of post-traumatic collapse, which, combined with the gastro-enteric disorders that affected most of the army in the Crimea, resulted in his return to England on medical grounds in December 1854. On 15 July 1856, Cambridge was promoted to general and became General Commanding-in-Chief of the British Army. He remained at the head of the British Army for the next thirty-nine years, becoming Field Marshal Commanding-in-Chief on 9 November 1862, when he was promoted to this rank, and Commander-in-Chief on 20 November 1887, when he was awarded this title by Royal Patent to mark his fifty years of commissioned service. He was closely involved with the Army reforms of the immediate post-Crimean period and, following the abolition of the post of Master General of the Ordnance, became colonel of the Royal Artillery and the Royal Engineers in May 1861.

Cambridge, a conservative in both military and civil matters, treated the emergence of Rifle Volunteer corps in 1859 and the early 1860s with caution, as he was suspicious of their military efficiency and, initially at least, of their political reliability. He opposed most of the reforms that transformed the British Army in the 1870s and 1880s, arguing that the old system was well suited for an Army that existed primarily to garrison a colonial empire. Cambridge resisted the abolition of the purchase of commissions and the introduction of short-service enlistment. He also objected to the concept of reorganizing the infantry into "territorial" regiments, composed of Regular, Militia, and Volunteer units (all previously quite separate from each other), arguing that this would weaken the *esprit de corps* of the former regiments of Foot. Cambridge was especially concerned to preserve the status of the Army by emphasizing its (and his own) loyalty to the monarch rather than to the government ministers of the day. When finally obliged to move his department from the Horse Guards to the new War Office, he insisted on using a separate entrance.

Cambridge, though claiming not to be clever himself, encouraged officers to study their profession and approved the establishment of a new Staff College in the grounds of the Royal Military College at Sandhurst. Cambridge Town, the village that grew up at the Staff College gate, later became better known as Camberley (a made-up name, adopted to avoid confusion with the University city from which he took his title). At the same time he frowned on those who sought posts on the staff as a way of avoiding duty with their regiments. He disapproved of careerists and of any officer whose conduct appeared to fall below what was expected of him, but was always ready to give a personal hearing to individuals seeking redress of grievance. He supported the preservation of well-earned regimental distinctions of dress, but refused to allow fanciful departures from the regulation pattern. His Royal connections, coupled with his long continuity in office, enabled him to slow down the pace of change urged by reformers such as Sir Garnet Wolseley [67], who personally disliked Cambridge and despised him for leaving the Crimea.

The Hartington Commission of 1890–1891 proposed the abolition of the post of Commander-in-Chief of the British Army. This was opposed by both Cambridge and by the Queen, who wished her son, the Duke of Connaught [73] to succeed him. Cambridge reluctantly agreed to retire, on grounds of age, on 31 October 1895. He was colonel of the Scots Fusilier Guards (later the Scots Guards) from September 1852 to December 1861, when he became colonel of the Grenadier Guards. He was appointed colonel-in-chief of the 60th Rifles (later the King's Royal Rifle Corps) in March 1869 and was subsequently colonel-in-chief of the Royal Artillery, the Royal Engineers and the Duke of Cambridge's Own (Middlesex Regiment). He remained colonel or honorary colonel of various other corps, including the 10th Bengal Lancers (Duke of Cambridge's Own); the Middlesex Yeomanry (Duke of Cambridge's Hussars); the 1st City of London Rifle Volunteer Corps (later the London Rifle Brigade) and the Cambridge Dragoons of the Hanoverian and German Armies. Cambridge died of a stomach haemorrhage at Gloucester House, London, on 17 March 1904 and was buried beside his wife, Mrs FitzGeorge, at Kensal Green cemetery.

Cambridge was C-in-C of the British Army for longer than any other occupant in the history of this post. Appointed by virtue of his Royal blood, he was thereafter outside party and beyond ambition and was respected by most officers as the personification of the link between the Army and the Crown. His main achievement was the preservation of the spirit and traditions of the old long-service Army. He was by no means the unintelligent reactionary that his opponents made him out to be. The success with which he defeated or delayed unwelcome developments, while protecting his own post, owed much to the strength and skill of his arguments. The military reformers eventually climbed the wall on which he stood, but not during his watch.

GIBBS
Sir ROLAND CHRISTOPHER, GCB, CBE, DSO, MC
(1921–2004) **[130]**

Roland Gibbs, the younger son of a gentleman who had served as an officer in the North Somerset Yeomanry during the First World War, was born on 22 June 1921. He was educated at Eton College and entered the Royal Military College, Sandhurst, in the summer of 1939, as a member of what proved to be the last batch of gentlemen cadets. Immediately before the beginning of the Second World War on 3 September 1939, together with the rest of the junior term, he was attested as a soldier in the Territorial Army. This was an administrative device enabling the gentlemen cadets to be paid and rationed at public expense on the outbreak of war, when the College was closed and the TA was embodied. He was immediately remustered with the other infantry cadets as an officer cadet in the Infantry Wing of the new Officer Cadet Training Unit (RMC) at Sandhurst. Gibbs joined the King's Royal Rifle Corps, as second lieutenant in the Regular Army, on 31 December 1939. He was promoted to lieutenant on 1 January 1941 and served in the North African campaign, where he was awarded the Military Cross (gazetted on 15 October 1942). He became acting major and officer commanding "C" Company, 2nd Battalion, the King's Royal Rifle Corps, (a motorized battalion in the 7th Armoured Division) in March 1943. Gibbs remained in this appointment for the rest of the war, with promotion to war substantive captain and temporary major on 25 June 1943, and took part in the campaigns in Tunisia, Italy, Normandy, the Low Countries and north-west Germany, where hostilities ended in May 1945.

Between August and October 1945, Gibbs was a General Staff officer, grade 2, at HQ Allied Land Forces, South-East Asia. He then served as a GSO 2 in the 3rd Division until April 1946 and became a substantive captain on 1 July 1946. From July 1946 to July 1947, he was brigade major of a parachute brigade in Palestine. After a further period of regimental duty, he became an instructor at the Royal Military Academy Sandhurst, in December 1948. During 1951 Gibbs attended the Staff College, Camberley. He was promoted to temporary major on 29 January 1952 and to substantive major on 31 December 1952. Between January 1952 and December 1953 he was brigade major of an infantry brigade. In 1955 Gibbs married Davina Merry, with whom he later had two sons. He attended the Joint Services Staff College, Latimer, Buckinghamshire, in 1956 and served at the War Office as GSO 2 in an Inter-Service planning team, between August 1957 and August 1959.

Gibbs transferred to the Parachute Regiment on 29 February 1960, with promotion to lieutenant colonel and appointment as commanding officer of its 3rd Battalion. From April 1962 to October 1963 he was in the United States as GSO 1 in the British Army Staff, Washington, DC. He was promoted to temporary brigadier on taking command of 16 Parachute Brigade Group on 6 December 1963 and became a substantive colonel on 4 July 1964. He was Chief of Staff, Middle East Command, from May 1966 to November 1967, with promotion to substantive brigadier on 6 December 1966. During 1968 Gibbs attended the Imperial Defence College. He commanded the British Land Forces in the (Persian) Gulf area from April 1969 to December 1971, with promotion to major general on 6 September 1969.

Gibbs became a lieutenant general on 14 January 1972, when he was given command of I (British) Corps in Germany, with the award of the KBE. Sir Roland Gibbs remained in this post until January 1974 and was promoted to general on 1 April 1974, when he became C-in-C, United Kingdom Land Forces. In May 1976 he became Chief of the General Staff. His period in office as CGS coincided with severe problems of recruitment and retention, caused largely by the government's policy of paying low wages at a time of high inflation. He ensured that the Army's interests were properly represented and, together with the professional heads of the other two Armed Services, twice exercised his right of personal access to the Prime Minister of the day on this issue. Sir Roland Gibbs was promoted to field marshal on 13 July 1979, one day before his retirement from active duty. He was colonel commandant of the 2nd Battalion, the Royal Green Jackets (the successor of the King's Royal Rifle Corps) from January 1971 to January 1979, as well as of the Parachute Regiment from December 1972 to December 1977. He died on 31 October 2004.

GLOUCESTER
HRH DUKE OF, see **HENRY WILLIAM FREDERICK** [121]

GLOUCESTER AND EDINBURGH
HRH 1st DUKE OF, see **WILLIAM HENRY** [13]

GLOUCESTER AND EDINBURGH
HRH 2nd DUKE OF, see **WILLIAM FREDERICK** [27]

GOMM
Sir WILLIAM MAYNARD, GCB (1784–1875) [48]

William Gomm, the eldest son of a lieutenant colonel in the 55th Foot, was born in 1784, on his maternal grandfather's plantation in Barbados. Colonel Gomm fell in the British attack on Guadeloupe in 1794 and his widow died two years later. Their orphaned children were brought up by her sister-in-law, Miss Jane Gomm, a former governess in the Royal Household. In recognition of his late father's services, William Gomm was granted a free commission on 24 May 1794 as an ensign in the 9th Foot. He became a lieutenant in this regiment on 16 November 1794, while continuing his education at a private military school in Woolwich. In 1799 his guardian (an old comrade of his late father) agreed to Gomm joining the expedition to the Helder, where he served with the 9th Foot at Bergen (19 September 1799); Alkmaar (4 September 1799) and Egmont (2 October 1799). He took part in the British descent on Ferrol (August 1800) after which he returned to the UK. Gomm was promoted to captain on 25 June 1803 and joined the Senior Division of the Royal Military College, at High Wycombe, in 1804. Despite a brief break in his studies to go with the force sent to Hanover in 1805, he obtained his College certificate at the end of 1806 and thus became one of the few properly-trained staff officers in the British Army of the period.

Gomm served on the staff in the expedition against Copenhagen (August 1807) after which he returned to regimental duty in Ireland. In July 1808 he joined the staff of the army sent to the Peninsula under Sir Arthur Wellesley [24]. He was at Rolica (17 August 1808) and Vimiero (21 August 1808) and returned with the army to England after the Convention of Cintra (Sintra). Gomm went back to the Peninsula at the end of September 1808 as a staff officer in Sir John Moore's army and served with it in the winter retreat to Corunna. He next served in the expedition that landed in Walcheren in July 1809 and was at the siege of Flushing (Vlissingen, 1–18 August 1809). Here, like most of the army, he contracted the malaria that eventually forced the British to abandon this campaign.

In March 1810 Gomm went to the Peninsula with the 9th Foot. He joined Wellington's staff in September 1810 and remained with him for the rest of the Peninsular War. He was at Busaco (27 September 1810), where his horse was shot under him; Fuentes d'Onoro (3 and 5 May 1811); Ciudad Rodrigo (stormed Jan 1812); Badajoz (stormed 6 April 1812), where he was wounded; Salamanca (22 July 1812); Burgos (16 September–21 October 1812); Vittoria (21 June 1813); San Sebastian

(July-August 1813); the Nivelle (10 October 1813) and the Nive (December 1813), where he was again wounded. He was promoted to major on 10 October 1811 and to lieutenant colonel on 17 August 1812. At the end of the campaign he was awarded the KCB and became a regimental captain in the Coldstream Guards. Sir William Gomm took part in the Hundred Days campaign on the staff of the 5th Division, at Quatre Bras (16 June 1815) and Waterloo (18 June 1815). After the end of the war, he remained with the Army of Occupation in France until 1817. In the same year he married Sophia Penn, a granddaughter of William Penn, the founder of Pennsylvania.

Between 1817 and 1839 Gomm held various staff appointments in the UK, where he was promoted to colonel on 16 May 1829 and to major general on 10 January 1837. After the death of his first wife, he married, in 1830, Elizabeth, eldest daughter of Major General Lord Robert Kerr, a younger brother of the 5th Marquess of Lothian. He commanded the British troops in Jamaica from 1839 to 1842 and in Mauritius from 1842 to 1849, with appointment as colonel of the 13th Foot on 10 March 1846 and promotion to lieutenant general on 9 November 1846. In 1849 Gomm sailed for Bengal in anticipation of succeeding Lord Gough [44] as C-in-C, India. He arrived to find that, in response to public outcry at Gough's reverses in the Second Sikh War, this appointment had been given to the veteran Sir Charles Napier, the conqueror of Sind. Gomm returned to the United Kingdom, where he was nominated as C-in-C, Bombay. Following Napier's resignation after a dispute with Lord Dalhousie, the Governor-General of India, Gomm became C-in-C, India in December 1850. He remained in this post until January 1856, with promotion to general on 20 June 1854. Like most of his contemporaries, he failed to foresee the Mutiny that broke out eighteen months after his departure from India, but he made a valuable contribution to the efficiency of the Bengal Army by supporting the introduction of promotion examinations for its officers. Sir William Gomm became colonel of the Coldstream Guards on 15 August 1863 and a field marshal on 1 January 1868. He died without issue on 15 March 1875. Lady Gomm died in 1877 and bequeathed funds to endow the Field Marshal Gomm Scholarships at Keble College, Oxford, open to all qualified candidates, but with preference given to the family of the Marquess of Lothian.

GORT
VISCOUNT, see VEREKER, JOHN, [110]

GOUGH
Sir HUGH, 1st Baronet, 1st Viscount Gough, KP, GCB, GCSI (1779–1869) [44]

Hugh Gough, the fourth son of Lieutenant Colonel George Gough of Woodstone, County Limerick, was born on 3 November 1779 and was first commissioned in 1793 in the Limerick Militia, of which his father was at that time the commanding officer. He became an ensign in a locally raised regiment of infantry on 7 August 1794 and a lieutenant in the 119th Foot (later disbanded) on 11 October 1794. He transferred to the 78th Highlanders in June 1795 and served with them in the British seizure of the Cape of Good Hope (3 September 1795). In December 1795 Gough became a lieutenant in the 87th (Prince of Wales' Irish) Regiment. He joined this regiment in the West Indies in 1797 and took part in the expedition against Dutch Guiana in 1799. Gough returned to the UK and became a captain in his regiment's newly-raised 2nd Battalion on 25 June 1803. He was promoted to major in this battalion on 12 February 1807. Shortly afterwards, at a military ball in Plymouth, he met Frances Maria Stephens, daughter of an artillery general commanding the garrison there. On the morning of the ball this lady told her father that she had dreamt of a handsome officer in a red coat with green facings, who would become her husband. When Gough, in the regimentals of the 87th, entered the ballroom, she at once recognized her dream figure. They were married later in the year and subsequently raised five children.

Gough went with his battalion to the Peninsula in January 1809 and commanded it at Talavera (28 July 1809). He was wounded and left behind in the subsequent retreat, but managed to crawl away and evade capture. In recognition of his services, Gough was promoted to brevet lieutenant colonel on 20 July 1809. He commanded the 87th at Barossa (5 March 1811); Tarifa (October 1811-January 1812); Vittoria (21 June 1813) and the Nivelle (19 November 1813), where he was wounded so badly that he took no further part in the Peninsular War. Gough was awarded a knighthood in June 1815 and went onto the half-pay in 1817, when the 2nd Battalion, the 87th Foot, was disbanded. Sir Hugh Gough was promoted to colonel on 12 August 1819. Between 1819 and 1826 he commanded the 22nd Foot, mostly in his native Ireland, where he became a landlord and magistrate in County Tipperary. He became a major general on 22 July 1830. In 1837 he went to Southern India to command the Mysore division of the Madras Army. He became colonel of the 99th Foot in December 1839 and retained this appointment to March 1841, when he became colonel of his old regiment, redesignated the 87th Royal Irish Fusiliers.

In March 1841 Gough was sent to take command of the British forces taking part in the "Opium War" against China. He arrived with reinforcements and stormed the defences of Canton on 26–27 May 1841, before handing over the command to Admiral Sir William Parker, as the senior British officer present, in July 1841. Gough personally led the assault on the Amoy Forts (26 August 1841) and was wounded at Chusan (1 October 1841). He was promoted to lieutenant general on 23 November 1841 and commanded his troops in the subsequent engagements of this war, including Chapu (8 March 1842) and Chinkiang (21 July 1842). He was awarded a baronetcy and returned to India to become C-in-C, Madras. Gough became C-in-C, India, in August 1843 and, as such, commanded in the field at Maharajpur (29 December 1843) in a brief campaign against the Maratha kingdom of Gwalior. Lady Gough found herself caught up in this battle, together with three other ladies, including her daughter Frances (the future wife of Gough's aide-de-camp, Patrick Grant [59]), Juana, Lady Smith (the spirited Spanish wife of the equally spirited Peninsular hero, Sir Harry Smith, who later gave her name to a South African town) and Mrs Curtis (the wife of a junior staff officer). Lady Ellenborough, wife of the Governor-General of India, later presented them each with a jewelled version of the campaign medal.

Gough again commanded in the field in the First Sikh War, at Mudki (18 December 1845), Ferozeshah (21–22 December 1845) and Sobraon (10 February 1846). He was joined in the field by the Governor-General, Sir Henry Hardinge [41], who considered himself a better general and had volunteered to serve as his second-in-command, an offer which Gough could not refuse. Hardinge, although junior to Gough in military terms, was his senior as the head of government and was therefore able to over-rule Gough in the strategic direction of the campaign. Gough was raised to the peerage as Baron Gough, of Chinkanfoo and of Maharajpore and the Sutlej. He was still in post as C-in-C, India, on the outbreak of the Second Sikh War in 1848, where he again commanded in person at Ramnagar (21 November 1848) and Chilianwala (13 January 1849). As in the previous campaign, Lord Gough was much criticized for relying on a frontal assault by infantry as his standard tactic, rather than using his superiority in artillery. Sir Charles Napier, the veteran conqueror of Sind, was nominated to replace him but, before Napier's arrival, Gough achieved a decisive victory at Gujarat (21 February 1849). He was rewarded by an advancement of one rank in the peerage, becoming Viscount Gough of Goojerat, and of Limerick, and was promoted to general on 2 June

1854. Viscount Gough was appointed colonel-in-chief of the 60th Rifles in January 1854, colonel of the Royal Horse Guards in June 1855 and honorary colonel of the 28th Middlesex (London Irish) Rifle Volunteer Corps in 1860. He was promoted to field marshal on 9 November 1862 and died at St Helen's, Booterstown, County Dublin, on 2 March 1869. He was succeeded as 2nd viscount by his only son.

Gough commanded in more battles than any British general apart from Marlborough and Wellington. With his Irish brogue, extrovert character and reckless disregard for his personal safety in battle, he was a popular figure with his troops, despite the heavy casualties that generally resulted from his plan of attack.

GRANT
Sir PATRICK, GCB, GCMG (1804–1895) [59]

Patrick Grant, the second son of Major John Grant of Auchterblair, Inverness-shire, was born on 11 September 1804. He became an ensign in the East India Company's Bengal Infantry on 16 July 1820, a lieutenant on 11 July 1823, and a captain on 14 May 1832. Grant held various regimental and army staff appointments in Bengal and northern India, prior to serving in the campaign against Gwalior in 1843. He was at Maharajpur (29 December 1843), under the command of his future father-in-law, Sir Hugh Gough [44], the C-in-C, India. Also present were his future second wife, Frances, and her mother, Lady Gough, both of whom were caught up in the battle, together with two other ladies (one, Juana, Lady Smith, the wife of Sir Harry Smith, a divisional general, and the other, Mrs Curtis, the wife of a staff officer). The four were later presented by Lady Ellenborough, wife of the Governor-General of India, with jewelled versions of the campaign medal. Grant had married his first wife, Jane Fraser Tytler, of Aldourie, Inverness-shire, in 1832. She died in 1838, leaving two small sons. In September 1844 Grant married Frances Gough, with whom he later had five more sons.

Grant was promoted brevet major on 30 April 1844. In the First Sikh War he was at Mudki (18 December 1845), where he was wounded twice and had his horse shot under him; Ferozeshah (21–22 December 1845) and Sobraon (10 February 1846). He became adjutant general of the Bengal Army in March 1846 and was promoted brevet lieutenant colonel on 3 April 1846. In the Second Sikh War he was at Chilianwala (13 January 1849) and Gujarat (21 February 1849), on his father-in-law's staff. After this war, he served against the hill tribes of the

North-West Frontier in a campaign led by Sir Charles Napier (Gough's successor as C-in-C, India). He was promoted to brevet colonel on 2 August 1850 and to major general on 28 November 1854.

Grant was appointed C-in-C, Madras, in January 1856, so becoming the first and only officer of the Company's service to hold this post. He was awarded the KCB in January 1857. During the early part of the Indian Mutiny, when General the Honourable George Anson, C-in-C, India, died of cholera on his way to Delhi in June 1857, Sir Patrick Grant, as the next senior C-in-C in British India, took his place. He stabilized the British position in Bengal and prepared to march against the mutineers in Oudh (Awadh), but was forestalled by the arrival from Europe of Sir Colin Campbell [46], the new C-in-C, India. Grant was the only officer of the East India Company's service to act as C-in-C, India, and many felt that he was not allowed to retain this command only because he did not belong to the British Army. He returned to Madras, from where he had already sent his toughest European troops to join the campaign against the mutineers. The Madras sepoys remained faithful to their oath to the East India Company and the local princes made no move against the British, so that the rest of his command was spent in watchfulness rather than warfare. Like all the Company's officers, Grant was transferred to the service of the Crown in India in 1858. He left Madras at the expiry of his appointment in January 1861. In September 1862 he became colonel of the 104th Bengal Fusiliers, one of the former East India Company's European regiments remustered as part of the British Army in the post-Mutiny reorganization. He was promoted to lieutenant general on 24 October 1862 and became colonel of the 78th Seaforth Highlanders in October 1863. Between 1867 and 1872 Sir Patrick Grant was Governor and C-in-C Malta. He was promoted to general on 19 November 1870 and to field marshal on 24 June 1883, thus becoming the first officer of the Indian Army to reach that rank. Grant became Governor of the Royal Hospital, Chelsea in 1874 and was appointed colonel of the Royal Horse Guards in October 1885. He died at the Royal Hospital on 28 March 1895 and was buried in Brompton Cemetery.

GRENFELL
Sir FRANCIS WALLACE, 1st Baron Grenfell, GCB, GCMG (1841–1925) [77]

Frances Grenfell, the fourth son of a minor landholder and ironmaster who came from a cadet branch of the prominent Buckinghamshire family, was born at Maesteg House, Swansea, on 29 April 1841. He was educated at Milton Abbas, Dorset, and purchased his first commission as second lieutenant in the 3rd Battalion, the 60th Rifles, on 5 August 1859. He purchased promotion to lieutenant on 16 July 1863 and to captain on 21 October 1871, in the last batch of officers to do so before the purchase system was ended. Seeing little prospect of advancement, Grenfell had decided to leave the Army when, in 1874, he was offered a post as aide-de-camp to Sir Arthur Cunynghame (late of the 60th Rifles), the newly appointed C-in-C in South Africa. Grenfell served in the Kaffir War of 1878–79, where he was at Quintana (7 February 1878) and was promoted to brevet major on 4 November 1878. He also took part in the Zulu War and was at Ulundi (4 July 1879), where he served as a staff officer. On returning to England, he became a brigade-major at Shorncliffe, with promotion to brevet lieutenant colonel on 29 November 1879. He went back to South Africa, where he served on the staff during the Boer War of 1881. In the Egyptian campaign of 1882, Grenfell was a senior staff officer under Sir Garnet Wolseley [68] and was at Tel-el-Kebir (13 September 1882). He was promoted to colonel on 18 November 1882 and remained in Egypt as deputy to Sir Evelyn Wood [74], the newly-appointed Sirdar (C-in-C) of the Egyptian Army, then being reorganized under British officers. During the Gordon Relief Expedition of 1884 Grenfell commanded the Egyptian troops stationed at Aswan. He succeeded Wood as Sirdar of the Egyptian Army in April 1885 and led his Egyptian troops in combat against the Mahdist forces at Ginnis (30 December 1885). Grenfell was awarded the KCB in 1886 and in the following year married Miss Evelyn Wood, the daughter of a major general. Sir Francis Grenfell remained in Egypt and commanded his army at Gamazia (20 December 1888) and Toski (3 August 1889).

Grenfell was promoted to major general in the British Army on 3 August 1889. He was replaced as Sirdar of the Egyptian Army in 1892, when a new Khedive (who had previously taken a dislike to him) succeeded to the Egyptian throne. Grenfell then went to the War Office as Deputy Adjutant General (from 1884, Inspector General) for the reserve and auxiliary forces, before returning to Egypt in 1897 to command the British troops there. He was promoted to lieutenant general on 1 April 1898. For political reasons, he played no part in the re-conquest of the Sudan, which was led by Sir Herbert Kitchener [79] (his junior in the British Army), as Sirdar of the Egyptian Army. Grenfell was Governor and C-in-C, Malta, from January 1899 to 1902, after which he was raised to the peerage as Baron Grenfell, of Kilvey. Lord Grenfell was promoted to general on 16 March 1904 and served as C-in-C, Ireland, from 1904 until 1908. He was colonel of the 2nd Life Guards from April 1905 to April 1907, when he became colonel of the 1st Life Guards. In June 1908 he became colonel commandant of the 1st Battalion, the King's Royal Rifle Corps (formerly the 60th Rifles). Grenfell became a field marshal on 11 April 1908. His first wife having died without offspring four years earlier, he married in 1903 the Honourable Margaret Majendie, daughter of an Essex MP. They had a daughter and two sons, the elder of whom succeeded to the barony after Lord Grenfell's death, at Windlesham, Surrey, on 27 January 1925.

GRIFFIN
(WHITEWELL), Sir JOHN GRIFFIN, 4th Baron Howard de Walden and 1st Baron Braybrooke KB (1719–1797) [18]

John Griffin Whitewell, born in 1719 at Oundle, was the eldest son of William Whitewell, a country gentleman who was possessed of ample means and a noble wife. These factors assisted the young Whitewell in obtaining a commission in 1739 as an ensign in the 3rd Foot Guards and lieutenant in the Army. During the War of the Austrian Succession he served with the Pragmatic Army in Germany, where he was promoted to captain in his regiment and lieutenant colonel in the Army in March 1744. In 1749 Whitewell inherited the substantial fortune and extensive estates (including the great house of Audley End, near Saffron Walden) of his maternal aunt, Elizabeth, Countess of Portsmouth. At the same time he adopted her family name, Griffin, which he already bore as a baptismal name, as his own surname. Griffin entered Parliament in 1749, as the member for Andover, and continued to represent that borough until 1784. He was promoted to colonel on 29 May 1756 and to major general on 25 June 1759, followed by appointment as colonel of the 50th Foot in October 1759. Griffin became colonel of the 33rd Foot in May 1760 and commanded a brigade at Corbach (Korbach, 10 July 1760) and Warburg (31 July 1760), in the Seven Years War. He was promoted to lieutenant general on 19 January 1761 and became a Knight of the Bath on 26 May 1761. Sir John Griffin played no further part in military affairs other than as colonel of the 1st Troop of Horse Grenadier Guards, from March 1766 until March 1788, and then as colonel of the 4th Dragoons. He was promoted to general on 2 April 1778. In 1784 he was permitted to inherit the title of 4th Baron Howard de Walden, through his mother (a granddaughter of James Howard, 4th Earl of Suffolk). He was granted a new peerage in 1788 as Baron Braybrooke. Lord Howard de Walden became a field marshal, along with the other five senior generals in the Army, on 30 July 1796. He died on 2 June 1797, having married twice, but leaving no offspring.

GROSVENOR
THOMAS (1764–1851) [36]

Thomas Grosvenor, a nephew of the 1st Earl of Grosvenor, was born on 30 May 1764. He was educated at Westminster School and was first commissioned on 1 October 1779 as an ensign in the 3rd Foot Guards and lieutenant in the Army. His first active duty was as commander of the picquet sent to guard the Bank of England at the time of the Gordon Riots in June 1780. He was promoted to lieutenant in the regiment and captain in the Army on 20 April 1784 and to captain in the regiment and lieutenant colonel in the Army on 25 April 1793. During the French Revolutionary War Grosvenor served with the Foot Guards in Flanders in the campaigns of 1793-94 and 1794–95, including the winter retreat into Germany. He became MP for Chester, a seat owned by his family, in 1795 and remained a member of the House of Commons until 1830. He was promoted to colonel on 3 May 1796 and in the following year married Elizabeth, the daughter of Sir Gilbert Heathcote, a wealthy baronet and an MP for Rutlandshire. After promotion to major general on 29 April 1802, Grosvenor held various brigade commands in southern England between 1803 and 1805. He was appointed colonel of the 97th Foot in 1807 and commanded a brigade in the British descent on Copenhagen (August-September 1807). He was promoted to lieutenant general on 25 April 1808 and took part in the Walcheren expedition of August-December 1809, where he served as deputy commander under General Sir Eyre Coote. After the disbandment of the 97th Foot, Grosvenor became colonel of the 65th Foot on 8 January 1814. He was promoted to general on 12 August 1819 and to field marshal on 9 November 1846, when three new field marshals were created to celebrate the fifth birthday of the Prince of Wales [54]. After the death of his first wife, Grosvenor married, in 1831, Anne Wilbraham, the daughter of a Cheshire MP. Field Marshal Grosvenor died on 20 June 1851, at his Surrey home, Mount Ararat, Richmond on Thames.

HAIG
Sir DOUGLAS, Earl Haig, GCB, OM, GCVO, KCIE
(1861–1928) **[85]**

Douglas Haig, the youngest son in a family of eleven children of a long-established Border whisky distiller, was born in Edinburgh on 19 June 1861. He was educated at Clifton College, where, on the deaths of his father and mother in 1878 and 1879 respectively, he inherited very substantial funds. In 1880 he entered Brasenose College, Oxford, where he established a reputation for diligence in his studies, combined with a preference for the society of other rich undergraduates from influential backgrounds. Haig's money and determination allowed him to become an expert horseman and polo-player. He passed his final examinations, but, having missed a term's residence through ill-health, left Oxford without completing the residential period necessary for the award of his degree. Abandoning an earlier idea of entering the Indian Civil Service, Haig decided to join the Army and entered the Royal Military College, Sandhurst, just under the upper age limit, in 1883. Older and more highly educated than the great majority of his fellow gentlemen cadets, Haig established a reputation both for aloofness and for attention to study. He excelled at polo and equitation, became the under officer in charge of his division and was awarded the Anson Memorial Sword, given to the cadet passing out with the highest marks. Haig was first commissioned on 7 February 1885 as a lieutenant in the 7th (Queen's Own) Hussars. He spent the next nine years at regimental duty and went to India with his regiment in 1886. He became a captain on 23 January 1891 and returned to the United Kingdom in 1893 to study for the Staff College entrance examination. He failed both the mathematics paper and the medical test, which found that he suffered from a relatively common form of colour-blindness, the inability to distinguish red from brown.

Haig returned briefly to his regiment in 1894 and then went back to the UK to renew his attempt to enter the Staff College, Camberley. In 1895 he became an aide-de-camp to the Inspector General of Cavalry and made the acquaintance of Sir Evelyn Wood **[74]**, Quartermaster General of the Army. Through these contacts he obtained a staff appointment at the War Office, to complete the new cavalry training manual (begun by the future Sir John French **[83]**, who also met and befriended Haig at this time). With Wood's support, Haig appealed successfully against his medical disqualification and passed into the Staff College in January 1896. He maintained his reputation both for industrious study and for aloofness, while at the same time making no effort to disguise the contacts that his wealth had enabled him to establish in fashionable society. His fellow students made clear their opinion of him by electing as Master of the Staff College Draghounds, not Haig (who was the better rider) but another cavalryman, Edmund Allenby [90]. At this period Haig lent substantial sums to French, who was then heavily in debt. He justified this decision to his trustees on the grounds that French (considerably his senior) was a personal friend and a good officer who would otherwise have been lost to the Army.

Haig passed out of the Staff College at the end of 1897 and gained an appointment as squadron commander in the cavalry of the Egyptian Army. In the campaign for the re-conquest of the Sudan, he served under Sir Herbert Kitchener [79] at Abadar (22 March and 5 April 1898); the Atbara (8 April 1898) and Omdurman (2 September 1898). He was promoted to brevet major on 16 November 1898 and in May 1899 was appointed brigade major of the 1st Cavalry Brigade at Aldershot. On the approach of the South African War, when French was nominated to command the Cavalry Division, he selected Haig as his assistant adjutant general. The two arrived in South Africa as the war began and were sent to join Sir George White [75], commanding the British troops in Natal. Haig was at Elandslaagte (29 October 1899) and then, as the Boers advanced to besiege Ladysmith, escaped with French, under fire, in the last train to leave. When the Cavalry Division was formed, the new C-in-C in South Africa, Lord Roberts [68] overruled French's protests and appointed the better-qualified Colonel Lord Erroll as its assistant adjutant general. Haig then became deputy assistant adjutant general, at the level of staff appointment appropriate to his rank as major. He served as such with the Cavalry Division at Klip Drift (15 February 1900) and in the advance to the relief of Kimberley. On 22 February 1900 he was given local promotion to lieutenant colonel and became assistant adjutant general in place of Erroll, who had joined Roberts' own staff. Haig became a substantive lieutenant colonel on 29 November 1900. Early in 1901 he transferred to the 17th (Duke of Cambridge's Own) Lancers as commanding officer. He was welcomed neither by the officers, whose promotion prospects were damaged by the appointment of someone from outside the regiment, nor by the troopers, who had heard of him as a stern and remote disciplinarian. Haig and his regiment spent the rest of the war in the fruitless pursuit of Boer commandos, including one led by Jan Smuts [108], and returned to the UK in September 1902. He was four times mentioned in despatches and was promoted to brevet colonel on 22 August 1902.

156

In October 1903 Haig was appointed Inspector General of Cavalry in India. He imposed a number of reforms, despite complaints by the Indian cavalry that they were being "dragooned" by the introduction of standardized practices conforming to those of the British Army. He was promoted to major general on 1 May 1904 and, after returning to the UK on leave, was invited to Windsor Castle by Edward VII [54], an old sporting and polo acquaintance. There he met one of the Queen's ladies-in-waiting, the Honourable Dorothy Vivian and, three days later, asked her to marry him. With parental and royal approval, they became, on 11 July 1905, the first non-royal couple to be married in the private chapel of Buckingham Palace. They later had a son and two daughters. In 1906, with the help of the influential and enigmatic Lord Esher, the King's friend and adviser, Haig was appointed Director of Military Training (and later Director of Staff Duties) at the War Office. There, in a rare moment of eloquence and emotion, he played an important part in ensuring the survival of the newly-formed General Branch of the staff (copied from the German model) by challenging its opponents to devise a better alternative. Haig became a favourite of the Liberal Secretary of State for War, Richard Haldane, and supported him in raising the Territorial Force as a separate army of part-time locally-based volunteers, complete with field artillery and divisional troops.

Haig returned to India to become Chief of Staff at Army HQ in October 1909. He encouraged the development of the new Indian Staff College at Quetta, and took an enlightened view on the question of Indian self-government. Having seen Egyptian officers in command of Egyptian regiments, he did not share the view widely held by British officers of the time that Indians could not be trained to command Indian regiments. He was awarded the KCVO (given for personal services to the Royal Family) in 1909, after a Royal visit to India. The death of Edward VII in 1910 reduced Sir Douglas Haig's access to Royal circles, but he gained the favour of George V [80], whom he had met as Prince of Wales. Aided by his wife's continued employment at Court, Haig was able throughout the rest of his career to meet and correspond with the King, without the need to go through official channels. He was promoted to lieutenant general on 31 October 1910 and left India in December 1911.

Haig was appointed GOC-in-C Aldershot Command in March 1912, after being selected for this prestigious post over the heads of several officers senior to him. On the outbreak of the First World War in August 1914, the troops of Aldershot Command became I Corps of the British Expeditionary Force, sent to France under Sir John French.

Haig's Corps covered the retreat from Mons and took part in the subsequent advance to the Aisne. It then moved to Flanders with the rest of the BEF and was at the first battle of Ypres (19 Oct–22 Nov 1914). Haig was promoted to general on 16 November 1914. When the BEF grew large enough to be divided into two armies, Haig became GOC First Army, consisting of I, IV and the Indian Corps. Haig commanded this army at Neuve Chapelle (10–13 March 1915); Festubert (15–25 May 1915) and Loos (25 September–14 October 1915). The heavy casualties and lack of success at Loos ended French's career as a battlefield commander. Haig had for some time been writing to his influential friends in London to say that Sir John French lacked the military and intellectual ability to command a great army. He reported to the King that French was obstinate and conceited. George V told Kitchener, who had become Secretary of State for War, that this savoured of "sneaking". Haig also complained to Herbert Asquith, the Prime Minister, about French's violent mood swings and hot temper. Asquith decided to replace French by Haig, who accordingly became C-in-C of the BEF on 19 December 1915. Relations between Haig and French, his one-time patron, were thereafter marked by mutual hatred and contempt.

Haig's first great offensive, on the Somme, began on 1 July 1916 and cost 57,470 casualties in the first twenty-four hours, the greatest losses ever suffered by the British Army on a single day. By the end of the battle in November 1916, Haig had lost some 420,000 men in repeated offensives, inflicting heavy casualties on the Germans, but making few territorial gains. George V had earlier proposed Haig's promotion to field marshal, but was persuaded by Asquith that such a move would be premature. The King took the opportunity of Asquith's fall to make Haig a field marshal on 1 January 1917. Haig persuaded the War Cabinet that he could win the war by a great offensive that would break out of the Ypres salient and reach the Belgian coast. Officially known as the third battle of Ypres, but more generally, from the final point of the British advance, as Passchendaele, this operation began on 31 July 1917. Appalling and unseasonable weather played a major part in the ultimate failure of the British offensive, with heavy casualties on both sides. Along with the battle of the Somme, Passchendaele entered the British folk memory as a costly and futile disaster.

In February 1918, David Lloyd George, Prime Minister since December 1916, succeeded in removing Sir William Robertson [92] from the post of Chief of the Imperial General Staff. Haig had previously supported Robertson, whose policy had been to concentrate on the

Western Front at the expense of other theatres. He now abandoned him and expressed a willingness to serve under whoever the Cabinet chose. This was Sir Henry Wilson [91], whom Haig subsequently described as "a humbug". Lloyd George sent the South African General Jan Smuts, who had become a member of the War Cabinet, to tour the Western Front and find a replacement for Haig. Smuts reported that none could be found, a view that Lloyd George regarded not as a compliment to Haig, but a sad reflection on the quality of British generals. The major German offensive of Spring 1918 cost the British heavily in men, supplies and ground and led Haig finally to agree to the establishment of a unified Allied command (given to the French General, later Marshal, Ferdinand Foch [88]). With the aid of reserves and reinforcements from other theatres, the BEF was able to halt the German advance and to begin a counter-offensive. Further advances carried the British over the Hindenburg Line at the end of September 1918 and hostilities ended on 11 November 1918.

Haig returned to the UK in July 1919, where he succeeded French as C-in-C Home Forces and retained this post until it was abolished in June 1920. He was raised to the peerage as Earl Haig, of Bemersyde, on ending his full-time service in January 1921. He had previously, through the influence of Lady Haig, taken an interest in schemes to find employment for officers invalided out of the Army in the course of the war. With the coming of peace, he played an important part in the formation of the British Legion, as a politically neutral, but officially recognized, benevolent organization and pressure group, to which all ex-servicemen could belong. He gave his name to the Earl Haig Fund, which, with the Flanders poppy as its symbol, supported those whom the war had left disabled and dependent on the tender mercy of the British Treasury. Despite his stern and unapproachable manner, Haig remained, in his lifetime, a generally popular figure both with his own veterans and the public as a whole. He was appointed colonel of the 17th Lancers in May 1912 and remained as colonel of its successor, the 17th/21st Lancers, when this was formed in 1922. He became colonel of the Royal Horse Guards in July 1919 and of the King's Own Scottish Borderers in September 1923. He was also honorary colonel of the 14th (County of London) Battalion, the London Regiment (London Scottish) from July 1919. Earl Haig died suddenly, in London, on 30 January 1928. He was buried near his Border home, Dryburgh Abbey, Bemersyde, which had been purchased for him from the proceeds of a nationwide subscription. As C-in-C of the British Expeditionary Force, he commanded the largest field army in British military history.

HAILE SELASSIE
HIM Emperor of Ethiopia, KG, GCB, GCMG
(1892–1975) [125]

Tafari Makkonen, baptized into the Ethiopian Coptic Church as Haile
Selassie ("Power of the Trinity"), was born on 23 July 1892 at
Ejarsogoro, Harar, a territory conquered by the Emperor Menelik of
Ethiopia (the country then more usually referred to by Europeans as
Abyssinia) five years earlier. Tafari's father, Ras (Duke) Makonnen was
a successful general who had been rewarded for his part in this campaign with the governorship of Harar and later became one of the
Emperor's most trusted ministers. Ras Makkonnen entrusted the education of Tafari, his tenth and only surviving son, to French
missionaries. At the same time Tafari was brought up in the traditional
faith of the Ethiopian Church, in which he was ordained as a deacon
in 1900. On the death of Ras Makonnen in 1906, Menelik declined to
appoint the young Tafari as his successor, but gave him the governorship of a less strategically important province instead. During the
power struggle following Menelik's illness in 1908, Tafari remained
neutral. He was rewarded by being at last appointed Governor of Harar
in 1910. Control of Ethiopia passed to Tafari's cousin, Lij Iyasu, who
ruled as the head of a Regency Council. Lij Iyasu made a number of
concessions to his Muslim subjects, with the intention of unifying the
different peoples of the Ethiopian Empire, but succeeded only in alien-
ating the dominant Christian majority. During the First World War his
opponents accused him of seeking to bring Ethiopia into the war on the
side of Muslim Turkey and the other Central Powers, with the aim of
gaining the Italian and British possessions in the Horn of Africa. In
October 1916 Lij Iyasu was overthrown amid accusations of apostasy.
Menelik's daughter, Zawditu (Judith) was proclaimed Empress, while
Tafari, raised to the status of a Ras, was named as the new Regent. In
the brief civil war that ensued, Ras Tafari was at Segele (27 October
1916), after which he established himself as the effective head of the
Ethiopian government.

   Ras Tafari began to modernize the Ethiopian revenue and criminal
justice systems and employed Western technical experts to improve
the public services. In 1923, in order to gain Ethiopia's admission to
the League of Nations, he decreed the abolition of the slave trade
within his territories and that the children of existing slaves would,
from then on, be born free. He toured Egypt, Italy, France, the UK and
other European states in 1924, where he was greeted with the honours
due to a ruling prince. In London King George V [80] returned to him

the Ethiopian crown that had been brought back to Queen Victoria by Lord Napier of Magdala [58]. Tafari made no other tangible gains and returned to his unsettled country, where in 1928 he assumed the title of Negus (king). This was followed in 1929 by a serious rebellion, led by the Empress's husband, Ras Gugsa. This nobleman was killed in battle after his army had been routed by Negus Tafari's new Imperial Air Force (composed of two aircraft operated by European mercenaries). The Empress died two days after her husband's defeat and Negus Tafari succeeded to the Ethiopian throne as Negusa Negast (King of Kings, or Emperor). He was crowned by his baptismal name, as Haile Selassie, on 2 November 1930. His coronation was attended by representatives of various Western powers, including the Duke of Gloucester [121] on behalf of the British Crown. The recognition given to him on this occasion played a part in the rise of the Rastafarian cult (the "Rastas"), a group of Afro-Caribbean origin whose members regarded conventional Christianity as an instrument of white domination. The ruler of the last African kingdom not under European control, Haile Selassie appeared to them as a messianic figure.

Increasing tension between Italy and Ethiopia led to the outbreak of war in October 1935. Haile Selassie, hoping for international assistance, invoked the collective security clauses of the Covenant of the League of Nations, while withdrawing from his frontier districts to delay the onset of fighting. An agreement brokered by the British and French foreign ministers was rejected by liberal opinion in both countries, more from a dislike of the fascist government in Italy than from any sympathy with the people of Ethiopia. The League ordered economic sanctions against Italy, but these failed to have the desired effect of halting the war and only drove Italy into the arms of Nazi Germany. Led by Marshal Badoglio, the Italian forces pressed forward, making full use of the resources of Western civilization, including bomber aircraft and chemical weapons. Haile Selassie's army was finally routed by Italian mountain troops at Amba Aradam on 31 March 1936, where the Emperor manned a machine gun during the closing stages of the battle. The Ethiopian soldiery fled in disorder, becoming prey to Muslim Galla bandits among their fellow-countrymen or taking to banditry on their own account. In Addis Ababa, the capital city, numbers of Europeans were murdered or raped before Badoglio's troops arrived to restore order. Ethiopia was annexed to the Italian Empire on 9 May 1936. Haile Selassie and his immediate entourage escaped through the French Red Sea territory of Djibouti and eventually found refuge in England, where they settled at Bath.

161

After Italy entered the Second World War in June 1940, Haile Selassie, with the encouragement of Winston Churchill, the British Prime Minister, went to the Sudan to encourage Ethiopian guerrillas fighting against Italian rule. He was given a small group of military advisers (including the charismatic Orde Wingate) and re-entered Ethiopia in January 1941. Some local British officials had not been entirely sorry to see the replacement of an independent African state by a colonial regime that at least shared their notions of stable government. They were inclined to regard him with suspicion (referring to him by the punning name of "Highly Suspicious") and ensured that he did not reach Addis Ababa until it had been taken by British and South African troops. The Cabinet, however, decided that Ethiopia was to be regarded as a liberated country, rather than (as it technically was) an occupied enemy territory, and Haile Selassie was acknowledged as the legitimate ruler on 31 January 1942. He was allowed to sign the Charter of the United Nations as the head of an independent nation and British bombers assisted him to recover control of the province of Tigre from its local Muslim rulers in 1943.

Haile Selassie issued a revised constitution in 1955. He sought to rule as an absolute monarch, but brigands and warlords still controlled outlying areas, while the slow pace of economic and social development alienated many young members of the Western-educated *élite* that he himself had brought into being. An attempted rising in December 1960, during his absence on a state visit to Brazil, was put down by loyal troops, but stories of greed and corruption in the government continued to circulate. Haile Selassie was a leading figure in the foundation of the Organization of African Unity, which was set up with its headquarters in Addis Ababa in 1963. He became one of Africa's elder statesmen, despite the rivalry of other post-colonial leaders, who, as radicals and democrats, disapproved of his position as a crowned monarch. He mediated in a number of intra-African disputes and upheld the OAU principle of respecting the frontiers inherited from the colonial powers. Nevertheless, in 1962, he annexed Eritrea to his dominions, thus beginning a war that lasted until Eritrea recovered its independence in 1980. Increasingly, visitors to Ethiopia were shocked by the high levels of poverty and illiteracy, the absence of medical and educational facilities and the extent to which land-ownership remained in the hands of the great noble families. The Emperor, who grew more conservative with age, refused to consider reform. Instead, he increased expenditure on his personal pomp and prestige. He maintained cordial relations with his erstwhile British allies, sending his best cadets to the Royal Military Academy Sandhurst, (which he visited several times and to which he made a number of generous gifts) and encouraging British officers to explore his country. He was made a British field marshal on 20 January 1965.

Ethiopia's economic position worsened during the 1960s. Unemployed graduates ridiculed their Emperor's claim to semi-divine status as "the Lion of Judah". Public servants went on strike for decent wages. Soldiers mutinied for decent burial, as, in the continuing war with Eritrea, only the bodies of officers were recovered, while those of private men were left where they fell. A series of famines caused widespread distress, but the regime, for reasons of international prestige, denied their existence and rejected foreign offers of aid. Too late, the Emperor appointed a new, reformist prime minister. The Army, on the model of the Russian Soviets of 1917, elected a 120-strong *derg* (council) to investigate the government. For several months the new ministry and the *derg* existed side by side, until on 12 September 1974 the *derg* arrested many ministers and nobles, and announced that the Emperor had been deposed. Haile Selassie was confined to a palace room and was not again seen in public. His death from "circulatory failure" was announced on 28 August 1975 and he was buried in an unmarked grave within the palace grounds.

HAINES
Sir FREDERICK PAUL, GCB, GCSI, CIE (1819–1909) [65]

Frederick Haines, the youngest child of a commissariat officer who had prospered from his services in Wellington's campaigns, was born at Kirdford, Sussex, on 10 August 1819. He became an ensign in the 4th Foot on 21 June 1839 and sailed for India to join his eldest brother, who had recently married a daughter of the commanding general at Mysore, Sir Hugh Gough [44]. Haines was promoted to lieutenant on 15 December 1840. When Gough became C-in-C, India, in 1843, he appointed Haines as one of his aides-de-camp. Haines was on Gough's staff throughout both Sikh Wars, serving at Mudki (18 December 1845); Ferozeshah (21 December 1845), where he was wounded; Ramnagar (21 November 1848); Chilianwala (13 January 1849) and Gujarat (21 February 1849). In this period he became a captain in the 10th Foot on 16 May 1846, exchanged to the 21st Royal North British Fusiliers in March 1847 and was promoted to brevet major on 7 June 1849. He became a brevet lieutenant colonel on 2 August 1850.

During the Crimean War Haines was with his regiment at the Alma (20 September 1854); Balaklava (25 October 1854) and

Inkerman (5 November 1854), where, as the senior officer present, he held the Barrier for six hours. He was promoted to brevet colonel on 28 November 1854 and remained before Sevastopol, serving under Sir Colin Campbell [46] (who remembered him from Chilianwala and had some reservations about his judgement). Ordered home as supernumerary, he joined the staff at Aldershot in February 1855. In 1856 he married Charlotte Miller, daughter of a colonel in the Madras Amy. He then became military secretary to the C-in-C, Madras, Sir Patrick Grant [59], and remained on his staff during the Indian Mutiny (1857–58). During 1860–61 Haines commanded the 8th Foot in the UK. He was promoted to major general on 25 November 1864 and, from 1865 to 1870, held command of the Mysore division of the Madras Army. He was then for a short period Quartermaster General in London, after which he was awarded the KCB and returned to India in May 1871 as C-in-C, Madras. Sir Frederick Haines was promoted to lieutenant general on 23 May 1873 and became colonel of the 104th Bengal Fusiliers (later the 2nd Battalion, the Royal Munster Fusiliers) in May 1874.

In April 1876 he succeeded Lord Napier of Magdala [58] as C-in-C, India, with promotion to general on 1 October 1877. Lord Lytton, the new Viceroy and Governor-General of India, arrived with instructions to establish a British diplomatic presence in Afghanistan. Lytton had been provided with a military secretary, Colonel George Colley (a member of the "Ring" led by Sir Garnet Wolseley [67]) who acted as his unofficial adviser on questions of strategy. Colley, a former professor at the Staff College, but with no experience of command, considered Haines to be out-of-date and parochial. Haines described Colley as the finest theoretical soldier he ever met. In 1878, during the preparations for the Second Afghan War, Lytton objected to the mobilization of a large force and suspected that Haines (whom he regarded as "an unintelligent mediocrity") wished to lead a huge army in person. Haines insisted that it would be a false economy to send an army that was inadequate for its task. Lytton was unable to over-rule his C-in-C in military matters, but the Indian Government's lack of funds meant that, when the campaign began, the troops in the field lacked logistic and administrative support. During the war Lytton attempted to by-pass Haines by dealing directly with the commanders in the field. Haines left India in 1881 and declined the offer of a baronetcy, feeling slighted that his subordinates, Sir Donald Stewart [66] and Sir Frederick Roberts [68], the main field commanders during the Afghan campaign, had been given this honour ahead of him. Haines was promoted to field marshal on 21 May 1890 and became colonel of the Royal Scots Fusiliers in

October 1890. He died in London on 11 June 1909, and was buried in Brompton Cemetery, leaving three sons.

HAMILTON
Lord GEORGE, 1st Earl of Orkney, KT (1666–1737) [1]

Lord George Hamilton was born in February 1666 at Hamilton Palace, Lanark. He was the fifth son of William Douglas, 3rd Duke of Hamilton, who had gained his title by virtue of his marriage to Anne Hamilton, Duchess of Hamilton in her own right. Lord George's first commission was dated 9 May 1684, in the regiment (later the 1st Foot, the Royal Scots) of which his uncle, the Earl of Dumbarton, was colonel. Dumbarton, a staunch Roman Catholic, remained loyal to James II and followed him into exile, but Lord George, like his father, supported William III and the Protestant cause. In June 1689 Lord George Hamilton was appointed lieutenant colonel of Lloyd's Regiment of Enniskilling Foot. Lloyd died on active service with his regiment in Ireland during the harsh winter of 1689–90. Hamilton, with the rank of brevet colonel, succeeded to the command of his regiment and led it at the Boyne (1 July 1690); Athlone (June 1691); Aughrim (12 July 1691) and the siege of Limerick (capitulated 3 October 1691). At the end of this campaign Hamilton's services were rewarded with the colonelcy of the Royal Fusiliers (later the 7th Foot), which he commanded in the Nine Years War at Steenkerke (23 July 1692), covering the Allied retreat. After this combat he was made colonel of the Royal Scots in place of Sir Robert Douglas, who had been killed in the battle. Hamilton remained in the field until July 1695, when he was wounded at the siege of Namur.

Hamilton's reward from a grateful William III, under whom he had served in two campaigns, was the hand in marriage of the King's mistress, Elizabeth Villiers. Elizabeth, possessed of ample funds granted to her through William's influence, was then aged 38, nine years older than her new husband. She proved an excellent match, bearing him three daughters and remaining influential in court circles throughout the reigns of Queen Anne and George I. Dean Swift described her as "squinting like a dragon", but also as the wisest woman he ever knew. Hamilton was created Earl of Orkney, in the Scottish peerage, in January 1696. Shortly afterwards he purchased the two adjoining Thameside estates of Taplow Court and Cliveden, Buckinghamshire, where he was able to entertain Royal guests and other notables during his subsequent political career. In the War of the Spanish Succession

Orkney served under Marlborough in Flanders, where he became a major general on 9 March 1702 and a lieutenant general on 1 January 1704. He was at the siege of Stevenswaert (capitulated 5 Oct 1702); Blenheim (13 August 1704); the relief of Liège (June 1705); Ramillies (23 May 1706); the siege of Menin (July 1706); Oudenarde (11 July 1708); the passage of the Scheldt (November 1708); the siege of Tournai (June 1709) and Malplaquet (11 September 1709), a battle so costly that Orkney declared he hoped never to see another. He became general of the Foot in 1710. After Marlborough's recall Orkney continued in this post under the Duke of Ormonde, until hostilities ended in 1713, and served at the sieges of Douai and Bouchain. Orkney continued to play an active part in public life. Following the 1707 Act of Union, he sat in the House of Lords at Westminster as a representative Scottish peer. He was appointed Governor of Virginia (a post which at that time did not require the holder to reside there) in December 1714. When the rank of field marshal was introduced into the British Army on 12 January 1736 he was, as the senior general in the Army, the first to be promoted. He died in London on 29 January 1737 and was buried at Taplow Court, in the vault of the ancient parish church of St Nicholas (later demolished). Orkney had no sons. His eldest daughter, Anne, the wife of William O'Brien, 4th Earl of Inchiquin, succeeded him by special remainder as 2nd Countess of Orkney in her own right.

HARCOURT
WILLIAM, 3rd Earl Harcourt, GCB (1743–1830) [30]

The Honourable William Harcourt, younger son of Simon, 1st Earl Harcourt, of Stanton Harcourt and Nuneham Park, Oxfordshire, was born on 20 March 1743. He was first commissioned on 10 August 1759 as an ensign in the 1st Foot Guards and lieutenant in the Army. In October 1759 he became captain in the 16th Light Dragoons, a regiment that his father had raised earlier as Harcourt's Black Horse. Earl Harcourt's elder son, who eventually succeeded him as 2nd Earl, had severe learning difficulties and it was therefore William who joined their father as a member of the Royal Household. He remained at Court until going as an aide-de-camp with Lord Albemarle in the expedition against Havana (8 June–30 July 1762), in the Seven Years War. Harcourt became lieutenant colonel of the 31st Foot in 1764 and then of the 18th Light Dragoons in 1765, before returning to the 16th Light Dragoons as their commanding officer. He sat as MP for Oxford from 1768 to 1774 and from August to October 1776. Harcourt served with the 16th

Light Dragoons during the American War of Independence, where he led the British cavalry charge at White Plains (28 October 1776). On 13 December 1776 he surprised and captured Charles Lee, one of the ablest American generals, but played no other major part in this war. Harcourt returned to England in 1778 where he married Mrs Mary Lockhart, a young widow. He became colonel of the 16th Light Dragoons on 20 October 1779 and was promoted to major general on 20 November 1782 and to lieutenant general on 12 October 1793.

At the beginning of the French Revolutionary War Harcourt commanded the British cavalry in the Flanders campaign of 1793–1794 and was in command of the whole army during the winter retreat into Germany. He was promoted to general on 1 January 1798. In 1799 he became the first Governor of the newly-formed Royal Military College. He succeeded his brother as 3rd Earl in 1809. When George IV decided to mark his coronation by creating two additional field marshals, Earl Harcourt was the second senior general in the Army after the Marquis of Drogheda [29] and was promoted with him on 17 July 1821. Harcourt died on 18 June 1830, at his country house, St Leonard's Hall (a future "Legoland") on the western outskirts of Windsor Great Park, Berkshire. His countess, who survived him by three years, had no children and his titles became extinct.

HARDING
Sir "JOHN" ALLAN FRANCIS, 1st Baron Harding of
Petherton, GCB, CBE, DSO, MC (1896–1989) [120]

Allan Harding was born in South Petherton, Somerset, on 10 February 1896, the only son among the four children of a solicitor's clerk and his strong-minded wife, the daughter of a local draper. Of diminutive stature, he was educated as a weekly boarder at Ilminster Grammar School until 1911, when he joined the staff of the Post Office Savings Bank in London as a boy clerk. He studied for promotion in the Civil Service and joined the Territorial Force on 15 May 1914 as a second lieutenant in the 11th (County of London) Battalion (Finsbury Rifles), the London Regiment. On mobilization at the outbreak of the First World War in August 1914 Harding was among those who accepted liability for service overseas. He became the machine-gun officer of his battalion and, attached to the newly-formed Machine Gun Corps, was promoted to acting captain on 22 June 1915. Harding landed with his battalion in Gallipoli as part of the 54th (East Anglian) Division in August 1915 and was wounded in the leg at Kidney Hill on 16 August

1915. He became a substantive lieutenant in the Territorial Force on 7 January 1916, a temporary captain in the Machine Gun Corps on 25 April 1916 and a substantive captain in the Territorial Force on 7 June 1916. Harding was granted a commission in the Regular Army on 22 March 1917, as a lieutenant in Prince Albert's (Somerset Light Infantry), but remained attached to the Machine Gun Corps and was at the third battle of Gaza (27 March 1917), where he was again wounded. After medical treatment at Alexandria, he became the machine-gun staff officer of the 54th Division, with promotion to acting major on 11 October 1917. He was with this formation at the fourth battle of Gaza (1–2 November 1917) where he was awarded the Military Cross. Harding served as the machine-gun staff officer of XXI Corps from April to July 1918, when he became the acting commanding officer of the 54th Battalion, the Machine Gun Corps (disbanded in Egypt in 1919).

In 1919 Harding joined the 12th Battalion, the Machine Gun Corps, at Shorncliffe, as a company second-in-command and temporary captain. His adjutant decided that "Allan" was not a suitable name for an officer of the Regular Army and told him that he would be called "John", the name that Harding accordingly adopted. He was posted with his battalion to India in 1919 where, on the disbandment of the Machine Gun Corps in 1921, he joined the 2nd Battalion, the Somerset Light Infantry, at Lucknow. He was battalion adjutant from 1922 to 1925, with substantive promotion to captain on 11 October 1923. After failing his Staff College entrance examination, he returned on leave to the UK, where he met and proposed to Mary Rooke, the sister of an officer in his battalion and the elder daughter of a Cheshire solicitor. Despite her family's reservations about Harding's modest background and lack of private income, they were married in April 1927 and their only child, John, was born the following year. Harding entered the Staff College, Camberley, in January 1928 and passed out at the beginning of 1930. After a few months of regimental duty as a company commander, he became a General Staff officer, grade 2, at HQ Southern Command. In May 1933 Harding became brigade major of the 13th Infantry Brigade at Catterick. Between January 1935 and April 1936 he was once more a company commander in the 2nd Battalion, the Somerset Light Infantry, with promotion to substantive major on 1 July 1935. He then returned to the staff as GSO 2 in the Directorate of Military Operations at the War Office. Harding was promoted to lieutenant colonel on 1 January 1938 and became commanding officer of the 1st Battalion, the Somerset Light Infantry, in India, on 1 August 1939.

After the outbreak of the Second World War on 3 September 1939 Harding's unit remained on the North-West Frontier of India. It took part in minor operations against the dissident Fakir of Ipi in March-May 1940, during which Harding was mentioned in despatches. He feared that (as had happened to the 2nd Battalion, the Somerset Light Infantry in the First World War) his battalion would be kept in India, with the result that he would miss the career opportunities offered by service in an active theatre. He was therefore happy to go to Middle East Command in September 1940 as GSO 1. He was promoted to substantive colonel and acting brigadier on 14 December 1940 and, a week later, was appointed Brigadier, General Staff, of the Western Desert Force, under Lieutenant General Sir Richard O'Connor. When Harding's two immediate superiors, O'Connor and Sir Philip Neame, were both captured during the British retreat from Cyrenaica in April 1941, Harding assumed temporary command and was largely responsible for the initial decision to hold Tobruk. He was awarded the DSO for his services during the British offensive of May-June 1941. He remained in this theatre as BGS of XIII Corps from August 1941 to February 1942. He was awarded a bar to his DSO for organizing the local defence of his Advanced HQ, in the operations to relieve Tobruk at the end of November 1941. After the British withdrawal to Gazala in February 1942, Harding became Director of Military Training at GHQ in Cairo. He was promoted to major general with effect from 26 January 1942 and was appointed GOC 7th Armoured Division on 17 September 1942. During the battle of El Alamein (23 October–4 November 1942) he led his tactical HQ forward to the minefield area and commanded his division first from a tank and then from a jeep, where his ADC was killed beside him. He took part in the subsequent pursuit of the Axis forces until 17 January 1943, when he was wounded by shell splinters in the chest, thigh and arm and lost three fingers from his left hand. He was awarded a second bar to his DSO for his conduct in these operations.

Harding was invalided back to the UK, where, on 11 November 1943, he was promoted to acting lieutenant general and given command of VIII Corps. At the end of December 1943 he was appointed Chief of Staff to Sir Harold Alexander [113], the Allied commander in Italy. On 26 July 1944, Harding was knighted in the field by George VI [106], who insisted on dubbing him as Sir Allan Harding on the grounds that John was not among Harding's Christian names. The King nevertheless told him he might be known as Sir John Harding if he so wished. Harding asked his wife for a decision. Lady Harding preferred "Sir John", by which style he thereafter went. He became temporary lieutenant general on 10 November 1944 and substantive lieutenant general on 1 January 1945. Early in March 1945 he was given command of XIII Corps in Italy. His troops reached Trieste on 3 May 1945, a day after the German surrender, and Harding remained there as the representative of the Western powers during a period of strained relations with their erstwhile Yugoslav allies. Between November 1946 and July 1947 he was Commander, Central Mediterranean Force (the successor of the Eighth Army) in Italy.

After returning to the UK, Harding served as GOC-in-C Southern Command until July 1948 when he became C-in-C, Far Eastern Land Forces. In August 1951 he was appointed C-in-C, British Army of the Rhine. With the re-armament of the Federal German Republic as part of the Western Alliance, Harding had the task of changing his army from an occupation force into one trained for field operations in the defence of a friendly country. He succeeded Sir William Slim [117] as Chief of the Imperial General Staff on 1 November 1952. Together with Earl Alexander [113], the then Minister of Defence, Harding supported the withdrawal of British troops from the Suez Canal Zone and the establishment of a new Middle East base area in Cyprus. He was promoted to field marshal on 21 July 1953.

In October 1955, on completion of his tour as CIGS, Harding was appointed Governor of Cyprus. The British decision to establish a new Middle East base there, with the assumption that Cyprus would remain under colonial rule indefinitely, had led to militant disaffection among the Greek Cypriot community. The long-standing demand for "Enosis" (union with Greece) was revived, to be countered by demands from the minority Turkish Cypriot community for "Taksim" (partition). Harding held office in Cyprus for two years, during which time he led a successful counter-insurgency campaign against the Greek Cypriot terrorist organization, EOKA.

Harding was raised to the peerage as Baron Harding of Petherton, of Nether Common, in January 1958. He entered the world of commerce as a director of several major firms and, in 1961, became the first chairman of the Horse Race Betting Levy Board. Lord Harding was colonel of the 6th Queen Elizabeth's Own Gurkha Rifles from 1951 to 1961; the Somerset Light Infantry from April 1953 to October 1959 and its successor, the Somerset and Cornwall Light Infantry, from October 1959 until April 1960, and the Life Guards from April 1957 to January 1965. He was honorary colonel of the North Somerset Yeomanry (amalgamated with the 44th Royal Tank Regiment in 1956) from 1949 to 1959. Lord Harding also maintained his connection with the Finsbury Rifles (remustered as a Territorial anti-aircraft unit of the Royal Artillery) and regularly dined with its Old

Comrades Association until late in his life. Lord Harding died at his home in Sherborne, Dorset, on 20 January 1989 and was succeeded as 2nd baron by his son.

HARDINGE
Sir HENRY, 1st Viscount Hardinge, GCB (1785–1856) **[41]**

Henry Hardinge, the third son of a wealthy clergyman, was born on 30 March 1785 at Wrotham, Kent. His first commission, dated 8 October 1798, was as an ensign in the Queen's Rangers, a colonial corps localized in Upper Canada. On 25 March 1802 he became a lieutenant in the 4th Foot, on the half-pay list. He transferred to the 1st Foot, the Royal Scots, on the full-pay list in 1803 and exchanged to the 57th Foot with promotion to captain on 7 April 1804. Between February 1806 and November 1807 he attended the Senior Department of the newly-formed Royal Military College, High Wycombe, and so became one of the British Army's first properly trained staff officers. As such, he obtained a staff appointment in the contingent sent to reinforce the British army in Portugal in August 1808 and was at Rolica (17 August 1808) and Vimiero (21 August 1808), where he was wounded. He returned to the Peninsula in Sir John Moore's army later in 1808, where he served as a staff officer in the retreat to Corunna. Hardinge was at the battle of Corunna (16 January 1809) and was involved in organizing the subsequent British embarkation. Hardinge was promoted to major on 13 April 1809 and was selected for service with the Portuguese Army under the command of Marshal Beresford. He was with the Portuguese at the passage of the Douro (Oporto, 12 May 1809); Busaco (27 September 1810); Albuera (16 May 1812); Ciudad Rodrigo (8–19 January 1812); Badajoz (6 April 1812); Salamanca (22 July 1812); Vittoria (21 June 1813), where he was wounded; the Pyrenees (27–30 July 1813); Pamplona (August-September 1813); the Nivelle (10 October 1813); the Nive (10–18 December 1813); Orthez (27 February 1814) and Toulouse (10 April 1814). Hardinge became a lieutenant colonel in the British Army on 30 May 1811 and in the 40th Foot on 12 April 1814. He joined the 1st Foot Guards on 25 July 1814, as a captain in the regiment and lieutenant colonel in the Army, and was awarded the KCB in January 1815. In the Hundred Days campaign Sir Henry Hardinge was appointed British commissioner with the Prussian army under Field Marshal Prince von Blücher. He was wounded at Ligny (16 June 1815), where he lost a hand. He rejoined the Prussians in Paris two weeks later and remained with them until the Army of Occupation was withdrawn in November 1818.

Hardinge entered Parliament as MP for Durham in 1820 and retained his seat until 1844. He was promoted to colonel on 19 July 1821 and married, in December 1821, Lady Emily James, the widowed half-sister of the 2nd Marquess of Londonderry. He became Clerk of the Ordnance in 1823, when the Duke of Wellington [24] became Master General of the Ordnance. Hardinge was appointed Secretary at War in May 1828 and, as such, acted as Wellington's second in his duel with Lord Winchilsea. He was a government minister as Secretary for Ireland from July 1828 to November 1830 and from July to December 1834, during which time Daniel O'Connell, the Irish political leader, publicly referred to him as a "one-handed miscreant". Hardinge was promoted to major-general on 22 July 1830 and became colonel of the 97th Foot on 4 March 1833. He again became Secretary at War, this time as a member of Sir Robert Peel's second Cabinet, in September 1841. He was promoted to lieutenant general on 23 November 1841 and was appointed colonel of the 57th Foot on 31 May 1843.

In May 1844, Hardinge was appointed to succeed his brother-in-law, Lord Ellenborough, as Governor-General of India. On the outbreak of war with the kingdom of Lahore (the 1st Sikh War) in 1845, Hardinge offered his services to Sir Hugh Gough [44], C-in-C, India, as his second-in-command and served as such at Ferozeshah (21 December 1845) and Sobraon (10 February 1846). He was junior to Gough in military rank, but considered himself the better general and, as the head of the Government of India, was able to over-rule him in the strategic conduct of the campaign. After the British victory Hardinge was raised to the peerage as Viscount Hardinge, of Lahore and King's Newton. He remained in India as Governor-General until January 1848. Lord Hardinge became Master General of the Ordnance at the beginning of 1852 and succeeded Wellington as Commander-in-Chief on 28 September 1852. He was reluctant to alter arrangements that had satisfied his old chief and so was later blamed for weaknesses revealed by the Crimean War of 1854–56. He was promoted to general on 20 June 1854 and to field marshal on 2 October 1855. After being affected by a stroke, he retired on 15 July 1856 and was succeeded by the Duke of Cambridge [45]. Hardinge died on 24 September 1856 at his residence, South Park, Fordcombe, near Penshurst, Kent. He was buried at the nearby St Peter's church, the construction of which owed much to his generosity. His viscountess, who died in 1865, left him two daughters and two sons, of whom the eldest succeeded to his peerage.

HAY

GEORGE, 8th Marquess of Tweeddale, KT, GCB
(1787–1876) **[53]**

George Hay, by courtesy Earl of Gifford, was born at his family seat, Yester, Haddingtonshire, on 1 February 1787. He succeeded his father as 8th Marquis of Tweeddale in August 1804, two months after first being commissioned as an ensign in the 52nd Light Infantry. Tweeddale was promoted to lieutenant on 12 October 1804 and served as an aide-de-camp with the British army in Sicily in 1806. He became a lieutenant in the 1st Foot Guards and captain in the Army on 12 May 1807. Tweeddale joined the Peninsular campaign as a staff officer under Wellington **[24]** and was at Busaco (27 September 1810), where he was wounded. On 14 May 1812 he became a major in the 41st Foot, but remained on the staff and was at Vittoria (21 June 1813), where he was again wounded He was promoted lieutenant colonel on the same date and, after a period of sick leave, joined the 41st Foot in the American War of 1812–14. Tweeddale took command of the 100th Foot (later disbanded) just before the battle of Chippewa (5 July 1814), where he was wounded for the third time and taken prisoner by the Americans, who chivalrously frustrated his attempt to fight to the death.

After this war Tweeddale lived mostly on his family estate at Yester and improved his income by introducing more efficient methods of farming. He was nevertheless a prominent figure in Regency society and a noted horseman and whip. In March 1816 he married Lady Susan Montagu, a younger daughter of the 5th Duke of Manchester, with whom he later had seven sons and six daughters. Tweeddale became a colonel on 27 May 1825 and a major general on 10 May 1837. He resumed public office between 1842 and 1848, when he served as Governor and C-in-C, Madras. He became colonel of the 30th Foot on 7 February 1846 and was promoted to lieutenant general on 9 November 1846. Thereafter, he returned quite literally to his plough, as he continued his agricultural improvements and pressed on with the conversion of common pasture into arable land. Tweeddale was promoted to general on 20 June 1854 and to field marshal on 29 May 1875. He was made colonel of the 42nd Foot (Black Watch) in March 1862 and of the 2nd Life Guards in September 1863. He died at Yester on 10 October 1876.

HENRY WILLIAM FREDERICK ALBERT
HRH 1st Duke of Gloucester, KG, KT, KP, GCB, GCMG, GCVO (1900–1974) **[121]**

Prince Henry, third son and fourth of the six children of the then Duke and Duchess of York (later HM George V **[80]** and Queen Mary) was born at Sandringham, Norfolk, on 31 May 1900. He was educated at Eton College and the Royal Military College, Sandhurst, and was commissioned as a second lieutenant in the 2nd Battalion, the Rifle Brigade (the Prince Consort's Own) on 16 May 1919. For political reasons the King refused to allow him to join this battalion, which at that time was stationed in Ireland, and Prince Henry spent the following year at the Rifle Brigade depot in Winchester. An enthusiastic horseman, he was given an attachment to the 13th Hussars and was subsequently transferred from the Rifle Brigade to the 10th (Prince of Wales's Own) Royal Hussars. As this regiment also was serving in Ireland, he was not allowed to join it until 1922, when it was posted to Canterbury. In the meanwhile Prince Henry acted as extra ADC to Lord Cavan **[101]**, GOC-in-C Aldershot Command, and was promoted to lieutenant on 16 July 1921.

Prince Henry was promoted to captain on 11 May 1927 and was created Duke of Gloucester and Earl of Ulster in April 1928. He was then detached from his regiment for an official visit to the Far East, where he presented the insignia of a Knight of the Garter to the Emperor Hirohito of Japan **[99]**. The Duke of Gloucester rejoined the 10th Royal Hussars in Egypt, but political considerations prevented him from going with his regiment when it was posted to India and he was placed on the half-pay in July 1929. In October 1930 he represented King George V at the coronation of the Ethiopian Emperor Haile Selassie **[125]**. Gloucester returned to the full-pay list in March 1931, when he was appointed as a staff captain in the 2nd Cavalry Brigade at Tidworth, Salisbury Plain. A year later he was attached to the 11th Hussars in command of a squadron of armoured cars. He rejoined the horsed cavalry in January 1934, attached to the 16th/5th Lancers as a squadron commander and was promoted to brevet major on 2 August 1934 and to substantive major on 6 July 1935. In November 1935, urged by his royal parents to take a wife, he married Lady Alice Montagu Douglas Scott, third daughter of the 7th Duke of Buccleuch and a sister of Gloucester's closest friend, Lord William Scott. They proved a devoted couple and later had two sons.

The Duke of Gloucester entered the Staff College, Camberley, in January 1936, but his active military career ceased on the abdication of his eldest brother, Edward VIII [104] in the following December. Gloucester then stood third in line of succession to the throne, after the two young daughters of his brother George VI [106], and was nominated as Regent Designate in the event of the King's death or incapacity. George VI promoted him to major general on 1 January 1937, so ending his last hopes of commanding his regiment. Gloucester then retired from the Army, on his major's pension, and devoted himself to farming the estate he had purchased at Barnwell Manor, Northamptonshire. After the outbreak of the Second World War on 3 September 1939 he was appointed Chief Liaison Officer on the staff of Lord Gort [110], C-in-C of the British Expeditionary Force in France. The Duke was slightly wounded on 15 May 1940, when his staff car came under German air attack. With the retreat of the BEF towards the sea, he was ordered home and reached London on 20 May 1940. His contribution to the war effort thereafter consisted of morale-boosting visits to various locations in the UK, the Mediterranean, the Middle East and India. He was promoted to lieutenant general on 17 September 1941, but reverted to the rank of colonel so that he could broaden his experience by serving for a time as deputy commander of the 20th Armoured Brigade.

Gloucester ceased to be Regent Designate when the Princess Elizabeth came of age on 21 April 1944. He was promoted to general on 27 October 1944 and in December 1944 was nominated as the first member of the Royal Family to be Governor-General of Australia. After arriving there in January 1945, he undertook a series of tours and visited the bases in Queensland and Bougainville, from which Sir Thomas Blamey [118] was waging his Pacific Islands campaign. Gloucester's time in Australia was accompanied by numerous bouts of ill-health, affecting not only the Duke himself, but also his family. Gloucester was not gregarious by nature and was not comfortable in his dealings with Australian politicians. He gave up office after only two years and returned to the UK, where he headed the Council of State set up during the absence of King George VI, Queen Elizabeth and the Princesses Elizabeth and Margaret in South Africa (February-May 1947).

Thereafter, Gloucester represented the King and (after her accession in 1952) Queen Elizabeth II on numerous visits to foreign and Commonwealth countries. He became a field marshal on 31 March 1955. The Duke of Gloucester suffered a minor stroke in March 1965, while on an official visit to Australia. In early 1966 he returned to London from a state visit to Malaysia and Singapore, amid increasing anxiety for his health. Late in May 1968 a further series of strokes left him confined to a wheelchair and unable to communicate. His elder son, Prince William, was killed in a flying accident on 28 August 1972.

Gloucester was nursed by his Duchess until his death on 9 June 1974, when he was succeeded as 2nd Duke by his younger son, Prince Richard.

The Duke of Gloucester was colonel-in-chief of the 10th Royal Hussars; the Gloucestershire Regiment; the Gordon Highlanders; the Royal Inniskilling Fusiliers and its successor, the Royal Irish Rangers, formed in 1968; the Rifle Brigade and its successor, the 3rd Green Jackets, formed in 1958, and the Royal Army Service Corps and its successor, the Royal Corps of Transport, formed in 1965. He was also colonel of the Scots Guards and, in the Territorial Army, honorary colonel in the Royal Artillery and the Cambridge University Contingent, Officers Training Corps. In Commonwealth Armies, the Duke was colonel-in-chief of the Royal Canadian Army Service Corps; the Royal Winnipeg Rifles; the Royal Australian Armoured Corps; the Royal Australian Army Service Corps; the Royal New Zealand Army Service Corps; the Ceylon Light Infantry and the Natal Mounted Rifles.

HIROHITO
HIM Emperor of Japan, KG, GCB, GCVO (1901–1989) **[99]**

The future Emperor Hirohito was born in Tokyo on 29 April 1901, the eldest of three sons of the Crown Prince (later Emperor) Yoshihito **[87]**. He was educated at the Gakushuin, or Peers' School, for the sons of the Japanese royal and noble families. There, under the headmastership of a noted guardian of traditional Japanese values, he was indoctrinated with the ideals of *bushido*, the code of the Japanese warrior class, based on the military virtues of discipline, courage and hardihood. Hirohito's frail physique, short sight and stooping posture made him ill-fitted to the harsh regime that this imposed on him. Despite a feeling among influential courtiers that he should be passed over in favour of his more robust younger brother (later Prince Chichibu), Hirohito was declared Crown Prince on 9 September 1913, the year after his father's accession to the throne. Hirohito was commissioned as a sub-lieutenant in the Imperial Navy and a second lieutenant in the army. He displayed no great enthusiasm for military training and devoted his studies mostly to the liberal arts and sciences, developing a special interest in marine biology. In 1918 he broke with tradition by making his own choice of a future bride, selecting a lady of noble birth, but not from the family into which it had been expected that he would marry.

In 1921 Hirohito travelled to Europe, the first Japanese Crown Prince to do so. He visited England and was made a general in the British Army on 9 May 1921. On returning from Europe in September 1921, he was declared Regent by virtue of his father's mental incapacity and succeeded to the Japanese throne on Emperor Yoshihito's death on 25 December 1925. After returning to Japan from the UK, Hirohito had begun to appear in public more frequently, following the example of the British Royal Family, but an assassination attempt on 27 December 1927 drove him back into seclusion.

Hirohito gave his new reign the name Showa (" Enlightened Peace") but political events soon overtook this. The Anglo-Japanese alliance, which had been of great benefit to both parties, was effectively ended by the Washington Naval Agreement of 1922. The British were forced by economic factors to accept equality in capital ships with the USA, while Japan was obliged to accept inferiority to the two great Western Navies. Under pressure from the governments of Canada and Australia, British ministers made it clear that, in the rivalry between Japan and the USA for power in the Pacific, they had no choice but to support the Americans. The Japanese, seeing this as a decision based on racial grounds, grew more nationalist and anti-Western. After the Depression of 1927, which had a drastic effect on the Japanese economy, Japan became increasingly militarist and xenophobic. Officers of the Army and Navy increasingly intervened in political decisions and the Ministers for War and the Marine (both of whom were serving officers) were able to veto Cabinet decisions by the threat of resignation. Civilian politicians who resisted the military were assassinated. Hirohito, to whom all Japanese officers and soldiers were bound by religious as well as military duty, expressed apprehension at these developments. Nevertheless, he acted against them only once, in February 1936, when he denied the publicity of a court-martial to military assassins who were subsequently executed for a particularly shocking set of political murders.

Hirohito was made a Knight of the Garter in 1928 (the insignia being presented to him by the Duke of Gloucester [121]) and became a British field marshal on 26 June 1930, but these gestures did little to improve Anglo-Japanese relations. He made no move to prevent Japan going to war either with China in 1937, or with the USA, the British Commonwealth, the Netherlands and the Philippines in December 1941. He played a minor part in the conduct of Japanese strategy, though the atrocities committed by Japanese personnel acting ostensibly in their Emperor's name made him the most hated of the Axis leaders. He supported his ministers while the war went well for Japan, but used his personal powers to order a Japanese surrender on 15

August 1945, after the destruction of Hiroshima and Nagasaki by atomic bombs.

Despite calls for him to be tried as a war criminal, Hirohito was kept on the throne on the advice of General Douglas MacArthur, the head of the Allied forces occupying Japan. MacArthur saw him as the only person with the authority to bring resistance to an end and also as a figurehead under whom Japan could be rebuilt as a democratic state. The sole concession to liberal opinion was that Hirohito was required to renounce his divinity as a living god, a status that he himself had earlier felt to be an anachronism in the modern world. In the post-war period Hirohito emerged as a constitutional monarch, reigning over a country which, under American tutelage, rebuilt itself from the ravages of war and became one of the dominant economies of the capitalist world. He lived quietly, devoting himself to research into marine biology and undertaking occasional public appearances in a non-political role. In 1971, during a state visit to the United Kingdom, Hirohito was restored to his position as a Knight of the Garter but not to the rank of field marshal of which he had been stripped on the outbreak of the Pacific War. He died of cancer of the pancreas at Tokyo on 7 January 1989, after the longest reign in the history of the Japanese monarchy, and was succeeded by his son, Akihito (born 22 December 1933).

Though Hirohito was not a military man, he was served and worshipped by the soldiers of a great Army, the brilliance of whose initial victories was later dimmed by barbaric crimes against helpless non-combatants and prisoners of war. His apologists argued that his ability to prevent or influence the conduct of the war was limited by the power of his ministers, whom he saw it as his duty to support. Others argued that he was a man of guile and ambivalence, whom no Japanese of any rank would have defied, had he declared himself against a policy of aggression.

HODGSON
STUDHOLME (1708–1798) [19]

Studholme Hodgson, a member of an obscure Cumbrian family, was born in 1708. He entered the Army on 2 January 1728, as an ensign in the 1st Foot Guards and lieutenant in the Army. It was not until 3 February 1741 that wartime expansion gave him the chance to rise to lieutenant in his regiment and captain in the Army. He served as an aide-de-camp at Fontenoy (11 May 1745) and Culloden (16 April 1746), where he was nicknamed "the old boy" by the Honourable Henry

Conway [12] and other young officers on Cumberland's staff. Hodgson was promoted to captain in his regiment and lieutenant colonel in the Army on 18 May 1747. He became the colonel of a newly-raised regiment (later the 50th Foot) on 30 May 1756 and served with it, as a brigade commander, in the expedition to Rochefort under Sir John Mordaunt and the Honourable Henry Conway in September 1757. Hodgson was promoted to major general on 25 June 1759 and became colonel of the 5th Foot in October 1759. Profiting from the lessons of Rochefort, he led the expedition that captured Belle-Île after a two-month siege, on 7 June 1761. Hodgson became a lieutenant general on 19 January 1761, was appointed colonel of the 4th Foot in November 1768 and was promoted to general on 2 April 1778. He was colonel of the 7th Dragoon Guards from June 1782 to March 1789, when he became colonel of the 11th Light Dragoons. He was promoted to field marshal with the six other senior generals in the army on 30 July 1796. His wife, Catherine, was the sister of another field marshal, Sir George Howard [14]. She died in April 1798, leaving two daughters and three sons. Field Marshal Hodgson died at Old Burlington Street, London, on 20 October 1798.

HOWARD
Sir GEORGE, KB (c.1720–1796) [14]

George Howard was one of four sons of Lieutenant General Thomas Howard, a distant relative of the influential family of the Earls of Effingham. Born sometime around 1720, he was appointed to his first commission on 20 February 1725, as a lieutenant in his father's regiment (later the 24th Foot). In 1737 Thomas Howard became the colonel of a more senior regiment (later the 3rd Foot, the Buffs), in which his son George then became a captain. George Howard reached military age a few years later and served in Germany during the War of the Austrian Succession. He was promoted to lieutenant colonel on 2 April 1744 and commanded the Buffs at Fontenoy (11 May 1745) before returning with them to the United Kingdom to meet the Jacobite Rising. During the subsequent campaign in Scotland he was at Falkirk (17 January 1746) and Culloden (16 April 1746), where he served under the Duke of Cumberland. Howard himself was condemned by Jacobite sympathizers for being conspicuously harsh in implementing Cumberland's measures against the defeated highlanders. He returned with Cumberland to the Continent and fought under his command at Laffeldt (La Val, 2 July 1747).

Howard succeeded his father as colonel of the Buffs on 21 August 1749 and was promoted to major general on 10 January 1750. He took part in the unsuccessful descent upon Rochefort led by Sir John Mordaunt and the Honourable Henry Conway [12] in September 1757 and later joined the Allied army in Germany under Prince Ferdinand of Brunswick. He became a lieutenant general on 22 February 1760 and commanded a brigade at the battle of Warburg (31 July 1760). Howard entered Parliament in 1762, where he sat as MP for Lostwithiel until 1766 and for Stanford from 1768. He was made a Knight of the Bath in 1763 and became colonel of the 7th Dragoons on 18th August 1763. Sir George Howard was promoted to general on 29 August 1777 and became colonel of the 1st King's Dragoon Guards on 21 August 1779. When the rank of field marshal was revived on 12 October 1793, he was the third senior general in the Army, after Conway and the Duke of Gloucester [13], and was promoted with them. He died at Sackville Street, London, on 16 July 1796. Howard was married to Mary Morton, daughter of the Bishop of Meath, and had a family. His sister, Catherine, was married to another field marshal, Studholme Hodgson [19].

HOWARD DE WALDEN
LORD, see **GRIFFIN**, Sir JOHN, [18]

HULL
Sir RICHARD AMYATT, KG, GCB, DSO (1907–1989) [126]

Richard Hull was born at Cosham, Hampshire, on 7 May 1907. He was the only son and youngest of the three children of a brevet major in the Royal Scots Fusiliers who later became a major general and commanded the 56th (London) Division in the First World War. Hull was educated at Charterhouse School and Trinity College, Cambridge, where he gained a pass degree before being commissioned as a second lieutenant on 7 May 1928. He joined the 17th/21st Lancers from the General List shortly before their departure for Egypt in October 1928. Hull became a lieutenant on 7 May 1931 and was promoted to captain on 1 June 1933, before going with his regiment to India in October 1933. In 1934 he married Antoinette Labouchère de Rougement, the daughter of an official in the Bank of Egypt, and later had a son and two daughters. When the 17th/21st Lancers were mechanized in 1938 Hull, as adjutant, drove the first tank to arrive in the regiment. He attended the

Indian Staff College, Quetta, in 1938–1939, before returning to the UK with his regiment in the summer of 1939. Hull served in the Directorate of Staff Duties at the War Office as a General Staff officer, grade 3, from February to June 1940, and as a GSO 2 until February 1941. He was promoted to temporary major on 1 March 1941, when he became the officer commanding "C" Squadron, the 17th/21st Lancers. After a brief return to staff duty, he was given command of the regiment, replacing an exercise fatality, with promotion to acting lieutenant colonel on 22 August 1941. He became a GSO 1 in June 1942 and served on the staff of the Canadian Armoured Division and of No.2 Group, Royal Armoured Corps, until September 1942.

Hull was then given command of Blade Force, an independent regimental group formed around the 17th/21st Lancers. This landed in Algeria in November 1942 and advanced rapidly to the outskirts of Tunis. He was awarded the DSO for his conduct at Tebourba Gap (30 November 1942). When Blade Force was broken up at the end of this phase of the campaign, Hull became second in command of the 26th Armoured Brigade. On 17 April 1943 he became a war substantive lieutenant colonel, temporary colonel and acting brigadier in command of the 12th Infantry Brigade. He later returned to the 26th Armoured Brigade, which he commanded until the end of the Tunisian campaign. Between December 1943 and August 1944 he was Deputy Director, Staff Duties, at the War Office. Hull then became acting major general as GOC 1st Armoured Division, which he commanded at Coriano (5 September 1944) in an unsuccessful attempt to outflank the German defence line in Northern Italy. He was promoted to substantive major on 7 May 1945 and to war substantive colonel and temporary major general on 12 August 1945.

Hull remained in command of his division until May 1946, when he became commandant of the Staff College, Camberley, with substantive promotion to major general on 21 October 1946. Between September 1948 and November 1950 he was Director of Staff Duties at the War Office. Throughout 1951 and 1952 he was a chief instructor at the Imperial Defence College. Hull served as Chief of Staff, Middle East Land Forces, from January 1953 to June 1954, after which he became the last GOC British Troops, Egypt. He was promoted to lieutenant general on 29 September 1954 and was awarded the KCB in 1956. Sir Richard Hull was Deputy Chief of the Imperial General Staff from October 1956 to April 1958. He then served as C-in-C Far Eastern Land Forces between June 1958 and May 1961. He became, in November 1961, the last Chief of the Imperial General Staff, and remained in that office (renamed Chief of the General Staff in April 1964) until 7

February 1965. His period as CIGS coincided with the despatch of British troops to Kuwait to forestall an Iraqi invasion in 1961, confrontation with Indonesia in Borneo and a militarily successful counter-insurgency campaign in the Radfan. He was on bad terms with the Chief of Defence Staff, Earl Mountbatten, whom Hull, like the Chiefs of the other two Services, considered unscrupulous and deceitful.

Hull was promoted to field marshal on 8 April 1965 and became Chief of the Defence Staff in July 1965. In this post, faced with demands by the Labour Secretary of State for Defence, Denis Healey, for further reductions in expenditure, he supported the Royal Air Force against the Royal Navy by recommending that large aircraft carriers were no longer needed. This period also saw the withdrawal of British forces from Singapore and Aden, together with the successful defiance of British authority by the government of Rhodesia. He retired from active duty at the end of his tour as CDS in August 1967 and became a director of a large brewing company. He was colonel of the 17th/21st Lancers from July 1947 to June 1957, colonel commandant of the Royal Armoured Corps from April 1968 to April 1971 and honorary colonel of the Cambridge University Contingent, Officers Training Corps, from May 1958 to May 1968. He retired from business in 1976 to his family home at Pinhoe, near Exeter, where he died of cancer on 17 September 1989. After a state funeral at Windsor, he was buried in the churchyard of St Michael and All Angels, Pinhoe. He was awarded the KG in 1980.

HULSE
Sir SAMUEL, GCH (1747–1837) [32]

Samuel Hulse, the second son of a baronet from an eminent medical family, was born in 1747. He was first commissioned on 17 December 1761, as an ensign in the 1st Foot Guards and lieutenant in the Army, and was promoted to lieutenant in the regiment and captain in the Army on 2 August 1769. He saw no active duty until June 1780 when, as a captain in his regiment and lieutenant colonel in the Army, he was called out to deal with the Gordon Riots in London. Hulse became a colonel in the Army on 20 November 1782. He was promoted to major in his regiment on 12 March 1789 and commanded its 1st Battalion in the 1793 Flanders campaign at Valenciennes (May-June 1793) and Dunkirk (August 1793). Hulse was promoted to major general on 17 October 1793. During the 1794 Flanders campaign he was in command of a brigade at Willems (10 May 1794) and in the winter retreat into Germany. Between 1795 and 1797, Hulse commanded troops in the

Brighton area. He was promoted to lieutenant general on 1 January 1798 and was sent to Ireland at the time of the 1798 rebellion, but returned without being actively engaged. Hulse served in the expedition to the Helder in September and October 1799. He became GOC South-East District, with promotion to general on 25 September 1803.

Hulse was colonel successively of the 56th Foot from March 1795, the 19th Foot from January 1797 and the 62nd Foot from June 1810. He served for many years as a member of the household of the Prince Regent and was made a knight of the Guelphic Order of Hanover on the Prince's succession to the throne as George IV in 1820. In the same year he was appointed Governor of the Royal Hospital, Chelsea. When William IV created two field marshals to mark his coronation, Sir Samuel Hulse was the second senior general in the Army after Sir Alured Clarke [31] and was promoted with him on 22 July 1830. Hulse, who never married, died at the Royal Hospital on 1 January 1837. and was buried in his family vault at Erith, Kent.

INGE
Sir PETER ANTHONY, 1st Baron Inge, KG, GCB (1935-)
[138]

Peter Inge was born on 5 August 1935. He was educated at Wrekin College, Shropshire, and entered the Army as a National Serviceman in September 1953. After attending Eaton Hall Officer Cadet School, he joined the Royal Military Academy Sandhurst (Burma Company, Victory College) in March 1955 and was commissioned as a second lieutenant in the Green Howards (Alexandra, Princess of Wales's Own Yorkshire Regiment) on 27 July 1956. He was promoted to lieutenant on 27 July 1958 and served with the 1st Battalion of his regiment in Hong Kong from 1958 to 1959. During this period, he undertook an operational tour in Malaya, attached to the Rifle Brigade. He served with his battalion at Iserlohn, in the British Army of the Rhine, from 1959 to 1960, before becoming aide-de-camp to the GOC 4th Division. In 1960 Inge married Letitia Thornton-Berry, with whom he later had two daughters. He was promoted to captain and became adjutant of his battalion on 26 July 1962. After a period of regimental duty in Libya, Inge entered the Staff College, Camberley, in 1965. On 19 January 1967 he became an acting major on appointment as a General Staff officer, grade 2, in the Army Staff Duties Directorate at the Ministry of Defence. Inge was promoted to substantive major on 31 January 1967. He returned to his battalion as a company commander at the beginning of 1969 and in June-August 1970 took part in operational duties in aid of the civil power in Northern Ireland. During 1971 he was at the Joint Services Staff College at Latimer, Buckinghamshire. Inge was brigade major of the 11th Armoured Brigade from August 1971 to October 1972, with promotion to lieutenant colonel on 30 June 1972. Between October 1972 and December 1974 he was an instructor (GSO 1) at the Staff College, Camberley. He was commanding officer of the 1st Battalion, the Green Howards, from December 1974 to February 1977, during which period his unit undertook two operational tours in aid of the civil power in Northern Ireland (April-August 1975 and April-May 1976) before moving to Berlin in 1976. Inge was promoted to colonel on 30 June 1976. From February 1977 to December 1979 he was commandant of the Staff College's Junior Division, Warminster. He was given command of Task Force "C"(later the 4th Armoured Brigade) in the British Army of the Rhine in December 1979, with promotion to brigadier on 30 June 1979.

Inge remained in Germany as Chief of Staff of I (British) Corps, from February 1982 until December 1983, when he became GOC North Eastern District and 2nd Infantry Division, based at York. Between February 1986 and May 1987, he was in London as Director General, Logistics Policy (Army) in the Quartermaster General's Department at the Ministry of Defence. He was promoted to lieutenant general on 8 August 1987 on assuming the command of I (British) Corps and was created a KCB. In November 1989, Sir Peter Inge became the commander of NATO's Northern Army Group and C-in-C, BAOR. He was promoted to general on 3 September 1990 and returned to the UK in February 1992, when he was appointed Chief of the General Staff. At short notice Inge became Chief of the Defence Staff, with promotion to field marshal, on 15 March 1994, after his predecessor, an officer in another service, resigned over a matter of personal conduct. Sir Peter Inge served in this appointment until the expiry of the normal three-year period of tenure in April 1997.

His time in office as CGS and CDS coincided with demands by the Conservative government of the day for continued economies in defence expenditure. In 1995 one of a number of reviews of defence questions (the Betts report, headed by an eminent businessman) included in its findings a recommendation that the existing practice of promoting the Chiefs of the three armed services (on their retirement) and the Chiefs of the Defence Staff (on their appointment) to be Admirals of the Fleet, Field Marshals, or Marshals of the Royal Air Force respectively should be discontinued. The original proposal of the Betts report was to abolish these ranks altogether, but it was subsequently agreed that they should remain available for award in the event of a major war or other special circumstances. Sir Peter Inge thus became the last field marshal to be promoted to that rank as a normal consequence of serving as CGS or CDS. He was granted a life peerage as Baron Inge of Richmond in 1997. Lord Inge was colonel commandant of the Army Physical Training Corps from September 1988 to April 1997 and of the Corps of Royal Military Police from 1987 until April 1992. He was colonel of the Green Howards from July 1982 to December 1994. After retiring from active duty, Lord Inge undertook a wide range of charitable commitments, as well as a number of consultancies and directorships in the defence and electronics industries. He was awarded the KG in April 2001.

IRONSIDE
Sir WILLIAM EDMUND, 1st Baron Ironside, GCB, CMG, DSO (1880–1959) [107]

Edmund Ironside was born in Edinburgh on 6 May 1880, the only son and second child of Surgeon Major William Ironside MD, an officer who spent most of his career as a regimental surgeon with the Royal Artillery. Surgeon Major Ironside died in January 1881, leaving his widow in reduced circumstances. For a time she travelled with her young children on the Continent, where Edmund developed a facility for foreign languages which would play an important part in his career. Edmund Ironside was educated at Tonbridge School and the Royal Military Academy, Woolwich, before being commissioned as a second lieutenant in the Royal Artillery on 25 June 1899. He joined the field artillery as a section commander in the 44th Battery and served with this unit during the South African War from February 1900 until May 1902. Ironside was at Kheis Drift (28 May 1900) and took part in various operations during the guerrilla phase of the war. He was promoted to lieutenant on 16 February 1901 and was mentioned in despatches in September 1901.

After the war Ironside spent two years in German South-West Africa (Namibia) using his language skills to disguise himself as a Boer oxwagon-driver and to gain employment by the German military authorities as a scout. He eventually came under suspicion when the Germans noticed that his pet bulldog was wearing a collar with the name, rank and regiment of a British officer. The writer John Buchan later based the character "Richard Hannay" in his novel *The Thirty-Nine Steps* on this period in Ironside's career. Ironside then returned to regimental duty, first in I Battery (Bull's Troop), Royal Horse Artillery, in northern India, and then with Y Battery, Royal Horse Artillery, in Pretoria from 1907. He was promoted to captain on 18 February 1908 and was appointed a brigade major on 26 September 1908, remaining in South Africa where he served with both cavalry and infantry formations. In 1913 Ironside went to the Staff College, Camberley, from which he passed out the following year. He also studied the Russian language and qualified as an Army linguist.

At the beginning of the First World War in August 1914 Ironside obtained a staff appointment at the British disembarkation port of Boulogne. When the 6th Division arrived in France in mid-September 1914 Ironside joined it as a General Staff officer, grade 3. He served in this division on the Aisne and at the first battle of Ypres (19 October–21 November 1914), with promotion to major on 30 October 1914. Ironside became a GSO 2 in the 6th Division in February 1915 and remained with it until the end of February 1916. He was then recalled to the UK to become GSO 1 of the newly-formed 4th Canadian Division. This formation was commanded by a Canadian Militia officer, Major General D Watson, who in civil life was the wealthy proprietor of a Montreal newspaper and, as a businessman, made full use of Ironside's expertise in staff duties. Ironside became a brevet lieutenant colonel on 3 June 1916. The 4th Canadian Division moved to France in August 1916, to be kept in reserve as part of II Corps during the later stages of the battle of the Somme. It then joined the Canadian Corps, under Sir Julian Byng [100]. Ironside served with the 4th Canadian Division in all its operations, including Vimy Ridge (9–14 April 1917) and the third battle of Ypres (31 July–6 November 1917) until the beginning of 1918. Then, with the Canadian Army able to provide its own staff officers, Ironside was appointed commandant of the British Army's Machine Gun Corps school at Camiers, as a temporary lieutenant colonel. During the German offensive of Spring 1918 he was sent with his school's guns and staff to hold a gap in the British line. On 27 March 1918, Ironside was given command of the 99th Infantry Brigade, as a battle casualty replacement. He was promoted to temporary brigadier general and commanded this formation in the fighting around Albert and Bapaume until 6 September 1918, when he was unexpectedly ordered back to London.

Ironside was then appointed chief of staff of the British contingent in the Allied force occupying Archangel (Archangelsk). Shortly after Ironside's arrival, the British GOC in Archangel decided to return to England on leave. Ironside assumed command and was appointed C-in-C Allied Forces, with promotion to temporary major general on 19

186

October 1918. The Armistice of 11 November 1918 made little immediate difference to the situation at Archangel, where Allied policy was to
support the White forces in what had become a Russian civil war.
Ironside commanded a multinational force composed of British, French,
Americans, Poles and a Slav Legion of Russian soldiers in British pay.
He waged a minor campaign in support of the Whites during the winter
of 1918–1919, but a vigorous counter-offensive by the Red Army,
coupled with a series of mutinies among his own forces, prevented him
from achieving any real success. He returned to the UK with a lasting
antipathy to the cause of international socialism. He had become a
substantive colonel on 1 January 1919 and reverted to that rank until 11
November 1919, when he was awarded the KCB and promoted to
substantive major general in recognition of his services in North Russia.

Sir Edmund Ironside was placed on the half-pay list until February
1920. Having learned the Magyar language when a subaltern, he was
then sent to report on the situation in Hungary, where a Regency had
been established by the counter-revolutionary Admiral Horthy. Ironside
was disposed to sympathize with the Hungarians, who had been on the
defeated side in the First World War and had lost territory in the post-
war settlement. He also approved of Horthy's suppression of the
Hungarian Communists and accepted at face value his assurances that
no kind of "White Terror" had taken place.

In July 1920 Sir George Milne [97], British C-in-C in the area
surrounding the Black Sea, asked the War Office to send him a young
fighting major general who could speak French. Ironside fitted these
requirements and accordingly was given command of a division-sized
British force holding Ismid (Izmit) on the eastern side of the Sea of
Marmora. Ironside now sympathized with the defeated Turks, as he had
with the Hungarians, but after a few weeks at Ismid, he was ordered to
hand over the city to the Greeks, in accordance with the recently-signed
Treaty of Sevres. In mid- August 1920, for the second time within a
year, he found himself organizing the evacuation and dispersal of his
command. His services were then asked for by Sir Aylmer Haldane, the
British commander in Mesopotamia, with whom Ironside had served in
France in 1918. He was given command of the North Persian Force, a
large all-arms brigade of British and Indian troops, and played a part in
securing the dismissal of the White Russian (and by this time anti-
British) officers of the Shah's Persian Cossack Brigade. Ironside's
troops engaged in a number of minor combats against local warlords
and others whom he saw as agents of the Russian Bolsheviks, but once
again soon found himself ordered to withdraw British stores and troops
from the theatre in which he commanded.

At the Cairo conference of 1921, where the future form of British rule in the Middle East was settled, Ironside represented the Mesopotamia (renamed Iraq) Command. He had long been on friendly terms with Winston Churchill, the British Colonial Secretary of the time, whom he had met during the South African War. Despite the strong disapproval of Haldane and of most other Army officers, Ironside supported the proposal (first made by Churchill as Minister for Air) that responsibility for the defence and internal security of Iraq should be given to the Royal Air Force. Churchill chose Ironside to succeed Haldane, but taking over his new command, Ironside was involved, on 8 April 1921, in his second flying accident within a year. Unscathed on the first occasion, he now broke his legs so seriously that both were shortened by an inch and a half, reducing his immense height, from which he derived the nickname "Tiny", to six feet four inches (1.9 metres). Convalescent, he spent his time learning Arabic. His injuries preventing him from taking command in Iraq, he was sent back to the UK in July 1921 and placed on the half-pay. Despondent at his prospects, he considered leaving the Army, but was then appointed commandant of the Staff College, Camberley, where he assumed office in April 1923.

Ironside became GOC 2nd Division at Aldershot in 1926, followed by appointment as GOC Meerut District, Northern India, in 1928. He was promoted to lieutenant general on 1 March 1931 and returned to the half-pay list. In January 1932 he became a colonel commandant of the Royal Artillery. He went back to India as Quartermaster General in 1933 and was promoted to general on 30 June 1935. He returned to the UK to become GOC-in-C Eastern Command in April 1936. Ironside was appointed Governor and C-in-C, Gibraltar, in November 1938, with the prospect of becoming C-in-C, Middle East, in the event of a major war. He returned to London in July 1939 to become Inspector General of Overseas Forces. As relations between the British and German governments deteriorated, Ironside was sent on an official visit to Poland and returned with an optimistic assessment of the abilities of the Polish Army. On mobilization at the beginning of the Second World War in September 1939, Ironside expected to be given command of the British Expeditionary Force. He sent his staff to make preparations in Aldershot while he waited in London for orders, only to find that command of the BEF was given to Lord Gort [110], the Chief of the Imperial General Staff, and that he was appointed as CIGS in Gort's place.

Ironside's period as CIGS was not a happy one. He had never served in the War Office, and felt irritated and frustrated by long conferences that seemed to him to settle nothing. He was critical of what he saw as a lack of proper organization and was confirmed in his existing view that Gort had been out of his depth as CIGS. Like Gort, Ironside disliked the Secretary of State for War, Leslie Hore-Belisha, partly because of his extrovert and self-advertising manner and partly because he concerned himself with what the generals considered purely professional matters. When the Prime Minister, Neville Chamberlain, removed Hore-Belisha from the War Office in January 1940, Ironside recorded a feeling of intense relief. Ironside had maintained his friendship with Winston Churchill during the latter's years out of office, even to the extent of passing on to him information he acquired during official pre-war visits to Germany and Poland. Churchill, who became First Lord of the Admiralty in September 1939, gave strong support to Ironside's appointment as CIGS. Ironside, still anti-Bolshevik in his sympathies, backed the abortive proposal to send troops to support Finland against the Soviet Union at the end of September 1939. The Norwegian campaign of April-June 1940, ending in disaster for the Allies, led him for the first time to question the judgement of his old friend Churchill (who had pressed for, and largely directed, this adventure). At the same time, the appointment of Sir John Dill [109] to the newly created post of Vice Chief of the General Staff, taking over many of the day-to-day duties of the CIGS, indicated that his own ability was being called into question.

The opening of the German offensive in the West on 10 May 1940 came shortly after Ironside had been quoted in the *Daily Express* as saying that, confident in the ability of the Allies to meet it, he would welcome just such an attack. Ten days later, learning that Gort was preparing to retreat to the coast, Ironside went to France with instructions from Churchill (Prime Minister since 9 May 1940) that he should join in a proposed French counter-offensive. Having seen the situation for himself, Ironside despaired of the French Army's willingness to fight and accepted Gort's view that, for the BEF, evacuation was the only option. On 27 May 1940, on Churchill's prompting, Ironside resigned as CIGS and was appointed C-in-C Home Forces. This post, in which Ironside would have commanded the Home Forces in battle in the event of a German invasion, was more congenial to his temperament, but ambitious rivals who had experienced German *Blitzkrieg* tactics in France, criticized his strategy, based on a series of static "stop-lines", as out-of-date. Churchill lost confidence in Ironside and on 19 July 1940 replaced him as C-in-C Home Forces by Sir Alan Brooke [112]. Ironside was promoted to field marshal on 20 July 1940 and was raised to the peerage as Baron Ironside, of Archangel and of Ironside. He retired to his home at Hingham, Norfolk, and took no further part in

189

public life. Ironside married, in 1915, Mariot Ysabel Cheyne, the daughter of a retired colonel of the Indian Army. They had later a daughter and a son, who succeeded as second baron on Ironside's death at the Queen Alexandra Military Hospital, Millbank, London, on 22 September 1959.

JACOB
Sir CLAUD WILLIAM, GCB, GCSI, KCMG
(1863–1948) **[96]**

Claud Jacob, the son of Lieutenant (later Major General) William Jacob, an officer in the 19th Bombay Native Infantry, was born in Mahidpur, India, on 21 November 1863. He was educated at Sherborne School, Dorset, and the Royal Military College, Sandhurst, before being commissioned on 9 September 1882 as a lieutenant in the Worcestershire Regiment. He joined this regiment in India and, in 1884, having completed the obligatory period of service with a British unit, transferred to the Bombay Staff Corps, the body to which all officers of the Bombay Army at this time belonged. In July 1886 he became adjutant of the 30th Bombay Infantry (Jacob's Rifles), a regiment that had been raised by another member of his family, Sir John Jacob, for service on the Upper Sind Frontier. Claud Jacob was with this unit in the Zhob Valley Expedition of 1890 and joined the 24th Bombay Infantry at Loralai, Baluchistan, in 1891. He spent the next twenty years as a regimental officer on the North-West Frontier, where his appointments included command of the Zhob Valley Levy Corps and the 106th Hazara Pioneers, a regiment that he raised in 1906. Jacob was promoted to captain on 9 September 1893, major on 10 July 1901, lieutenant colonel on 1 October 1904 and colonel on 1 January 1911. In 1894 he married Clara Wyatt, the daughter of a missionary at Trichinopoly. They later had a son who became a general in the Second World War.

Jacob left the frontier in 1912 to become a General Staff officer in the Meerut Division. After the outbreak of the First World War in August 1914 he went with this formation to France as part of the Indian Corps and took part in the final stages of the battle of La Bassée (24 October–1 November 1914). In January 1915 he became brigadier general of the Dehra Dun Brigade, which he commanded at the battles of Neuve Chapelle (10–13 March 1915) and Aubers Ridge (9 May 1915). He was appointed GOC Meerut Division on 6 September 1915 and commanded this formation during the battle of Loos (25 September–13 October 1915). When the Indian Corps was withdrawn from the

Western Front at the end of October 1915, Jacob remained in that theatre and was given command of the 21st Division, with promotion to temporary major general on 18 November 1915. He became a substantive major general on 1 January 1916. In March 1916 he was wounded by a German shell that hit his divisional HQ and killed his senior staff officer. In September 1916, Jacob became a temporary lieutenant general on appointment to command II Corps, just before the British attack at Thiepval (26 September 1916). He was made a substantive lieutenant general on 3 June 1917 and was awarded the KCB. Sir Claud Jacob remained in command of II Corps during the third battle of Ypres (31 July- 6 November 1917) and in the campaigns of 1918. At the end of the war he served with this Corps in the British Army of Occupation in the Rhineland, before returning to India as Chief of the General Staff at Army HQ in January 1920. He was promoted to general on 31 May 1920. Between 1924 and 1925 he was GOC-in-C, Northern Command, India. On the death in office of Lord Rawlinson in 1925, Jacob took over as officiating C-in-C, India. When the permanent appointment was given to Sir William Birdwood [95], Jacob became Secretary of the Military Department at the India Office in London. He held this post from 1926, with promotion to field marshal on the Indian establishment on 30 November 1926, until his retirement from active duty in 1930. He became colonel of the 2nd Battalion, 10th Baluch Regiment, in 1928 and was colonel of the Worcestershire Regiment from February 1927 to November 1938. Sir Claud Jacob died on 2 June 1948.

KENT AND STRATHEARN
HRH DUKE OF, see **EDWARD AUGUSTUS [23]**

KENT
HRH 2nd DUKE OF, see **EDWARD GEORGE NICHOLAS PAUL [137]**

KITCHENER
Sir Herbert Horatio, 1st Earl Kitchener, KG, KP, GCB, OM, GCSI, GCMG, GCIE, (1850–1916) **[79]**

Herbert Kitchener was born on 24 June 1850 in Listowel, County Kerry, the second son of a former major of the 9th Foot who had no

Irish connections, but bought an estate there after selling his commission in 1845. Major Kitchener made himself unpopular with his neighbours and tenants and eventually moved to Switzerland, where his three sons completed their education at Montreux. After the death of his first wife in 1864, he remarried and went to live in France. Herbert Kitchener entered the Royal Military Academy, Woolwich, in 1868. Always a Francophile, he visited his father at Dinant, from where he joined the Army of the Loire, one of the French armies fighting in the Franco-Prussian War of 1870–71. Notionally a member of a field ambulance unit, he took the chance of a balloon ascent, caught a chill and nearly died of pleurisy. On recovering, he was summoned before the Duke of Cambridge [45], C-in-C of the British Army, who reproved him in colourful language for this breach of neutrality by a British gentleman cadet and then told him to go away and never do it again. Kitchener was commissioned as a lieutenant in the Royal Engineers on 4 January 1871. He had developed an interest in biblical studies and in the history of Palestine and in 1874, after serving at Chatham and Aldershot, was lent to the Palestine Exploration Fund. He spent the next four years undertaking surveys of Palestine, at that time a province of the Ottoman Empire. In the process, he became fluent in Arabic. In September 1878, Kitchener was sent to join the survey of Cyprus (newly-acquired as a British protectorate under the Anglo-Turkish agreement of June 1878). He was employed in this project until 1883, with a brief and unauthorized visit to Egypt, where he landed in disguise at the time of the British naval bombardment of Alexandria in July 1882. In Cyprus, he developed a dislike for the High Commissioner, Sir Garnet Wolseley [67] and for Lady Wolseley, who, in the young Kitchener's view, was the one who "drove the coach".

Kitchener became a captain on 4 January 1883 and was released from the Cyprus survey to become one of the twenty-six British officers with whom Sir Evelyn Wood [74] began the reconstruction of the Egyptian Army. He became second-in-command of an Egyptian cavalry regiment in February 1883. During Wolseley's Sudan campaign (1884–85), Kitchener was employed in intelligence-gathering duties and, in Arab disguise, was the last British officer to maintain a link with Major General Charles Gordon before Khartoum fell to the Mahdi in January 1885. He was promoted to major in the Royal Engineers on 8 October 1884. After the Anglo-Egyptian forces abandoned the Sudan, he resigned his Egyptian commission in July 1885 and was appointed the British representative on the Zanzibar Boundary Commission. Kitchener was promoted to lieutenant colonel on 15 June 1885. In September 1886 he was appointed Governor of the Egyptian provinces of Eastern Sudan and Red Sea Littoral. In practice, Egyptian authority was confined to the area around Suakin, where the town was constantly threatened by Mahdist forces. Kitchener led his troops against them at Handub (17 January 1888), where he was wounded in the jaw. He remained in office as Governor and was promoted to brevet colonel on 11 April 1888. Shortly after repulsing a Mahdist attack on Suakin on 20 December 1890, he was posted to Cairo as Adjutant General of the Egyptian Army.

There, Kitchener found his *métier* as a military administrator, although he also served as a field commander and led the Egyptian cavalry at Toski (3 August 1889). He became Sirdar (C-in-C) of the Egyptian Army in April 1892 and was awarded the KCMG in 1894. He then prepared the campaign that made his reputation, the re-conquest of the Sudan. Sir Herbert Kitchener's successes at Firket (7 June 1896) and Hafir (19 September 1896) kindled popular support for the Sudan War among the British public, while his economical methods found favour among British politicians. He was promoted to major general on 25 September 1896. The Anglo-Egyptian army defeated the Mahdists at the Atbara (8 April 1898) and, decisively, at Omdurman (2 September 1898). Kitchener earned a rebuke from Queen Victoria for his desecration of the Mahdi's tomb, but was otherwise the hero of the hour and was raised to the peerage as Baron Kitchener of Khartoum, and of Aspall. Encountering at Fashoda a small French military column claiming access to the White Nile, he dressed tactfully in Egyptian uniform and withdrew, leaving an Egyptian garrison. Lord Kitchener was appointed Governor-General of the Sudan in December 1898 and, in a departure from his previous policy of parsimony, began an ambitious programme of public expenditure.

In December 1899, when, after the early British disasters in the South African War, Lord Roberts **[68]** was sent to South Africa as C-in-C, Kitchener went with him as Chief of Staff and was promoted to lieutenant general on 23 December 1899. Acting as a deputy commander rather than as a staff officer, he was at the relief of Kimberley (15 February 1900) and launched an unsuccessful attack at Paardeberg (18 February 1900) before the arrival of Roberts the following day. After Paardeberg, Kitchener was not present at any major engagements except for Venterskroon (7–9 August 1900). He succeeded Roberts as C-in-C, South Africa, on 29 November 1900. Faced with a guerrilla war, he eventually wore down Boer resistance by constructing lines of blockhouses (to restrict the mobility of the Boer commandos still in the field), burning farms (so as to deny them supplies) and putting their displaced families into concentration camps. He was promoted to general on 1 June 1902. After returning home to a hero's welcome, he came under pressure from the Cabinet to go to the War Office and undertake the post-war reform of the British Army. He declined, saying that he would only be thwarted by the politicians.

In 1902 Kitchener was advanced in the peerage to become Viscount Kitchener of Khartoum, and of the Vaal and of Aspall, and was appointed C-in-C, India, a post he had long sought. He changed the Army in India from a garrison force, organized primarily to hold India against the threat of another Mutiny, into a modern army with nine field divisions and corps troops kept up on a permanent basis, instead of being formed only when hostilities were imminent. To emphasize the unification of the Indian Army, he renumbered its regiments in a common sequence and abolished all reference to the former Bengal, Madras and Bombay Armies. Kitchener argued that Indian Army regiments should serve anywhere in the Indian Empire, including the North-West Frontier, and that all sepoys should be capable of facing European troops (in particular Russians, in a campaign in Central Asia). He therefore carried to extremes the policy of replacing South Indian sepoys by men from the so-called "martial classes", drawn mostly from the northern or western parts of the sub-continent. In 1902, he became colonel of the newly-raised 7th Gurkha Rifles. He believed that all military affairs should be concentrated under one authority and insisted on the abolition of the Government of India's Military Department (the "War Office" of British India), with the transfer of its functions to the C-in-C, India. In particular, he objected to the long-established practice whereby a general of long Indian experience, but of lower rank than the C-in-C, sat as Military Member of the Governor-General of India's Council. The Viceroy and Governor-General of the day, Lord Curzon, objected to Kitchener's plan, on the grounds that the Government of India would be left with only a single source of advice on military subjects. Both men used their contacts in London to press their respective arguments and each threatened to resign if not supported. The British Cabinet felt that it could not afford to lose the first soldier of the Empire (especially with the imminent prospect of a war against Russia in Central Asia) so that it was Curzon whose resignation was accepted in November 1905.

Kitchener became a colonel commandant of the Royal Engineers, in April 1905. His tour as C-in-C, India, was extended in 1907 for a further two years, at the end of which he was promoted to field marshal on 10 September 1909. After touring Australia and New Zealand, to advise the governments of these new dominions on the organization of their defence forces, Kitchener hoped that he would be nominated as the next Viceroy and Governor-General of India. Learning that this post would not be offered to him, Kitchener declined the Mediterranean Command (from which the Duke of Connaught [73] had just resigned) and sought, unsuccessfully, to be appointed the British Ambassador at Constantinople. In June 1911 he was given the post of Consul General in Egypt, through which the British ruled the country on behalf of a puppet Khedive. Kitchener came to regard Egypt as his spiritual home and departed from the practice of his predecessors by seeking to enter Egyptian society and by entertaining Egyptians at his official residence. Nevertheless, his pharaonic style of government offended Egyptian nationalists and humiliated the Khedive (with whom he had clashed earlier, when Sirdar of the Egyptian Army). Kitchener was given a further advancement in the peerage in June 1914, when he became Earl Kitchener of Khartoum and of Broome. On the outbreak of the First World War in August 1914 he was on leave in London.

On 5 August 1914 Earl Kitchener was persuaded by the Liberal Prime Minister, Herbert Asquith, to become Secretary of State for War. Despite some reservations by both men, the appointment was greeted with enthusiasm by the public. Kitchener was one of the few who forecast a long war. He persuaded his Cabinet colleagues to plan accordingly and called for thousands of volunteers to enlist in the Regular Army for the duration of hostilities. His idealized portrait appeared on one of the most potent recruiting posters in history and helped produce, in a matter of weeks, enough men for four new field armies, each of six divisions. Kitchener chose to disregard the Territorial Force as a vehicle for raising his New Armies. He was well acquainted with the Territorials and their predecessors, as he was honorary colonel of the Glasgow Engineers; the 6th Battalion, the Royal Scots (Lothian Regiment); the 1st County of London Yeomanry (Duke of Cambridge's Hussars) and the East Anglian Divisional Engineers. While acknowledging their patriotic spirit, he regarded them as amateurs, who were reluctant to accept the discipline expected of regular soldiers. What he had seen of some of the Yeomanry and Volunteer contingents that served under him in the South African War only strengthened this opinion. Nevertheless, despite his scathing description of the Territorials as a "Town Clerks' army", he made full use of municipal authorities in recruiting his new armies on a regional or local basis. Promising that those who enlisted together would serve together, he fostered the concept of "Pals' battalions" with sub-units from particular clubs, schools, or work-places.

On 1 September 1914 Kitchener rushed to France to prevent Sir John French [83], C-in-C of the British Expeditionary Force, from withdrawing his troops to rest and refit after a period of intense fighting. French, while complying with the instructions given by Kitchener as a member of the Cabinet, resented his appearance in the uniform of a field marshal (in which rank he was senior to French). He also suspected Kitchener of planning to arrive at the head of his new armies and to become the future victor in this campaign. French argued that the BEF was being starved of replacements and of experienced officers who were being diverted to the new armies. Although French and Kitchener had been on cordial terms in the South African War, they were not able to re-establish good relations and Kitchener greeted French's removal from command of the BEF at the end of 1915 with considerable relief.

Always distrustful of politicians and of any check on his authority, Kitchener disliked attending Cabinet meetings. David Lloyd George, at this time Chancellor of the Exchequer, later compared Kitchener's contribution to that of a lighthouse, illuminating the discussion with brief shafts of piercing light which then left everything as dark as before. Kitchener, who never married, withheld military information from his Cabinet colleagues on the grounds that they would pass it on to their wives, or, in the case of Asquith, to other people's wives. For a few months he was almost a military dictator and privately considered seeking the title of Captain General, with control over the entire war effort. By early 1915 his position began to weaken. There was a shortage of guns and shells, for which the War Office (and hence Kitchener) was blamed. In May 1915 a new Ministry of Munitions was formed, headed by Lloyd George, to take over responsibility for the supply of these items.

In deciding strategy, Kitchener formed the view that the German position on the Western Front had become a fortress that could not be stormed. He therefore supported a plan by Winston Churchill, the First Lord of the Admiralty, to outflank it by a campaign in the Dardanelles. The early failures of this campaign weakened Kitchener's influence and, when Asquith formed a Coalition government in May 1915, he was only retained in office at the insistence of the Unionists. With his Eastern experience, Kitchener argued that to abandon the Dardanelles campaign would inflict great damage to British prestige in Egypt and India. He was sent to examine the situation in person and visited the ANZAC beaches in November 1915. In his absence, Asquith took over the War Office and tried to persuade Kitchener to assume command of the Near Eastern theatre. Kitchener refused and returned to the UK to find that Sir Douglas Haig had taken French's place in command of the BEF and Sir William Robertson [92] had become Chief of the Imperial General Staff. Robertson insisted on being the Cabinet's sole adviser on strategy, with full control over the conduct of operations. Kitchener's functions were reduced to the War Office's peace-time role of administration. The concentration of military advice into the hands of one individual, the very principle for which Kitchener had fought so successfully in India, now meant that the Cabinet only heard the arguments in favour of concentrating on the Western Front, advocated by Robertson.

Kitchener, though no longer influential in Cabinet, was still too popular either to be dismissed or to be allowed to resign. In April 1916 he offered to head a British military mission to Petrograd to arrange moral and material aid to the war-weary Russians. Shortly after embarking in the cruiser *Hampshire* on 5 June 1916 he was drowned when the ship hit a mine and sank in bad weather off Orkney. His body was never found and wild rumours sprang up that the report of his death was deliberate disinformation and that he had survived and was living in a cave in the Hebrides to avoid reproach for the shell-shortage scandal, or that, like some legendary hero, he was merely waiting the call to return when the nation was in danger. Conspiracy theorists postulated that Irish extremists, German secret agents or an imagined secret society ("the Hidden Hand") had either planted a time-bomb or betrayed the cruiser, with its supposed cargo of gold, to a waiting U-boat. Kitchener's earldom was inherited, by special remainder, by his brother.

LAMBART
FREDERICK RUDOLPH, 10th Earl of Cavan, KP, GCB, GCMG, GCVO, GBE (1865–1946) [101]

The Honourable Frederick Lambart, the eldest son of the heir to an Irish peerage, was born on 16 October 1865, at the rectory of Ayot St Lawrence, Hertfordshire, the home of his maternal grandparents. He was educated at Eton College and at the Royal Military College, Sandhurst, from which he entered the Grenadier Guards as a lieutenant on 29 August 1885. Lambart assumed the courtesy title of Viscount Kilcoursie in 1887, when his father succeeded as the 9th Earl of Cavan. Between 1891 and 1893 Lord Kilcoursie was in Canada as aide-de-camp to the then Governor-General, Lord Stanley (later the 16th Earl of Derby). He then returned to regimental duty, where he became adjutant of his battalion and was promoted to captain on 16 October 1897. He served in the South African War from March 1900 to July 1902, commanding No 7 Company, the 2nd Battalion, Grenadier Guards, at Biddulphsberg (29 May 1900) and in minor engagements in the

Wittebergen area during July 1900. He succeeded his father as the 10th Earl of Cavan in July 1900. Lord Cavan took part in operations against Boer guerrilla forces during 1901 and was mentioned in despatches. He was promoted to major on 28 October 1902 and became second in command of the 2nd Battalion, Grenadier Guards, in July 1905. Cavan was given command of the 1st Battalion, Grenadier Guards, with promotion to lieutenant colonel, on 14 February 1908. He became a colonel on 4 October 1911 and went onto the half-pay list on 14 February 1912. After returning briefly to the full pay to command a brigade on manoeuvres in 1913, he transferred to the Reserve, to enjoy the life of a Hertfordshire country landowner and master of foxhounds.

Cavan was recalled to active duty on the outbreak of the First World War and was appointed a temporary brigadier general on 5 August 1914, in command of a Territorial brigade. On 17 September 1914, as a battle casualty replacement, he was given command of the 4th Guards Brigade, which included some of his former neighbours, serving in their local Territorial Force unit, the 1st Battalion, the Hertfordshire Regiment. He commanded this formation at the first battle of Ypres (19 October–22 November 1914) and at Festubert (May 1915). In June 1915, he became a temporary major general and GOC 50th (Northumbrian) Division. He became GOC the Guards Division in August 1915 and commanded it at Loos (25 September–13 October 1915). Cavan was given command of XIV Corps, with promotion to temporary lieutenant general, in January 1916 and served with this formation at the Somme during August 1916 and the third battle of Ypres (July-October 1917), becoming a substantive lieutenant general on 1 January 1917. He moved with XIV Corps to Italy in October 1917, after the victory of the Central Powers at Caporetto, and took over command of the British forces in Italy from Sir Herbert Plumer [89] in March 1918, when Plumer and many of his troops were recalled to meet the German offensive in France. Cavan withstood the Austro-Hungarian offensive of August 1918 and, commanding a small army of three British and two Italian divisions, launched a successful counter-attack on the Piave in September 1918.

After the end of hostilities, Cavan returned to the United Kingdom, where he was promoted to general on 2 November 1921 and appointed GOC-in-C Aldershot Command in 1922. He was appointed Chief of the Imperial General Staff in succession to Sir Henry Wilson [91] on 19 February 1922 and remained in this post until 1926, when he handed over to Sir George Milne [97]. He became colonel of the Irish Guards in May 1925 and of the Bedfordshire and Hertfordshire Regiment in December 1928, followed by promotion to field marshal on 31 October

1932. Cavan had married, in 1893, Caroline Crawley, who died without issue in 1920. In 1922 he married Lady Hester Mulholland, a niece of Viscount Byng [100] and the widow of an officer who had been killed in action during the First World War. They later had two daughters, but no sons, so that when he died in London on 28 August 1946 his earldom was inherited by his brother, the Archdeacon of Shrewsbury.

LENNOX
CHARLES, 3rd Duke of Richmond and Lennox, KG (1735–1806) [22]

Charles Lennox, born in London on 22 February 1735, was the third son of Charles, 2nd Duke of Richmond and Lennox, and Sarah, eldest daughter of the 1st Earl Cadogan. His parents' marriage had an unpromising start, as the bridegroom (at that time, as heir to the dukedom, known by the courtesy title Earl of March) entered the marriage only to settle a gaming debt between their respective fathers. March went abroad immediately after the wedding, without his bride, and undertook the "Grand Tour" then customary for young British noblemen. On his return three years later, he asked for an introduction to a lady whom he saw at the theatre, only to be informed that she, the reigning beauty in London, was his own countess. Their marriage was thereafter a happy one and they had twelve children (of whom the two elder boys died in infancy) before the 2nd Duke of Richmond's death in 1750 at the early age of 49. His duchess's death in 1751 was generally attributed to her grief at his loss.

Charles Lennox succeeded as 3rd Duke at the age of fifteen. Unable to sit as a peer until his twenty-first birthday, he finished his education at Westminster School and then attended Leyden University, where he graduated in 1753. He became a captain in the 20th Foot on 18 June 1753 and lieutenant colonel of the 33rd Foot on 7 June 1756. In April 1757 Richmond married Lady Mary Bruce, only child of the 3rd Earl of Elgin and his third wife, Caroline (the only sister of the 5th Duke of Argyll [16]). They had no children, though Richmond later acknowledged four natural daughters. His younger brother, Lord George Lennox, succeeded him as lieutenant colonel of the 33rd Foot in May 1758. During the Seven Years War Richmond himself served with the Allied army in Germany, under Prince Ferdinand of Brunswick. He was at Minden (1 August 1759), where he was mentioned in despatches The day before this battle, serving as one of Brunswick's ADCs and riding beside him on a high-mettled charger, he had accidentally jostled the

199

Prince and his horse into a deep ditch, where both nearly drowned. Richmond, who became colonel of the 72nd Foot and major general on 9 March 1761, remained in the field until the end of the war in 1763, after which his regiment was disbanded.

Richmond then embarked on the political career of a great nobleman of his time. He supported the party of the Duke of Cumberland until that prince's death in 1767 and opposed the policies of William Pitt the Elder. He was British Ambassador in Paris from August 1765 to May 1766. He then became Secretary of State for the Southern Department, only to resign when Pitt (newly created Earl of Chatham) resumed office in the following August. He was promoted to lieutenant general on 30 April 1770 and continued to oppose the government, especially over its policy towards the American colonies. Richmond entered the Cabinet in March 1782 as Master General of the Ordnance and remained in this post until 1783, becoming a general on 20 November 1782. He returned to office as Master General of the Ordnance in January 1784, in the ministry led by Pitt the Younger, where he remained until February 1795.

In his younger days, Richmond was in favour of political reform. With the advent of the French Revolution he became even more of a reactionary than Pitt, who had once been a noted reformer himself. In July 1795 he was appointed colonel of the Royal Horse Guards in recognition of his continuing support for the ministry. Richmond became a field marshal on 30 July 1796. He continued to speak in the House of Lords, where he supported the Act of Union of Ireland in 1801 and opposed the Treaty of Amiens in 1803. He died at his family seat, Goodwood Park on 29 December 1806 and was buried in Chichester Cathedral. He was succeeded as the 4th Duke of Richmond by his nephew, who, as Lieutenant Colonel Charles Lennox, had fought a duel with the Duke of York [15] and later became the British Ambassador whose Duchess gave the famous ball at Brussels on the eve of Waterloo.

LEOPOLD I

HM King of the Belgians, LEOPOLD GEORGE CHRISTIAN FREDERICK, HSH Prince of Saxe-Coburg and Gotha, KG, GCB, GCH (1790- 1865) [28]

Leopold, the third surviving son of the ruler of the minor German Duchy of Saxe-Coburg-Saalfeld, was born in Coburg on 16 December 1790. During the German War of Liberation (1813–14) he fought alongside the Russians and was given the rank of general in the Russian Army. His appearance in the list of British field marshals derives from the customary inability of the sovereigns of the House of Hanover to get on well with their heirs. In this instance, Princess Charlotte of Wales, only child of the Prince Regent, had alarmed her father by her un-inhibited personal life. She also irritated him by openly sympathizing with her mother, the sluttish Princess of Wales. He was therefore glad of the chance that arose in 1814 of marrying her to the Anglophile Prince William of Orange [34] (heir to the throne of the newly united Kingdom of the Netherlands and Belgium) and of shipping her out of England accordingly. The eighteen year-old princess gave her unenthusiastic agreement to the proposal until the 1814 victory celebrations brought to London the Emperor Alexander I of Russia and his sister, the Grand Duchess Catherine. Acting from a combination of personal and polit-ical motives, Catherine persuaded Charlotte that William was a poor match and that she should instead choose one of the handsome German princes who had fought like lions beside their Russian allies. At the same time the Prince Regent's political enemies told the princess that, once she was in the Netherlands, he would be able more easily to divorce the Princess of Wales, marry again and produce a male heir. Charlotte then, to spite her father, broke off her engagement to the Prince of Orange and declared that she would marry Leopold of Saxe-Coburg. Leopold's modest origins posed no dynastic problems, although his poverty reduced Charlotte to laughter when, at their wedding ceremony on 2 May 1816, he vowed to endow her with all his worldly goods. Leopold was appointed a field marshal on 25 May 1816 and colonel of the 5th (Princess Charlotte of Wales's) Dragoon Guards in October 1816. The couple seem to have been genuinely happy together, but Charlotte, subjected to the most fashionable obstetrician in London, died in child-birth on 6 November 1817, leaving her father without a direct heir and her husband prey to melancholy for the rest of his life. The unfortunate doctor later killed himself.

Leopold undertook no duties in the British Army other than as colonel of his regiment. At first he lived quietly on his country estate in England and declined to be considered for the proposed new thrones of either Mexico (in 1821) or Greece (in 1830). In June 1831, after a rising that gained them independence from the Netherlands, the Belgians offered their throne to Leopold, as the only candidate acceptable to both the British and the French. In renewed fighting, the Belgians were defeated by a Dutch army, led by the Prince of Orange (Leopold's one-time rival suitor for the hand of Princess Charlotte) but the international community eventually acknowledged Belgium as a separate kingdom. In August 1832 Leopold married Louise Marie, daughter of Louis Philippe, King of the French. As King of the Belgians, Leopold proved to be a capable ruler and, despite the small size of his kingdom, played an influential part in European diplomacy. Through his influence, one of his nephews, Ferdinand, became Prince Consort of Portugal, and another, Albert [33], became Prince Consort of the United Kingdom. Leopold died on 10 December 1865 and was buried at Laeken. He was succeeded by his eldest living son, a child of his second marriage, who reigned as Leopold II.

LIGONIER
Sir JOHN (JEAN) LOUIS, 1st Earl Ligonier, KT (1680–1770) [10]

Jean Louis Ligonier was born at Castres, in the Massif Central, on 7 November 1680, the second of five sons of Louis de Ligonier, Sieur of Monteuquet. Sieur Louis, a Huguenot, died in 1693, leaving his forty-one year-old widow to bring up a family of seven young children in a time of religious persecution. Like many other Huguenots, Jean Ligonier chose to go into exile. In 1697, with extremely limited funds, he made his way to Ireland to join his uncle, an officer in one of William III's Huguenot regiments. In the War of the Spanish Succession Ligonier served as a volunteer in Marlborough's army in Flanders, where he came to the notice of his superiors by leading a storming party at Liège (13–29 October 1702). A generous patron lent him the money with which to purchase a commission as captain in Lord North and Grey's Regiment, (later the 10th Foot) on 10 February 1703 and was later repaid by Ligonier from winnings at the gaming table. Ligonier fought at the Schellenberg (2 July 1704); Blenheim (13 July 1704); Ramillies (23 May 1706) and Malplaquet (11 September 1709), where he afterwards counted twenty-three bullet holes in his hat, coat and belt. He joined the British army in the Peninsular campaign in 1711, where he served first on the staff and then as lieutenant colonel of an infantry regiment (later the 12th Foot). In 1719 he was adjutant general of the expedition that captured Vigo, where he led a storming party of grenadiers in the assault on Fort Marin.

In July 1720 Ligonier was appointed colonel of a regiment of Horse (later the 7th Dragoon Guards). He was promoted to major general in 1739. During the War of the Austrian Succession he served in the Pragmatic Army with the Earl of Stair [5] in Germany. He was at Dettingen (27 June 1743) under George II, who made him a Knight of the Bath. In 1744 Sir John Ligonier was made a lieutenant general and took over from George Wade [7] (who had succeeded Stair) as commander of the British troops in the Pragmatic Army. He remained as general of the infantry when the Duke of Cumberland assumed command in April 1745 and was at Fontenoy (11 May 1745), where he was mentioned in despatches for his skilful handling of the infantry in the withdrawal. He then led the British troops that were recalled from Germany to meet the Jacobite Rising of 1745, until Cumberland arrived to take over command. Ligonier returned to the campaign on the Continent and commanded at Rocoux (Rocourt, 11 October 1746). Early in 1747 he again handed over to Cumberland and became general of the Horse. As such, he led the cavalry charge at the battle of Laffeldt (La Val, 2 July 1747), where he was taken prisoner. The French commander, Marshal Saxe, invited him to dinner at his table and presented him to Louis XV, who had observed the battle. King Louis released him on parole, with a message for Cumberland that played a part in opening the subsequent peace negotiations.

Ligonier entered Parliament as MP for Bath in March 1748. In 1749 he succeeded Wade as Lieutenant General of the Ordnance and gave up his colonelcy of his regiment of Horse to take that of a more senior regiment (later the 2nd Dragoon Guards). He retained this colonelcy until 1753, when he became colonel of the Royal Horse Guards. He was required to give up his Ordnance post in 1756 to allow the advancement of Charles, 3rd Duke of Marlborough. On 24 October 1757, following the resignation of the Duke of Cumberland, Ligonier was appointed Commander-in-Chief in England (the first professional soldier to hold this title) with a seat in the Cabinet and an Irish peerage as Viscount Ligonier, of Inniskilling (a title changed to Clonmell in 1762). King George II decided that he should be promoted to field marshal, a rank that had been left unfilled since the death of Viscount Cobham [6] in 1748. As Lord Ligonier was junior in the Army to Sir Robert Rich [8] and Lord Molesworth [9], these two generals were promoted to field marshal on 28 and 29 November 1757 respectively. This allowed Ligonier to be given this rank on 30 November without infringing the principle of promotion by seniority. He became colonel of the 1st Foot Guards in the same month. As C-in-C during the Seven Years War, he worked closely with the Prime Minister (William Pitt the Elder), providing him with detailed advice on military questions at all levels and playing an important part in strategic as well as administrative decisions. In 1763 he was made a peer of the United Kingdom as Baron Ligonier, of Ripley. He remained in the Cabinet as C-in-C until August 1766, when he was succeeded by the Marquis of Granby. Between 1759 and 1762, he was also Master General of the Ordnance. On 10 September 1766 he was advanced in the UK peerage as Earl Ligonier, of Ripley.

Ligonier never married, though he established a liaison with a Miss Miller of Southwark by whom he had a natural daughter, Penelope, in 1727. He acknowledged and provided for his daughter, who took his surname and in the course of time married and was accepted in respectable society as the mother of Lord Ligonier's grandchildren. With his Gallic charm, Ligonier had a reputation as a great lady-killer and in his later years was noted as the constant friend and companion of various beautiful actresses or opera singers. He conducted a series of *affaires* with young (generally extremely young) women and scandalized London society by keeping four mistresses at the same time, whose combined ages did not exceed fifty-eight years. At the age of eighty-one, he paid court to a wealthy widow, with a view to gaining possession of her fortune. He led her to believe that he was a mere seventy-four years of age, but a newspaper (giving one of several premature reports of his death) revealed his true age, with the result that the lady ended their connection. Ligonier sued the editor for defamation, but the defence successfully pleaded that the obituary contained only creditable material and that the age given was the true one. During forty-seven years of active soldiering, Ligonier took part in nine pitched battles and nineteen sieges without a serious wound. In his day he was a popular, even heroic, figure, who served his adopted country well. He died on 28 April 1770, at his country estate in Ripley, Cobham, Surrey, and was buried in the local parish churchyard. His grave is not marked, but a monument to him stands in Westminster Abbey. His titles in the UK peerage died with him and his Irish viscountcy was inherited, by special remainder, by his nephew

LUCAN
LORD, *see* **BINGHAM,** CHARLES, **[63]**

MAHENDRA BIR BIKRAM SHAH DEVA MAHARAJADHIRAJA
HM King of Nepal (1921–1972) **[124]**

King Mahendra of Nepal was born in 1921 and succeeded to the throne on the death of his father, King Tribhuvan, in 1955. He encouraged measures for the economic and social progress of his country, but was wary of the suitability of Western-style liberal democracy for his people. He allowed a General Election for the Nepali Parliament, based on universal adult suffrage, in 1959, but was soon faced with a crisis over demands for land reform. In December 1960 he dissolved parliament, suspended the constitution, outlawed political parties and arrested the leading members of the majority Congress Party. King Mahendra replaced the parliamentary form of government with the traditional system of locally-elected councils (*panchayats*), free from party politicians. These councils were established at all levels of local and regional government, but central government remained in the hands of the King and of the ministers personally nominated by him. King Mahendra continued the policy of allowing the recruitment of his Gurkha subjects into the British and Indian Armies. He did not hold any British regimental appointments, but was made a field marshal in the British Army on 17 October 1960. He died in January 1972 and was succeeded by his son, King Birenda [131].

METHUEN
PAUL SANDFORD, 3rd Baron Methuen, GCB, GCMG, GCVO (1845–1932) [81]

The Honourable Paul Methuen, eldest son of the 2nd Baron Methuen, of Corsham, was born on 1 September 1845 at his family seat, Corsham Court, Wiltshire. After attending Eton College, he became a cornet in the Royal Wiltshire Yeomanry and then obtained his first regular commission as an ensign in the Scots Fusilier Guards (later the Scots Guards) and lieutenant in the Army on 22 November 1864. Methuen was promoted to lieutenant in the regiment and captain in the Army on 25 December 1867 and served as adjutant of the 1st Battalion of his regiment from 1868 to 1871. He was appointed brigade major, Home District, in 1871. During the Ashanti War Methuen served on the staff of Sir Garnet Wolseley [67] and was at Amoafu (21 January 1874). He was promoted to lieutenant colonel on 15 July 1876. In 1878 Methuen became the British military attaché in Berlin and married Evelyn Bathurst, the eldest daughter of the owner of Clarendon Park, Wiltshire. She died a year after their marriage. Methuen became a colonel on 1 July 1881. He again served on the staff under Wolseley in the Egyptian campaign of 1882, where he was at Tel-el-Kebir (13 September 1882). Between 1884 and 1888, he served in counter-insurgency operations in Bechuanaland, where he raised a local corps of mounted riflemen, Methuen's Horse. In 1884 he married his cousin, Mary Sandford, whose father was then serving in South Africa as an official in the colonial government. Methuen remained in South Africa, as a staff officer in the adjutant general's branch, from 1888 to 1891. He was promoted to major general on 21 May 1890 and returned to England after succeeding his father as 3rd baron in 1891. Lord Methuen was GOC Home District from 1892 to 1897. He then went to India to take part in the Tirah campaign in 1897, where he acted as press censor at the Field Force HQ. He was promoted to lieutenant general on 1 April 1898.

On mobilization for the South African War Methuen was given command of the 1st Division. After landing at Cape Town, he advanced to the relief of Kimberley and was at Belmont (23 November 1899), Graspan (25 November 1899) and Modder River (28 November 1899), where he was slightly wounded. His encounter with the Boer General Cronje at Magersfontein (11 December 1899) was one of the three British disasters of "Black Week" that led to the despatch of Lord Roberts [68] to take over command in South Africa. Methuen's criticism of the performance of the Highland Brigade under his command at Magersfontein raised a storm of protest. Lord Lansdowne, Secretary of State for War, gave orders for Methuen to be relieved of his command, and Roberts, though friendly with Methuen, decided that he could not again be trusted with a senior post.

During the guerrilla stage of the war, Methuen led a brigade-sized force hunting the Boer commandos still in the field. He achieved a minor success at Klerksdorp (19 February 1901), but was not able to catch his opponents. At Tweebosch (7 March 1902), they caught him. After most of his men had fled, Methuen fought on with his regular infantry and artillery alone until all were killed or taken. In this engagement, he was wounded twice and suffered a broken leg when his horse was shot and fell on him. Some of his captors, including their field-chaplain, felt that Methuen's zeal in implementing the British policy of burning Boer farms, killing Boer cattle and herding Boer women and children into concentration camps made him liable to punishment as a war criminal. Their commander, Commandant de la Rey, nevertheless treated him with chivalry and sent him under flag of truce to the nearest British hospital, with a letter of sympathy addressed to Lady Methuen. He was the highest ranking British officer (and the only British general) captured by the Boers in the South African War.

Methuen was promoted to general on 26 May 1904 and became colonel of the Scots Guards in June 1904. At the same time, he was given command of IV Army Corps (reorganized as Eastern Command in 1905). Lord Methuen returned to South Africa as C-in-C in April 1908 and became Governor and C-in-C, Natal, in 1910. He was promoted to field marshal on 19 June 1911. During the First World War, Methuen was Governor and C-in-C, Malta, from February 1915 to May 1919. After the war he devoted himself to ex-servicemen's organizations and to the interests of the Brigade of Guards. He died on 30 October 1932 at his family home, Corsham Court (later occupied by the Royal Army Educational Corps). By his second marriage, he had two daughters and three sons, of whom the eldest succeeded to his peerage.

MICHEL
Sir JOHN, GCB (1804–1886) [60]

John Michel, the eldest son of a wealthy general, was born on 1 September 1804 at his family seat, in Dewlish, Dorset. He was educated at Eton and purchased his commission as an ensign in the 57th Foot on 3 April 1823. Michel transferred first to the 27th Foot and then to the 64th Foot, stationed in Gibraltar, with promotion to lieutenant on 28 April 1825. He purchased the captaincy of an unattached company on 12 December 1826 and became a captain in the 64th Foot, still in Gibraltar, in February 1827. In February 1832 Michel went to the Senior Department of the Royal Military College at Sandhurst. He gained his College certificate in November 1833 and so became one of the few trained staff officers in the British Army at this period. He rejoined the 64th and served in Ireland until 1835, when he exchanged to the 3rd Foot (the Buffs) at that time stationed in Bengal. Between 1835 and 1839 Michel was aide-de-camp to the C-in-C, India, (his maternal uncle, Sir Henry Fane). In May 1838 he married Louise Churchill, the daughter of a British major general then serving in India. They later had two sons and three daughters. On 6 March 1840, he purchased a majority in the 6th Foot. This caused some ill-feeling among officers of the regiment, which had been in India since 1825 and was due to return to England. Its lieutenant colonel was about to retire and these two factors raised the price of the major's commission to a level which only a rich man such as Michel, who was junior as a captain to some of those in the regiment, could afford. He returned to the UK with the 6th Foot and purchased its lieutenant colonelcy on 15 April 1842.

Between 1847 and 1852 Michel commanded the 6th Foot in South Africa. In the Kaffir Wars, he served in the Transkei region and was at Iron Mountain (Waterkloof, 15 March 1851) and Mount Chaco (9 December 1851). He then went to the 98th Foot, on the half-pay list, with promotion to brevet colonel on 20 January 1854. During the Crimean War he served as Chief of Staff of the British Army's Turkish

Contingent. In 1856, when another Kaffir war seemed imminent, he went back to South Africa as a local major general, but the crisis passed and he was ordered to join the British forces in the Second China War. He was shipwrecked *en route*, landed at Singapore in July 1857 and went to India with the troops recalled from China on the outbreak of the Indian Mutiny. In the Bombay Army's campaign against the mutineers in Central India, Michel commanded the Malwa Field Force in a series of marches covering over 1,700 miles and was at Biowra (15 September 1858), Mangrauli (9 October 1858) and numerous minor engagements. He was on good terms with his officers and, during quiet periods, tried to teach them the mathematics that formed an important part of a staff officer's training at this period. His educational efforts were defeated by the soporific effect of the Central Indian climate. He was promoted to major general on 26 October 1858 and was awarded the KCB.

In the renewed campaign against China Sir John Michel commanded the 1st Division of the army under Sir Hope Grant. He was at Sinho (12 August 1860), at Tang-ku, where his horse, (the only Allied casualty of the day) was shot under him, and at the Taku Forts (21 August 1860). Together with Sir Hope Grant and Sir Robert Napier [58], Michel protested at the official destruction of the Summer Palace, Peking (Beijing) and, like them, refused his share of the prize money. He was appointed colonel of the 86th Foot (later the 2nd Battalion, the Royal Irish Rifles) in August 1862 and was promoted to lieutenant general on 25 June 1866. He became a general on 28 March 1874. Between 1875 and 1880 he was C-in-C, Ireland, where his social qualities and ample means made him very popular. He was made field marshal on 27 March 1886 and died at Dewlish on 23 May 1886.

MILNE
Sir GEORGE FRANCIS, 1st Baron Milne, GCB, GCMG, DSO (1866–1948) [97]

George Milne, the only son and youngest child of a local bank manager, was born at Aberdeen on 5 November 1866. After attending the Aberdeen Gymnasium and the Royal Military Academy, Woolwich, Milne was commissioned as a lieutenant in the Royal Artillery on 16 September 1885. He joined a field battery (1/Q, renumbered as 38 Battery in 1889) at Trimulgherri, southern India, and served there until 1889, when he was selected for the Royal Horse Artillery and posted to D Battery at Aldershot. In September 1891 he went back to India, where he served in C Battery, Royal Horse Artillery, at Meerut, near

Delhi. With promotion to captain on 4 June 1895, he joined No.2 Company, Southern Division, Royal Artillery, in the garrison artillery at Malta. Milne was with the British contingent that guarded Suakin in 1896, while its Egyptian garrison of Sudanese troops took part in the Dongola campaign under Sir Herbert Kitchener [79]. He then returned to the field artillery as battery captain (second-in-command) of 37 Battery at Hilsea, from where he entered the Staff College at Camberley in 1897. He was allowed to return to 37 Battery to take part in the Sudan campaign of 1898, where he was at Omdurman (2 September 1898). In the final stage of this battle, he directed the shelling of the Mahdi's tomb, unaware that Kitchener, commanding the Anglo-Egyptian army in this campaign, was already there. Milne rejoined his course at the Staff College and passed out in 1899.

Milne was promoted to major on 1 November 1899. In the South African War he was appointed deputy assistant adjutant general on Kitchener's staff in February 1900. He was at Poplar Grove (7 March 1900); Vet River (5–6 May 1900); Zand River (10 May 1900) and Diamond Hill (12 June 1900). During this campaign, he was mentioned in despatches and was awarded the DSO. Milne was promoted to brevet lieutenant colonel on 22 August 1902 and joined the newly-formed Intelligence Branch at the War Office. In 1905 he married Claire Maitland, the daughter of a baronet; they later had a son and daughter. He was promoted to brevet colonel and substantive lieutenant colonel on 3 November 1905, but was still a regimental major. When his staff appointment expired, he was given a major's command, that of the 59th Battery, Royal Field Artillery, at Brighton. He obtained another post on the staff in April 1908, as General Staff officer, grade 2, in the newly-formed North Midland Division, a Territorial Force formation, based at Lichfield. Milne was promoted to substantive colonel on 1 November 1909, when he became GSO 1 of the 6th Division, at Cork. He became Brigadier General, Royal Artillery, of the 4th Division, located at Woolwich, in October 1913.

On the outbreak of the First World War in August 1914 Milne went to France with the 4th Division, as part of the British Expeditionary Force. He commanded the divisional artillery in various operations, including those at Le Cateau (27 August 1914); the Marne (6–9 September 1914); the Aisne (13–20 September 1914) and the first battle of Ypres (3 October–25 November 1914), until 27 January 1915, when he was appointed Brigadier General, General Staff, in III Corps. Milne became Major General, General Staff, of III Corps on 23 February 1915 and served in this post during the operations of the second battle of Ypres (15 April–25 May 1915), where he was mentioned in despatches. He became GOC 27th Division on 16 July 1915 and was sent with this formation to Salonika (Thessaloniki) in January 1916. On arrival, he was immediately given command of the newly-formed XVI Corps, with promotion to temporary lieutenant general.

On 5 May 1916 Milne assumed command of all British troops in Macedonia. He became a substantive lieutenant general on 1 January 1917, when he was raised to the status of a C-in-C. His freedom of action was limited by the political need to co-operate with the Allied commander in this theatre, who was always a French general. At the same time he was starved of resources by Sir William Robertson [92], Chief of the Imperial General Staff, who considered all operations outside the Western Front to be "side-shows". Milne's troops suffered numerous casualties, mostly from malaria or exposure, but also as the result of unsuccessful offensives undertaken to support his French and Serbian allies. In mid-September 1918 the Allied armies finally broke out from Salonika, forcing Bulgaria to sign an armistice on 27 September 1918 and so opening the way into Central Europe. With the collapse of the Central Powers, Milne became responsible for British military administration of a vast area around the Black Sea, with some of his troops occupying Constantinople and others located in the Caucasus and on the Caspian. He had also to deal with internal disorders in these regions, following the Russian and Turkish revolutions. He was awarded the KCB in 1918.

Sir George Milne was given substantive promotion to general and became a colonel commandant of the Royal Artillery on 26 April 1920. He spent the next two years on the half-pay list until 1922, when he became GOC-in-C Eastern Command. He was appointed Chief of the Imperial General Staff in 1926 and retained this post, with a two-year extension of the normal five-year tenure, until 1933. He supported the concept of mechanization and the development of armoured formations, but was cautious about re-equipping with machines that could soon become obsolete. Government policy inhibited planning for a major war, so that the Army was committed primarily to imperial policing, for which horsed cavalry and conventional infantry were well suited. Retention of these arms enabled Milne both to conciliate the military traditionalists and to keep up regimental morale at a time of continued reductions in defence spending, while the Royal Navy and Royal Air Force claimed priority for such funds as were available. His critics argued that he clung to office for too long and became old, tired and depressed, acting as a block on the promotion of those below him, while the efficiency of the British Army steadily declined.

During his last three years in office Milne was chairman of the Chiefs of Staff Committee. He was promoted to field marshal on 30 January 1928 and was raised to the peerage as Baron Milne, of Salonika and of Rubislaw, on his retirement from active duty in 1933. With the approach of the Second World War Lord Milne became an air raid warden in the Civil Defence organisation for Westminster. In 1940 he was appointed colonel commandant of the Pioneer Corps, newly-formed to provide the Army's labour resource service, and retained this post until he retired on age grounds in 1945. Between 1929 and 1946 Milne held the appointment of Master Gunner, St James's Park. He died on 23 March 1948 and his ashes were scattered in his native Aberdeen.

MOLESWORTH
RICHARD, 3rd Viscount Molesworth (1680–1758) [9]

Richard Molesworth, born in 1680, was the second son of an eminent Anglo-Irish supporter of William of Orange. He was sent to study law in London, but abandoned his books in order to join the Nine Years War in the Low Countries. Accompanied by his manservant, he made his way to the British camp, where he presented himself to his father's old friend, Lord George Hamilton [1]. He served as a volunteer in Hamilton's Regiment (later the 1st Foot, the Royal Scots) during the final stages of this campaign. He became an ensign in this regiment in 1701 and served with it, as a captain, at Blenheim (13 August 1704) in the War of the Spanish Succession. Molesworth was at Ramillies (23 May 1706), where he was ADC to the Duke of Marlborough and gave up his own mount to allow Marlborough, who had been unhorsed in a cavalry *mêlée* to escape. Molesworth himself, wounded by several sabre cuts, was overlooked in the subsequent pursuit, so that he was able to recover Marlborough's own charger and restore it to its owner. On 5 May 1707 he was appointed captain in the Coldstream Guards and lieutenant colonel in the Army. He remained in the Flanders campaign until 1710, narrowly escaping injury in the explosion of a mine during the siege of Mons (9 September–20 October 1709). He then became colonel of an infantry regiment (later disbanded) with which he served in the campaign in Spain from 1711 to 1712. In 1714 he was elected to the Irish Parliament as MP for Swords.

During the Jacobite Rising of 1715 Molesworth raised and commanded a regiment of dragoons and was wounded at Preston (13 November 1715). On the disbandment of his dragoons, Molesworth was made colonel of the Enniskillen Regiment of Foot (later the 27th Royal Inniskilling Fusiliers) in March 1725. He succeeded his elder brother as 3rd Viscount Molesworth, of Swords, County Dublin, in October 1731 and was appointed colonel of a regiment of dragoons (later the 9th Queen's Royal Lancers) in May 1732. Lord Molesworth retained this post until 1737, when he became colonel of a more senior regiment (later the 5th Royal Irish Dragoons). He was promoted to major general on 18 December 1735 and became a lord justice for Ireland in December 1736. In 1739 he became a lieutenant general on the Irish establishment, followed by appointment as Master General of the Ordnance for Ireland in 1740. Molesworth was promoted to lieutenant general on the English establishment in July 1742, but spent the rest of his career in Ireland. He became general of the Horse on the Irish establishment on 24 March 1746 and commander of the forces there in September 1751. He was promoted to field marshal on 29 November 1757 and died on 12 October 1758, in post as Governor of the Royal Hospital, Kilmainham. He married twice, firstly to Jane Lucas, from Dublin, with whom he had a son (who died in infancy) and three daughters. After his first wife's death, Molesworth married Mary Usher (daughter of the Archdeacon of Clonfert) with whom he had seven daughters and a son who inherited his title as 4th viscount.

MONTANDRE
MARQUIS OF, see **DE LA ROCHEFOUCAULD, FRANCIS, [4]**

MONTGOMERY
Sir BERNARD LAW, 1st Viscount Montgomery, KG, GCB, DSO (1887–1976) **[114]**

Bernard Montgomery was born at St Mark's Vicarage, Kennington Oval, on 17 November 1887. He was the third son and the fourth of nine children of the Reverend Henry Montgomery, whose own father, a scion of the Anglo-Irish Protestant Ascendancy, had been lieutenant-governor of the Punjab and held land in County Donegal. The Reverend Henry, a younger son, relied on his stipend to keep his wife (who also came from Anglo-Irish Protestant stock) and his growing family. Mrs Montgomery, engaged at fourteen, married when barely sixteen to her father's curate (a man then twice her age) and the mother of five children before she was twenty-five, was a dominant personality. She controlled her husband, his limited purse and their children with equal strictness. Bernard, whose defiant ways gained him frequent canings from his mother, feared and respected her, but gave his love to his kind, weak father. Between 1889 and 1902 the Right Reverend Henry Montgomery was Bishop of Tasmania. The family then returned to London, where Bernard Montgomery was educated as a day-boy at St Paul's School.

Having decided on a military career, Montgomery entered the Royal Military College, Sandhurst, in January 1907. Lacking the private means on which most officers of the British Army relied to meet their regimental expenses, he planned to join the Indian Army, where pay and promotion prospects were good and the cost of living was low. At this period there was great competition among those in similar circumstances to obtain one of the limited number of vacancies available to each batch of Sandhurst cadets. Montgomery became a cadet lance-corporal but was subsequently reduced to the rank of gentleman cadet and threatened with expulsion for rowdiness and violence. He began to work harder, but those who passed out senior to him in the final order of merit took all the Indian vacancies allotted to his batch. Montgomery therefore decided to join the British Army and chose the 1st Battalion, the Royal Warwickshire Regiment, a unit that was then serving in India, where he could live on his pay. He was commissioned as a second lieutenant on 19 September 1908 and was promoted to lieutenant on 1 April 1910. He served with the 1st Battalion, the Royal Warwickshire Regiment, at Peshawar on the North-West Frontier until 1910 and then at Bombay until 1912, when the battalion returned to the UK. By this time, Montgomery had formed a high opinion of the sepoys of the Indian Army but a low opinion of their British officers, whose abilities and energies he considered to be sapped both by the climate and their expatriate life-style. Montgomery himself used neither alcohol nor tobacco and held puritanical views about those who became dependent on these substances.

Montgomery remained at regimental duty as adjutant of the 1st Battalion, the Royal Warwickshire Regiment, at Shorncliffe. On the outbreak of the First World War he landed in France with his battalion on 23 August 1914 as part of the British Expeditionary Force and was soon in combat at Haucourt, near Le Cateau (26 August 1914). He took part in the retreat from Mons and in various minor engagements on the Aisne. During the first battle of Ypres, he was at Meteren (13 October 1914), where he was badly wounded in his right lung and left leg. Montgomery was then invalided home, with the award of the DSO for his conduct in this engagement and promotion to captain on 14 October

1914. He returned to duty in February 1915, acting as brigade major first of the 112th Infantry Brigade and then of the 104th Infantry Brigade, under training in Lancashire. Montgomery went to France with the 104th Brigade and was with it at the Somme (1 July–18 November 1916). As an acting major, he became a General Staff officer, grade 2, in the 33rd Division in January 1917 and served with this formation at Arras (9 April –16 May 1917). In July 1917 he became GSO 2 in IX Corps. He was in this post during the third battle of Ypres (31 July–6 November 1917) with promotion to temporary major on 25 February 1918 and brevet major on 3 June 1918. Montgomery became an acting lieutenant colonel on 16 July 1918, when he was appointed GSO 1 of the 47th (London) Division. He remained in this post until the end of the First World War, during which he was mentioned in despatches six times and received the French Croix de Guerre.

On 5 September 1919 Montgomery was given command of the 17th Battalion, the Royal Fusiliers (the City of London Regiment), part of the Army of Occupation in the Rhineland. When this unit was disbanded in November 1919, he joined the staff of the army commander, Sir William Robertson [92] through whose influence he was nominated to attend the Staff College, Camberley. After qualifying as a trained staff officer, he was appointed brigade major of the 17th Infantry Brigade at Cork, where he was engaged in counter-insurgency operations during the final months of British rule in southern Ireland. On the withdrawal of the British garrisons from the Irish Free State, he was appointed brigade major of the 8th Infantry Brigade at Plymouth in May 1922. Montgomery was appointed GSO 2 in a Territorial Army formation, the 49th (West Riding) Division, in May 1923. When his tenure of this post expired, he returned to his old battalion at Shorncliffe as a company commander in May 1925, with promotion to substantive major on 25 July 1925. He went back to the Staff College, Camberley, as an instructor, in January 1926. There he met another instructor, Alan Brooke [112]. Each recognized the abilities of the other and they established valuable bonds of friendship.

On holiday in Switzerland in 1926, Montgomery met and fell in love with Betty Carver, widow of a Territorial captain in the East Lancashire Royal Engineers, who had been killed in Gallipoli, and sister of the future Lieutenant General Sir Percival Hobart. They were married in July 1927 and their only child, David, was born in August 1928. Montgomery later recorded that he had never thought it possible that such love and affection could exist. He was promoted to brevet lieutenant colonel on 1 January 1928 and, after ending his tour at the Staff College in January 1929, returned to the 1st Battalion, the Royal

Warwickshire Regiment, to command its Headquarters Company. He was posted to the War Office in the summer of 1929, where he served as secretary of a committee revising the Infantry Training Manual. In July 1930, he became second-in-command of his battalion, followed by appointment as its commanding officer, with promotion to substantive lieutenant colonel, on 17 January 1931.

Montgomery's imperious ways, his refusal to allow sentiment to interfere with efficiency and his emphasis on hard training, led to some unrest in his battalion, which moved to Palestine early in 1931. There, he caused offence by tactless criticism of senior officers. He was promoted to brevet colonel on 1 January 1932 and, at the end of 1933, went with his battalion to Poona (Pune), where he made no secret of his view that India was a military backwater. He was appointed GSO 1 and Chief Instructor of the Junior Division at the Indian Staff College, Quetta, in June 1934, with substantive promotion to colonel, backdated to 1 March 1932.

At the end of his three years at Quetta Montgomery returned to England to take command of the 9th Infantry Brigade at Portsmouth, with promotion to temporary brigadier on 5 August 1937. He cast himself as a relentless moderniser and the apostle of a professional approach to soldiering. In this role, both Montgomery and his brigade major, the future General Sir Frank Simpson, were easily persuaded by the commanding officer of the Royal Wiltshire Yeomanry (a noted practical joker) that his regiment would deal with opposing machine guns by a mounted charge. Neither of the two Regulars ever realized that this officer and many of his yeomen had fought as infantry during the First World War and were as personally familiar with the effects of machine-gun fire as were Montgomery and Simpson themselves.

Montgomery's personal happiness was destroyed by the death of his wife on 19 October 1937 from septicaemia following an insect bite. Grief-stricken, he sought solace by concentrating ever more intensely on his profession and reverted to the solitary way of life, out of which his wife, with her wide social and artistic interests, had taken him. He was promoted to major general on 21 May 1938 and, at the end of that year, returned to Palestine to command the 8th Division. He waged a vigorous counter-insurgency campaign against Arab extremists, achieving a number of successes, but condemning the senior British officers of the para-military Palestine Police as useless. He returned to England in July to take command of the 3rd Division, doing so just before all postings were stopped on mobilization for the Second World War on 3 September 1939.

Montgomery went to France with his division as part of the British

Expeditionary Force and used the period of the "Phoney War" to prepare for active operations and to weed out inefficient officers. He was not liked by Lord Gort [110], his C-in-C, whom Montgomery considered to lack the intellect required in so high an appointment (though he later gave Gort full credit for courage and determination). Brooke (at this time Montgomery's Corps commander) had to defend Montgomery from Gort's wrath for publishing an order on the subject of venereal disease, couched in terms which the C-in-C and his senior chaplains thought obscene. When the German offensive began on 10 May 1940 Montgomery commanded his division with great skill both in the advance into Belgium and the subsequent retreat to the Channel coast. As the size of the BEF dwindled, Montgomery was given a brief command of II Corps, at Dunkirk, from 30 May to 1 June 1940. On returning to England he resumed command of the 3rd Division and became responsible for the defence of the Sussex coast. He succeeded Lieutenant General Claude Auchinleck [116] as GOC V Corps, with promotion to acting lieutenant general on 22 July 1940. At the same time, Auchinleck took over from Brooke as GOC-in-C Southern Command, so that Montgomery came under Auchinleck's command. Although both officers were keen advocates of realistic training and physical fitness, they did not get on well together. Montgomery personified the British Army's prejudice against Auchinleck as an Indian Army officer and rarely agreed with him on any subject. As far as possible, he disregarded Auchinleck's existence and ignored his orders, until the latter was succeeded by Sir Harold Alexander [113] at the end of 1940. Montgomery took command of XII Corps, in Kent, at the end of April 1941, with promotion to temporary lieutenant general on 22 July 1941. He became GOC-in-C South Eastern Command (comprising the XII and Canadian Corps) on 17 November 1941 and was involved in the initial planning for the ill-fated raid on Dieppe (19 August 1942).

Montgomery left the UK for North Africa on 10 August 1942. His first assignment was to command the First Army, destined to land in French North Africa. This appointment was cancelled when Lieutenant General "Strafer" Gott, who had been selected to take over command of the Eighth Army in the Western Desert, was killed in an air crash. Montgomery was appointed in his stead and immediately set himself to introduce a new spirit into his army. He announced that contingency plans for any further withdrawal (drawn up as a precautionary measure by Auchinleck when C-in-C Middle East) were cancelled. Any kind of "belly-aching" or discussion of the merits of orders was explicitly forbidden. Determined to create his own personality to rival that of Field Marshal Erwin Rommel, commander of the German army in

North Africa, Montgomery made extensive visits to his front-line troops. He accepted a slouch hat from the Australians and, when this proved popular, experimented with various other kinds of head-dress. He finally settled on what would be his characteristic feature, the black beret of the Royal Tank Regiment (in which he had never served), worn with a second cap-badge, that of his rank as a general officer.

Montgomery repulsed an attack by Rommel at Alam el Halfa (31 Aug– 4 September 1942) and then carefully prepared his own offensive. His success at El Alamein (23 October– 4 November 1942) was the first major victory of British over German land forces in the Second World War. He was promoted to general on 11 November 1942 and was awarded the KCB. Sir Bernard Montgomery remained with the Eighth Army during the campaign in Sicily (10 July–18 August 1943) and the subsequent invasion of Italy. At the end of December 1943, he was ordered back to England to be the commander of 21 Army Group and C-in-C Allied Land Forces, in preparation for the invasion of Normandy. He embarked on a series of visits to the units of all the nationalities under his command, as well as to groups of factory and transport workers, stressing to everyone the importance of their respective roles and inspiring them with his confidence in the certainty of ultimate Allied victory.

He remained as C-in-C, Allied Land Forces, during the Normandy landings of June 1944 and subsequent operations, including Operation Goodwood (18–19 July 1944) where the failure of British armoured formations to make headway was his first serious reverse. On 31 August 1944, in accordance with existing plans, General Dwight D. Eisenhower took over as C-in-C, ALF, while retaining the post of Supreme Commander, Allied Expeditionary Force. Montgomery was promoted to field marshal on 1 September 1944. He led 21 Army Group north-westwards into the Low Countries and liberated Antwerp on 17 September 1944, but the defeat of the British 1st Airborne Division at Arnhem (17–25 September 1944) diminished his prestige. His proposal to advance into Germany in a single powerful thrust to take the Ruhr was disregarded by Eisenhower, who favoured an approach to the Rhine on a broad front. During the German offensive in the Ardennes (the "Battle of the Bulge", 16 December-25 January 1945) Montgomery was given temporary command of the American divisions north of the threatened sector. He displayed his old confidence and ability, but offended his United States allies (to whom he had shown little tact or courtesy when serving in the Mediterranean theatres) by giving the impression that he personally had saved them from defeat.

At Luneberg Heath, Hanover, on 4 May 1945, after humiliating the

German envoys, Montgomery accepted the surrender of all enemy armed forces in North West Germany, the Netherlands, and Denmark. He became C-in-C, British Forces of Occupation, and British member of the Allied Control Commission for Germany on 23 May 1945. As such, he ruled the British Zone of Germany with a series of edicts, deliberately couched in dictatorial terms, regulating the infrastructure of government, education, transport, the distribution of food and the revival of democratic institutions.

On 1 June 1946 Montgomery became Chief of the Imperial General Staff. Raised to the peerage as Viscount Montgomery of Alamein, of Hindhead, he immediately began a tour of British troops in Egypt, Palestine, Greece and India. He considered the results so beneficial that he established a pattern of spending one month in three on overseas tours. In 1947 he made an extensive tour of Africa. In 1948 he proposed the amalgamation of British African territories into three great federations, whose mineral resources and raw materials could be developed under British enterprise. He criticized the European settlers for their comfortable life-style and declared that the African was a complete savage, quite incapable of developing the country himself. The Emperor Haile Selassie of Ethiopia [125] was described by Montgomery as a pathetic figure, living in a state of medieval feudalism, surrounded by an atmosphere of suspicion and mistrust. Montgomery declared that his own plan for Africa would be essential to the survival of the British in the event of any future world conflict. Those who opposed it should, he said, be ruthlessly eliminated. "Belly-achers" should be stamped on. Arthur Creech Jones, Colonial Secretary in the Labour Government of the day, rejected Montgomery's proposals on the grounds that Africa was a poor continent that could only be exploited at great expense.

Montgomery did not get on well with the Chiefs of the other two Services nor with the Minister of Defence, A. V. Alexander, but his habit of plain speaking enabled him to establish a rapport with Emmanuel Shinwell, a former conscientious objector who had become the Secretary of State for War. His plan for the post-war Army was for a long-service regular cadre, with a large well-trained reserve in the form of a Territorial Army made up mostly of men undertaking the part-time element of their compulsory national service. The Cabinet considered that only one year of National Service should be spent with the colours. Montgomery stated that, as not enough recruits were being attracted into the Regular Army, this would not be practicable unless British military commitments overseas were liquidated. By this period the Prime Minister, Clement Attlee, was losing patience with Montgomery's self-proclaimed determination to make himself a nuisance in Whitehall. The Berlin Crisis of 1948 had led to the creation of the Western European Union, a military alliance aimed at the Soviet Union. Montgomery was nominated by the British government to be the first Chairman of the Commanders-in-Chief of the five nations involved and took up this post in October 1948.

With the establishment of the NATO Alliance, Montgomery became Deputy Commander in the Supreme Headquarters of the Allied Powers in Europe (SHAPE) on 2 April 1951 and served in this post until his retirement from active duty in September 1958. His *Memoirs*, published in 1958, caused much offence, especially in the USA, where Eisenhower (who had in fact treated Montgomery with much forbearance) had become President. Montgomery then began a series of international goodwill visits. He went to the Soviet Union in April 1959, where he spoke of the absurdity of two great power blocs spending vast resources on armaments that neither wished to use against the other. He visited the leaders of the People's Republic of China, in both 1960 and 1961, and expressed a high opinion of their personal qualities. After a visit to South Africa in 1962, he outraged conventional liberal opinion by expressing a degree of understanding for the policy of separate development (apartheid) adopted by the South African government of the time. Montgomery was colonel of the Royal Warwickshire Regiment from January 1947 to October 1953 and of the Parachute Regiment from 1944 to 1955. He was also colonel commandant of the Royal Armoured Corps from May 1947 to July 1958, of the Royal Tank Regiment from 1945 to 1956 and of the Army Physical Training Corps from 1947 to 1961. After a serious illness in 1972, Viscount Montgomery reluctantly began to withdraw from public life. He gradually faded away to die of heart failure at his home, Isington Mill, near Alton, Hampshire, on 24 March 1976. He was buried in the nearby parish churchyard of Holy Cross, Binsted, and was succeeded as 2nd viscount by his only son.

MONTGOMERY-MASSINGBERD
Sir ARCHIBALD ARMAR, GCB, GCVO, KCMG
(1871–1947) [103]

Archibald Montgomery was born on 6 December 1871 at Blessingbourne, Fivemiletown, County Tyrone, the second son of Hugh de Fellenberg Montgomery, a local landholder with connections to many other Anglo-Irish Protestant military families. After attending Charterhouse School and the Royal Military Academy, Woolwich, he was commissioned as a second lieutenant in the Royal Artillery on 4 November 1891. In 1892 he joined a field artillery unit, 65 Battery, serving in India, where he was promoted to lieutenant on 4 November 1894. He returned with 65 Battery to the UK in 1896 where he married Diana Langton, whose mother was heiress to the extensive estates of the Massingberd family at Gunby Hall, Lincolnshire. Montgomery was promoted to captain on 8 March 1900 and served in the South African War in command of an ammunition column. He was at Magersfontein (11 December 1899); Paardeberg (17–26 February 1900); Poplar Grove (7 March 1900); Dreifontein (10 March 1900) and the Caledon River (27–29 November 1900), where he was slightly wounded. During the guerrilla stage of the war, he took part in various minor operations in the Orange River Colony and Cape Colony, before being posted to base duties at Cape Town. He was mentioned in despatches and returned to regimental duty in 1902 as battery captain (second-in-command) of the 114th Battery, Royal Field Artillery, at Bulford. Between January 1905 and December 1906, Montgomery was a student at the Staff College, Camberley. After passing out, he was appointed staff captain in the Inspectorate of Horse and Field Artillery and, in August 1908, became a General Staff officer, grade 3, in Aldershot Command. He was promoted to major on 5 June 1909, followed by appointment as an instructor and GSO 2 at the newly-formed Indian Staff College, Quetta, with the local rank of lieutenant colonel. In 1911 he exchanged with an opposite number at the Staff College, Camberley, and returned to the UK to become an instructor there.

On mobilization at the outbreak of the First World War in August 1914, Montgomery joined the 4th Division as a GSO 2. He continued to use his local Staff College rank and was soon appointed GSO 1. In September 1914 command of this division was given to Major General (later General Lord) Rawlinson, who formed a high opinion of Montgomery's abilities and thereafter retained him in his personal entourage. When Rawlinson assumed command of IV Corps in October 1914 he appointed Montgomery as his Chief of Staff, with the local rank of brigadier general. He became brevet lieutenant colonel and temporary colonel on 18 February 1915. In February 1916 Rawlinson was given command of the Fourth Army and Montgomery went with him as Chief of Staff of this new formation, with promotion to temporary major general on 5 February 1916 and substantive major general on 1 January 1917. When Rawlinson was appointed British Military Representative at the Allied Supreme War Council at Versailles in January 1918, he took Montgomery with him on his staff. At the time of the German offensive in March 1918, when Rawlinson was given command of a new Fourth Army (formed mostly from the remnants of the Fifth), Montgomery was again his Chief of Staff. In the final British offensives on the Western Front, Montgomery effectively acted as deputy commander of the Fourth Army, rather than a staff officer, and played an important part at Amiens (8 August–3 September 1918) and subsequent British victories. After the Armistice of 11 November 1918 he became Chief of Staff of the British Army of the Rhine under Sir William Robertson [92] and was awarded the KCMG. When Rawlinson was appointed C-in-C, India in February 1920, Sir Archibald Montgomery became Deputy Chief of the General Staff, India.

Montgomery returned to the United Kingdom in March 1922 to become GOC 53rd (Welsh) Division in the Territorial Army. In June 1923 he was appointed GOC 1st Division at Aldershot. He was transferred to the half-pay on promotion to lieutenant general on 16 March 1926. In the same year Lady Montgomery inherited the Massingberd family lands. Montgomery added the name Massingberd to his own and spent the next two years on his wife's Lincolnshire estates. Montgomery-Massingberd became a colonel commandant of the Royal Artillery in November 1927 and returned to active duty on being appointed GOC-in-C Southern Command in June 1928. He was promoted to general on 1 October 1930 and became Adjutant General in March 1931. He was appointed Chief of the Imperial General Staff in February 1933. He felt strongly that the Army should be armed and trained to fight a major campaign on the Continent and now believed that large armoured formations would play an important part in conventional warfare. Montgomery-Massingberd was able to make some limited progress towards mechanization, but the ministerial policy of maintaining the Army primarily for imperial defence, while giving priority to the needs of the Royal Navy and Royal Air Force, meant that funds for further modernization were not available. He was promoted to field marshal on 7 June 1935 but soon afterwards announced his intention of retiring, ostensibly on health grounds. He left office, two years early, in March 1936, partly out of frustration and partly so as to ease the promotion block caused by his predecessor, Sir George Milne [97], who had remained in office for two years longer than usual. He settled at Gunby Hall, where he died, without offspring, on 13 October 1947. He had become colonel commandant of the Royal Tank Corps in December 1934, of the Royal Malta Artillery in May 1937 and of the Burma Rifles in 1935. In the title of his book *The Story of the Fourth Army in the Hundred Days* (published in 1919) he gave the name of the famous and decisive campaign of 1815 to the final stages of the war on the Western Front in 1918, where his own reputation was made.

MOORE
CHARLES, 1st Marquess of Drogheda, KP
(1730–1821) [29]

Charles Moore, the eldest son of the 5th Earl of Drogheda, was born on 29 June 1730 and was first commissioned on 18 November 1755 as a cornet in the 12th Dragoons. He sat in the Irish Parliament as MP for St Canice from 1756 until October 1758, when he succeeded his father as 6th Earl. In December 1759 Drogheda raised a regiment of Light Horse, later remustered as the 18th Light Dragoons, of which he became colonel in August 1762. He commanded this regiment between 1762 and 1764 in operations in aid of the civil power in Waterford and Tipperary, against the Whiteboys (an underground organization that attacked deer-parks, orchards and similar economic targets, in protest against excessive rents and tithes). Lord Drogheda was a member of the government as Chief Secretary to the Lord Lieutenant for Ireland from July 1763 to June 1764 and became a Lord Justice for Ireland (one of the officers of state who governed Ireland in the Lord Lieutenant's absence) in 1766. In February 1766 he married Anne Seymour Conway, daughter of the 1st Marquess of Hertford, and niece of the Honourable Henry Seymour Conway [12]. They later had eight children. As a prominent member of the Irish establishment, Drogheda opposed the administrative reforms attempted by Viscount Townshend [20] while Lord Lieutenant of Ireland between 1767 and 1772. He became major general on 30 August 1770, lieutenant general on 29 August 1777 and general on 12 October 1793. Drogheda remained in command of the 18th Light Dragoons (mostly *in absentia*) until 1799 and continued as colonel until the regiment was disbanded in 1821.

Lord Drogheda sat in the Westminster Parliament as MP for Horsham from 1776 to 1780. His support for the ministry was rewarded in July 1791 by his advancement to the rank of marquess in the Irish peerage and he was created a baron of the United Kingdom on the Act of Union in 1801. At the time of the accession of the Prince Regent as King George IV, the Marquess of Drogheda was the senior ranking general in the Army. Together with Earl Harcourt [30], he was made a field marshal on 19 July 1821, in the awards granted to mark the new monarch's accession. Drogheda died at Dublin on 22 December 1821 and was buried at the town from which he took his title. His eldest son, who had severe learning difficulties, succeeded him as the 2nd Marquess of Drogheda and died unmarried, in 1837.

NAPIER
Sir ROBERT CORNELIS, 1st Baron Napier of Magdala, GCB, GCSI (1810–1890) [58]

Robert Napier was born on 6 December 1810 at Colombo, Ceylon (Sri Lanka), a settlement taken by the British from the Dutch some fourteen years earlier. His mother was the daughter of a Barbados plantation owner. His father, a major in the Royal Artillery, was badly wounded in the assault on the Lines of Cornelis in the Dutch East Indies in August 1811 and died on his way home, having given the name of his fatal battle to his infant son. In February 1825 Napier obtained a cadetship at the East India Company's Military Seminary, Addiscombe, from which he was commissioned as a second lieutenant in the Bengal Engineers on 15 December 1826. He was promoted to lieutenant on 28 September 1827, while still at the Company's depot at Chatham. After arriving in India in November 1828, he was employed in various garrison and public works projects until 1836, when he became entitled to leave in Europe on medical certificate. On the expiry of his three-year furlough, Napier returned to India, where in June 1840 he married Anne Pearse, daughter of a surgeon in the Madras Medical Service. They later had three sons and three daughters before she died in childbirth in 1849.

Napier was promoted to captain on 25 January 1841 and became garrison engineer at Sirhind in 1842. On the outbreak of the First Sikh War he hastened to join the field army under Gough [44]. In this campaign he was at Mudki (15 December 1845) where his horse was shot under him; Ferozeshah (21 December 1845), where he was wounded, again with his horse being shot under him, and Sobraon (10 February 1846). He was promoted to brevet major on 3 April 1846 and was chief engineer at the siege of Kot Kangra (May 1846). During the Second Sikh War he was at the siege of Multan, where he was wounded on 12 September 1848 and took part in the assault on 23 January 1849. Napier was promoted brevet lieutenant colonel on 7 June 1849 and remained in the Punjab as civil engineer to the new British administration. After holding subordinate commands in expeditions against the hill tribes of the North-West Frontier in 1852–53, Napier became increasingly at odds with Sir John Lawrence, lieutenant-governor of the Punjab, who introduced a policy of restricting expenditure on public works. He became brevet colonel on 28 November 1854 and lieutenant colonel in his corps on 15 April 1856. After a furlough in England, he returned to India and arrived there shortly after the outbreak of the Indian Mutiny in May 1857.

Napier joined the staff of the column led by Sir James Outram and took part in the first relief of Lucknow (25–26 September 1857), where he remained as chief engineer until the arrival of the final relief column under Sir Colin Campbell [46], on 17 November 1857. He was wounded, but rejoined Outram and was present in the operations of 4–21 March 1858, when Lucknow was recaptured by the British. He was then appointed to succeed Sir Hugh Rose [57] in command of the Central India Field Force. Before he could take over, a sudden threat caused by the mutiny of the troops of the Maharaja Sindia of Gwalior, a British ally, led Rose to resume command. Napier served as his second-in-command in the various combats leading to Sindia's restoration and then took over when Rose finally left on 29 June 1858. The campaign against scattered but determined opponents continued until the end of the year, with Napier proving an able leader of cavalry and mounted infantry in counter-insurgency operations and being rewarded with the KCB. Like all the East India Company's officers, he was transferred to the service of the Crown in India in 1858.

Sir Robert Napier commanded the 2nd Division in the China War of 1860, fighting at the Taku Forts (21 August 1860), where he counted six bullet holes in his clothing and equipment. He was at the subsequent occupation of Peking (Beijing) and the destruction of the Summer Palace. Although not a wealthy man, he was one of the three senior British officers (the others being Sir Hope Grant and Sir John Michel [60]) who refused to accept any share of the prize-money allotted to the army after this event. He became a major general on 15 February 1861, after which he was transferred, with all other officers of the Bengal, Madras and Bombay Engineers, to the Corps of Royal Engineers in the British Army. In April 1861 he married Maria Cecilia Smythe Scott, the daughter of a general of artillery, with whom he had six sons and three daughters. From 1861 to 1865, the period in which the Indian armies were reorganized after the Mutiny, Napier sat as the Military Member of the Governor-General of India's Council (in effect, the War Minister of British India). He then became C-in-C, Bombay, with promotion to lieutenant general on 1 March 1867.

Napier's reputation for caution, together with his record of success in the field, led to his selection in July 1867 to command the expedition against the Emperor Theodore of Abyssinia (Tewodros of Ethiopia). After establishing a firm logistic base on the Red Sea coast, he began his advance through difficult mountainous country in January 1868. Theodore's army was defeated at Arogie (10 April 1868) and Theodore himself committed suicide on the fall of his capital city, Magdala (13 April 1868). The expedition re-embarked in June 1868, carrying with it numerous trophies of historical and cultural interest, including Theodore's crown, which was laid before Queen Victoria. Napier was raised to the peerage as Baron Napier of Magdala and of Caryngton. From April 1870 to April 1876 Lord Napier was C-in-C, India. He became a general and colonel-commandant of the Royal Engineers (Bengal) on 1 April 1874, was Governor and C-in-C, Gibraltar, from September 1876 to January 1881 and was promoted to field marshal on 1 January 1883. He died of influenza at Eaton Square, London, on 14 January 1890 and was buried in St Paul's Cathedral. He was the first officer of engineers to command a British army in the field.

NICHOLAS II,
HIM Emperor (Tsar) of Russia, KG (1868–1918) [84]

The future Emperor Nicholas II was born in St Petersburg on 18 May 1868. He was the eldest son of the then Tsarevich Alexander, who succeeded to the Russian throne as Alexander III on the assassination of his own father, Alexander II, in 1881. Alexander III rejected his father's liberal views and saw it as his duty to rule as an absolute monarch. Of impressive physical strength and size, he became an object of hero-worship to his small and slightly-built heir, who accepted without question his father's opposition to any kind of constitutional reform. Nicholas' tutors included instructors from the St Petersburg Military Academy, but he displayed little interest in the Army, or indeed in any other subject, until 1887, when he was given command of a squadron of Hussars of the Imperial Guard during exercises. In 1888 he was appointed to command the 1st Battery of the Horse Artillery, where he delighted in the comradeship and social activities of life in the Officers' Mess. He was then sent on a world tour, during which, in Japan, he was attacked and wounded by a religious fanatic, an experience that left him with a lasting hostility towards the Japanese. On his return to regimental duty, he was promoted by his father (who still doubted Nicholas's ability as a potential sovereign) to be colonel of the Preobrazhensky Guard Regiment, an honour in which Nicholas thereafter took great pride. It was, in fact, the highest rank he ever held in the Russian Army.

In 1893 Nicholas visited London for the wedding of his cousin, the Duke of York, the future George V [80], whom he physically much resembled. In 1894 he proposed to Princess Alix of Hesse-Darmstadt, to whom he had for some time been devoted. Alix was reluctant to accept the necessary conversion from her Lutheran religion to the

Russian Orthodox Church, but was persuaded by her grandmother (Queen Victoria) and her cousin (the German Emperor William II [71]) to yield on this point. The couple visited Alix's sister, the Princess of Battenberg, at her home in England. They were feted at Windsor and became popular with the British sporting public through the foundation of a new horse-race, named in Nicholas' honour (using the French system of transliteration) as the Cesarewitch.

Nicholas succeeded his father as Emperor on 1 November 1894 and married Alix (received into Orthodoxy as Alexandra Fedorovna) on 26 November 1894. As a wedding present from Queen Victoria, he was appointed colonel-in-chief of the Royal Scots Greys (2nd Dragoons). His reign began inauspiciously. Even before his coronation, he alienated liberal opinion by declaring that the idea of representative government was a "senseless dream", ill-chosen words for which the new Empress, as reactionary as she was wilful, was held responsible. The coronation festivities were marred by the death of 2,000 people, trampled to death when a crowd panicked. The disasters to Russian arms in the Russo-Japanese War of 1904–5 weakened the prestige of the Emperor, who, like all monarchs of the period, was identified with his country's armed forces. In St Petersburg a peaceful procession of workers, seeking their ruler's aid to achieve a living wage and basic civil rights, was fired on by his troops. This episode, the original "Bloody Sunday" (9 January 1905), horrified public opinion at home and abroad and fatally undermined the traditional image of the Russian Tsar as "the little father of his people". Popular unrest continued to grow until, faced by a general strike, Nicholas was forced in October 1905 to concede the establishment of an elected parliament, the Duma.

The Empress, after producing four daughters, turned to religious mysticism in her anxiety for a male heir. In July 1904 she bore a son, Alexei, but it soon became clear that, like other descendants of Queen Victoria, Alexandra carried haemophilia, a genetic illness passed on through the female line, but apparent only in the male. As the infant Tsarevich grew older, his sufferings became more severe. A putative holy man, Gregori Efimovich Rasputin, who seemed to have mystical healing powers over the Tsarevich's condition, emerged from Siberia and became a trusted adviser of the Imperial Family, to the scandal of St Petersburg society. In August 1914 Nicholas for once disregarded his Empress (and Rasputin) and agreed to sign the order for mobilization. Then, in response to an appeal from his cousin the German Emperor, who appreciated that this order would lead to the outbreak of war between their two countries, he reduced the mobilization from "general" to "partial". Under pressure from his generals, Nicholas then changed the order to full mobilization, thus making war inevitable. His Army staff then disconnected their telephone to prevent any further countermands.

In August 1915, with the Russian armies in retreat, Nicholas decided to take personal command. He was encouraged to do so by the Empress, who disliked the commander-in-chief, Grand Duke Nicholas (the Tsar's cousin), partly for his failure to crush the revolution of 1905 and partly because of his threat to hang Rasputin if ever he appeared among the troops. In a gesture of Allied solidarity, King George V appointed Nicholas a field marshal in the British Army on 1 January 1916. A Russian offensive in Galicia obliged the Germans to transfer eighteen divisions from the battle for Verdun, on the Western Front, but cost the lives of over a million men. On Rasputin's advice, relayed by the Empress, Nicholas ended the battle. Continued losses were now blamed on the Tsar's incompetence, or on the treachery of the German-born Tsarina. Russian soldiers, with little idea of why they were fighting, but knowing that their families were starving, lost heart. In February 1917 a bread riot in the capital turned into a general strike. Soldiers, sent to restore order, fraternized with their class comrades. The government collapsed within a few days. Liberals and socialists united in demanding the end of the monarchy. Nicholas, learning from his generals that the Army would not support him, abdicated on 2 March 1917. He and his family were placed under confinement, at first in their palace outside Petrograd (St Petersburg) and then in a mansion in Siberia. The British Cabinet agreed to a request from the Provisional Government to offer them asylum, but reneged in response to pressure from George V, who feared that the arrival of a fallen tyrant with an unpopular German-born wife would place his own throne at risk.

After the Revolution of October 1917 Nicholas and his family were subjected to increasing hardships and indignities. On 16 July 1918, on the orders of the Bolshevik authorities, Nicholas, Alexandra, their children and their personal attendants were murdered in a cellar in Yekaterinburg. Eighty years later, after the fall of the Soviet system, their remains (except for those of the Tsarevich Alexei) were identified by analysis of genetic material, including that from a distant relative, HRH Philip, Duke of Edinburgh [119]. The Russian Orthodox Church (the exiled part of which had canonized Nicholas shortly after his death) refused to accept the accuracy of this identification and none of its bishops attended the ceremony of re-interment in the cathedral of St Peter and Paul, St Petersburg, on 16 July 1998. The President of the Russian Federation, Boris Yeltsin, made this ceremony an act

227

of atonement and reconciliation. The Royal Scots Dragoon Guards, the successor of the Royal Scots Greys, sent a piper and escort to mark the association of their regiment with the last Tsar.

NICHOLSON
Sir WILLIAM GUSTAVUS, 1st Baron Nicholson, GCB
(1845–1918) **[82]**

William Nicholson, the youngest son of a Yorkshire landowner, was born at Roundhay Park, Leeds, on 2 March 1845. He was educated at Leeds Grammar School and the Royal Military Academy, Woolwich, where he passed out first in his batch and was awarded the Pollock **[51]** medal. Nicholson was commissioned into the Royal Engineers as a lieutenant on 21 March 1865 and served in the United Kingdom until 1868, when he was sent to Barbados. In 1871 he married Victorie d'Allier, after having gained an appointment as a military engineer in India, where he was subsequently employed on various public works. He was promoted to captain on 16 March 1878 and, at the beginning of the Second Afghan War, was in the column that advanced to Kandahar in November 1878. On the renewal of the war in 1879 Nicholson served under Sir Frederick Roberts **[68]** as a field engineer at Shutargardan (2 October 1879); Charasia (6 October 1879); Sherpur (11 and 23 December 1879) and Kandahar (1 September 1880). Nicholson was three times mentioned in despatches and was promoted brevet major on 2 March 1881.

Nicholson took part in the Egyptian campaign of 1882 under Sir Garnet Wolseley **[67]** and was at Tel-el-Kebir (13 September 1882). He then returned to India, where he conducted a survey of Baluchistan in 1884 and was assistant adjutant general, Royal Engineers, from 1885 to 1890. During this period, he served under Roberts (at that time C-in-C, India) in the Burma campaign of 1886. Nicholson received a further mention in despatches and was promoted to brevet lieutenant colonel on 1 July 1887. Between 1890 and 1893 he was on Roberts' staff as Military Secretary, with promotion to colonel on 1 January 1891. In 1893 when Roberts returned to the UK, Nicholson returned to military engineering duties on the North-West Frontier. He was appointed adjutant general of the newly-created Punjab Command in 1895 and served as deputy adjutant general and Chief of Staff in the Tirah campaign of 1897, where he was at Dargai (18 October 1897); Sampagha Pass (29 October 1897); Arangha Pass (31 October 1897); Saran Sar (9 November 1897) and operations in the Bara and Bazar valleys at the end of December 1897. He was awarded the KCB and became Adjutant General, India, in 1898.

On assuming command of the British troops in the South Africa War at the end of 1899, Roberts appointed Sir William Nicholson as his Military Secretary, with promotion to major general on 23 December 1899. He became Director of Transport in South Africa in February 1900 and implemented Roberts' controversial policy of organizing the transport service as a centralized resource. He was at Paardeberg (17–26 February 1900); Poplar Grove (7 March 1900); Dreifontein (10 March 1900); Vet River (5–6 May 1900); Zand River (10 May 1900) and Diamond Hill (11–12 June 1900) and was twice mentioned in despatches. After the occupation of the Boer capitals, Nicholson returned with Roberts to the United Kingdom in November 1900. He became Director of Military Operations at the War Office (under Roberts as C-in-C of the British Army) and was promoted to lieutenant general on 4 November 1901. In 1904 he was sent to Manchuria as the senior British observer with the Japanese Army in the Russo-Japanese War. He succeeded Sir Herbert Plumer [89] as Quartermaster General at the War Office in December 1905, with promotion to general on 23 October 1906.

In April 1908, Nicholson became the first Chief of the newly-formed General Staff. With the energetic support of Douglas Haig [85] (first as Director of Military Training and then as Director, Staff Duties), he secured the acceptance of this new staff branch, despite objections from traditionalists who saw it as an alien concept, copied from the Germans. In 1910 the General Staff at the War Office was renamed the Imperial General Staff. Nicholson became a field marshal on 19 June 1911 and was raised to the peerage as Baron Nicholson, of Roundhay, after handing over as CIGS to Sir John French [83] in March 1912. Lord Nicholson was then appointed as the head of a committee set up to consider the defence of India. Under the influence of Sir William Meyer (the Finance Member of the Governor-General of India's Council and thus, in effect, the Treasury Minister of British India), Nicholson recommended that defence expenditure should be kept to a fixed sum, regardless of the defence consequences. He remained a member of the Committee for Imperial Defence and, during the First World War, sat as a member of the Parliamentary Select Committees of Inquiry into the Mesopotamian and Dardanelles campaigns. His own capitulation to the parsimony of Meyer and of the British Cabinet had played a part in the logistical shortcomings of the Mesopotamian campaign, but the blame for them was mostly shifted to Lord Kitchener [79], who by this time had been lost with the cruiser *Hampshire*. Nicholson was appointed a colonel commandant of the Royal Engineers in October 1916. He had no children and his title became extinct with his death, in London, on 13 September 1918.

NORMAN
Sir HENRY WYLIE, GCB, GCMG, CIE (1826–1904) [72]

Henry Norman was born in London on 2 December 1826, the son of a trader and seafarer who conducted most of his business in the West Indies, before moving to Calcutta, then the capital of British India. Norman joined the family firm as a clerk in 1842. In Calcutta he persuaded his reluctant father to obtain him a nomination for a cadetship in the East India Company's Bengal Army. He was appointed while still in India, despite being so small and thin as to barely pass the medical examination, and was commissioned as an ensign in the 1st Bengal Native Infantry on 1 March 1844. He transferred to the 31st Bengal Native Infantry in March 1845 and went with it to Lahore, in the Punjab, in 1846. Norman was promoted to lieutenant on 25 December 1847 and served in the Second Sikh War at Ramnagar (21 November 1848); Sadulapur (3 December 1848); Chilianwala (13 January 1849) and Gujarat (21 February 1849). He then joined the staff at Peshawar, on the North-West Frontier, and took part in the Kohat campaign of 1850. In 1853 he married Selina Davidson, the daughter of a senior member of the Bengal Medical Service. He returned to regimental duty to take part in suppressing the Santhal Rising of 1855, after which he became an assistant adjutant general on the staff of the C-in-C, India, in May 1856.

After the outbreak of the Indian Mutiny in May 1857 Norman took the field with Army HQ and was at the siege of Delhi (June-September 1857), where he served as a staff officer in the adjutant general's branch. After the storming of Delhi he was at the relief of Lucknow (16 November 1857), where his horse was shot under him; Cawnpore (Kanpur, 6 December 1857); the recapture of Lucknow (March 1858) and various engagements in Rohilkhand, where he was wounded on 5 May 1858. With the grasp of statistics that was one of his distinguishing characteristics as a staff officer, he calculated that he was present at some eighty combats during his career, ranging from regular sieges and pitched battles to skirmishes and affairs of outposts.

In August 1858 Norman, along with all the other officers of the East India Company, was transferred to the service of the Crown in India. He was promoted to captain on 1 March 1859 and returned to England in 1860, with promotion to brevet major on 3 December 1860 and brevet lieutenant colonel on the following day. His experience of both combat and staff duty in India made him much in demand and he was appointed to the Hotham Committee, set up to consider the future of the Government of India's European troops. In September 1860 he was appointed to the staff of the Duke of Cambridge [45], C-in-C of the British Army, in the newly created post of assistant military secretary for liaison with India. Norman went back to India in 1861, on appointment as deputy adjutant general of the Bengal Army. In January 1862, he became secretary to the Government of India in the Military Department. He played an important part in the adoption of two fundamental principles for the reconstruction of the Indian armies. One was that units should be organized on the "Irregular system", whereby command at sub-unit level was left to Indian officers, with British officers serving only as the regimental staff and field officers. The other was the Staff Corps concept, whereby British officers belonged to a central pool, with automatic promotion by length of service, rather than to separate regiments or corps in which promotion depended upon the random occurrence of vacancies.

Selina Norman died of fever at the age of 30, leaving her husband with four young daughters. In 1863, he married Jemima Temple, the widow of a captain in the Bengal Army. She died in 1865, in an outbreak of typhoid fever which Norman himself also contracted. After being promoted to colonel on 8 September 1868 and to major general on 23 March 1869, he married Alice Sandys, the daughter of a Bengal Civil Servant, in 1870. They had two sons and a daughter and Norman's later career was much assisted by his wife's contribution to his official and domestic life.

In 1870, Norman joined the Governor-General of India's Council as Military Member, so becoming, in effect, the War Minister of British India. As such, he maintained the policy that the Indian Army should be less well-armed than the British troops in India, in case of another Mutiny. Would-be reformers of his earlier arrangements were met with a series of well-argued and elegantly written minutes, some so long as to be divided into chapters, supported by statistics that enabled him to overwhelm every proposal for change. He was awarded the KCB, with promotion to lieutenant general on 1 October 1877. Sir Henry Norman was appointed to the Council of India at the India Office in London in February 1878, where he sat as chairman of its military committee until the end of 1882. He was promoted to general on 1 April 1882 and, after the expiry of his five-year term in the Council of India, was appointed Governor of Jamaica. He implemented the decision of the Colonial Office in London to introduce a new constitution for this colony and end the long-established autonomy of its local Assembly (previously dominated by the white plantation owners). In 1889, Norman became Governor of Queensland, where he had the difficult task of cutting public expenditure (including his own pay). As in Jamaica, he managed to get on with the local politicians, who respected his administrative skills and his personal good nature, and with the population as a whole, through his donations to good causes (a generosity that, with a wife and several daughters, he could ill afford). In 1893, the British Cabinet, faced with difficulty in finding a new Viceroy and Governor-General of India, offered this post to Norman. He initially accepted, but, faced with strong protests by Indian nationalists, who saw him as a relic of a former age, withdrew on the grounds that his age and health would not stand another five years of the Indian climate. At the expiry of his tenure of office in Australia, he returned to England, where he was appointed Governor of the Royal Hospital, Chelsea, in 1901 and was promoted to field marshal on 26 June 1902. He died on 26 October 1904 at the Royal Hospital, Chelsea, and was buried at Brompton cemetery. His admirers instituted a memorial to him in the form of a prize medal for the best cadet joining the Indian Army from each batch of gentleman cadets at the Royal Military College, Sandhurst.

NUGENT
Sir GEORGE, 1st Baronet, GCB (1757–1849) [35]

George Nugent, illegitimate son of the Honourable Edmund Nugent (a younger son of the 1st Earl Nugent), was born in 1757 and educated at Charterhouse School and the Royal Military Academy, Woolwich. He did not complete his course at the Academy (the school for future artillery and engineer officers) but instead obtained a commission as an ensign in the 39th Foot, on 5 July 1773. He served with the 39th in Gibraltar from February 1774 to March 1776 and was promoted to lieutenant on joining the 7th Royal Fusiliers, in New York, in September 1777. He took part in the American War of Independence, where he served in the campaign on the Hudson, including the storming of Forts Montgomery and Clifton (6 October 1777), and at Philadelphia until the British evacuation in July 1778. Nugent became a captain in the 57th Foot on 28th April 1778 and a major on 3 May 1782. He returned to England to become lieutenant colonel in the 97th Foot on 8 September 1783. This regiment was disbanded in the post-war reductions and Nugent was placed on the half-pay list. In 1787 he joined the 13th Foot and returned to full pay.

Nugent was then given a post in Dublin, on the staff of his cousin, the 1st Marquess of Buckingham, who became Lord Lieutenant of Ireland in November 1787. In 1789, when Buckingham left this office, Nugent joined the 4th Dragoon Guards. He transferred in 1790 to the Coldstream Guards, as captain in the regiment and lieutenant colonel in the Army. He became an MP in 1790 and represented various Buckinghamshire constituencies until the reform of Parliament in 1832. At the beginning of the French Revolutionary War he went with the Foot Guards to Flanders, where he was at Valenciennes (May-June 1793); Lincelles (18 August 1793) and Dunkirk (August 1793). During the winter of 1793–94, Nugent used his local connections to raise a new regiment, the Buckinghamshire Volunteers, (later the 85th Light Infantry), of which he became colonel on 1 March 1794. He was promoted to major general on 1 May 1796 and subsequently held various commands in Ireland. He also sat as MP for Charleville, County Cork, until the Irish Parliament was abolished on the Act of Union of 1801. In November 1797, he married Maria Skinner, seventh daughter of the attorney general of the State of New Jersey. Between April 1801 and February 1806, Nugent was lieutenant governor and C-in-C, Jamaica, with promotion to lieutenant general on 25 September 1803. He became colonel of the 62nd Foot in December 1805 and retained this appointment until March 1806, when he became colonel of the 6th Foot. He was created a baronet on 28 November 1806.

Between 1806 and 1809, Sir George Nugent held various commands in southern England. He was C-in-C, India, from January 1812 to October 1813, with promotion to general on 4 June 1813. Along with the other two senior generals in the Army, he was promoted to field marshal on 9 November 1846, to celebrate the fifth birthday of the Prince of Wales [54]. Nugent died at Waddesdon House, his home on the outskirts of Marlow, Buckinghamshire, on 11 March 1849, leaving a family of three sons and two daughters. He was the first field marshal to have attended (although not actually to have passed out from) the Royal Military Academy.

O'HARA
JAMES, 1st Baron Kilmaine and 2nd Baron Tyrawley,
(1690–1773) [11]

James O'Hara was born in Ireland in 1690, the eldest son of General Sir Charles O'Hara, (a Protestant Irish officer who would be raised to the peerage in 1710 and end his active military career as commander of the forces in Ireland). He was first commissioned on 15 March 1703 as a lieutenant in the Royal Fusiliers (later the 7th Foot), the regiment of which Sir Charles O'Hara was at that time colonel. The young O'Hara was promoted to captain in 1705 and served in the Peninsular campaign in the War of the Spanish Succession, at Barcelona (May 1706) and Almanza (25 April 1707), where he was wounded. In 1708 O'Hara joined Marlborough's army in the Low Countries, where he was badly wounded at Malplaquet (11 September 1709). After recovering, he became lieutenant colonel of the Royal Fusiliers and was appointed colonel of the regiment on 29 January 1713. He served with the Royal Fusiliers in the garrison of Minorca in 1713–14 and took part with them in a minor campaign in Sicily and Naples late in 1718. His services were rewarded with the grant of an Irish peerage as Baron Kilmaine on 2 January 1722. Lord Kilmaine succeeded his father as the 2nd Baron Tyrawley in 1724.

From 1728 to 1741, Lord Tyrawley was the British Ambassador at Lisbon. He became a popular figure in Portuguese society, spending freely and eventually returning to London with, it was said, three wives, fourteen children and a reputation for licentiousness. He became a major general in 1739 and lieutenant general on 31 March 1743. Between November 1743 and February 1745, he was British Ambassador at St Petersburg. He gave up his colonelcy of the Royal Fusiliers to become, successively, colonel of a regiment of Horse on the Irish establishment (later the 4th Royal Irish Dragoon Guards) from August 1739; the 2nd Troop of Horse Grenadier Guards from April 1743; the 3rd Troop of Horse Guards from April 1745; a regiment of infantry (later the 10th Foot) from December 1746; a junior regiment of dragoons (later the 14th Dragoons) from July 1749; a senior regiment of dragoons (later the 3rd Dragoons) from July 1752 and the Coldstream Guards from April 1755. Tyrawley became a general on 7 March 1761. He returned to Portugal in 1762 as both British Ambassador and commander of the British troops sent to assist Portugal against Spain during the Seven Years War. He was superseded in effective command by the younger and more active General John Burgoyne and returned to the UK in protest. Tyrawley was promoted to field

234

marshal on 10 June 1763. He died at Twickenham on 14 July 1773 and was buried at the Royal Hospital, Chelsea. He had no children by his lawful wife, Mary Stewart, the daughter of Lieutenant General Lord Mountjoy. Tyrawley was the last officer to be promoted to field marshal for thirty years. After his death the rank was left unfilled until its revival in1793. Except for royal personages, he was colonel of more regiments (eight) than any other officer in the history of the British Army.

ORKNEY
EARL OF, see **HAMILTON,** GEORGE, **[1]**

PAGET
HENRY WILLIAM, 1st Marquess of Anglesey and 3rd Earl of Uxbridge KG, GCB, GCH (1768–1854) **[37]**

Henry, by courtesy Lord Paget, the eldest son of the 2nd Earl of Uxbridge, was born in London on 17 May 1768. He was educated at Westminster School and Christ Church, Oxford, and entered public life in 1790 as MP for Carnarvon, which he represented until 1810. Lord Paget began his military career as an officer in the Staffordshire Militia, of which his father was colonel. In September 1793 he raised a regiment of infantry (later the 80th Foot) recruited mostly from his own militia-men. In the French Revolutionary War Paget served in the Flanders campaign of 1794–95, where he commanded first his own regiment and then, during the winter retreat into Germany, a brigade. Although colonel of his regiment, with the rank of lieutenant colonel, Paget at this period had not been granted a commission in the Regular Army. To remedy this, without the need for purchase, a series of exchanges and promotions had to be arranged. During 1795 his name appeared on the rolls of the 7th Royal Fusiliers (as lieutenant), the 23rd Royal Welsh Fusiliers (as captain), the 65th Foot (as major) and the 16th Light Dragoons (as lieutenant colonel) without his doing duty with any of them. He gave up his colonelcy of the 80th Foot on becoming lieutenant colonel of the 16th Light Dragoons on 15 June 1795. During the same year, he married Lady Caroline Villiers, with whom he later had eight children.

Paget was promoted to colonel in the Army on 3 May 1796 and became a lieutenant colonel in the 7th Light Dragoons on 6 April 1797. In the expedition to the Helder (September-October 1799), he commanded a cavalry brigade at Egmont (Bergen, 2 Oct 1799) and

Kastrikum (6 Oct 1799). Paget became colonel of the 7th Light Dragoons (Hussars) on 16 May 1801, followed by promotion to major general on 29 April 1802 and to lieutenant general on 25 April 1808. He went to the Peninsula in August 1808 and returned there with Sir John Moore's army later that year, where he was at Sahagun (21 December 1808), Benavente (29 December 1808) and in the retreat to Corunna (evacuated 17 January 1809). Paget then took part in the Walcheren campaign of August-December 1809, where he commanded an infantry division.

In 1810, Paget's wife was granted a divorce, on the grounds of his adultery with Lady Charlotte Wellesley (daughter of the Earl Cadogan and sister-in-law of the future Duke of Wellington [24]). Forced into a duel by Lady Charlotte's indignant brother, he fired wide, so as to do no further injury to her family. Paget married Lady Charlotte after she was divorced by her husband, and Caroline Paget married another general, her long-standing admirer, the 6th Duke of Argyll.

Paget succeeded his father as 3rd Earl of Uxbridge on 13 March 1812. Despite the dash and ability he had shown both on the Helder and, under Moore, in the Peninsula, he remained in disgrace and was not employed in Wellington's Peninsular campaigns. In the Hundred Days Campaign, however, he was given command of the Allied cavalry and became, in effect, Wellington's second-in-command. Uxbridge was at Quatre Bras and Genappe (14 June 1815) and Waterloo (16 June 1815). In the closing moments of the battle, he lost a leg by cannon-shot. He recovered from this wound and, both encouraging and benefiting from contemporary developments in the science of pros-thetics, was later fitted with an articulated false limb. Uxbridge was created Marquess of Anglesey on 4 July 1815 and became a general on 12 August 1819. He was, from 1 May 1827 to January 1828, the last Master General of the Ordnance to sit as a member of the British Cabinet. On 27 February 1828, Anglesey became Lord Lieutenant of Ireland. He argued against conceding Roman Catholic Emancipation in response to terrorist outrages, but nevertheless became convinced that this measure was justified on other grounds and recommended it accordingly. This policy was unacceptable to the ministers of the day and in January 1829 the office of Lord Lieutenant of Ireland was given to the Duke of Northumberland. After the fall of the Tory ministry, Anglesey was re-appointed as Lord Lieutenant of Ireland in December 1830, and remained as such until September 1833.

During this period, Anglesey was faced with widespread agitation for further reforms, especially for repeal of the 1801 Act of Union. In accordance with ministerial policy, he implemented a series of repressive measures, but also introduced improvements in elementary education from which the Roman Catholic majority of the population benefited. He again became Master General of the Ordnance in 1846 and held this post until the fall of the Whig ministry in February 1852. Anglesey became colonel of the Royal Horse Guards on 20 December 1842. He was one of the three senior ranking generals in the Army who were promoted to field marshal on 9 November 1846 on the occasion of the fifth birthday of the Prince of Wales [54]. Anglesey died in London at Uxbridge House, Burlington Gardens, on 29 April 1854 and was buried in his family vault at Lichfield Cathedral.

PAULET
Lord WILLIAM, GCB (1804–1893) [62]

Lord William Paulet, fourth son of the 13th Marquess of Winchester, was born on 7 July 1804. He was educated at Eton College and was commissioned as an ensign in the 85th Light Infantry on 1 February 1821. He became a lieutenant in the 7th Royal Fusiliers on 23 February 1822 and captain of an unattached company on 25 February 1825. Paulet then exchanged to the 21st Royal North British Fusiliers. He became a major in the 68th Light Infantry on 10 September 1830 and subsequently served with this regiment in the United Kingdom, Gibraltar, Jamaica and Canada. He was promoted to lieutenant colonel on 21 April 1843 and served as commanding officer of his regiment until 1848, when he exchanged to the half-pay list. At the beginning of the Crimean War Paulet joined the staff of the Cavalry Division under Lord Lucan [63]. He was at the Alma (20 September 1854); Balaklava (25 October 1854) where he had his hat shot away; Inkerman (5 November 1854) and in other operations in the invest-ment of Sevastopol. He was given command of the rear maintenance area on the Turkish coast, with promotion to brevet colonel, on 28 November 1854. Paulet's responsibilities included the base hospital at Scutari, where, having experienced conditions in the Crimea at first hand, he gave his support to Florence Nightingale in her struggle with the military medical establishment. At the end of the campaign, he briefly took command of the Light Division. He became a major gen-eral on 13 June 1858 and commanded South-West District from 1860 to 1863. He was colonel of the 87th Foot from July 1863 to April 1864, when he became colonel of the 68th Light Infantry (later the 2nd Battalion, the Durham Light Infantry). His last active employment was between 1865 and 1870, as Adjutant General. Paulet became a lieutenant general on 8 December 1867, general on 7 October 1874 and field marshal on 10 July 1886. He died on 10 May 1893.

PHILIP
HRH Duke of Edinburgh, KG, KT, OM, GBE, AC, QSO
(1921–   ) [119]

Prince Philip of Greece was born in Corfu on 10 June 1921, the only son in a family of five children born to Prince Andrew of Greece and his wife Princess Alice (Victoria Alice Elizabeth Julia Maria), the daughter of Prince Louis of Battenberg. Prince Andrew was a younger brother of King Constantine I of the Hellenes. Their paternal grandfather was Christian IX of Denmark, whose daughter Alexandra married the future King Edward VII [53] and the two were therefore cousins of King George V [80]. Princess Alice's mother, Princess Victoria of Hesse-Darmstadt, was a granddaughter of Queen Victoria and a sister of Alexandra, wife of the Emperor Nicholas II of Russia [84]. Princess Alice, in her youth, was said to be the most beautiful princess in Europe. A woman of determined character, who overcame the challenge of being born profoundly deaf, she became in later life a nun in a Greek Orthodox community. Her father, Prince Louis of Battenberg, made his career in the British Navy. By the time of the outbreak of the First World War in 1914, Prince Louis had risen to the post of First Sea Lord. Despite his loyalty to his adopted country and his value to the Service of which he had become the professional head, he was driven to resign his office by the public hysteria against anything that could be connected with Germany. When the British Royal Family disclaimed its German titles in 1917, Prince Louis of Battenberg anglicized his name as Mountbatten and was granted a peerage as the Marquess of Milford Haven. He was promoted to admiral of the fleet in August 1921, in a belated compensation for the injustice that had been done him in 1914. The marquess's younger son, Lord Louis Mountbatten, (later Admiral of the Fleet Earl Mountbatten of Burma) was thus a brother of Princess Alice of Greece and the uncle of her only son, Prince Philip.

Following the establishment of a republican regime in Greece, Prince Andrew went into exile with his family in 1922. They took refuge with his mother in Paris, from where Prince Philip was sent, in 1930, to Cheam Preparatory School. In 1934, he spent two terms in Germany, before going to a school newly-founded by an eminent German educationalist, at Gordonstoun, Morayshire. Prince Philip decided on a naval career and, in May 1939, became a cadet at the Royal Naval

College, Dartmouth. On the advice of Lord Louis Mountbatten, he sought naturalization as a British subject when the Second World War began in September 1939, but found that this process had been placed in abeyance for the duration of hostilities. Prince Philip joined the fleet as a sea officer but, as the national of a neutral state, was kept away from operational zones until after the Italian invasion of Greece in October 1940. He then joined the battleship *Valiant* in the eastern Mediterranean and was at Cape Matapan (28 March 1941), where he was mentioned in despatches. Prince Philip subsequently served in destroyers in the Mediterranean, the North Sea and the Pacific.

After his return to duty in the UK in 1946, Prince Philip's name became increasingly linked with that of the Princess Elizabeth, heiress to the British throne. He was granted British citizenship, disclaimed his title as a prince of Greece and (largely through the influence of his uncle, who had made the name famous through his wartime exploits) assumed the surname Mountbatten. Lieutenant Philip Mountbatten and Princess Elizabeth were married in Westminster Abbey on 20 November 1947. On the following day he was granted the style of Royal Highness and was created Duke of Edinburgh (a title which had been held by Queen Victoria's second son, Alfred, who had served as a naval officer himself). The Duke returned to sea duty in the Mediterranean, where he served as First Lieutenant of the destroyer flotilla leader *Chequers* and, after promotion to lieutenant commander in July 1950, as commanding officer of the frigate *Magpie*. Princess Elizabeth succeeded to the throne on 6 February 1952 on the death of her father, King George VI [106]. The Duke of Edinburgh's naval career then came to an end as he took up the duties of a Royal consort.

The Duke of Edinburgh became an Admiral of the Fleet, Field Marshal and Marshal of the Royal Air Force on 15 January 1953. Later in 1953 he was appointed colonel-in-chief of the 8th King's Own Royal Irish Hussars, later amalgamated to form the Queen's Own Royal Irish Hussars, subsequently renamed the Queen's Royal Hussars (the Queen's Own and Royal Irish), of which the Duke became deputy colonel-in-chief; the Duke of Edinburgh's (Wiltshire Regiment), later amalgamated first to form the Duke of Edinburgh's Royal Regiment (Berkshire and Wiltshire) and subsequently the Royal Gloucestershire, Berkshire and Wiltshire Regiment; and the Queen's Own Cameron Highlanders, later amalgamated first to form the Queen's Own Highlanders (Seaforth and Camerons) and subsequently the Highlanders (Seaforth, Gordons and Camerons). The Duke of Edinburgh became colonel-in-chief of the Royal Electrical and Mechanical Engineers in 1969 and of the Intelligence Corps in 1977.

He was colonel of the Welsh Guards from 1953 to 1975, when he became colonel of the Grenadier Guards. In the Territorial Army, he was appointed honorary colonel of the Leicestershire Yeomanry (Prince Albert's Own), later amalgamated to form the Leicestershire and Derbyshire Yeomanry (Prince Albert's Own) and subsequently disbanded, and of the Edinburgh University (later Edinburgh and Heriot Watt Universities) Contingent, Officers Training Corps. In the Australian Army, he became a field marshal in 1954 and colonel-in-chief of the Royal Australian Electrical and Mechanical Engineers in 1959. In the Canadian forces, he was appointed colonel-in-chief of the Royal Canadian Regiment; the Royal Hamilton Light Infantry; the Queen's Own Cameron Highlanders of Canada (Militia); the Seaforth Highlanders of Canada (Militia) and the Cameron Highlanders of Ottawa (Militia). He was appointed a field marshal in the New Zealand Army, where he became colonel-in-chief of the Hawkes Bay Regiment; the Otago and Southland Regiment and the Royal New Zealand Electrical and Mechanical Engineers (later disbanded). The Duke of Edinburgh's interest in young people, exemplified by his creation of the Duke of Edinburgh's Award scheme to encourage endeavour and self-reliance, had its military expression in his appointment as colonel-in-chief of the Army Cadet Force in the British Army and the equivalent organizations in Canada and Australia. In 1957, to mark the occasion of their tenth wedding anniversary, Queen Elizabeth II awarded her husband the title of a Prince of the United Kingdom.

PLUMER
Sir HERBERT CHARLES ONSLOW, 1st Viscount Plumer, GCB, GCMG, GCVO, GBE (1857–1932) **[89]**

Herbert Plumer, the elder son of a wealthy Yorkshireman, was born in Sussex Place, London, on 13 March 1857. He attended Eton College from 1870 to 1876 and was commissioned as a lieutenant in the 65th Foot (later the 1st Battalion, the York and Lancaster Regiment) on 11 September 1876. He joined the 65th in India and became battalion adjutant in 1879, followed by promotion to captain on 29 May 1882, when his regiment was posted to Aden. From there, he went on leave to the United Kingdom and became engaged to his second cousin, Annie Goss, a sensible young woman to whom, after their marriage, he left all the important decisions in his life. In 1884, Plumer and his regiment took part in the operations in the eastern Sudan, in support of the Gordon Relief Expedition. He was at El Teb (29 February 1884) and

Tamai (13 March 1884) and was mentioned in despatches. After returning to the United Kingdom, he married his fiancée in July 1884; they later had three daughters and a son. He attended the Staff College at Camberley from 1886 to 1888 and was appointed deputy assistant adjutant general in Jersey in 1890. He was promoted to major on 22 January 1893 and joined the 2nd Battalion, the York and Lancaster Regiment, in Natal.

Plumer remained in South Africa, where he was appointed assistant military secretary to the GOC, Cape Colony, in December 1895. He was sent to Rhodesia early in 1896 to supervise the disarming of the British South Africa Company Police, following their part in the unsuccessful Jameson Raid. Later that year he returned to command the 750-strong Matabele Relief Force, hastily raised from local volunteers in response to the Matabele ('Ndbele) rising. After six months of counter-insurgency operations he returned to the United Kingdom as deputy assistant adjutant general at Aldershot, with promotion to lieutenant colonel on 8 March 1897. In 1899, on the approach of the South African War, Plumer was sent back to Rhodesia to raise a force of mounted infantry, in which many of his Matabele War veterans enlisted. When Mafeking came under siege he assumed command of the Rhodesian troops remaining in the field. Their attempt to relieve Mafeking was defeated on 31 March 1900, when Plumer himself was wounded. After another combat at Jan Massibi (15 May 1900) he entered Mafeking as part of a larger relieving column. He was promoted to colonel on 29 November 1900. Between January and March 1901 he commanded a mixed force of Rhodesians, Canadians, Australians and New Zealanders in the pursuit of the Boer Commandant De Wet. Plumer established a good rapport with his independently-minded colonial troops and captured De Wet's wagon train at Hamelfontein (12 February 1901). At the end of the war he was mentioned in despatches and given command of the 4th Brigade at Aldershot.

Plumer was promoted to major general on 22 August 1902 and became GOC Eastern District in December 1903. In February 1904 he was appointed Quartermaster General, with a seat on the newly-created Army Council. He became identified with the controversial reforms proposed by H.O.Arnold-Foster, Secretary of State for War in the Unionist Cabinet of the day, and consequently was removed from office in December 1905, when a new Liberal ministry came to power. He was made a KCB and, after a brief period on half-pay, was given command of a division in Ireland. Sir Herbert Plumer was promoted to lieutenant general on 4 November 1908. When the tenure of his divisional command expired in 1909, he returned to London on the half-pay.

Bitter at being superseded by officers junior to him, he considered taking up an offer of lucrative employment outside the Army, but was persuaded to remain by Lord Roberts [68], an old friend who pointed out that, with the deteriorating international situation, he might expect opportunities for advancement in his chosen profession. In 1911 he became GOC-in-C, Northern Command, where he remained when the First World War began in August 1914.

Plumer went to the Western Front in January 1915, to command the newly-formed V Corps. In May 1915, at the end of the second battle of Ypres, he was given command of the Second Army, with promotion to general on 11 June 1915. He remained in the Ypres salient, where he launched a limited but successful attack at Messines in June 1917. From 31 July to 7 November 1917 he commanded the Second Army in the third battle of Ypres. Plumer had established a reputation for caution and reliability, but the combined effect of prolonged unseasonable rainfall and strong German defences resulted in extremely heavy losses for limited territorial gains. His "bite and hold" strategy forced the Germans to incur heavy casualties in attempting to regain lost ground, but the battle (generally known as Passchendaele) joined the Somme in British folklore as a synonym for futile slaughter. After the victory of the Central Powers at Caporetto (24 October–19 November 1917) he was then given command of a force of five British and six French divisions sent as reinforcements to Italy. With the Italian front stabilized, Plumer and most of his men returned to France in March 1918. During the German offensives of March-April 1918, the Second Army was driven back from Messines, Wytschaete and Passchendaele, but, in a determined resistance, held on to Ypres. In the Allied counter-offensive, its initial role was in support of the British Fourth Army. In September 1918, the supreme Allied commander, Marshal Foch [88] placed Plumer and the Second Army under command of King Albert I of the Belgians [94], as part of the Flanders Army Group. This made extensive gains before the end of hostilities on 11 November 1918, after which the Second Army then became the British Army of Occupation on the Rhine. As C-in-C and the head of the military government, Plumer put down outbreaks of revolutionary disorder, but secured food for the starving civilian population under his control.

After being succeeded in command of BAOR by Sir William Robertson [92] in April 1919, Plumer was granted a peerage as Baron Plumer, of Messines and of Bilton, and was promoted to field marshal on 31 July 1919. He became Governor and C-in-C, Malta in June 1919, where he was faced with the problem of economic hardship among the Maltese population, compounded by the demands of local nationalists for self-determination (one of the principles declared by the Allies to be an important feature of the post-war settlement). From August 1925 to July 1928 he was High Commissioner in Palestine, (and latterly also in Transjordan) where he dealt firmly and impartially with both Zionists and Arab nationalists. After retiring from public service Plumer was made a viscount in 1929. He became colonel of the York and Lancaster Regiment (later disbanded) in August 1917 and honorary colonel of the Inns of Court Regiment, Territorial Army, in November 1928. He died in London on 16 July 1932 and was buried in Westminster Abbey. The rotund figure and white moustache that marked Plumer's appearance during his later years were said to have inspired David Low's famous cartoon character "Colonel Blimp".

POLLOCK
Sir GEORGE, 1st Baronet, GCB, GCSI (1786–1872) [51]

George Pollock was the youngest son of a Charing Cross saddler who included the Royal Household among his fashionable customers. The father's business prospered so well that he was able to raise his first two sons to become eminent lawyers and obtain a nomination in the East India Company's service for the third. After attending the Royal Military Academy, Woolwich, George Pollock was commissioned as lieutenant fireworker in the Bengal Artillery on 14 December 1803 and was promoted to lieutenant on 19 April 1804. Pollock served in the battle of Deig (Dig, 13 November 1804) and the subsequent siege of that city (2–24 December 1804) and in the siege of Bharatpur (2 January–21 April 1805), with promotion to captain-lieutenant on 17 September 1805. In 1810 he married Frances Webbe Barclay, daughter of the sheriff of Tain, Easter Ross. Pollock was promoted to captain on 12 March 1812, major on 12 August 1819 and lieutenant colonel on 1 May 1824. During the First Burma War he commanded the British artillery in operations around Prome (November-December 1824) and at Pagan (9 February 1826). He was promoted to brevet colonel on 1 December 1829, to colonel commandant in the Bengal Artillery on 3 March 1833 and to major general on 28 June 1838.

During the First Afghan War Pollock was given command of the force sent to relieve Jalalabad, besieged following the British retreat from Kabul in January 1842. He went on to the offensive at the end of March 1842, took Jamrud, at the entrance to the Khyber Pass, by a surprise attack on 5 April 1842 and reached Jalalabad on 16 April 1842. He remained there until August 1842, when he marched to meet a British army approaching Kabul from Kandahar, under Major General Nott. After defeating the Afghans at Gandamak (24 August 1842), Jagdalak (8 September 1842), and Tezin (12–13 September 1842), Pollock reached Kabul two days ahead of Nott. The joint force, under Pollock's command, recovered the British hostages who had been left behind in the earlier retreat, blew up the main bazaar and then returned to India. Pollock was awarded the GCB and in 1844 was for a short time British Resident at Lucknow. Sir George Pollock then served as Military Member of the Governor-General of India's Council from 1844 until 1848, when he returned to England. To mark his achievements in Afghanistan, a medal, originally funded by the British inhabitants of Calcutta, was instituted in his name, to be awarded to the most deserving cadet in each batch at the East India Company's Military Seminary, Addiscombe. This prize was awarded from 1848 until this establishment closed in 1860 and, from then on, at the Royal Military Academy, Woolwich, until the Academy closed in 1939. Lady Pollock died in 1849, leaving a family of five children. Her widowed husband later married Henrietta Wollaston, the daughter of a private gentleman living in South London.

Pollock was promoted to lieutenant general on 11 November 1851 and from 1854 to 1856 sat as one of the three government-appointed members of the East India Company's Court of Directors. On the ending of the Company's government in August 1858, together with all its other military and civil servants, he was transferred to the service of the Crown in India. He was promoted to general on 17 May 1859 and, on the amalgamation of the three Indian Regiments of Artillery with the Royal Regiment in 1861, was appointed colonel commandant on the Royal Artillery's Bengal list. In 1861 Pollock became honorary colonel of the 1st Surrey Rifle Volunteer Corps. He was promoted to field marshal on 24 May 1870 and was made a baronet in March 1872. He outlived his second wife by eight months and died on 6 October 1872, at Walmer Castle, his official residence as Warden of the Cinque Ports. He was buried in Westminster Abbey. Sir George Pollock was the first officer of artillery to be given command of a British army in the field and the first field marshal to have begun his career in the East India Company's service. He was succeeded as 2nd baronet by his eldest son, who became Sir Frederick Montagu-Pollock.

RAGLAN
LORD, see **SOMERSET,** Lord FITZROY, **[38]**

RICH
Sir ROBERT, 4th Baronet, 1685–1768 [8]

Robert Rich, the second son of a Suffolk landowner and courtier, distantly connected to the Earls of Warwick and Holland, was born at Roos Hall, Beccles, on 3 July 1685. He began his career as a page of honour to William III and was first commissioned on 10 June 1700, as ensign in the 1st Foot Guards and lieutenant in the Army. During the War of the Spanish Succession Rich served in Marlborough's early campaigns in Flanders. He was at the Schellenberg (2 July 1704), where he was wounded, and Blenheim (13 August 1704), after which he was promoted to lieutenant in his regiment and captain in the Army. Rich succeeded his brother as 4th baronet in October 1706 and was promoted to captain in his regiment and lieutenant colonel in the Army on 9 March 1708. In June 1708, he fought a duel with another baronet, Sir Edward Bacon and ran him through. Sir Robert Rich had to lie low for a time, but Bacon recovered and lived until 1755. In 1710 Rich married Elizabeth Griffin, whose father was a colonel in the Army and secretary to Prince George of Denmark, the consort of Queen Anne. The marriage produced one daughter and three sons, of whom the second eventually succeeded to his title as 5th baronet. Between 1715 and 1722 Rich sat as member of Parliament for the borough of Dunwich. He returned to Parliament in 1727, where he represented various different constituencies until 1744.

During the Jacobite Rising of 1715 Rich was appointed colonel of a newly-raised regiment of dragoons but did not take part in active operations After the disbandment of this regiment, he became colonel, successively, of a junior regiment of dragoons (later the 13th Hussars) in 1722, of a more senior one (later the 8th Hussars) in 1725, of a regiment of Horse (later the 6th Dragoon Guards) in 1731, of the 1st Troop of Horse Grenadier Guards (later disbanded) in 1733 and, finally, of a senior regiment of dragoons (later the 4th Hussars) in 1735. Rich became a major general on 12 November 1735 and lieutenant general on 2 July 1739. During the War of the Austrian Succession, he served in the Pragmatic Army under the Earl of Stair [5] and fought at Dettingen (16 June 1743). He later returned to the UK with an appointment in the home forces and was promoted to general on 29 March 1747. Ten years later, when George II decided to revive the rank of field marshal for the benefit of Lord Ligonier [10], the newly-appointed C-in-C, Rich was the senior ranking general in the British Army. He was accordingly promoted to field marshal on 28 November 1757, two days ahead of Ligonier and one day ahead of the second senior general, Lord

Molesworth [9]. Rich died on 1 February 1768, in post as Governor of the Royal Hospital, Chelsea.

RICHMOND
DUKE OF, *see* **LENNOX,** CHARLES, **[22]**

ROBERTS
Sir FREDERICK SLEIGH, 1st Earl Roberts, VC, KG, KP, GCB, OM, GCSI, GCIE, VD (1832–1914) **[68]**

Frederick Roberts, later familiarly known as "Bobs", was born on 30 September 1832 at Cawnpore (Kanpur) in northern India. He was the younger son of a senior officer in the East India Company's Bengal Army, and a member of a family long-established in the Anglo-Irish Protestant Ascendancy. Roberts was educated at Eton College, before attending the Royal Military College, Sandhurst, and the East India Company's Military Seminary, Addiscombe. At first remarkable only by his diminutive stature (barely over five feet tall), Roberts was commissioned on 15 December 1851 as a second lieutenant in the Bengal Artillery. In 1852, he became ADC to his father, who was at that time commanding the British garrison at Peshawar, on the North-West Frontier. Roberts joined the Bengal Horse Artillery, the élite of the Company's Army, in 1854 and obtained a staff appointment at Peshawar in 1856. He was promoted to lieutenant on 31 May 1857. On the outbreak of the Indian Mutiny in May 1857 he formed part of the column sent from the Punjab to Delhi, where he served both on the staff and in the siege batteries and was wounded in June 1857. He took part in the final relief of Lucknow (14–17 November 1857) and in its re-capture by the British (11–19 March 1858). Roberts was awarded the Victoria Cross for valour at Khudaganj (2 January 1858) where, on the staff of the Cavalry Division, he captured an enemy standard in hand-to-hand combat. In 1858, like all other officers of the East India Company, he was transferred to the service of the Crown in India.

Having qualified for leave out of India on medical certificate, Roberts returned to the United Kingdom, where he met and married Nora Henrietta Bews, daughter of a retired captain of the 73rd Foot. He was promoted to captain on 12 November 1860 and to brevet major on 13 November 1860. In February 1861, along with the rest of the Indian artillery, Roberts was transferred to the Royal Regiment of Artillery in the British Army. He continued to serve in India on the staff of the

Bengal Army, taking part in various minor campaigns on the North-West Frontier and going with the Bengal contingent in the expedition to Abyssinia (Ethiopia) in 1868. Roberts became a brevet lieutenant colonel on 15 August 1868 and a brevet colonel on 30 January 1875. Between 1875 and 1878 he was Quartermaster General of the Bengal Army.

Roberts then became a favourite of Lord Lytton, the newly-arrived Viceroy and Governor-General of India, a keen proponent of expanding British power across the North-West Frontier into Afghanistan. In March 1878 he was given command of the Punjab Frontier Force (a body which came directly under the Governor-General rather than under the C-in-C, India), with promotion to acting major general. When the British invaded Afghanistan in November 1878, Roberts commanded the Kurram column and achieved a victory at Peiwar Kotal (2 December 1878). In the distribution of honours for this campaign he was awarded the KCB with promotion to substantive major general on 31 December 1878. Roberts was sent back into Afghanistan in September 1879, with orders to exact retribution for the murder by an Afghan mob of Sir Louis Cavagnari, the British envoy at Kabul. After defeating an Afghan force at Charasia (6 October 1879) he occupied Kabul and carried out a policy of reprisals that made the war unpopular at home and stirred up resistance in Afghanistan. Roberts was defeated outside Kabul at Sherpur (11 December 1879) and was besieged there until relieved two weeks later. At the end of April 1878 Sir Donald Stewart [66] arrived from Kandahar and assumed command as the senior ranking general. This, together with the resignation of his patron, Lord Lytton, seemed to spell the end of Roberts' career. He was saved by a sudden requirement for troops to go to the relief of Kandahar in August 1878. This allowed his friend Stewart to give Roberts command of a flying column that covered the 280 miles from Kabul to Kandahar in twenty days. Roberts then secured a victory at Kandahar (1 September 1880) that restored British prestige and his own reputation.

Roberts returned to England as a hero. In March 1881 he was sent to Natal to command the British forces after the Boer victory at Majuba, but, after arriving to find that peace had been agreed, returned immediately to London. Roberts declined the offered post of Quartermaster General, but accepted that of C-in-C, Madras. He made genuine attempts to improve the efficiency of the Madras Army, but became confirmed in his prejudice against South Indian troops. Roberts was promoted to lieutenant general on 26 July 1883 and became C-in-C, India, in November 1885. Between November 1886 and February 1887 Roberts commanded the British forces at Rangoon, in the Third

Burma War, following the death of the previous field commander, Sir Herbert Macpherson, who had succeeded him as C-in-C, Madras. He remained as C-in-C, India, until April 1893, with promotion to general on 28 November 1890 and elevation to the peerage as Baron Roberts, of Kandahar and of Waterford, in January 1892. He had not sought this unusually long tenure of command in India, as it prevented him from becoming Adjutant General in succession to Sir Garnet Wolseley [67]. Wolseley, however, did not wish to become C-in-C, India, and the only other candidate was the Duke of Connaught [73], whose candidature was pressed by Queen Victoria (his mother) and by the Duke of Cambridge [45] (his cousin) as a way of grooming him to succeed Cambridge as C-in-C of the British Army. The Cabinet had no desire to see another royal commander-in-chief and therefore declined to nominate him as C-in-C, India. Roberts felt aggrieved that he was not even allowed home on leave.

During his time as C-in-C, India, Lord Roberts became the recognized expert on the Indian Army and, as such, advocated that its sepoys should be recruited only from selected "martial classes" (mostly located in northern India and the Punjab). These groups alone, he believed, had the physique and temperament needed for service against European troops (especially the Russians whom he saw as a likely enemy in Central Asia) or the tough and wily Pathan tribesmen of the North-West Frontier. On his return to England he used a period out of employment to write his *Forty-One Years in India*, an influential autobiography in which he expounded his views on Indian military organization. His popularity was enhanced by the hero-worship he attracted from Rudyard Kipling, the best-selling writer and poet of his day, who portrayed Roberts as a great but self-effacing master of war and incorporated many of Roberts' opinions into his own works.

Roberts had hoped to succeed Cambridge as C-in-C of the British Army, but this post was given to Wolseley. This period saw the peak of the "battle of the Rings", the struggle for influence and promotion between the "Wolseley Ring", made up mostly of officers who had served under Wolseley in Africa, and the "Roberts Ring", made up mostly of those who had served under Roberts in India. Roberts became C-in-C in Ireland in 1895, with promotion to field marshal on 25 May 1895 and appointment as a colonel commandant of the Royal Artillery in October 1896. After the disasters of "Black Week" at the beginning of the South African War (where his only surviving son was posthumously awarded the Victoria Cross after being mortally wounded at Colenso, 15 December 1899), Roberts secured his own appointment as C-in-C in South Africa. He issued new operational instructions, centralized the army's transport system and, leaving his predecessor Buller (a member of the Wolseley Ring) to continue the campaign in Natal, advanced against the Boers in the western theatre. Despite heavy losses in horses as he outdistanced his supply columns, this offensive proved successful. Roberts commanded in person at Paardeburg (19–27 February 1900); Poplar Grove (7 March 1900); Dreifontein (10 March 1900); Vet River (5–6 May 1900); Zand River (10 May 1900); Diamond Hill (12 June 1900) and Machadodorp (28 July 1900). With the Boer capitals in British hands, Roberts considered the war was over. After initiating a policy of reprisals against Boer civilians living near the scene of guerrilla attacks, he handed over command to his Chief of Staff, Lord Kitchener [79], and returned to the UK. Roberts became, in October 1900, the first colonel of the newly-formed Irish Guards. His success in South Africa was rewarded by advancement in the peerage to become Earl Roberts of Kandahar and Pretoria, and of Waterford, with a special remainder in the female line. In 1902 he was appointed colonel of the 5th Gurkha Rifles (Frontier Force) in the Indian Army. In the auxiliary forces, he became honorary colonel of the North Somerset Yeomanry.

Roberts succeeded Wolseley as C-in-C in January 1901 and began the reform of Army training to take account of the lessons of the South African War. He engineered the removal of Wolseley's protégé, Sir Redvers Buller, from his command at Aldershot and appointed his own favourite, Sir William Nicholson [82], as Director of Military Operations at the War Office. Roberts' period in office as C-in-C came to an unhappy end in February 1904, when this historic post was abolished with so little ceremony that he arrived at his office to find his desk had been removed. He was given a place on the Committee of Imperial Defence, set up to deal with long-term strategic questions, but found that he had little influence on the development of policy. He resigned in November 1905 to become president of the National Service League, where he campaigned for introduction of conscription on the model of the great Continental powers, with a long-service regular army to provide the imperial garrisons. Roberts opposed reliance on the Territorial Force (created from the Yeomanry and Volunteers in 1908) as an alternative to conscription and argued that part-time training would not achieve the required standard of efficiency. This, he thought, would especially be so in the most powerful arm, the field artillery. He was appointed Master Gunner, St James's Park, in December 1904. In the reserve army, he accepted the appointment of honorary colonel of the 3rd (Militia, later Special Reserve) Battalion, the Sherwood Foresters (Nottinghamshire and Derbyshire Regiment).

Like many other officers of Anglo-Irish descent, Roberts viewed the prospect of Home Rule in Ireland with growing alarm. He selected the first chief of staff for the para-military Ulster Volunteer Force, formed in 1912, and gave encouragement to the pro-Unionist activities of Sir Henry Wilson [91], one of his own favourites, who was at that time Director of Military Operations at the War Office. In the Curragh incident of March 1914 a number of Anglo-Irish officers declared that they would resign rather than lead their troops to enforce the provisions of the Home Rule Bill on Ulster. Roberts told Sir John French [83], the Chief of the Imperial General Staff, that if the Cabinet used troops against the Ulstermen, there would be a civil war. He also, with great emotion, assured King George V [80] that half the officers in the Army would resign rather than obey such orders. French, who was obliged to resign following this episode, blamed Roberts for stirring up much of the trouble. When the First World War began in August 1914, Roberts repaid his debt to Kipling by using his influence to obtain a commission in the Irish Guards for the poet's under-age, short-sighted, only son, who was later killed on the Western Front. Roberts himself died in France in the line of duty, on 14 November 1914. Appointed as the colonel-in-chief of the Indian troops sent to France, he arrived at a review to find that the sepoys had no greatcoats. He declined to wear his own, caught a chill and contracted pneumonia. Roberts died at St Omer on 14 November 1914 and was buried in St Paul's Cathedral. His earldom, by special remainder, was inherited by his eldest daughter.

ROBERTSON
Sir WILLIAM, 1st Baronet, GCB, GCMG, GCVO, DSO
(1860–1933) [92]

William Robertson, the only son of a village tailor, was born in Welbourn, Lincolnshire, on 29 January 1860. He attended the local church school, where the rector, Canon Leslie-Melville, saw in him a boy of some intelligence and arranged for him to be taught French with his own daughters. In 1875 Robertson entered domestic service as a footman, before enlisting (five months under-age) in the 16th Lancers in November 1877. His mother, a member of the respectable working class, shared the view of her peer-group that having a son in the Regular Army brought disgrace on the family. Distraught, she wrote to him that she would rather see him dead than in a red coat. Nevertheless, Robertson rose rapidly through the ranks to become troop sergeant major within seven years. Recommended by his officers and tutored by

Canon Leslie-Melville, Robertson passed the required examination and was granted a commission on 27 June 1888 as a second lieutenant in the 3rd Dragoon Guards. This unit was then in India, where a careful officer could live on his pay. To boost his income, Robertson used the hot seasons, when most officers took leave, to qualify in a total of six North Indian languages. He was promoted to lieutenant on 1 March 1891. In 1894 he married Mildred Palin, the second daughter of a lieutenant general in the Indian Army. Her family felt she had married beneath her, but their marriage was a long and happy one, with Mildred Robertson giving her husband much help in his professional studies.

Robertson's skill as a linguist gained him a staff post in the Intelligence department at Army HQ, India, where he became a captain on 3 April 1895. He served as an intelligence officer in the Chitral Relief Expedition of 1895 and was present at Malakand (3 April 1895), but shortly afterwards was badly wounded (with his own sword) when attacked by his bearer when on a reconnaissance. Robertson's services in this campaign were rewarded with the DSO. He returned to England, where he entered the Staff College and passed out, second in his course, in December 1898. He was noticed by Sir Henry Brackenbury, Director of Military Intelligence at the War Office, and was posted to the Intelligence department as a staff captain, in April 1899.

At the end of 1899 Robertson joined the intelligence staff in the South African War, where he was promoted to major on 10 March 1900. Robertson was present at Paardeberg (17–26 February 1900); Poplar Grove (7 March 1900); Dreifontein (10 March 1900); Vet River (5–6 May 1900) and Zand River (10 May 1900). He received a mention in despatches and returned to the Intelligence department at the War Office in October 1900. He became a brevet lieutenant colonel on 29 November 1900. He worked closely with Sir William Nicholson [82], the Director of Military Operations, and was promoted to brevet colonel on 29 November 1903. When his tenure of this appointment expired in January 1907, he was placed on the half-pay list, where he turned his attention to translating German and Austro-Hungarian army manuals. Robertson became assistant quartermaster general at Aldershot Command in May 1907 and was appointed Brigadier General, General Staff, there at the end of that year.

In June 1910 Robertson was selected by his old patron Nicholson (by this time Chief of the General Staff) to be commandant of the Staff College, with promotion to major general on 21 November 1910. Following German military theories, Robertson urged his staff and students to concentrate on training for war against the strongest likely enemy. In June 1913 he was awarded the KCVO by George V [80], with whom he became a favourite, despite (or possibly because of) his humble origins. Robertson's correspondence shows that he wrote clear and grammatical English, while his abilities as a linguist demonstrate his mastery of the aspirate. Nevertheless, he affected a demotic turn of phrase, commonly countering reasoned argument with the remark "I've 'eard different".

Sir William ("Wully") Robertson became Director of Military Training in October 1913. On the outbreak of the First World War in August 1914 he went to France as Quartermaster General of the British Expeditionary Force, where he served in the campaign of 1914 and was appointed Chief of Staff in preference to Sir Henry Wilson [91] in January 1915. He was promoted to lieutenant general on 28 October 1915. In accordance with what he had been taught at the Staff College, derived from the German military theorists, Robertson believed that victory could be achieved only by the defeat of the enemy's strongest army and that therefore the Western Front was the decisive theatre. On the same principle, he believed that the BEF should not operate as an independent army, but conform to the strategy of its French allies, to avoid dispersal of resources. With a Germanic dislike of peripheral campaigns, he opposed the Dardanelles expedition. After Lord Kitchener [79], the Secretary of State for War, had been discredited by its failure, Robertson was able to write his own terms of reference, when he was appointed Chief of the Imperial General Staff in December 1915. He insisted that the CIGS alone should determine strategy, leaving the Secretary of State for War to deal with the Army's administration, finance and supplies, as had been the normal arrangement prior to Kitchener's appointment. Like Kitchener, he withheld information from the Cabinet, ostensibly for security reasons, but also to minimize the influence of civilian politicians on the conduct of the war. Robertson was promoted to general on 3 June 1916. He continued to stress the importance of concentrating on what was to him the decisive theatre, the Western Front, and described campaigns elsewhere as "sideshows".

He finally met his match in David Lloyd George, who became Prime Minister in December 1916. In February 1918 the Allied Supreme War Council at Versailles decided to set up a committee of its own military advisers to control the Allied reserves and so decide the direction of strategy. Lloyd George proposed Robertson as the British representative. Robertson realized that if he ceased to be CIGS he would be unable to oppose Lloyd George's policy of diverting British resources from the Western Front to other, more successful, theatres, but that if he no longer controlled his own reserves, he could no longer influence events on the Western Front. He therefore opposed the plan. George V and several ministers in the coalition government indicated their support for Robertson, but Lloyd George made the issue one of confidence, so that Robertson was removed from office on 18 February 1918.

Robertson was appointed GOC Eastern Command and then, in June 1918, C-in-C Home Forces. In April 1919 he became C-in-C of the British Army of Occupation on the Rhine. This was his last command. He was created a baronet and was promoted to field marshal on 29 March 1920. He became colonel of the Royal Scots Greys in March 1916 and of the 3rd/6th Dragoon Guards (Prince of Wales's), later the 3rd Carabiniers, in December 1925. Sir William Robertson held this appointment, together with that of colonel of the Royal Horse Guards (to which he was appointed in January 1928), until his death in London on 12 February 1933. He had two daughters and two sons, the younger of whom predeceased him at the age of eighteen.

ROSE
Sir HUGH HENRY, 1st Baron Strathnairn, GCB, GCSI (1801–1885) [57]

Hugh Rose, the third son of a diplomat, Sir George Rose, was born in Berlin on 6 April 1801. Sir George was at Berlin as British minister in 1813–1815 and Hugh Rose received private military tuition there from officers of the Prussian army. He was commissioned as an ensign in the 93rd Highlanders on 8 June 1820, before joining the 19th Foot in Ireland on 6 October 1820. Rose was promoted to lieutenant on 24 Oct 1821, captain on 22 July 1824 and major, unattached, on 30 December 1826. He became major in the 92nd Highlanders on 19 February 1829 and was appointed equerry to Adolphus, 1st Duke of Cambridge [26] in July 1830. Rose returned to regimental duty with the 92nd Highlanders in July 1832 and served with them in Tipperary, Gibraltar and Malta. On 17 September 1839 he became a lieutenant colonel, unattached.

Rose was one of the group of British military advisers sent into Syria in 1840 to assist the Ottoman government against Mehemet Ali, ruler of Egypt. When Mehemet Ali recalled his army in response to international pressure, the Ottomans, led by Omar Pasha, took the offensive. Rose served on Omar's staff at El-Mesden (15 January 1841) and took command of the British military mission later in 1841,after the sickness and death of his two senior officers. Rose became British consul general in Syria and the Lebanon in August 1841, at a period of continued intercommunal tension between the Druse and Maronite Christians. He negotiated with the various local factions for the protection of British subjects and other Christians, and personally escorted a group of American missionaries from Mount Lebanon to Beirut in May 1845. In November 1848 he transferred from the Consular to the Diplomatic Service and joined the British Embassy at Constantinople.

Rose was promoted to colonel on 11 June 1852 and, on the commencement of the Crimean War in 1854, was made British commissioner with the French contingent of the Allied army. He demonstrated personal courage as well as diplomatic skill and was awarded the Legion of Honour for putting out a fire in an ammunition dump. He was with the French Zouaves at the Alma (20 September 1854), where he was wounded; at Inkerman (5 November 1854) and in the assault on the Mamelon (6 June 1855). He was promoted to major general on 12 December 1854 and was awarded the KCB in October 1855. Sir Hugh Rose returned to service with the British Army and, following the outbreak of the Indian Mutiny, was given command of the Poona division in Bombay on 19 September 1857. He was at first regarded with some derision by the Bombay officers, who considered his cultured diplomatic ways more suited to a drawing-room than a battlefield. When his command was mobilized as the Central India Field Force, he established a reputation as a successful field commander by fighting his way to Sagar in January 1858. Rose was at Baroda (30 January 1858); Jhansi (21–31 March 1858) and Kalpi (23 May 1858). With British control over this area apparently restored, he obtained leave on medical grounds and was ordered to hand over to Robert Napier [58]. Before Napier could arrive, the troops of the Maharaja Sindia of Gwalior, a British ally, joined the Mutiny. In this crisis, Rose resumed command and restored Sindia to his throne with a victory at Gwalior (19 June 1858). Napier, who served as Rose's deputy in this operation, then succeeded him in command, while Rose received a rebuke from Lord Clyde [46], C-in-C, India, for having remained in post contrary to the regulations.

Rose became colonel of the 45th Foot in July 1858 and was promoted to lieutenant general on 28 February 1860. He was appointed C-in-C, Bombay, in March 1860 and became C-in-C, India, in November 1860. This period coincided with the reconstruction of the Indian Armies after the Mutiny. Rose set his face against the prejudices which led many officers to press for the exclusion of low-caste men who had been recruited by the British during the emergency. Instead, he advocated a balance between a wide number of communities, to minimize the chances of another combination against the British. He returned to Europe in March 1865 and was C-in-C, Ireland, from July 1865 to June

1870. Rose became colonel of the 92nd Highlanders on 25 June 1866 and was raised to the peerage as Baron Strathnairn on 28 July 1866. He became a general on 4 February 1867, colonel of the Royal Horse Guards in March 1869 and a field marshal on 2 June 1877. Lord Strathnairn died unmarried, in Paris, on 23 October 1885 and was buried in his family tomb at Christchurch Priory, Hampshire.

ROSS
Sir HEW DALRYMPLE, GCB (1779–1868) [49]

Hew Ross, the third of four sons of Major John Ross, of Balkiel, Galloway, was born on 5 July 1779. He was named for his godfather and maternal cousin, Sir Hew Dalrymple, who became best known as the general who, in August 1808, ordered Sir Arthur Wellesley [24] to sign the Convention of Cintra (Sintra), on terms favourable to the defeated French army. After attending the Royal Military Academy, Woolwich, Ross was commissioned as a second lieutenant in the Royal Artillery on 6 March 1795 and was promoted to first lieutenant on 10 May 1795. He served in Ireland with the horse artillery (at that time an experimental body, but soon to be recognized as the élite branch of the Royal Artillery) and took part in counter-insurgency operations during the Irish Rebellion of 1798. He was promoted to captain lieutenant on 19 July 1804 and was appointed adjutant of the 5th Battalion, Royal Artillery, at the regimental depot, Woolwich. On 24 July 1806 he was promoted to captain and given command of the Chestnut Troop (later "A" Troop), Royal Horse Artillery.

Ross and his troop joined the army under Sir Arthur Wellesley [24] in the Peninsula in July 1809 and subsequently served at Almeida (20 July 1810); the Coa (24 July 1810); Busaco (27 July 1810); Pombal (11 March 1811), Rodinha and Casal Novhal (12–15 March 1811), where he was twice slightly wounded; Sabugal (3 April 1811); Fuentes d'Onoro (3 April 1811); Aldea de Ponte (27 September 1811); Ciudad Rodrigo (stormed 19 January 1812); Badajoz (stormed 6 April 1812), where he was wounded in the assault; Salamanca (22 July 1812); Vittoria (21 June 1813); the Pyrenees (July 1813); the passage of the Bidassoa (7 October 1813); the Nivelle (10 November 1813); the Nive (8–10 December 1813), where he had his horse shot under him, and the siege of Bayonne (27 February-13 April 1814). Ross became a major in the Army on 31 December 1811 and lieutenant colonel in the Army, while still a captain in the Royal Artillery, on 21 June 1813. In the Hundred Days campaign, he arrived in time to command his troop at Waterloo (18 June 1815), where he had three horses shot under him and ended the day with only three of his six guns still in action. Ross served with his troop in the Army of Occupation in Paris and subsequently in various stations in England and Ireland. In 1816 he married Elizabeth Graham, the daughter of a Cumberland squire. Their son, born in 1829, later became a general.

Ross was awarded the KCB and became a lieutenant colonel in the Royal Artillery on 29 July 1825. Between 1825 and 1840 Sir Hew Ross was the artillery commander, Northern District, with delegated command of the four northern counties of England. He was promoted to colonel in the Army on 22 July 1830 and in the Royal Artillery on 10 January 1837. He became deputy adjutant general, Royal Artillery, in April 1840 and remained in this post until May 1854. He became a major general on 23 November 1841 and colonel commandant of the 12th Battalion, the Royal Artillery, on 1 November 1848. Ross was promoted to lieutenant general on 11 November 1851 and became colonel commandant of the Royal Horse Artillery on 11 August 1852. In May 1854 he was appointed Lieutenant General of the Ordnance and as such was responsible for organizng the artillery component of the army sent to the Crimea under Lord Raglan [38] later that year. Ross was promoted to general on 28 November 1854. When the Board of Ordnance was abolished in the post-Crimean War reforms, he joined the C-in-C's staff in the newly-created post of Adjutant General, Royal Artillery. He remained in this appointment until April 1858, when he retired from active duty. He became Master Gunner, St James's Park in 1864. Ross, the first officer of the Royal Artillery to reach this rank, was promoted to field marshal on 1 January 1868 and died in London on 10 December 1868. He served in twenty pitched battles and was a brilliant pioneer in the use of horse artillery by the British Army.

ROWAN
Sir WILLIAM, GCB (1789–1879) [55]

William Rowan, the son of Robert Rowan of Mullans, County Antrim, was born in the Isle of Man on 18 June 1789. He was commissioned as an ensign in the 52nd Light Infantry on 4 November 1803 and was promoted to lieutenant on 15 June 1804. Rowan served with his regiment in Sicily in 1806-07 and in Sweden in 1808, before becoming a captain in its 2nd Battalion on 19 October 1808. In 1809 he fought in the Peninsula under Sir John Moore, where his regiment covered the retreat to Corunna before embarking at Vigo. Rowan was then in the expedition to Walcheren, and served at the siege of Flushing (1–18 August 1809). He returned with the 52nd Light Infantry to the Peninsula, where he was at Sabugal (3 April 1809); Vittoria (21 June 1813); the Pyrenees (July 1813); the passage of the Bidassoa (31 August 1813); the Nivelle (10 November 1813); the Nive (9 December 1813); Orthez (27 February 1814) and Toulouse (10 April 1814). Rowan was promoted to brevet major on 3 March 1814 in recognition of his conduct at Orthez. He was with the 52nd Light Infantry throughout the Hundred Days campaign, at Waterloo (18 June 1815) and subsequently in the Army of Occupation in Paris.

Rowan was promoted to lieutenant colonel in the Army on 21 January 1819 and exchanged to the 58th Foot as a regimental major in 1826. Between 1823 and 1829 he was in Canada on staff duty. He was on the half-pay from July 1830 until 10 January 1837, when he rejoined the full-pay list on promotion to colonel, unattached. He became a major general on 9 November 1846, returned to Canada in 1849 and was C-in-C there until 1855, with promotion to lieutenant general on 20 January 1854. Rowan became colonel of the 19th Foot in June 1854 and was awarded the GCB in 1856. In March 1861 Sir William Rowan gave up his colonelcy of the 19th when he was appointed colonel of his old regiment, the 52nd Light Infantry. He was promoted to general on 13 August 1862 and to field marshal on 2 June 1877. Rowan died at Bath on 26 September 1879 and was buried there at the Lansdown cemetery.

SEATON
LORD, see **COLBORNE**, Sir JOHN, **[42]**

SHANNON
VISCOUNT, *see* **BOYLE**, RICHARD, **[3]**

SIMMONS
Sir JOHN LINTORN ARABIN, GCB, GCMG
(1821–1903) **[64]**

Lintorn Simmons, the fifth of nine sons in a family of twelve children of Captain Thomas Simmons, Royal Artillery, was born at Langford, Somerset, on 12 February 1821. After attending Elizabeth College, Guernsey, and the Royal Military Academy, Woolwich, he was commissioned as a second lieutenant in the Royal Engineers on 14 December 1837 and was promoted to lieutenant on 15 October 1839. From 1839 to 1845 Simmons served in Canada on survey and fortress construction duties along the border with the United States. He then became an instructor in fortification at the Royal Military Academy, with promotion to second captain on 9 November 1846. In the same year he married his cousin Ellen Lintorn Simmons of Keynsham, Somerset. She died in 1851, leaving him with a young daughter. Simmons became an inspecting engineer with the Railways Commission and served with the Board of Trade's railway section until 1853.

On the approach of the Crimean War, Simmons was ordered to the lower Danube to report on the defences of this part of the Turkish Ottoman Empire. He was promoted to captain on 17 February 1854 and was appointed British commissioner with the Ottoman army under Omar Pasha, with whom he served throughout the war. He was involved in the defence of Silistra in June 1854 and led the Ottoman forces at Giurgevo (Giurgiu, 7 July 1854). He became a brevet major on 12 July 1854 and a brevet lieutenant colonel on 14 July 1854. Simmons landed with the Turks in the Crimea at Eupatoria (Yevpatoriya) in January 1855 and repulsed a Russian attack on his field defences (17 February 1855). He was with Omar at Sevastopol and later accompanied him to the Trans-Caucasus theatre, where Simmons commanded a division of the Ottoman army at the Ingur (6 November 1855).

After the Crimean War Simmons was one of the British members of the international boundary commission set up to settle the Russo-Turkish frontier. In 1856 he married Blanche Weston, the daughter of a private gentleman. He was promoted to brevet colonel on 12 December 1857 and was British consul in Warsaw from 1858 to January 1860, when he became Commander, Royal Engineers, at Aldershot. Between 1865 and 1868 Simmons commanded the engineer school at Chatham, with promotion to major general on 6 March 1868. He then was appointed to command the Royal Military Academy, Woolwich, where, first as lieutenant-governor and then as Governor, he introduced many improvements in the training of future artillery and engineer officers. He was awarded the KCB in June 1869. When the Prince Imperial (the only son of the exiled French Emperor Napoleon III) became a gentleman cadet at the RMA, Sir Lintorn Simmons established cordial relations with the Imperial family and later assisted the widowed Empress Eugenie to settle at Farnborough Hill (later a convent school), in north-east Hampshire. He was promoted to lieutenant general and appointed a colonel commandant of the Royal Engineers on 27 August 1872. On leaving the Royal Military Academy in 1875, Simmons was appointed Inspector General of Fortifications. He served as Governor and C-in-C, Malta, from April 1884 to September 1888, when he retired from public life. After the deaths of Lady Simmons and his elder (unmarried) daughter in 1901, he lived with his younger daughter, Blanche (the only child of his second marriage) and her husband at Hawley House, Blackwater, Hampshire, on the western outskirts of Camberley. Sir Lintorn Simmons was promoted to field marshal on 25 May 1890. He died at Hawley House on 14 February 1903 and was buried beside his first wife at Churchill, Somerset.

SLIM
Sir WILLIAM JOSEPH, 1st Viscount Slim, KG, GCB, GCMG, GCVO, GBE, DSO, MC (1891–1970) [117]

William ("Bill") Slim was born at Bishopston, Bristol, on 6 August 1891, the younger son of a gentle but impractical wholesale ironmonger and his strong-minded wife. The family moved to Edgbaston in 1904, where the young Slim attended St Philip's, a Roman Catholic day school chosen by his devout mother (though he later lapsed from her religion). In 1907, after the failure of his father's business, family funds were available only for the education of Slim's elder brother, a medical student at Birmingham University. William Slim became first a pupil-teacher at an elementary school in a deprived area of Birmingham and then a junior clerk in a metal-tube factory. In 1912 he joined the Birmingham University Contingent, Officers Training Corps, although he had no direct connection with the university.

After the outbreak of the First World War, Slim was commissioned from the OTC on 22 August 1914, as a temporary second lieutenant in the 9th Battalion, the Royal Warwickshire Regiment, and was promoted to temporary lieutenant on 1 February 1915. After training in the UK, Slim's battalion landed in Gallipoli early in August 1915 and fought at Sari Bair (7–8 August 1915), where Slim was wounded in the shoulder and the lung, so dangerously as to be given the last rites. He was invalided home and obtained a commission in the Regular Army, choosing the unfashionable but inexpensive West India Regiment. Slim became a lieutenant in this regiment on 1 June 1916, but never actually served with it. Still medically unfit for front-line duty, he served as a draft-conducting officer, taking reinforcements from the UK to units of the Royal Warwickshire Regiment in France in April 1916 and Mesopotamia (Iraq) in August 1916. In Mesopotamia he rejoined his old company, with promotion to temporary captain on 2 September 1916, and took part in the campaign of 1916–17. After the British occupation of Baghdad (11 March 1917), Slim was given his first independent command, made up of two companies of infantry and a section of field artillery. He was wounded at the Marl Plain (Duqma, 29 March 1917), where he won the Military Cross. He was invalided to India and, in November 1917, on again becoming fit for duty, was appointed a General Staff officer, grade 3, at Army HQ. He was promoted to temporary major and GSO 2 in November 1918.

Slim transferred to the Indian Army as a substantive captain on 31 May 1919. In March 1920 he joined the 1st Battalion, 6th Gurkha Rifles, from which he was attached to the Kurram Militia, a border guard force. He returned to his battalion to take part in a punitive expedition against the Tochi Wazirs, on the North-West Frontier, later that year and was at Char Khan (12 October 1920). Between March 1921 and November 1924 he served as battalion adjutant. He then went on leave to the UK, where he studied for the Staff College entrance examination. On his return voyage to India, he met Aileen Robertson, the daughter of an Edinburgh minister in the Church of Scotland. In a shipboard romance, Slim made a proposal of marriage and, on being refused, pursued her to Kashmir, where he was finally accepted. The bride's family had reservations as much about Slim's religion as his profession, and the couple went through two wedding ceremonies, one Presbyterian and one Roman Catholic. Slim entered the Indian Staff College, Quetta, in February 1925 and passed out in 1928. He was promoted to brevet major on 5 June 1929 and subsequently served as GSO 2 in the Directorate of Military Operations at Army HQ, India, between 1930 and 1934. During this period his two children, John and Una, were born. Slim became substantive major on 19 May 1933. In 1934 he was appointed an instructor at the Staff College, Camberley, with promotion to brevet lieutenant colonel on 1 January 1935. After completing his tour at Camberley, Slim attended the 1937 course at the Imperial Defence College, London. He then returned to India, where he assumed command of the 2nd Battalion, 7th Gurkha Rifles, with promotion to substantive lieutenant colonel on 2 May 1938. He was appointed commandant of the Senior Officers School at Belgaum in April 1939. On the outbreak of the Second World War in September 1939 he became commander of the newly-formed 10th Indian Infantry Brigade at Jhansi, as a local brigadier, and was later given promotion to substantive colonel and temporary brigadier, back-dated to 1 January 1938 and 8 June 1939 respectively.

Slim went with his brigade to Eritrea as part of the 5th Indian Division in August 1940 and commanded in an independent action at Gallabat (6 November 1940). At the end of January 1941, while leading his brigade forward, Slim was wounded in the buttocks by fire from an Italian aircraft. He was invalided back to India, where he returned to Army HQ as Director of Operations and Intelligence. He was given command of the 10th Indian Division with promotion to acting major general on 1 June 1941 and joined the British force at Baghdad later that month. He led his division in the campaign against the Vichy French in Syria in July 1941 and commanded a composite force of armour and infantry in the British occupation of Iran at the end of August 1941.

Early in March 1942 Sir Harold Alexander [113], commanding the British forces in Burma, asked for Slim as a corps commander. Slim was accordingly given command of I Burma Corps on 19 March 1942, with promotion to acting lieutenant general. He conducted a fighting retreat to the Indian border, doing all in his power to maintain the morale and cohesion of his troops and finally reaching Imphal on 20 May 1942. At the end of June 1942 he assumed command of XV Corps and became responsible for the defence of Bengal, Bihar, and Orissa, including their sea-coasts and the Indo-Burmese frontier. Slim became a temporary lieutenant general on 19 March 1943. After the failure of its offensive in the Arakan, he was placed in operational control of India's Eastern Army and once more conducted a skilful withdrawal. He ordered his men not to abandon their positions when outflanked, but to hold their ground and ambush the advancing Japanese. Logistic, headquarters and medical units were taught to conduct their own defence, rather than relying on the infantry for protection.

In October 1943 Lord Louis Mountbatten, Supreme Allied Commander designate of the new South East Asia Command, selected Slim to command the Fourteenth Army, the renamed Eastern Army. Convinced that, man for man, his troops were the equal of their Japanese enemy, Slim set himself to improve their leadership, morale and self-confidence. He stressed the need for senior officers to talk to their soldiers and, learning that his British troops referred to him as "Uncle Bill", took to introducing himself as such in his broadcasts to them. Slim prepared to take the offensive in north-west Burma in the spring of 1944. He was forestalled by a Japanese attack in the Arakan, but rapidly redeployed his forces to meet this threat. In the ensuing battle, Slim achieved the first major victory of British over Japanese arms in the course of the war. A determined Japanese offensive in the north reached Imphal and Kohima, but was defeated by Slim's strategy of

261

holding pre-stocked strong points and re-supplying them from the air. When the Japanese were forced to retreat at the beginning of June 1944, Slim began an advance that continued throughout the monsoon season and proved that he was as skilful in the attack as he had been in the defence. He was promoted to substantive lieutenant general, with the award of the KCB in December 1944. The Fourteenth Army reached Mandalay on 20 March 1945 and ended the Burma campaign with the recovery of Rangoon on 6 May 1945.

On 7 May 1945 Sir Oliver Leese, commander of the Allied Land Forces, South East Asia, notified Sir William Slim that he would be transferred to a new formation, the Twelfth Army, formed for garrison duty in Burma. Slim took this as evidence that he no longer held Leese's confidence and decided to resign from the Indian Army as soon as he could hand over to a replacement. Mountbatten, alerted by Slim's staff to the disastrous effects on the morale of the Fourteenth Army of losing their victorious commander in such circumstancess, consulted Sir Claude Auchinleck [116], who was C-in-C, India, and the senior officer of the Indian Army. When Auchinleck replied that appointments in another Command were outside his area of responsibility, Mountbatten sought the opinion of Sir Alan Brooke [112], Chief of the Imperial General Staff. On Brooke's advice, Mountbatten dismissed Leese and retained Slim in post. Slim was promoted to general on 1 July 1945 and succeeded Leese at HQ ALFSEA, Ceylon (Sri Lanka), on 16 August 1945. He was responsible for dealing with the surrender of Japanese forces in his area, for the re-establishment of British garrisons in Malaya and for suppressing the Burmese National Army (which had co-operated with Slim in fighting the Japanese, but now resisted the return of the pre-war colonial administration). Early in 1946 Slim became the first post-war commandant of the Imperial Defence College. After the achievement of independence by India and Pakistan in August 1947, he retired from the rolls of the former British Indian Army on 1 April 1948.

Slim had already become, in January 1948, Deputy Chairman of the newly-nationalized British Railways. In this post he established a rapport with Clement Attlee, the Labour Prime Minister (with whom he shared reminiscences of their service in Gallipoli). Attlee decided that Slim should succeed Viscount Montgomery [114] as Chief of the Imperial General Staff. Montgomery argued that Slim was an ex-officer of the Indian Army with no experience of high command in Europe and was ineligible for appointment as he had retired. Attlee met these objections by restoring Slim to the active list as a general in the British Army. Sir William Slim became CIGS on 1 November 1948 and was promoted to field marshal on 4 January 1949. The Cabinet had already accepted that, for lack of voluntary recruits to the Regular Army, conscription should be continued, but was reluctant to agree that the period of service with the colours should be longer than one year. Slim, after securing the agreement of his colleagues on the Naval and Air staffs to resign on this issue if necessary, persuaded Attlee that a minimum of eighteen months full-time service was essential. Slim encouraged national servicemen to remain in the Territorial Army at the end of the part-time element of their compulsory service and declared that anyone who volunteered for the TA was "twice a citizen". He was colonel of the West Yorkshire Regiment (The Prince of Wales's) from May 1947 to June 1960, of the 7th Gurkha Rifles from March 1944 to May 1956 and of the 1st Gurkha Rifles, in the Army of the Republic of India, from 1949 to 1956. He also became honorary colonel of the Royal Engineers Special Reserve.

On completing his term as CIGS, Slim was appointed Governor-General of Australia, at the request of the Australian government. He took up office at the end of April 1952 and soon became well-liked by the average Australian, never more so than when he declared that Australian women were the most beautiful in the world and that Australian infantrymen were the toughest soldiers in history. Early in his married life, he had supplemented his income by writing stories under the pen-name "Anthony Mills". While Governor-General, remarking that field marshals had learned to sell their lives dearly, he published *Defeat into Victory*, a widely acclaimed account of his campaign in Burma. His normal five-year tour as Governor-General was extended by a further two years until January 1960, when he left Australia and was raised to the peerage as Viscount Slim, of Yarralumla, and of Bishopston.

Lord Slim then joined the boards of several large companies, but continued to give much of his time to ex-servicemen's organizations and regularly attended rallies of the Burma Star Association. From the late 1960s onwards, a series of strokes progressively impaired his faculties and, in the last year of his life, he retired to Eaton Mansions, Chelsea, where he died on 14 December 1970. After a funeral in St Paul's Cathedral, he was cremated privately. His son succeeded him as 2nd viscount. Slim was among the greatest army commanders of the Second World War. While remaining personally likeable and modest, he inspired all those who met or served with him and his teachings on leadership became a standard text for the officer cadets of the Royal Military Academy Sandhurst.

SMUTS
JAN CHRISTIAN, OM, CH, DTD, KC (1870–1950) [108]

Jan Smuts, the second son of a Boer farmer and politician, was born at his father's farm, Bovenplaatz, near Riebeek, Cape Colony (later Cape Province), on 24 May 1870. He was educated at Victoria College, Stellenbosch, where he devoted all his time to academic work, and won a scholarship to go overseas for study. In the autumn of 1891 Smuts entered Christ's College, Cambridge. He graduated with a First Class degree in law in 1894 and was admitted a barrister in the Middle Temple. He then returned to Cape Colony, where he began a career as an advocate and supported Cecil Rhodes, the colonial prime minister, in his aim of achieving a union of South Africa, with equal rights for all civilized (meaning European) men south of the Zambezi. In 1898, disillusioned by Rhodes' complicity in the Jameson Raid, Smuts repudiated his status as a British subject and became state attorney of the South African Republic. In the same year, he married Sybella (Isie) Krige, the daughter of one of his father's neighbours and formerly a fellow student at Stellenbosch. She proved an intelligent, loyal and practical wife, who bore him eight children and, disregarding his occasional infidelities, provided a home to support him throughout his career. During 1899 Smuts represented his adopted government in negotiations with the British. When the South African War began in October 1899, he hoped that arms and military advisers could be obtained from Germany and proposed an attack to seize the British port of Durban, in Natal.

In July 1900, with both Boer capitals in British hands, Smuts joined General de la Rey's commando as government adviser. He assumed the rank of Acting Assistant Commandant General but did not secure an independent command until August 1901. Smuts then led a raid into Cape Colony, with a force of 340 men, in one of the most remarkable feats of perseverance, good fortune and endurance of the entire war. He evaded four British columns sent against him and inflicted a humiliating defeat on the 17th Lancers at Modderfontein (17 September 1901). At the end of the war he attended the peace negotiations at Vereeniging and persuaded a majority of the Boer delegates that the harsh British terms had to be accepted.

Smuts re-entered political life in January 1905. He played a prominent part in negotiations in London that led to the restoration of local autonomy to the Transvaal and, in 1906, became a minister in the new colonial government. When the Union of South Africa was created in 1910, Smuts became Minister for Mines, Defence and the Interior, in the Cabinet headed by the Boer veteran General Louis Botha. He planned a Defence Force, consisting of a small regular army, supplemented, in time of emergency, by commandos raised from the rural areas, on the traditional Boer system. In 1913, when the Rand miners struck for better conditions and backed their arguments with armed force, the new South African Defence Force had not been fully formed. The Colonial Office refused to allow the British troops in South Africa to be used in aid of the local government and Smuts was forced to yield to the miners' demands. In January 1914, when the Natal miners went on strike, Smuts was ready for them and they were crushed in a swift operation that gained him a reputation among his own countrymen as a man of blood.

On the outbreak of the First World War in August 1914 the Union government called out its Defence Force to relieve the British Army garrisons in South Africa for service elsewhere. In April 1915 Smuts assumed the title of general and joined Botha in a campaign against German South-West Africa (later Namibia). Their victory in July 1915 was the first significant Allied success of the war and led to Smuts being given command of the British forces in German East Africa (later Tanzania), with the rank of lieutenant general in the British Army. He was faced with major difficulties of terrain and climate but, by January 1917, had succeeded in occupying practically all the areas of strategic importance. Smuts handed over command early in 1917 in order to represent Botha at a conference in London of all the British Commonwealth prime ministers. The British prime minister, David Lloyd George, saw Smuts as a kindred figure, a lawyer and politician who succeeded where professional generals failed. Comparing Smuts's victories in Africa favourably with the costly stalemate on the Western Front, Lloyd George asked him for his views on the future conduct of the war. Smuts recommended concentrating the weight of the British war effort against Turkey. He proposed ending the Allied presence at Salonika (Thessaloniki), with the aim of allowing the British contingent there to go to Palestine, while the French contingent returned to France and relieved the British Expeditionary Force for service elsewhere. Lloyd George did not take up this plan, but offered Smuts command of the British forces in Palestine. Smuts declined, on being told by Sir William Robertson [92], Chief of the Imperial General Staff, that the Western Front would remain the decisive theatre and no reinforcements could be spared for "side-shows". At Lloyd George's invitation, Smuts joined the British War Cabinet in June 1917. Lloyd George then asked Smuts to suggest another commander for the BEF. Smuts toured the Western Front, but returned to say that its existing C-in-C, Sir Douglas Haig [85], was better than any of the other generals. A more constructive contribution to the success of British arms came in August 1917, when Smuts drew together outstanding proposals for the co-ordination of air-power and recommended the creation of a new service, the Royal Air Force, under a separate Air Ministry.

Smuts left the War Cabinet in 1919 and represented South Africa at the Versailles Peace Conference. With memories of the Vereeniging Conference, he argued for showing magnanimity to the defeated Germans and, on failing to carry his point, signed the peace treaty only to give South Africa the status of a signatory in international agreements. He took South Africa into the League of Nations without enthusiasm, though he was one of the originators of the concept of "mandated territories", seeing it as a means whereby the victors might retain control of captured German colonies (especially South-West Africa). In August 1919 Smuts became Prime Minister of South Africa following the death of his old friend Botha. During 1922 he acted as a mediator between the British government and the Irish nationalists, in the negotiations leading to the establishment of the Irish Free State. At home, in the post-war period, he used his troops in a series of bloody actions to suppress strikes by miners, white as well as black.

Smuts was defeated at the polls in 1924, after he had failed to persuade Southern Rhodesia (later Zimbabwe) to join the Union. He remained in opposition until 1933, when he entered a coalition as deputy prime minister under General Herzog. When the British declared war on Germany on 3 September 1939, Herzog adopted a policy of neutrality. He was defeated in the South African Parliament and Smuts, who succeeded him as Prime Minister, brought South Africa into the Second World War on 6 September 1939. During the war, Smuts was on cordial terms with Winston Churchill, the British Prime Minister, each sharing the other's experience as combatants in the South African War and strategists in the First World War. Smuts, who had retained his title as general in the South African Defence Force, was appointed a British field marshal on 24 May 1941. At the San Francisco conference of 1945 he subscribed to the founding of the United Nations Organization, though he had reservations about its Charter's declaration of equal rights for all people. In 1948 Smuts was defeated by his Nationalist opponents in a general election. He remained leader of the Opposition until his death, from a coronary thrombosis, on his farm at Irene, near Pretoria, on 11 September 1950.

Smuts was the only British field marshal to attain this rank after having previously fought against the British Army and was the only member of a Dominion parliament to sit as a minister in the British

Cabinet. He was essentially a politician, whose skill in this profession brought him the Afrikaans epithet of "slim", meaning "crafty". His goal was to bring together the British and Boer communities in his country, though he saw no place in its government for the Bantu peoples who formed the majority population.

SOMERSET
Lord FITZROY JAMES HENRY, 1st Baron Raglan, GCB (1788–1855) [38]

Lord Fitzroy Somerset was the thirteenth child and eighth son of Henry, 5th Duke of Beaufort. He was born on 30 September 1788 at his family seat, Badminton House, Gloucestershire, and was educated at Westminster School. Somerset was commissioned on 9 June 1804 as a cornet in the 4th Light Dragoons. He was promoted to lieutenant on 30 May 1805 and to captain on 5 May 1808, when he joined the 43rd Foot. Through family influence, he was appointed an aide-de-camp to Sir Arthur Wellesley [24] in the army sent to the Peninsula in July 1808. This began a close association which lasted for the rest of their lives. Somerset was with Wellesley at Rolica (17 August 1808) and Vimiero (21 August 1808) before the army was recalled to the UK. He returned with Wellesley (later Wellington) to the Peninsula in May 1809 and was at the passage of the Douro (Oporto, 12 May 1809); Talavera (27–28 July 1809) and Busaco (27 September 1810), where he was wounded. Somerset was appointed acting military secretary on 28 November 1810 and was confirmed in this post on 1 January 1811. He was at Pombal (11 March 1811); Sabugal (3 April 1811); Fuentes d'Onoro (3–5 May 1811) and El Bodon (25 September 1811), with promotion to brevet major on 9 June 1811. At the storming of Badajoz (6–7 April 1812), Somerset entered the town after walls had been stormed and, by unexpectedly appearing from a deserted quarter, secured the surrender of the castle of San Christobal. He was promoted to brevet lieutenant colonel on 27 April 1812 and was with Wellington at Salamanca (21 July 1812); Valladolid (29 July 1812); Burgos (16 March–21 October 1812); Vittoria (21 June 1813); San Sebastian (August-September 1813); the Pyrenees (27–30 July 1813); the Nivelle (7 October 1813); the Nive (10–13 December 1813); Orthez (27 February 1814) and Toulouse (10 April 1814).

In 1814, when Wellington became British Ambassador to the restored French monarchy, Somerset remained with him as his secretary. In August 1814 he married one of Wellington's nieces,

Emily, the daughter of the future 3rd Earl of Mornington. In the Hundred Days campaign he served on Wellington's staff at Quatre Bras (16 June 1815) and at Waterloo (18 June 1815), where he was badly wounded in the arm. After an amputation in the field hospital, he called back the severed limb so as to retrieve the ring his wife had given him. Somerset was promoted to colonel in the Army on 28 August 1815. He continued with Wellington at the Paris Embassy and in the Army of Occupation until 1816 and at the Board of Ordnance from 1818 to 1827. In the parliaments of 1818–20 and 1820–26, Somerset was MP for Truro. He was promoted to major general on 27 May 1825. When Wellington became Commander-in-Chief in January 1827, Somerset was appointed Military Secretary, a post that he retained until Wellington's death in 1852. He became colonel of the 53rd Foot on 19 November 1830 and a lieutenant general on 28 June 1830. Somerset, who had become identified with Wellington's opposition to any change in the British military system, was not selected to succeed to the post of Commander-in-Chief when Wellington died. Instead, in October 1852, he was made Master General of the Ordnance and was raised to the peerage as Baron Raglan.

After the outbreak of war with Russia in 1854 Raglan was given command of the British army sent to the Crimea, with promotion to general on 20 June 1854. He was at the Alma (20 September 1854); Balaklava (25 October 1854) and Inkerman (5 November 1854) and was promoted to field marshal on 5 November 1854. Raglan was the first field marshal since Wellington himself to be appointed in the field, without regard to seniority, and passed over thirty-four generals senior to him, of whom four later became field marshals themselves. Nevertheless, he soon incurred criticism for the army's administrative shortcomings and also for the ill-fated charge of the Light Brigade at Balaklava. He died on 28 June 1855, from a combination of gastro-enteric illness and clinical depression. His body was taken back to England and buried at Badminton. Raglan had two sons, of whom the elder predeceased him in 1855, dying of wounds received during the First Sikh War, and the younger succeeded him as 2nd baron. Raglan was one of the few field marshals to command a British army in the field in that rank and the only one to die on active service.

STAIR
EARL OF, see **DALRYMPLE, JOHN, [5]**

STANIER
Sir JOHN WILFRED, GCB, MBE (1925-) [133]

John Stanier was born on 6 October 1925 and was educated at Marlborough College. He entered the Army in October 1944 and, after serving in the ranks and as an officer cadet, was granted a Regular Army emergency commission as a second lieutenant in the Royal Armoured Corps on 19 April 1946. Stanier became a war substantive lieutenant on 19 October 1946 and served with the 7th Queen's Own Hussars in north-west Italy. From January 1949 to August 1950 he was with the British Element, Trieste Forces, in the Free Territory of Trieste, first as an intelligence officer and then as a General Staff officer, grade 3. On 16 January 1948 Stanier was granted a Regular commission in the 7th Queen's Own Hussars, with seniority from 1 November 1947. He was at regimental duty in Germany from 1950 to 1954, serving at Luneberg and Fallingbostel, with promotion to captain on 6 October 1952. In April 1954 he became an instructor in the Royal Armoured Corps wing of Mons Officer Cadet School, Aldershot. In 1955 he married Cicely Constance Lambert, with whom he later had four daughters. After qualifying at the Staff College, Camberley, Stanier served from March 1958 to May 1959 as GSO 2 in the Directorate of Military Operations, at the War Office. He was promoted to temporary major on 20 March 1958 and became an officer of the Queen's Own Hussars when this was formed by the amalgamation of the 3rd King's Own Hussars and the 7th Queen's Own Hussars in November 1958. Between July 1959 and January 1961 Stanier served at the War Office as military assistant (GSO 2) to the Vice Chief of the Imperial General Staff, with promotion to substantive major on 6 October 1959. In 1961 he attended the Joint Services Staff College at Latimer, Buckinghamshire. He was appointed an instructor (GSO 2) at the Staff College, Camberley, with promotion to local lieutenant colonel on 18 May 1963, and remained there until December 1963.

Stanier transferred to the Royal Scots Greys (2nd Dragoons) on 1 January 1966 and was promoted to substantive lieutenant colonel on 2 February 1966, when he became the commanding officer of this regiment. In December 1968 he was appointed an instructor (GSO 1) at the Imperial Defence College, with promotion to brigadier on 30 June 1969. Between January 1970 and December 1971 Stanier commanded the 20th Armoured Brigade. He then went to the Ministry of Defence as Director of Public Relations (Army) and held this post until October 1973, with promotion to major general on 5 May 1973. He was GOC 1st Division in Germany from October 1973, until November 1975.

Between December 1975 and March 1978 he was commandant of the Staff College, Camberley. He was promoted to lieutenant general on 1 May 1978, followed by the award of the KCB and appointment as Vice Chief of the General Staff in June 1978. Sir John Stanier left this office in December 1980 and was promoted to general on 1 January 1981. From April 1981 to July 1982 he was C-in-C, United Kingdom Land Forces. In August 1982 he became Chief of the General Staff at the Ministry of Defence, where he remained until his retirement from active duty on 19 July 1985. Sir John Stanier was promoted to field marshal on 10 July 1985. He was colonel commandant, Royal Armoured Corps, from April 1982 to August 1985 and colonel of the Royal Scots Dragoon Guards (Carabiniers and Greys), the successor of the 3rd Carabiniers and the Royal Scots Greys, from January 1979 to May 1984.

STEWART
Sir DONALD MARTIN, 1st Baronet, GCB, GCSI, CIE (1824–1900) [66]

Donald Stewart, the son of a Highland gentleman, was born on 1 March 1824, at Dyke, Morayshire. He attended various local academies and the Aberdeen Gymnasium before joining the East India Company's service, as an ensign in the 9th Bengal Native Infantry, on 12 October 1840. Stewart was promoted to lieutenant on 3 January 1844. In 1847 he married Marina Davine, the daughter of a naval captain and the niece of an officer in the Bengal Political Service; they later had two sons and three daughters. She proved a capable financier and made it her first task to deal with the debts that Stewart had run up in his bachelor days. Stewart was promoted to captain on 1 June 1854 and served with the 9th Bengal Native Infantry in operations against the hill tribes on the North-West Frontier in 1854–55. During the Indian Mutiny campaign of 1857 Stewart was at the siege of Delhi (8 June –20 September 1857), where he served as a deputy assistant adjutant general. After the storming of Delhi, he became assistant adjutant general on the staff of Sir Colin Campbell [46], C-in-C, India, and was with him at the recapture of Lucknow. Stewart was promoted to major on 19 January 1858 and to lieutenant colonel on 20 July 1858. Between 1862 and 1865 he was deputy adjutant general of the Bengal Army, with promotion to colonel on 20 July 1863. In the expedition led by Sir Robert Napier [58] against Abyssinia (Ethiopia) in 1868, he commanded the Bengal brigade that provided the base area troops.

Stewart was promoted to major general on 24 December 1868. From

1869 to 1872 he was commandant of the convict settlement in the Andaman Islands and was there when, during an official visit, one of the inmates assassinated Lord Mayo, the Viceroy and Governor-General of India. Stewart was exonerated by the subsequent enquiry and, after a period of leave in the UK, returned to duty in April 1876 in command of the British troops at Lahore. He was promoted to lieutenant general on 1 October 1877. During the Second Afghan War Stewart was awarded the KCB, for his services in command of the column that occupied Kandahar in January 1879. Sir Donald Stewart later marched from Kandahar to Kabul and, while on the way there, defeated Afghan forces at Ahmad Khel (19 April 1880) and Arzu (23 April 1880). As the senior general, he took over command of the troops at Kabul from his old friend Sir Frederick Roberts [68] and, at the end of the war, withdrew to India.

Stewart was made a baronet and sat as Military Member of the Governor-General of India's Council (in effect the War Minister of the Government of India) from October 1880 to April 1881. He then succeeded Sir Frederick Haines [65] as C-in-C, India, with promotion to general on 1 July 1881. In this post he was faced with constant demands for what the clumsy phraseology of a century later would term "efficiency savings". He proposed meeting them by unifying the three separate Armies of Bengal, Madras and Bombay into a single Indian Army. This was rejected by the India Office (largely through the influence of Sir Henry Norman [72] and the Duke of Cambridge [45]). Stewart used the Panjdeh crisis of March 1885, when for some weeks it seemed that the Cossack would cross swords with the sepoy on the banks of the Oxus, to secure an increase in the number of British Army troops in India. In October 1885 he retired to the United Kingdom. He became a member of the Council of India at the India Office in 1893 and played an important part in achieving the unification of the Indian Army that he had proposed ten years earlier. Sir Donald Stewart was promoted to field marshal on 26 May 1894. He died in Algeria on 26 March 1900 and was buried at Brompton Cemetery, London.

STRAFFORD
EARL OF, see **BYNG**, Sir JOHN, **[40]**

STRATHNAIRN
LORD, see **ROSE**, Sir HUGH, **[57]**

TEMPLE
Sir RICHARD, 3rd Baronet, 1st Viscount Cobham (1669–1749) [6]

Richard Temple, the eldest son of a baronet of the same name, was born in 1669. He joined the British Army on 30 June 1685 as an officer in an infantry regiment, later to be disbanded in 1689 after the Glorious Revolution. Temple then became a captain in Babington's Regiment (later the 6th Foot). He fought under William III in Ireland in 1689-91 and in the Low Countries until the end of the Nine Years War in 1697. In May 1697 Temple succeeded his father as 3rd baronet. He was elected to his father's old seat as MP for Buckingham in December 1698 and represented various Buckinghamshire constituencies during most of the next sixteen years. In 1702, at the beginning of the War of the Spanish Succession, Temple became colonel of a newly-raised regiment of Foot (later disbanded). He joined Marlborough's army on the Continent and was at Venlo (September 1702) and Roermond (October 1702). He became a major general on 1 January 1708 and was at Oudenarde (11 July 1708) and Lille (12 August–10 December 1708) before being sent home with the despatches in recognition of his conduct. He was at Malplaquet (11 September 1709) and was promoted to lieutenant general in January 1710. Temple was appointed colonel of a regiment of dragoons (later the 4th Queen's Own Hussars) in April 1710. When the incoming Tory ministry replaced Marlborough by the Duke of Ormonde in 1712, Temple, both as a Whig and as one of Marlborough's lieutenants, was denied a field command and was deprived of his colonelcy in the following year.

The accession of George I in 1714 restored Temple's fortunes. He was granted a peerage as Baron Cobham in October 1714 and was appointed colonel of the Royal Dragoons in the following year. In 1718 he was made a viscount. In September 1719 Lord Cobham was given command of an expedition sent to co-operate with the French in the invasion of northern Spain, where he landed at Vigo and destroyed the naval stores and dockyards. Cobham gave up his colonelcy of the Royal Dragoons in 1721, when he became colonel of the King's Own Regiment of Horse (later the 1st King's Dragoon Guards). He held various other appointments until 1733, when he broke with Sir Robert Walpole, the Prime Minister of the day, and was obliged to give up his colonelcy and all other public offices. Cobham's right to promotion by seniority in the Army was not affected, so that he became a general on 27 October 1735 and a field marshal on 28 March 1742. Cobham was appointed colonel of the 1st Troop of Horse Grenadier Guards in

December 1742, but resigned in December 1743, in protest against the Cabinet's policy of sending a British army to fight on the Continent. He was subsequently colonel of a regiment of Horse (later the 5th Dragoon Guards) from August 1744 until he became colonel of a regiment of dragoons (later the 10th Hussars) in the following year. He died on 13 September 1749 and was buried at his country estate, Stowe Park, Buckinghamshire. Temple was married to Anne Halsey, the daughter of a Buckinghamshire landowner, but died without issue and was succeeded by a cousin.

TEMPLER
Sir GERALD WALTER ROBERT, KG, GCB, GCMG, KBE, DSO (1898–1979) [122]

Gerald Templer was born in Colchester, Essex, on 11 September 1898. His father, who came from a Devonshire family, was at that time the junior captain in Princess Victoria's (Royal Irish Fusiliers). His mother, the daughter of an officer in the Indian Political Service, was a lady of small stature but great energy and character. Her family home was in Armagh, Northern Ireland, where in later life she became a noted Orangewoman. She was ambitious both for her husband, who rose to be a lieutenant colonel in the Army Pay Department, and for her son, her only child. Gerald Templer was educated between 1912 and 1915 at Wellington College, Crowthorne. Of slight and wiry build, he was bullied by his schoolfellows and was glad to pass into the nearby Royal Military College, Sandhurst, at the beginning of 1916. Templer was granted a commission in the Regular Army as second lieutenant in Princess Victoria's (Royal Irish Fusiliers) on 16 August 1916. As both regular battalions of this regiment were on the Western Front and Templer was below the age for service overseas, he was posted to the 3rd (Special Reserve) Battalion in Ireland. He subsequently joined the regiment's 7th / 8th Battalion, a new army unit that formed part of the 16th (Irish) Division. Early in November 1917 he was posted to his regiment's 1st Battalion, where he became a lieutenant on 16 February 1918. During the German offensive of spring 1918, Templer was on sick leave, suffering from diphtheria. He rejoined his battalion in mid-April 1918 and served with it in several engagements until 19 October 1918, when he was sent to a school for potential adjutants.

At the end of 1919 Templer served with the 1st Battalion, the Royal Irish Fusiliers, in Iraq and north-eastern Iran. He became the battalion intelligence officer and moved with his unit to Egypt in 1920. In

September 1926, on leave in the UK, Templer married Ethel Margery ("Peggy") Davie, the daughter of a Devon solicitor, despite her family's objections that he had no income but his lieutenant's pay and the Army's disapproval of married subalterns. Templer and his wife began married life frugally, living in Egypt, where Templer remained at regimental duty. They later had a son and a daughter. Templer passed into the Staff College, Camberley, at his third attempt, in January 1928 and transferred to the Loyal (North Lancashire) Regiment on 11 August 1928 in order to become a captain, as there were no immediate prospects of a promotion vacancy in his original regiment. After qualifying as a staff officer in December 1930, he served for three months at Aldershot, as second-in-command of a company in the 2nd Battalion, the Loyal Regiment. Templer then became a General Staff officer, grade 3, in the 3rd Division on Salisbury Plain, where his senior officer recommended his discharge on grounds of inefficiency arising from chronic ill-health. Following a successful appeal, Templer was posted in January 1933 to Northern Command, York, as GSO 2 (Weapon Training). In April 1935 he rejoined his battalion at Tidworth as a company commander, followed by promotion to brevet major on 1 July 1935.

Early in 1936 Templer was posted to the 1st Battalion, the Loyal Regiment, and joined it in Palestine on its arrival from India. He was awarded the DSO for successful operations against Arab terrorist gangs and returned to the UK in November 1936, to be GSO 2 in the Territorial 53rd (Welsh) Division. He took advantage of the revival of the 2nd Battalion of the Royal Irish Fusiliers (disbanded in 1922) to transfer back to his original regiment in May 1937, though he never again served with it. He became a brevet lieutenant colonel on 1 July 1938 and a substantive major on 1 August 1938. He was appointed GSO 1 (Military Intelligence) at the War Office in October 1938, with the task of finding specialists for a future Intelligence Corps and officers to perform general intelligence duties.

At the beginning of the Second World War Templer became GSO 1 (Intelligence) at the General Headquarters of the British Expeditionary Force in France, with promotion to acting lieutenant colonel from 1 September 1939. There his duties included the co-ordination of various clandestine and intelligence-gathering activities in France and the Low Countries. He was promoted to temporary lieutenant colonel on 1 December 1939. After the evacuation of the BEF from France, Templer was given command of a newly-formed unit, the 9th Battalion, the Royal Sussex Regiment. On 4 November 1940 he became an acting brigadier in command of the 210th Infantry Brigade, in Dorset. He was appointed Brigadier, General Staff, in V Corps, in May 1941 and was later given promotion to colonel, with seniority from 1 July 1941. He was promoted to major general on 10 April 1942 when he became GOC 47th (London) Division, based at Winchester. As such, he arranged a demonstration at Imber Down of the effects of ground attack by a fighter aircraft. Pilot error resulted in the attack being made on the spectators, with twenty-seven killed and eighty wounded, of whom Templer himself was one. Late in 1942 Templer became an acting lieutenant general and GOC II Corps. After the disbandment of II Corps in April 1943 he remained in East Anglia in command of XI Corps. Templer became a temporary major general on 10 April 1943 and, on 31 July 1943, was given command of the 1st Division, in Tunisia.

Templer was sent to Italy in October 1943 as a battle casualty replacement, to be GOC 56th (London) Division, in the middle of the battles on the River Volturno. This formation remained in continuous action until 15 November 1943, when it was withdrawn after failing to take Mount Camino. In the retreat Templer ordered the 201st Guards Brigade to abandon their dead and wounded. His orders were obeyed punctiliously, but he was thereafter conscious of a coolness towards him on the part of the Foot Guards. The 56th Division served under Templer in operations around Anzio during February 1944, after which it went to Egypt to rest and refit. Templer became GOC 6th Armoured Division on 24 July 1944. His tenure of this command ended on 5 August 1944, when an approaching army lorry, ordered by Templer to give way to his own vehicle, struck a roadside landmine. Templer was hit by fragments of the vehicle and its cargo (a looted piano) and suffered serious injuries to his lumbar vertebrae.

On again becoming fit for duty, he was attached to HQ, Special Operations Executive in London, as substantive colonel and local major general, from December 1944. Templer again became temporary major general on 17 March 1945, (later substantive, with seniority from 30 May 1944) and was appointed Director of Civil Affairs and Military Government at HQ 21 Army Group in Brussels. He thus became the executive head of government in the British Zone of occupied Germany, where, with the end of hostilities, he had the task of finding and distributing food and fuel in a country where the economy and infrastructure of society had been destroyed by war. The Burgomaster of Cologne, Dr Konrad Adenauer, who had held this office from 1919 to 1933 (when the Nazis dismissed him), had been re-appointed by the Americans before they handed over the city to British control. Templer, always intolerant of opinions contrary to his own, considered that Adenauer was an obstructionist and dismissed him.

Between March 1946 and January 1948 Templer was Director of

Military Intelligence at the War Office, where he played an important part in establishing the Intelligence Corps on a permanent basis. He was promoted to lieutenant general on 1 August 1946. He became Vice Chief of the Imperial General Staff on 1 February 1948 and was awarded the KBE in January 1949. Sir Gerald Templer became GOC-in-C Eastern Command in February 1950 with promotion to general on 4 June 1950. In February 1952 he was appointed High Commissioner for the Federation of Malaya and Director of Operations in the campaign against the Malayan Races Liberation Army (a Communist-front organization made up mostly of ethnic Chinese). As the holder of both military and civil authority, Templer combined vigorous measures against the insurgents' jungle bases with political reforms, designed to win the hearts and minds (a phrase he is said to have coined) of the Malayan population, including the Malay and Indian communities. He sympathized with the Malays and compared their position in respect of the industrious and energetic Chinese community with that of the Arabs and Jews respectively at the time of his service in Palestine. His insistence on close co-operation between the military, police and civil authorities, together with the encouragement of local Home Guard units, played an important part in re-establishing government control over most of the country. In addition to expanding the Malay Regiment, Templer formed two new corps, the Federation Regiment and the Federation Armoured Car Regiment, which were open to all races. In his relations with the expatriate British community, he established a rapport with the planters and miners, to whom his troops and policies gave protection, but his brusque manner made him less popular with officials of the Colonial Service. During his two years in Malaya Templer was at the head of what was, both politically and militarily, one of the most successful of the British Army's counter-insurgency campaigns during the end of its imperial role.

Templer returned to Europe with a promise from Sir John Harding [120], Chief of the Imperial General Staff, that he would be appointed C-in-C, British Army of the Rhine. The Cabinet disallowed this, on the grounds that the former Burgomaster of Cologne, peremptorily dismissed by Templer in 1945, was now the widely respected Chancellor of the Federal Republic of Germany, on the soil of which BAOR was based. Templer therefore remained out of office until September 1955 when he succeeded Harding as CIGS. On the nationalization by the Egyptian government of the Suez Canal in 1956, Templer was called upon to prepare the British army element of an Anglo-French force for an invasion of Egypt. Over-estimating the strength of the Egyptian position, Templer insisted on assembling a powerful force so as to mount a set-piece invasion on the lines of the Allied landings in Europe during the Second World War. This imposed lengthy delays during which international and domestic public opinion, initially favourable to the Anglo-French case, was given time to swing against it. The landings, eventually made in October 1956 were successful in military terms, but proved politically disastrous for the two European powers and the abandonment of the campaign in response to pressure from the United States and the United Nations Organisation signalled the end of their imperial prestige.

The post-Suez reorganization of the British defence forces included numerous reforms and reductions, opposed by Templer without success. He derived little satisfaction from his period as CIGS and retired from active duty when his tenure expired in September 1958. His health deteriorated during the 1970s and he died, of cancer of the lung, at his home in Chelsea on 25 October 1979. Sir Gerald Templer was colonel of the Royal Irish Fusiliers from 1946 to 1960; the Malay Federation Regiment from 1954 to 1959; the 7th Gurkha Rifles from 1956 to 1964 and the Royal Horse Guards from 1963 to 1969, as well as of its successor, the Blues and Royals, from 1969 until 1979. He was honorary colonel of the London Irish Rifles Company, the North Irish Militia (Territorial and Army Volunteer Reserve) from 1967 to 1971.

TOWNSHEND
GEORGE, 4th Viscount and 1st Marquess Townshend (1724–1807) [20]

George Townshend, the eldest son of the 3rd Viscount Townshend, was born on 28 February 1723. He belonged to one of the great ruling families of Georgian England and included King George I among the sponsors at his baptism. After attending St John's College, Cambridge, Townshend became captain of a troop in Sir John Cope's regiment of dragoons (later the 7th Hussars) in 1745 and was appointed an aide-de-camp to William Augustus, Duke of Cumberland, third son of King George II. During the War of the Austrian Succession Townshend served under Cumberland at Culloden (16 April 1746) and at Laffeldt (La Val, 2 July 1747), as an officer of Sackville's Regiment (later the 20th Foot). He became a captain in the 1st Foot Guards and lieutenant colonel in the Army on 25 February 1748. After quarrelling with Cumberland, he returned to civil life in 1750. A pamphlet published in 1751, containing detailed criticisms of Cumberland's military ability, was generally attributed to Townshend's pen.

In Parliament, Townshend sat as MP for Norfolk (a seat owned by his family) from 1747 to 1764 and was an ally of William Pitt the Elder. Impressed by the citizen reserve forces he had seen on the Continent, he became a keen proponent of a reformed militia and, after the beginning of the Seven Years War, was largely responsible for the Militia Act of 1757. George II dismissed Cumberland from his post as Captain General in October 1757 and Townshend rejoined the Army in April 1758. His parliamentary support for Pitt's ministry was rewarded with the command of a brigade in the expedition to Canada and appointment as colonel of the 64th Foot in June 1759. After the death of Major General James Wolfe at Quebec (13 September 1759), Townshend took command of the British force as the senior officer present and secured the capitulation of the city four days later. Unfortunately for Townshend's reputation, he couched his despatches in such a way as to make it appear that he was claiming the laurels rightly due to Wolfe. He gave up his colonelcy of the 64th Foot in October 1759, when he became colonel of the 28th. He was promoted to major general on 6 March 1761 and held the post of Lieutenant General of the Ordnance from May 1763 to August 1767. He succeeded his father as 4th Viscount Townshend in 1764.

Lord Townshend then became Lord Lieutenant of Ireland, where he was promoted to lieutenant general on 30 April 1770. He introduced a number of administrative and economic reforms, with a view to reducing corruption and improving the lot of the population, but in doing so he alienated many local vested interests. His autocratic ways, coupled with his undoubted talent as a caricaturist, made him unpopular with the Dublin establishment and he was replaced in September 1772. Townshend ceased to be colonel of the 28th Foot on being appointed colonel of the 2nd Dragoon Guards in July 1773. At the same time he became Master General of the Ordnance, a post he retained throughout most of the American War of Independence, until March 1782. He was promoted to general on 20 November 1782. His support to the ministry of the day was acknowledged in October 1786, when he was advanced in the peerage to be Marquess Townshend of Raynham. In the early years of the French Revolutionary War, between 1793 and 1796, he was commander of the troops in eastern England. Townshend was promoted to field marshal on 30 July 1796, but did not hold any further active command.

Townshend was married twice, first to Charlotte, Baroness de Ferrers in her own right and daughter of the Earl of Northampton. She died in September 1770, leaving four sons and four daughters. He subsequently married Anne Montgomery, daughter of an Irish MP. She gave him six more children and lived until 1819. Townshend himself died at his family seat, Raynham Hall, Norfolk, on 14 September 1807 and was buried there in the family vault.

TWEEDDALE
MARQUESS OF, see **HAY,** GEORGE, **[53]**

TYRAWLEY
LORD, see **O'HARA,** JAMES, **[11]**

UXBRIDGE
EARL OF, see **PAGET,** Lord HENRY, **[37]**

VEREKER
JOHN STANDISH SURTEES PRENDERGAST, 6th Viscount Gort, VC, GCB, CBE, DSO, MVO, MC (1886–1946) **[110]**

The Honourable John Vereker, elder son of the 5th Viscount Gort (an Irish peer whose family had long been domiciled in England) was born in London on 10 July 1886. He was educated at Harrow School and, while there, succeeded as 6th viscount on the death of his father in 1902. After attending the Royal Military College, Sandhurst, Gort was commissioned on 16 August 1905 as a second lieutenant in the Grenadier Guards. He then went to regimental duty in London, where he was promoted to lieutenant on 1 April 1907 and commanded the bearer party at the funeral of King Edward VII **[54]** in May 1910. Gort then went to Canada to hunt moose, but returned to the UK after accidentally shooting dead his Indian guide. In February 1911 he married his second cousin, the twenty year-old Corinna ("Kotchy" or "Connie") Vereker, a brilliant society beauty, with whom, in the course of the following three years, he had two sons and a daughter. Gort's study of his profession, together with his life-long taste for horseplay at the expense of those he disliked, made him a poor match for his fun-loving and artistic viscountess.

On the outbreak of the First World War, Gort was promoted to captain on 5 August 1914. He went to France with the British Expeditionary Force as an ADC in the 2nd Division and took part in the retreat from Mons during late August 1914. At Villers-Cotterets (1 September 1914) Gort collected a group of stragglers and led them in an impromptu counter-attack, during which he was hit by a spent bullet. He served in the field until 26 December 1914, when he became a General Staff officer, grade 3, at the headquarters of the newly-formed First Army. Gort became brigade major of the 4th Guards Brigade on 1 April 1915 and took part with it in numerous engagements during the following twelve months. He was mentioned in despatches five times and was awarded the Military Cross (gazetted on 23 June 1915). Gort moved to the headquarters of the BEF on 30 June 1916, as GSO 2, and remained there throughout the battle of the Somme (July-November 1916). He was promoted to brevet major on 8 June 1916, but chafed at being away from the battlefield and derived little satisfaction from being later awarded the DSO in recognition of his services on the staff.

Gort returned to regimental duty in April 1917, with promotion to acting lieutenant colonel in command of the 4th Battalion, Grenadier Guards. He led this unit during the third battle of Ypres and was at Pilckem Ridge (31 July 1917), where he was wounded and won a bar to his DSO. In the battle of Cambrai Gort was at Gonnelieu (1 December 1917), where he was again wounded. He was invalided home, but returned to France early in March 1918, where he commanded the 1st Battalion, Grenadier Guards, during the German offensive that began shortly afterwards. Gort won a second bar to his DSO at Arras (18 March 1918). He led his battalion in the subsequent Allied advance and was twice wounded at Premy Ridge (27 September 1918), where he gained the Victoria Cross. He was then sent back to England for medical treatment and reverted to the rank of brevet major on 28 September 1918. During the war, he was mentioned in despatches eight times.

After convalescing, Gort was posted to HQ London District. He was then given a place on the first post-war course at the Staff College, Camberley, with promotion to substantive major on 3 June 1919. He passed out of the Staff College in 1920 and returned to HQ London District, where he became a brevet lieutenant colonel on 1 January 1921. Between 1921 and 1923 he was an instructor at the Staff College, where he kept up a friendship that he had established with Basil Liddell Hart, the influential military writer, and gained a reputation as a progressive. He returned to regimental duty in London in 1924. His domestic life had become increasingly unhappy. His viscountess had become estranged from him during his absence on active service, especially after the death of their two year-old younger son in 1915. Complaining of her husband's parsimony and neglect, Lady Gort found consolation elsewhere and, in 1925, Gort obtained a divorce on the grounds of her adultery. He was promoted to colonel on 1 January 1925 and, in the following year, became GSO 1, London District, before going to Sheerness as a chief instructor at the Senior Officers School. In January 1927 he was appointed GSO 1 in the British force sent to protect the International Settlements at Shanghai. He was ordered back to the UK in July 1927, on appointment as GSO 1, 4th Division, at Colchester. Gort remained there until 1930, when he became Officer Commanding the Grenadier Guards Regimental District and HQ 4th Guards Brigade (a cadre composed of London Territorial Army battalions). His next post was as Director of Military Training, India, with promotion to temporary brigadier on 14 November 1932. Gort became a major general on 25 November 1935. He returned to the UK in March 1936, on appointment as Commandant of the Staff College. Gort was still close to Liddell Hart, who was then at the peak of his influence. He remained a progressive and told his students that learning to fly would be of greater military value than riding with the College Draghounds.

In May 1937 Neville Chamberlain, the Prime Minister of the day, unexpectedly appointed a young and rising politician, Leslie Hore-Belisha, as Secretary of State for War. Encouraged by Liddell Hart, who became his closest adviser, Hore-Belisha decided to replace the existing members of the Army Council by younger and less conservative men. Gort was appointed Military Secretary, with accelerated promotion to acting lieutenant general on 23 September 1937 and substantive general on 6 December 1937. His selection was welcomed by most of his contemporaries, though not by those whom he superseded, nor by the Chief of the Imperial General Staff, Sir Cyril Deverell [105]. Despite Deverell's opposition, Gort supported Hore-Belisha's reforms, including the promotion of a Territorial officer to major general and command of a London Territorial division (thereby alarming those Regular officers whose promotion, in a small Regular Army, depended on commands in the Territorial Army). In December 1937 Hore-Belisha, seeing Gort as a dynamic young general who would help modernize the Army, appointed him as CIGS in place of Deverell. Influenced by the need to attract recruits and retain existing personnel, Hore-Belisha made many improvements in the military's conditions of service. His most lasting reform was the introduction of a system of promotion for Regular officers by time, regardless of vacancies on the establishment (an agreeable arrangement much envied by their colleagues in the Territorials and in the Civil Service). He was therefore dismayed when Gort told him that they must not go too fast for fear of "upsetting the people in the clubs".

Forgetting that he owed his promotion to them, Gort came to resent Hore-Belisha's reliance on Liddell Hart. Like Deverell before him, Gort opposed the policy of giving the anti-aircraft defences of the UK priority over the needs of the field army. After February 1939, when the Cabinet decided that it would send an army to the Continent in the event of war with Germany, he was faced with the need to prepare for a major conventional campaign. His personal relations with Hore-Belisha grew worse, arising partly from the anti-Semitic prejudice common among officers of Gort's background and partly from Hore-Belisha's flamboyant and self-advertising ways. Hore-Belisha's announcement on 29 March 1939 that the Territorial Army would be doubled in size was made without reference to Gort. The re-introduction of conscription from July 1939 was undertaken in consultation with the military, but Gort and Hore-Belisha had ceased to work together. On the outbreak of the Second World War in September 1939, Hore-Belisha unexpectedly arranged for Gort to leave the War Office and become C-in-C of the British Expeditionary Force sent to France.

During the period of the "phoney war" Gort too often seemed more concerned with minor details of uniform and equipment rather than the strategic questions appropriate to a C-in-C. He complained bitterly to Sir Edmund Ironside [107], his successor as CIGS, about Hore-Belisha's well-meant criticism of the rate at which the BEF was building concrete "pill-boxes" in its defence lines. Both generals were greatly relieved when Chamberlain subsequently removed Hore-Belisha from the War Office. When Chief of the Imperial General Staff, Gort had arranged for the BEF, after arriving in France, to be placed under the command of the French Army. When the Germans invaded Belgium on 10 May 1940, Gort led the BEF forward to meet them in accordance with the orders of his French commanders. By 19 May 1940, with the collapse of the French line further south, he was preparing to retreat to the coast. Supported by Ironside, Gort decided to evacuate his army through Dunkirk. On 31 May 1940, in response to a direct order from Winston Churchill, the new Prime Minister, he returned to the UK, where most of his troops had already arrived. Although given credit for having saved the BEF, he was also seen as a defeated general who, despite his moral and physical courage, had been out of his depth as a C-in-C in mobile warfare. No other command was found for him by either of the generals who succeeded Ironside as CIGS (Sir John Dill [109] and Sir Alan Brooke [112]) both of whom had been superseded by him in 1937 and had later served under him as Corps Commanders in the BEF. He was found employment as Inspector of Training for the Home Guard. In February 1941 Gort's only surviving son, who had little sympathy with his father's profession, but had become an officer in the Royal Artillery, shot himself after being injured in a motor-cycle accident.

In April 1941 Gort was appointed Governor and C-in-C, Gibraltar. Both Churchill and King George VI [106] saw this as a post for which his temperament would be well suited, if Spain declared war on the side of the Axis powers and laid siege to this symbol of the British Empire. Gort himself regarded the appointment as a slight, but set himself to improve the fortress's defences and extended its airstrip. In April 1942 he became Governor and Supreme Commander in Malta, which was at that time under intense air attack. Gort played a forceful role there and kept the civilian population fed, while maintaining Malta's vital role as a base of Allied operations in the Mediterranean. He received severe burns in November 1942, while leading his staff in retrieving petrol cans from a fuel dump, set on fire by Axis bombers. He returned for medical treatment to the UK, where, on 1 January 1943, he was promoted to field marshal at the King's express wish. Gort resumed his post in Malta and was present with his daughter when her husband, Major William Sidney (later Viscount de Lisle) of the Grenadier Guards, was presented with the Victoria Cross. In October 1944 Gort was appointed High Commissioner in Palestine, where he was faced with quarrels between Jews and Arabs and by the dislike of both communities for British rule. Gort's health began to deteriorate during late 1945, with the return of a cancerous condition from which he had suffered during the First World War. He resigned office in November 1945 and returned to the UK, where his illness was diagnosed as inoperable. Gort was granted a viscountcy in the UK peerage in February 1946, but did not live to take his seat. He died on 31 March 1946 at his son-in-law's family seat, Penshurst Place, Kent, and was buried in the near-by parish church of St John the Baptist, Penshurst. His Irish peerage was inherited by his younger brother and his UK peerage became extinct for lack of male heirs. Gort was appointed colonel commandant of the Honourable Artillery Company in May 1943, but never held a regimental colonelcy.

VINCENT
Sir RICHARD FREDERICK, Baron Vincent of Coleshill, GBE, KCB, DSO (1931-) [135]

Richard Vincent was born on 23 August 1931. After attending Aldenham School, Elstree, Hertfordshire, he entered the Army on 16

November 1950 and, after serving in the ranks and as an officer cadet at Mons Officer Cadet School, Aldershot, was granted a National Service commission as a second lieutenant in the Royal Artillery on 7 July 1951. From 1951 to 1955 he served at regimental duty in the British Army of the Rhine. He obtained a Short Service (later permanent) Regular commission in the Royal Artillery as second lieutenant on 16 February 1953 (with seniority from 7 July 1951) and was promoted to lieutenant with effect from 13 March 1953. In 1955 Vincent married Jean Paterson, with whom he later had two sons (one of whom died at a young age) and a daughter. He was promoted to captain on 23 August 1958 and became a gunnery staff officer in 1959. In 1960–61 he was seconded to the Ministry of Aviation at the Radar Research Establishment, Malvern. He returned to BAOR in 1962 as a troop commander and Forward Observation Officer in a field artillery regiment. During 1963–64 Vincent attended the technical staff course at the Royal Military College of Science, Shrivenham, and in 1965 qualified at the Staff College, Camberley. He became a major on 23 August 1965 and, in 1966–68, served at regimental duty with the Commonwealth Brigade in Malaysia.

Vincent served at the Ministry of Defence as a General Staff officer, grade 2, in the department of the Master General of the Ordnance from August 1968 to October 1969. He became commanding officer of 12 Light Air Defence Regiment, Royal Artillery, on 27 February 1970, with promotion to substantive lieutenant colonel on 30 June 1970. He commanded this regiment in Germany (with tours in Northern Ireland in aid of the civil power, for which he was awarded the DSO) until May 1972. From August 1972 to October 1973 he was an instructor and GSO 1 at the Staff College. After attending the Administrative Staff College, Henley, Vincent served between January 1974 and December 1975 at the Royal Military College of Science, Shrivenham, as military director of studies. He was promoted to colonel on 30 June 1974 and to brigadier on 30 June 1975. He commanded 19 (Airportable) Brigade from December 1975 to December 1977, after which he went to the Royal College of Defence Studies. Vincent was again at the Ministry of Defence between January 1979 and July 1980 as one of the two deputy military secretaries in the department of the Parliamentary Under-Secretary of State for the Army. He was promoted to major general on 1 April 1980 and from July 1980 to April 1983 held the post of commandant of the Royal Military College of Science. Vincent was subsequently appointed Master General of the Ordnance, with promotion to lieutenant general on 1 September 1983 and was created a KCB in January 1982.

Sir Richard Vincent was promoted to general on 3 November 1986. He became Vice Chief of the Defence Staff in October 1987 and remained in this post until March 1992, when he was made Chief of the Defence Staff. He was promoted to field marshal on 2 April 1992. He ceased to be CDS in December 1993 and then served as Chairman of the North Atlantic Treaty Organization's Military Committee until 1996. He was granted a life peerage in 1996 as Baron Vincent of Coleshill, of Shrivenham. Lord Vincent became a colonel commandant of the Royal Artillery in January 1983 and was colonel commandant of the Royal Electrical and Mechanical Engineers from February 1981 to October 1987. He became honorary colonel of 100 (Yeomanry) Field Regiment, Royal Artillery (Volunteers), in the Territorial Army in December 1982. After the decision to appoint honorary colonels (previously known only in the auxiliary forces) to regular units of the Royal Artillery, Lord Vincent was honorary colonel of 12 Light Air Defence Regiment, Royal Artillery, from 1987 to 1991. On retiring from active duty, he took up a number of business directorships and, in 1996, was appointed Master Gunner, St James's Park.

WADE
GEORGE (1673–1748) [7]

George Wade, the third son of Jerome Wade of Kilavally, County Westmeath, was born in 1673 and was commissioned as an ensign in the Earl of Bath's Regiment (later the 10th Foot) on 26 December 1690. He was with this regiment at Steenkerke (23 July 1692) and served in Flanders during the remainder of the Nine Years War. Wade was promoted to lieutenant on 10 February 1693 and to captain of the grenadier company of his regiment on 13 June 1695. During the War of the Spanish Succession he was in Marlborough's army at the sieges of Kaiserswerth (18 April–15 June 1702); Venlo (29 August–25 September 1702); Roermond (26 September–6 October 1702) and Liège (13–29 October 1702). He became a major on 20 March 1703 and served as a lieutenant colonel at the siege of Huy (15–26 August 1703). In 1704 Wade was appointed adjutant general in the Earl of Galway's army in the Peninsula. He became colonel of an infantry regiment (later 33rd Foot), as a battle casualty replacement, at the siege of Alcantara, where he was wounded on 10 April 1706. He commanded a brigade at Almanaza (25 April 1707) and was second in command of the expedition to Minorca in the autumn of 1708. Wade commanded a brigade at the battle of Zaragoza (20 August 1710) and earned a recommendation for promotion to major general, though he did not actually achieve that rank until 3 October 1714. He entered Parliament as MP for Hindon, Wiltshire, in January 1715.

During the Jacobite Rising of 1715 Wade was employed on internal security duties at Bath, a city that was known to contain a number of sympathizers to the Stuart cause. In 1719 he served as second in command to Viscount Cobham [6] in the descent on Vigo. Wade became MP for Bath in 1722 and retained this seat throughout the rest of his life. He was sent to the Scottish Highlands in 1724, to undertake a military survey of the region. After being appointed to command the forces in Scotland, Wade began the great achievement of his career, the construction (mostly by military labour) of a network of roads and bridges that opened the Highlands to both military and commercial traffic. He became lieutenant general on 7 March 1727, general on 2 July 1739 and field marshal on 14 December 1743, when he was given command of the Pragmatic Army in Germany in the War of the Austrian Succession. Wade, well over the age for active campaigning, was relieved at his own request in March 1745.

On the Jacobite Rising later in 1745 Wade was in post as commander of the forces in England. He concentrated his troops at Newcastle, but the Jacobites invaded England via Carlisle. Wade, hampered by bad roads and heavy snow, was unable to march his freezing and starving men to intercept them, nor could he make contact with the Jacobite army when it eventually retreated. Although much criticized by younger and more vigorous generals, he remained a popular figure and his name appeared in a verse of the new patriotic anthem "God save the King". Wade was offered his old post as commander in Scotland, with the task of bringing the insurgency to an end, but refused it on the grounds of age and unfitness for active duty. He was then, at his own request, allowed to retire from active duty. In private life, Wade was something of a dandy and enjoyed great success with women. He never married, but had four natural children, whom he acknowledged and supported. He died on 14 March 1748 and was buried in Westminster Abbey. His lasting memorial was the network of Highland roads, celebrated in the couplet:

" Had you seen these roads before they were made,
You would lift up your hands and bless General Wade".

WAVELL
Sir ARCHIBALD PERCIVAL, 1st Earl Wavell, GCB, GCSI, GCIE, CMG, MC (1883–1950) [111]

Archibald Wavell, the only son and the second of three children of a major in the Norfolk Regiment (later a major general), was born in Colchester, Essex, on 5 May 1883. Major Wavell exchanged into the Black Watch (Royal Highlanders) in 1891 to become its commanding officer. The young Wavell won a scholarship to Winchester College in 1896, where he developed an interest in history and literature that remained with him for the rest of his life. He entered the Royal Military College, Sandhurst, in September 1900, passing in fourth in order of merit in his batch, and was commissioned as a second lieutenant in the 2nd Battalion, the Black Watch, on 8 May 1901. Wavell joined this unit in the South African War, where he served until October 1902, when he suffered a permanent injury to his shoulder in an inter-unit football match and was invalided home. He rejoined his battalion early in 1903, in the Punjab, and was promoted to lieutenant on 13 August 1904. In 1908, when attached to the staff, Wavell nominated himself to command an ammunition column formed for service in the Bazar Valley campaign and thus gained his first experience of active service. He then returned to the UK and passed into the Staff College, Camberley, in January 1909. After qualifying as a staff officer in 1911, he was sent to Moscow to learn Russian. In March 1912 he was appointed a General Staff officer, grade 3, in the Russian section at the War Office and was promoted to acting captain. He returned to Russia as an official observer at the autumn manoeuvres of 1912 and 1913, with promotion to substantive captain on 20 March 1913.

After mobilization on 4 August 1914 Wavell spent the first six weeks of the First World War at the War Office. On obtaining an appointment with the General Headquarters of the British Expeditionary Force in France, he became engaged to Eugenie Marie (Queenie) Quirk, the daughter of a colonel in the infantry. He was promoted to acting major in the Intelligence branch at GHQ on 28 September 1914. On 16 November 1914, he was appointed brigade major of the 9th Infantry Brigade, serving in the Ypres salient. Wavell married his fiancée on 22 April 1915. He remained as brigade major until 16 June 1915, when he was wounded and lost his left eye. He was awarded the newly-instituted Military Cross and invalided back to the UK. In October 1915 he became GSO 2 in the 64th (Highland) Division. Wavell returned to GHQ in France in December 1915, where he was promoted to substantive major on 8 May 1916, three days before the birth of his first child, a son.

In November 1916 Wavell became a temporary lieutenant colonel and was sent to Tiflis (Tbilisi) as acting British military representative at the headquarters of the Russian armies in the Caucasus. His wife arrived there the following month, having travelled, with her maid (neither of them Russian-speakers) via Sweden, Finland and Moscow. While in Russia, Wavell received promotion to brevet lieutenant colonel, with seniority from 3 June 1916. He returned to London in June 1917 and was appointed a liaison officer between Sir William Robertson [92], Chief of the Imperial General Staff, and Sir Edmund Allenby [90] the new C-in-C of the Egyptian Expeditionary Force. Wavell formed a great admiration for Allenby and later published a biography of him, together with several studies of his Palestine campaign. In January 1918, after returning from Palestine, Wavell joined the staff of Sir Henry Wilson [91], British Military Representative at the Supreme Allied War Council, Versailles. Disliking what he saw of the ways of politicians and political generals, he gave up his appointment at Versailles at the end of February 1918 and returned to Palestine as Brigadier General, General Staff, XX Corps, where he remained until the end of the First World War in November 1918.

Wavell served as BGGS at Headquarters, Middle East, first at Haifa and then at Cairo, from January 1919 until the spring of 1920. He then returned to regimental duty and commanded a company in the 2nd Battalion, the Black Watch, in the British Army of Occupation on the Rhine. He was promoted to substantive colonel on 3 June 1921 and became an assistant adjutant general in the War Office in the following December. He was GSO 1 in the Directorate of Military Operations from July 1923 to January 1926, when he was placed on the half-pay list. Wavell supplemented his income by writing on military subjects until he returned to full pay, as GSO 1 of the 3rd Division, on Salisbury Plain, in November 1926. He became an acting brigadier early in 1930, on appointment to command the 6th Infantry Brigade at Aldershot. He established a reputation for imaginative and enthusiastic infantry training, but insisted that even the most realistic exercises could not replace the experience of war. The best substitute, he told his officers, was a study of military history and of the great captains, "if properly done, which it very seldom is".

Wavell was promoted to major general on 16 October 1933 and was again placed on half pay until March 1935, when he was given command of the 2nd Division. In 1937 he became commander of the British troops in Palestine and Transjordan. In the quarrel between

Palestinian Arabs and the Zionists, he was inclined to sympathize with the former. Nevertheless, on the renewal of terrorist activity by the Palestinians, he took vigorous counter-measures, forming mobile columns from his British troops, and allowing one of his officers, Orde Wingate, to form the Special Night Squads, a local defence force of Jewish settlers. Wavell used his own interest in classical and biblical studies to help plan his counter-insurgency operations. He was promoted to lieutenant general on 21 January 1938 and returned to the UK in April 1938, to become GOC-in-C, Southern Command, with the award of the KCB in January 1939. A few weeks before the outbreak of the Second World War, Sir Archibald Wavell was appointed GOC-in-C Middle East, with promotion to local general on 28 July 1939.

Wavell's post was up-graded to C-in-C, Middle East, in January 1940. When Italy entered the war on 10 June 1940 he found himself greatly outnumbered in both East and North Africa. He accepted the loss of British Somaliland in August 1940, but turned back an attempted Italian invasion of Egypt at Sidi Barrani (16 September 1940). Wavell took the offensive on 9 December 1940 and captured Cyrenaica early in February 1941. He launched an offensive against the Italians in East Africa in February 1941, leading to the recovery of all British territory and the restoration of the Emperor Haile Selassie of Ethiopia [125] in May 1941. Wavell supported the despatch to Greece of a force under Sir Henry Maitland Wilson [115], in the hope of keeping German influence away from the Middle East, but the Germans overran the Greek mainland in late April 1941 and captured Crete a few weeks later. During the same period the Axis forces drove Wavell out of Cyrenaica and laid siege to Tobruk. Winston Churchill, the British Prime Minister, pressed Wavell to send troops into Iraq, where the anti-British Regent had seized power and opened negotiations with German agents. Wavell was reluctant to divide his resources, but eventually complied with this plan, so that a government friendly to the Allied cause was installed at Baghdad at the end of May 1941. In the Western Desert Wavell launched two offensives, on 15 May and 15 June 1941, both of which ended in failure. On 8 June 1941 he advanced into Syria and the Lebanon, where the Vichy French forces surrendered in early July 1941. Churchill had nevertheless lost confidence in Wavell and, on 21 June 1941, ordered him to hand over the Middle East Command to Sir Claude Auchinleck [116] and to take Auchinleck's place as C-in-C, India.

Wavell began his command with a successful action on India's western flank, in co-operation with the Soviet Union, to ensure that Iran remained within the Allied sphere of influence. Indian troops seized the oilfields at Abadan on 25 August 1941 and entered Tehran on 17 September 1941. The strategic situation changed fundamentally with the beginning of the Pacific War on 7 December 1941. At the suggestion of the United States, Wavell was appointed Supreme Allied Commander for the South-West Pacific area on 30 December 1941. With limited resources made up of the local American, British, Dutch, and Australian forces (ABDA Command), he was unable to withstand the onslaught of the Japanese, whose fighting abilities he greatly underestimated. As the Japanese advanced through Malaya, he made a visit to Singapore and decided that it could not be defended. The fall of this great naval base on 15 February 1942, the most humiliating defeat in the history of British arms, was followed by the dissolution of ABDA Command a week later. Wavell returned to his post as C-in-C, India, where he remained responsible for the overall conduct of the campaign in Burma (lost to the Japanese by May 1942). He began preparations for a counter-offensive in September 1942 and, in a return to his taste for the unorthodox, authorized the "Chindit" operations conducted behind Japanese lines by Major General Orde Wingate. Wavell ordered an attack in the Arakan in December 1942, but this made little headway and was ended with the approach of the monsoon in May 1943. He had by this time lost the confidence of both Churchill and the Americans. Wavell ceased to be C-in-C, India, in June 1943, when he was appointed Viceroy and Governor-General of India. He was raised to the peerage as Viscount Wavell of Cyrenaica and Winchester in July 1943.

Wavell was by this time a field marshal, having recommended himself in August 1942 on the grounds of the number of troops under his command and of the number of campaigns in which he had commanded. The promotion was resisted by the Secretary of State for War, P. J. Grigg, who said that Wavell had brains but no determination and had achieved no resounding successes. He also pointed out that the King believed Lord Gort [110] had a better claim. Despite this, both Churchill and Sir Alan Brooke [112], Chief of the Imperial General Staff, supported Wavell, who was accordingly promoted on the same day as Gort on 1 January 1943.

As Governor-General, Lord Wavell's first major task was to deal with a famine in Bengal. This disaster, in which over a million people died, arose from the loss of Burma's rice-fields to the Japanese and from the effect of the war on local transport systems. It was compounded by the selfishness of farmers and speculators and by the policies of government officials who believed that the free operation of market forces would solve the problem. Wavell introduced food rationing and used troops to

290

distribute food and provide aid to refugees. The demands of Indian politicians for constitutional progress were more difficult to deal with. Wavell was inclined to make some conciliatory gesture and released the imprisoned Congress Party leader, Mahatma Gandhi. The Labour government, elected in July 1945, determined to end British rule in India at the earliest moment, but failed to achieve any agreement between the various nationalist leaders. The "Calcutta killing" of August 1946 left thousands dead in the streets of the second city of the British Empire. Thousands more died in October and November 1946 as Hindus, Sikhs and Muslims attacked each other throughout northern India. Wavell told the Cabinet that the British must either send more troops, re-establish direct rule and stay in India for at least fifteen more years, or else withdraw from each province in turn before quitting India altogether by a pre-set date. Both alternatives were equally unacceptable. Clement Attlee, the Prime Minister, came to view Wavell as not only unpopular with the Indian nationalist leaders but also exhausted and irresolute. On 20 February 1947 he gave Wavell one month's notice that he would be replaced. Wavell then retired from public life, with the customary advancement of one rank in the peerage to mark his services as Viceroy and Governor-General. He became colonel of the Black Watch (the Royal Highland Regiment) in March 1946. Earl Wavell died on 24 May 1950, following an operation for jaundice, and was buried at Winchester College. He had two daughters and a son, who succeeded him as 2nd Earl and was later killed in action, serving as a major in the Black Watch in the Mau Mau rebellion, Kenya, after which his titles became extinct.

WELLESLEY
(WESLEY), Sir ARTHUR, 1st Duke of Wellington, KG, GCB, GCH (1769–1852) [24]

The Honourable Arthur Wesley, fourth son of an Irish peer, the 1st Earl of Mornington, was born in Dublin on or about 1 May 1769. He was educated at Eton College and a French military school at Angers, where he was sent by his widowed mother when the Earl's early death left her with limited funds. The young Wesley was commissioned on 7 March 1787 as an ensign in the 73rd Foot and then passed through the rolls of the 76th Foot (as lieutenant from 25 Dec 1787); the 41st Foot (23 Jan 1788); the 12th Light Dragoons (25 June 1788); the 58th Foot (as captain, from 30 Jun 1791) and the 18th Light Dragoons (31 Oct 1792). Wesley joined the 33rd Foot as a major on 30 April 1793, with promotion to lieutenant colonel on 30 September 1793. Between November 1787 and March 1793 he was on the staff of various Lords Lieutenant of Ireland at Dublin Castle. He also sat in the Irish Parliament from April 1790 to June 1795, as MP for Trim.

In the French Revolutionary War, Wesley, in command of the 33rd Foot, joined the British army in Flanders in June 1794. He was at Boxtel (14 September 1794) and commanded a brigade during the subsequent winter retreat into Germany. Wesley became a colonel in the Army on 3 May 1796, as almost the junior officer in a large number promoted on that day, possibly to allow him to be rewarded in this way for supporting the ministry in Ireland He followed his regiment to India, where he arrived in February 1797. His eldest brother, Richard, 2nd Earl of Mornington, (later 1st Marquess Wellesley) became Governor-General of Bengal in May 1798. He had long preferred to use the name Wellesley, as an older and fuller form of Wesley, and from then on, all his family spelt their name in this way. The Honourable Arthur Wellesley took part in the campaign against Tipu Sultan of Mysore early in 1799 and became Military Governor of Mysore after Tipu's defeat and death at Seringapatam (2 May 1799). Wellesley was promoted to major general on 29 April 1802 and commanded the British forces in the Deccan during the Maratha War, where he gained a series of victories at Ahmadnagar (12 August 1803); Assaye (23 September 1803); Argaon (29 November 1803) and Gawilghar (15 December 1803). These major actions were followed by a period of low-intensity operations, after which Wellesley was awarded the KB on 1 September 1804. His Indian campaigns earned him Napoleon's contemptuous description as "a sepoy general" but gained him valuable experience of the logistic problems associated with operations in a poor country.

Sir Arthur Wellesley returned to England in 1805 and, at the end of that year, was sent in command of a brigade to reinforce the British army in Hanover. This army was recalled to the UK, without having taken part in active operations, in February 1806. Wellesley became colonel of the 33rd Foot on 30 January 1806 and entered Parliament, as MP for Rye, in April 1806. He later represented Mitchell, in Cornwall and Newport, in the Isle of Wight, until he became a member of the House of Lords. Out of a characteristic sense of duty, he married, on 10 April 1806, the thirty-three year-old Catherine (Kitty) Pakenham, sister of the 2nd Earl of Longford. Wellesley had paid court to her when a young officer in Dublin, and she, to his surprise, had waited for him while he was in India. Between April 1807 and April 1809 he was part of the Tory ministry as Chief Secretary for Ireland, but continued his military career and served in the British descent on Copenhagen (31 July-30 September 1807), where he defeated a Danish force at Kioge (29 August 1807). He was promoted to lieutenant general on 25 April 1808 and was given command of an army intended for operations against the Spanish in Venezuela. When the peoples of Spain and Portugal rose up against Napoleon, it was sent to the Peninsula instead. Wellesley defeated the French at Rolica (17 August 1808) and Vimiero (21 August 1808) before being superseded by the arrival of over-cautious seniors, under whose orders he signed the Convention of Cintra (Sintra) on terms favourable to the French.

Exonerated by the subsequent official enquiry, Wellesley returned to Portugal at the head of an army in April 1809 and began the campaigns that, despite occasional reverses, gained him his reputation as one of the British Army's greatest captains of war. His battles and sieges included the passage of the Douro (Oporto, 12 May 1809); Talavera (27–28 July 1809), where he was hit by a spent musket-ball; Busaco (27 September 1810); Pombal (11 March 1811); Sabugal (3 April 1811); Fuentes d' Onoro (3–5 May 1811); El Bodon (25 September 1811); Ciudad Rodrigo (8–19 January 1812); Badajoz (16 March–7 April 1812); Salamanca (22 July 1812); Valladolid (29 July 1812); Burgos (19 September–21 October 1812); Vittoria (21 June 1813); the Pyrenees (27–30 July 1813); San Sebastian (stormed 31 August 1813); the passage of the Bidassoa, into France (7 October 1813); the Nivelle (10 October 1813); the Nive (10–13 December 1813); Orthez (27 February 1814), where he was slightly wounded by a spent musket-ball, and Toulouse (10 April 1814). During this period he became Marshal of the Portuguese Army in July 1809 and was promoted in the British Army to be a local general on 31 July 1812. He was raised to the peerage as Viscount Wellington in September 1809, with further advancement to an earldom in February 1812 and a marquessate in August 1812.

After the battle of Vittoria he sent the captured baton of the French Marshal Jourdain to the Prince Regent, who replied with a message that he was sending him, in return, the baton of a British field marshal. This was a metaphorical flourish, as British field marshals had not previously carried batons, at least since the revival of their rank in 1793, and one had to be made (designed by the Prince Regent himself) especially for the occasion. The design of the new baton was based upon that of a marshal of France, but covered in red, rather than blue, velvet and surmounted by a gold figure of St George slaying the dragon. Earlier field marshals and other commanding generals had carried a plain baton of polished wood with ferrules of yellow metal. Wellington's promotion, on 21 June 1813, was the first in which a general, other than a royal duke, was advanced to the rank of field marshal by passing over those senior to him. Wellington superseded eighty generals, of whom four (three of them royal dukes) subsequently became field marshals themselves. After the abdication of Napoleon in 1814, Wellington was rewarded with a dukedom and became British Ambassador to the restored Bourbon court in Paris. He was the British representative at the Congress of Vienna from early February to late March 1815, when he left to command the Allied armies assembling in the Low Countries to meet Napoleon's return to France. The Hundred Days campaign gave the Duke of Wellington his last and most famous victory, at Waterloo (18 June 1815), followed by command of the Army of Occupation and resumption of his Embassy at Paris.

Wellington continued to play an important part in both political and military life. He sat in the Cabinet as Master General of the Ordnance from December 1818 until April 1827 and was Commander-in-Chief of the British Army three times (from January to May 1827, from August 1827 to January 1828 and from August 1842 until his death in 1852). In January 1828 when both Whigs and Tories were so divided that neither party could form a government, Wellington became Prime Minister at the King's request. In April 1829 he reluctantly accepted the principle of Catholic emancipation, as the only way of avoiding a civil war in Ireland. Lord Winchilsea, a Protestant zealot, accused Wellington of deceit and of planning to introduce Popery. Wellington responded by challenging him to a duel. Both parties fired wide and Winchilsea made the desired apology. A conservative in political as in military matters, Wellington stood out firmly against the growing agitation for parliamentary reform and his ministry fell on this issue in November 1830.

On the fall of the Whig ministry in November 1834, Wellington became a caretaker Prime Minister pending the return of Sir Robert Peel, the Tory leader, from overseas. Wellington remained in the Cabinet as Foreign Secretary from December 1834 to April 1835. He was in Peel's Second Cabinet, as Tory party leader in the Lords, from September 1841 until the ministry fell in June 1846. He was appointed colonel of the Royal Horse Guards in 1813 and retained this post until 1827, when he became colonel of the Grenadier Guards. In 1820 he became colonel-in-chief of the Rifle Brigade. Despite his prestige and influence, Wellington was unable to prevent the usual peacetime economies in defence spending. He himself declared that he saved what was left of the Regular Army only by hiding it in the colonies. At the time of his death, the British Army had the resources neither to mount a major campaign overseas nor even to defend the Royal Navy's bases at home. Wellington died at Walmer Castle, his official residence as Lord Warden of the Cinque Ports, on 14 September 1852 and was buried in St Paul's Cathedral, London. His marriage to Kitty Pakenham brought little happiness to either party, but she bore him two sons, of whom the elder succeeded to his titles.

Wellington was the British Army's most illustrious field marshal. As a general commanding Allied as well as British armies, he was successful against the previously invincible troops of Revolutionary and Imperial France, before finally meeting and defeating Napoleon himself at Waterloo. In his personal character, Wellington was the model of the nineteenth-century English gentleman, austere in speech, Spartan in conduct, but at the same time enjoying all the personal pleasures available to his level in society. As a commander, he was generally frugal with his men's lives and, though a stern disciplinarian, inspired the confidence, even the affection, of his army. In him can be found all the military virtues of leadership, courage, practical common-sense, and, above all, regard for duty. To his Peninsular officers he was "the Beau" or "the Peer". To the British public, he was "the Iron Duke", who responded to alternate popularity and unpopularity with equal lack of outward emotion. In addition to his rank in the British Army, he was a marshal or field marshal in the armies of Austria, the Netherlands, Portugal, Prussia and Russia, as well as captain general of the army of Spain.

WELLINGTON
DUKE OF, see **WELLESLEY**, Sir ARTHUR, **[24]**

WHITE
Sir GEORGE STUART, VC, GCB, OM, GCSI, GCMG, GCIE, GCVO (1835–1912) **[75]**

George White, second son of James White of White Hall, County Antrim, was born on 6 July 1835. He was educated at King William's College in the Isle of Man and at the Royal Military College, Sandhurst, before being commissioned as an ensign in the 27th Foot on 4 November 1853. In 1854 he sailed with his regiment to India, where he was promoted to lieutenant on 29 January 1855. On the outbreak of the Indian Mutiny in May 1857 White was serving on the North-West Frontier at Peshawar. He remained there as part of the border defences and so saw no action in the Mutiny campaign. White became a captain in the 92nd Gordon Highlanders on 10 July 1863, shortly before returning with this regiment to the UK. He was promoted to major on 24 December 1863 and went back to India with the 92nd Highlanders in 1868. In 1874 White married Amy Baley, daughter of the Archdeacon of Calcutta, with whom he later had a son and two daughters.

During the absence of both its lieutenant colonels, White held command of his battalion as a major in 1875–76. During the Second Afghan War he served under Sir Frederick Roberts [68] at Charasia (6 October 1879) and in various operations around Kabul during December 1879. After three months as military secretary to Lord Ripon, the newly-appointed Viceroy and Governor-General of India, White rejoined his battalion in August 1880 and took part in Roberts' march from Kabul to Kandahar. He was awarded the Victoria Cross for his conduct at the battle of Kandahar (1 September 1880), coupled with that previously at Charasia. White was promoted to lieutenant colonel on 2 March 1881. He then went back to the United Kingdom with the 92nd (renamed the 2nd Battalion, the Gordon Highlanders in July 1881), where he remained as commanding officer until 1884. White then joined the staff of the British army in Egypt, with promotion to colonel on 2 March 1885.

In the following year, White commanded a brigade in the Third Burma War, where from November 1886 to February 1887 he once again served under Roberts (by this time, C-in-C, India). Roberts promoted White to local major general, (superseding 222 colonels senior to him) and left him in command of the operations in Burma when these dwindled into a series of minor engagements against local patriots and robbers. He was awarded the KCB in 1886 and became a substantive major general on 1 July 1887. Sir George White left Burma in 1889 to take command at Quetta, from where he conducted minor expeditions in the Zhob Valley and Baluchistan. In 1893 he succeeded Roberts as C-in-C, India, with promotion to lieutenant general on 1 April 1895. He was appointed colonel of the Gordon Highlanders in June 1897 and Quartermaster General of the British Army in 1898.

In early September 1899 White was surprised to find himself given command of the British forces in Natal, where hostilities with the Boer republics were imminent. While in India, after a fall from his horse, he had been left with a limp that made him unfit for field duty. Accepting the command, he told the C-in-C, Lord Wolseley [67], that at least he would not be able to run away. White arrived at Ladysmith the day after the outbreak of the South African War on 10 October 1899. He fought a series of engagements, at Elandslaagte (21 October 1899); Rietfontein (24 October 1899) and Nicholson's Nek (30 October 1899) before retreating into Ladysmith. Sir Redvers Buller, C-in-C, South Africa, advanced to his relief, but was defeated with heavy casualties. Unnerved, he sent a signal to White advising him to destroy his guns and stores and make the best terms he could. White replied that the capitulation of so many British troops would have a serious impact on the war and concluded his message with the words "I hold Ladysmith for the Queen". He did so by standing a four-months' siege, during which his courage and determination made him a popular figure among both his troops and the civil population. Invalided home after the eventual relief of Ladysmith on 1 March 1900, he was feted as a hero, with promotion to general on 9 October 1900 and field marshal on 8 August 1903. Sir George White was appointed Governor of the Royal Hospital, Chelsea, in 1905 and died there on 24 June 1912.

WILLIAM (WILLEM) II
HM King of the Netherlands, WILLIAM FREDERICK GEORGE LUDWIG, HSH Prince of Orange, GCB (1792–1849) [34]

Prince William of Orange, son of the heir to the Stadtholder of the United Provinces, was born in the Hague on 6 December 1792. He was educated in England, where his father took refuge with his family on the occupation of the Netherlands by Revolutionary France in the winter of 1794–5. In 1806, on his father's accession as Stadtholder, Prince William became Prince of Orange in his place. After attending Christ Church, Oxford, he was granted a commission as colonel in the British Army on 17 October 1811 and joined the Peninsular War on the staff of the British commander, Lord Wellington [24]. The Prince of Orange, nicknamed from his appearance "Slender Billy" or "the young frog", by his British fellow officers, was at Ciudad Rodrigo (January 1812); Badajoz (April 1812); Salamanca (22 June 1812); Vittoria (21 June 1813); the Pyrenees (July-August 1813) and at the operations on the Nivelle (10 November 1813). He was promoted in the British Army to be major general on 17 December 1813, lieutenant general on 8 July 1814 and general on 12 July 1814.

In the immediate post-war settlement the British secured the creation of a new United Kingdom of the Netherlands and Belgium, with the Stadholder William IV becoming King William I. To strengthen British influence over this state, a dynastic marriage was arranged between the

Prince of Orange and the Prince Regent's only child, Princess Charlotte of Wales. Charlotte at first gave her consent, as a way of escaping from her father's control, but was later persuaded that, if she went to the Netherlands, the Prince Regent would be able more easily to divorce the Princess of Wales, his estranged wife, marry again and produce a male heir. The Grand Duchess Catherine of Russia, in London with her brother the Emperor Alexander I for the victory celebrations of 1814, had dynastic plans of her own. She urged Charlotte to reject William and choose a more handsome German prince (especially one who had fought alongside the Russians in the War of Liberation). To spite her father, the princess thereupon broke her engagement to the Prince of Orange and later married Leopold of Saxe-Coburg [28].

The beginning of the Hundred Days campaign found the Prince of Orange in command of the Dutch-Belgian Army. As the senior officer present, in both his own and the British Army, he planned an immediate offensive, but was persuaded by Sir John Colborne [42], his military secretary, to wait the arrival of the Duke of Wellington as Allied commander in April 1815. As British reinforcements arrived, the Prince greeted his old comrades of the Peninsular War with such warmth as to earn a stern reminder from his royal father to pay more attention to his own Netherlands officers. He was given command of I Corps in the Allied army, but, over-anxious to impress his old chief, proved a difficult subordinate. Both at Quatre Bras (16 June 1815) and at Waterloo (18 June 1815), where he was wounded, the Prince of Orange was criticized for giving orders that led to his infantry being ridden down by the French cavalry. After the war he married in February 1816 the Grand Duchess Anna, youngest sister of the Emperor Alexander I of Russia, with whom he later had a daughter and four sons.

In 1830 the Belgians rose in rebellion and declared their independence from the Netherlands. Leopold of Saxe-Coburg, the Prince of Orange's one-time rival for the hand of Princess Charlotte of Wales, was elected King of the Belgians in June 1831. When the Belgians continued to occupy Luxembourg (of which the King of the Netherlands was Grand Duke), a Dutch army, led by the Prince of Orange, invaded Belgium in August 1831. He routed the Belgian army, took Louvain and was prevented from capturing Brussels only by French intervention. The Prince succeeded his father in 1840 and reigned as King William II of the Netherlands. In the early part of his reign, he resisted the growing demands for constitutional reform and only gave way when faced by the threat of revolution in 1848. He became a British field marshal on 28 July 1845. William II died at Tilburg on 17 March 1849 and was succeeded by his eldest son.

WILLIAM (WILHELM) II
HM German Emperor (Kaiser) and King of Prussia,
FREDERICK WILLIAM VICTOR ALBERT, KG, GCVO
(1859–1941) **[71]**

William of Prussia, the future "Kaiser Wilhelm", was born in Berlin on 27 January 1859. He was the first child and eldest son of Frederick, Crown Prince of Prussia, and Victoria, eldest daughter of Queen Victoria of England. Their marriage, in January 1858, was made for reasons of state, but proved to be something of a love-match between the strong-willed princess and her husband, in appearance the model of the Germanic warrior-hero and later a capable general in the Austro-Prussian and Franco-Prussian wars. Victoria, neither as Crown Princess nor Empress, ever considered herself to have become a German. Her habit of comparing all aspects of her adopted country unfavourably with those in England (despite her mother's advice to the contrary) soon made her unpopular in Berlin. William's birth, to a teen-age mother, was a difficult one, leaving him with a left arm which never grew to full size, an imbalance to one side of his body and, possibly, brain damage that contributed to his violent mood swings in later life. He made courageous and successful efforts to overcome his disability and became a good shot and an able horseman. He attended Bonn University in 1877 and was appointed a subaltern in the Potsdam Guards Regiment in 1879.

Prince William's military commission brought him into closer contact with his grandfather, the Emperor William I, who personified the traditional Prussian values that the young prince then adopted. He acquired a taste for military life and was thereafter never happier than when wearing uniform, riding at the head of his troops. In February 1881 he married Augusta Victoria ("Dona"), eldest daughter of the Duke of Schleswig-Holstein-Sonderburg-Augustenburg, with whom he later had six sons and a daughter.

Hopes that the Emperor Frederick, under his wife's forceful influence, would turn the new German Empire into a liberal and pro-British nation ended with his death from cancer of the throat at the age of 55, after a reign of ninety-nine days. William succeeded his father as German Emperor on 15 June 1888 and began his reign by impressing all whom he met with his personal charm, energy, enthusiasm, breadth of interests and receptiveness to new ideas for a new empire. With nobody willing to contradict him, he came to believe himself an expert on every subject, foreign policy in particular. His capricious and unstable character led him to alternate between chauvinism and conciliation, serving only to increase tension between Germany and the other Great Powers. William's attitude towards the British was one of extremes. On the one hand, he admired British power and influence and was proud to be the grandson of Queen Victoria (who died in his arms). On the other, he resented British reluctance to accept the emergence of Germany as a world power. In 1898 he visited the Holy Land and, wearing a flowing cloak, rode into Jerusalem, where he declared himself the protector of Islam. This alarmed the British as much as his description of the projected Baghdad railway as "my railway" and the general perception of this line as the "Berlin to Baghdad Railway". His open sympathy for the Boer Republics during the South African War, while shared by many of his subjects, placed considerable strain on Anglo-German relations. His enthusiasm for the German Navy, a new service created for the new empire and officered largely by the sons of its new industrial and commercial middle class, alienated the British still further.

In 1893 William suggested that the Prince of Wales (the future King Edward VII [54]) should take Queen Victoria's place as colonel-in-chief of the Prussian Dragoon Guard Regiment, to celebrate the twenty-fifth anniversary of the award of the Prince's first military commission. The Prince of Wales welcomed this proposal and suggested that, in reciprocity, William (who was already an honorary Admiral of the Fleet in the Royal Navy) should be made a field marshal in the British Army or the colonel-in-chief of a British regiment. The Queen had some reservations, on the grounds that the Emperors of Russia and Austria would expect similar honours (which indeed they later did receive). Her ministers thought that his rank in the Royal Navy was honour enough. William was made colonel-in-chief of the 1st Royal Dragoons in April 1894, but did not become a British field marshal until 27 January 1901, a week after King Edward VII's accession. William took this promotion seriously and sent the War Office a plan for the defeat of the Boers. He subsequently claimed credit for the ultimate British victory in South Africa. In his personal life he affected Germanic respectability, sharing a double bed with his Empress as an example of domestic bliss for his subjects to copy and expressing disapproval of the hedonistic ways of his royal uncle of England. Privately, he seems to have had a taste for sado-masochism and other unconventional sexual practices.

The approach of the First World War in 1914 found William cruising in his yacht in the Baltic. Shocked and surprised by the rapid escalation of the crisis, he first tried to persuade his cousin, the Emperor Nicholas II of Russia [84], not to mobilize, but failed both in this and in his subsequent attempt to persuade his generals to march against Russia rather than France. When the British declared war on Germany, William repudiated his appointments in the British armed forces and commanded his troops in France to "exterminate first the treacherous English" and walk over their "contemptible little army of mercenaries" (the British Expeditionary Force, composed of regular soldiers). He was compensated by his ally, the Emperor Francis Joseph [76], with the baton of a field marshal in the Austro-Hungarian Army. Like most of his contemporaries, he completely underestimated the probable length of the conflict. Sending his troops to the battle front, he promised them "You will be home before the leaves fall". During the war, despite his constitutional position as Supreme War Lord, William was ignored by his generals, who relegated him to ceremonial and morale-raising activities. He constantly sided with the military against his civilian ministers, as he had done throughout his reign, and eventually became a mere echo of Field Marshal Ludendorff, his Supreme Army Commander. At the beginning of November 1918 news that his government was seeking an armistice had a shattering effect throughout Germany. Faced with mutinies and the threat of a socialist revolution, William fled to the General Headquarters of his army on the Western Front. The generals told him that, with the survival of Germany and the German Army at stake, their oaths of allegiance to him meant nothing. On 9 November 1918, following the declaration of a German republic, he abdicated and fled to the neutral Netherlands. Despite popular cries of "Hang the Kaiser" and demands from the Allied governments for a show trial, William was given refuge by the Dutch government. He spent the rest of his life in exile in the Netherlands, at Doorn. His Empress died in 1921 and, in the following year, he married Princess Hermine of Reuss, a capable thirty-four year-old widow with five children. When Nazi troops invaded the Netherlands in 1940 he declined the offer of refuge made by the British government and continued to live as a private gentleman. William died at Haus Doorn on 4 June 1941 and was buried in the grounds of his estate there, in an impressive tomb of his own design.

WILLIAM FREDERICK
HRH 2nd Duke of Gloucester and Edinburgh, KG, GCB, GCH (1776–1834) [27]

Prince William Frederick, only son of King George III's younger brother, the 1st Duke of Gloucester and Edinburgh [13], was born on 15 January 1776 in the Teodoli Palace, Rome. The Gloucesters were at this time in self-imposed exile, following the refusal of the King to recognise the validity of their secret marriage. After their marriage was declared lawful they returned to England, where Prince William grew up. On the outbreak of war with Revolutionary France in February 1793, Prince William of Gloucester was granted a commission as captain in the 3rd Foot Guards and lieutenant colonel in the Army, with seniority from March 1789. He was promoted to colonel in the Army on 24 February 1794. Prince William took part in the Flanders campaign between March and May 1794 and was promoted to major general on 26 February 1795. He was appointed colonel of the 115th Foot (later disbanded) in May 1794 and retained this post until November 1795, when he became colonel of the 6th Foot. Prince William took part in the expedition to the Helder (September- October 1799), where he commanded a brigade of Foot Guards and was mentioned in despatches. He was promoted to lieutenant general on 13 November 1799 and succeeded his father as 2nd Duke of Gloucester and Edinburgh on 25 August 1805. Gloucester held various commands in the UK, before being promoted to general on 25 April 1808. He became a field marshal on 26 May 1816. In private life, he was happily married to his cousin, George III's fourth daughter, the Princess Mary. The couple patronized various charitable and philanthropic causes, including the abolition of slavery. They also supported Princess Charlotte of Wales in her determination not to marry the young Prince of Orange [34], notwithstanding her father's wishes to the contrary. Gloucester died on 30 November 1834 and was buried at St George's Chapel in Windsor Castle. He had no children and his titles became extinct until revived respectively for Alfred, Duke of Edinburgh (Queen Victoria's second son); Henry, Duke of Gloucester [121] (King George V's third son) and Philip, Duke of Edinburgh [119] (consort of Queen Elizabeth II).

WILLIAM HENRY
HRH 1st Duke of Gloucester and Edinburgh, KG
(1743–1805) [13]

Prince William Henry, a son of Frederick, Prince of Wales, and a younger brother of King George III, was born on 14 November 1743 at Leicester House, London. He was created Duke of Gloucester and Edinburgh in 1764 and was commissioned as colonel of the 13th Foot on 25 June 1766. Gloucester was promoted to major general and became colonel of the 3rd Foot Guards on 16 December 1767. He became a lieutenant general and colonel of the 1st Foot Guards on 30 April 1770, followed by promotion to general on 25 May 1772. When the rank of field marshal was revived on 12 October 1793, he was the second senior general in the British Army and was promoted at the same time as the Honourable Henry Conway [12] and Sir George Howard [14].

In September 1766 Gloucester married the widowed Countess Waldegrave, a lady of respectable character but of illegitimate birth, who was, on that account, not received at court. When another of his brothers, Henry, Duke of Cumberland, also married an unsuitable widow, George III took action to preserve the prestige of his House. This led to the Royal Marriages Act of 1772, a measure that, in effect, required the assent of the Sovereign before marriages by members of the Royal Family could be considered valid. As the Gloucesters had married in secret and as the only witness (the Countess's chaplain, who had conducted the ceremony) was by this time dead, a Commission was set up to investigate their claim to lawful wedlock. In the meanwhile, the Gloucesters withdrew to self-imposed exile in Italy and it was not until 1780, two years after official recognition of the legitimacy of their marriage and their children, that they were reconciled with the King and returned to London. In his later years Gloucester scandalized even Regency England by his open *affaire* with Lady Almeria Carpenter, his wife's lady-in-waiting. He died on 25 August 1805 and was buried in St George's Chapel, Windsor.

William, 1st Duke of Gloucester and Edinburgh, was the first member of the Royal Family to become a field marshal. Although he held a military commission for almost forty years, he was the first British field marshal to be appointed without actually having commanded troops or seen any kind of active service. His name was given to Fort William Henry, New York, where many members of the British and colonial garrison were massacred by native Americans in 1757, after surrendering to the French .

WILSON
Sir HENRY HUGHES, 1st Baronet, GCB, DSO
(1864–1922) [91]

Henry Hughes Wilson, the second son of parents whose families were long-established in the Anglo-Irish Protestant Ascendancy, was born at Currygrane, County Longford on 5 May 1864. The family employed French nursemaids, from whom Henry Wilson learned to speak French with a fluency that would shape his later career. Between 1877 and 1880 he attended Marlborough College and then, having failed to pass the entrance examinations for either the Royal Military Academy or the Royal Military College, decided to enter the Army via the Militia. Wilson obtained a commission in the former Longford Militia, the 6th Battalion, the Rifle Brigade (the Prince Consort's Own), from which he became a lieutenant in the Royal Irish Regiment on 12 November 1884. He immediately exchanged back to the Rifle Brigade and, in 1886, joined its 1st Battalion on counter-insurgency operations in Burma. On 19 June 1887, when attempting to arrest a bandit or patriot, Wilson was severely wounded over the eye. He was invalided back to Ireland to recover, where he met and decided to marry Cecil Mary Wray (a young woman of forceful character whom nobody liked to cross), the daughter of a Donegal squire. Her father was unwilling to bestow his daughter's hand on a subaltern with limited prospects and refused his consent until Wilson showed some evidence of taking his profession seriously. After Wilson passed the entrance examination to the Staff College, Camberley, the couple were married in October 1891.

On passing out from the Staff College in December 1892, Wilson was ordered back to his battalion in India, but a successful appeal on medical grounds delayed his departure long enough for him to find an attachment to the Intelligence branch at the War Office. He was promoted to captain on 6 December 1893 and gained an established post at the War Office as staff captain. He remained there until 1897, when he became brigade major of the 3rd Brigade, at Aldershot. In the South African War he went to Natal as brigade major of the 4th Brigade and served at Colenso (15 December 1899); Spion Kop (24–25 January 1900); Vaal Kranz (5–7 Feb 1900) and Pieter's Hill (19–27 February 1900). In August 1900 he joined the staff of Lord Roberts [68], C-in-C, South Africa, where Wilson served first as deputy assistant quartermaster-general and then as assistant military secretary.

Wilson became one of Roberts' favourites and returned with him to London on his personal staff in January 1901. He was awarded the DSO, followed by promotion to substantive major on 30 November 1901 and to brevet lieutenant colonel on 1 December 1901. In February 1902 he became commanding officer of the 9th Provisional Battalion at Colchester, where he was promoted to lieutenant colonel on 7 November 1902. After the minimum period of regimental duty he returned to the War Office in April 1903 as deputy assistant adjutant general in the new Department of Military Education and Training. In June 1904, he became assistant adjutant general in the same department, with special responsibility for the training of the auxiliary forces.

Wilson remained under the patronage of Roberts, who had become Commander-in-Chief, and was promoted to brevet colonel on 11 December 1904. He was involved in the reorganization of the War Office, following the abolition of the post of C-in-C and the creation of a General Staff, and became responsible for arranging the selection and training of staff officers.

On 1 January 1907 Wilson was appointed commandant of the Staff College, with promotion to substantive colonel and temporary brigadier general. As such, he encouraged staff officers to consider themselves as an élite in much the same way as was the case in the German Army. In 1909 he visited his opposite number at the French Staff College, Brigadier General Ferdinand Foch [88]. Wilson was at first inclined to look down on Foch for his petty bourgeois background, but soon fell under his influence. Impressed by the tempo at which Foch conducted his exercises, Wilson returned to Camberley and introduced a similar element of urgency and stress into the training there. When Lord Kitchener [79] visited the Staff College, Wilson's attempt to patronize the first soldier of the Empire (who was not himself a Staff College graduate) only led Kitchener to consider him presumptuous and arrogant. In August 1910 Wilson became Director of Military Operations on the General Staff at the War Office. An ardent Francophile, he began to prepare plans for the despatch of an Expeditionary Force to fight alongside the French in any future war with Germany. This alienated him from the Chief of the General Staff, Sir William Nicholson [82], with whom he had been friendly in South Africa. Nicholson's successor, Sir John French [83] was more amenable to Wilson's arguments and accompanied him on bicycle tours along the frontiers of northern France. Wilson, on his own initiative, drew up plans with the French staff for the landing and deployment in France of the British Expeditionary Force. He was promoted to major-general on 5 November 1913.

A Unionist by heredity and conviction, Wilson believed that the introduction of Home Rule in Ireland would be the first step in the break-up of the British Empire. Accordingly, he encouraged the Ulster Protestants in their opposition to the Home Rule Bill of 1913 and, together with his old patron Lord Roberts, gave moral support to the para-military Ulster Volunteer Force. At the time of the Curragh Incident in March 1914 Wilson intrigued with those officers who sought an assurance that they would not be called upon to use force against the Ulster Unionists. He encouraged Sir John French to agree to their demands and subsequently to resign, when this agreement was overruled by the Cabinet.

On the outbreak of the First World War in August 1914 Wilson pressed for immediate mobilization and co-operation with the French, as he had planned. He was dismayed by the appointment of Kitchener to be Secretary of State for War, partly because he knew Kitchener disliked him, and partly because he feared Kitchener would not endorse his plan of committing the British Army to a major campaign on the Continent. When the British Expeditionary Force (under the command of Sir John French) was sent to France, Wilson went with it as Sub-Chief of Staff. He established a close liaison with the French and helped them persuade Kitchener that the BEF should conform to their strategy, rather than fight as an independent British army. During the retreat from Mons, when Sir Archibald Murray's health gave way, Wilson took over from him as acting Chief of Staff. Despite support from Sir John French, Wilson was not confirmed in this post and, in January 1915, the Cabinet decided to appoint William Robertson [92] instead. When Wilson declined to serve under an officer junior to himself, French created a post for him in Paris, as principal liaison officer. Wilson became a temporary lieutenant general on 25 February 1915 and was belatedly awarded a KCB for his part in the 1914 campaign. Sir Henry Wilson's post in Paris was abolished at the end of 1915, when Sir Douglas Haig succeeded French as C-in-C.

Wilson was then given command of IV Corps, his first and only operational command. It carried little influence and prestige, especially when Haig transferred most of its units to II Corps during the battle of the Somme (July-November 1915). With little to do in France, Wilson appeared frequently in London, where he cultivated his political contacts with the Unionists and impressed many others (among them David Lloyd George, Kitchener's successor as Secretary of State for War) with his enthusiasm and optimism. He was then sent as head of a military mission to Russia, from where he returned to London just before the Russian Revolution of February (in the Western Calendar, March) 1917. Wilson was promoted to substantive lieutenant general on 16 March 1917 and was re-appointed to his old post of principal liaison officer with the French Army. He succeeded in establishing good relations between Haig and General Robert Nivelle, the French C-in-C, but his post was again abolished in May 1917, when General Philippe Pétain (who regarded Wilson as an intriguer) became C-in-C in Nivelle's place. At the end of July 1917 Wilson was placed on half-pay prior to becoming, in September 1917, GOC-in-C Eastern Command, a post that allowed him easy access to influential circles in London.

When a Supreme War Council, composed of the Allied prime ministers and their special military advisers, was set up at Versailles, Wilson was selected by Lloyd George (Prime Minister since December 1916) to be the British army representative, with promotion to temporary general on 1 December 1917. He emerged as a powerful figure, fully supportive of Lloyd George's policy of giving the Council effective control of Allied strategy. When Sir William Robertson, Chief of the Imperial General Staff, refused to accept any reduction of his own powers, Lloyd George dismissed Robertson and appointed Wilson in his place on 18 February 1918. Witty, clever and articulate himself, Wilson was better able than the taciturn Robertson to deal with politicians on their own terms. While still believing the Western Front to be the decisive theatre, he listened to Lloyd George's views and responded to them with reasoned arguments. Faced with the German successes in France in the spring of 1918, Wilson reinforced the BEF with some 500,000 men, drawn from the Middle East and the UK. He also pressed for the extension of conscription to include Ireland, something which even the Ulster Unionists opposed and which, when attempted, led to a final breakdown in negotiations with the Irish Nationalists.

After the end of the First World War, relations between Wilson and the Cabinet rapidly grew worse. He was outraged when, without consulting him, Lloyd George ordered the end of conscription immediately the armistice was signed on 11 November 1918. When a major rebellion developed in Ireland, Wilson supported the use of force against the nationalists and objected to the controversial special constabulary, "the Black and Tans", only on the grounds that they were less effective than regular soldiers. He opposed the idea of a League of Nations and urged intervention against the Bolshevik regime in Russia. Wilson was promoted to field marshal on 31 July 1919 and was granted a baronetcy. He had become colonel of the Royal Irish Rifles in November 1915 and retained this appointment when he became colonel of the 3rd Battalion of his old regiment, the Rifle Brigade, in October 1920. In January 1921 the title of the Royal Irish Rifles was changed to Royal Ulster Rifles, a change unpopular in the regiment, but one that Wilson assured its officers he had been unable to prevent, either as CIGS or as their colonel. Nevertheless, no other Irish regiment retained in the British Army after the establishment of the Irish Free State in 1922 was required to adopt the word *Ulster* in its title and, with two counties of Ulster lying within the Free State, the new province of the United Kingdom was officially called Northern Ireland. Wilson completed his tour as CIGS in February 1922 and was immediately elected, unopposed, as Ulster Unionist MP for North Down. In Northern Ireland, Wilson took an extremist line. He blamed the Anglo-Irish treaty for the civil war then in progress in the Free State and proposed a reorganization of Northern Ireland's military and police forces with a view to the reconquest of the South. On 22 July 1922, after unveiling the Great Eastern Railway's war memorial at Liverpool Street Station, London, he was shot dead outside his house in Eaton Place, in an impromptu attack by two Irish nationalists. Wilson was given a state funeral and was buried in St Paul's Cathedral. He had no children and his baronetcy became extinct.

WILSON
Sir HENRY MAITLAND, 1st Baron Wilson of Libya, GCB, GBE, DSO (1881–1964) [115]

Henry Wilson, eldest of three sons of a wealthy landowner, was born at his father's house, Stowlangtoft Hall, Suffolk, on 5 September 1881. After attending Eton College and the Royal Military College, Sandhurst, he was commissioned on 10 March 1900 as a second lieutenant in the Rifle Brigade (the Prince Consort's Own). "Jumbo" Wilson, so-called from his impressive height and physique, joined its 2nd Battalion on active service in the South African War. He took part in operations in the Transvaal in August 1900 and was promoted to lieutenant on 18 March 1901. In the final months of the war Wilson was employed as a railways staff officer. He subsequently accompanied his battalion to Egypt and then, in 1907, to India. Wilson was promoted to captain on 2 April 1908 and returned to the UK with the 3rd Battalion, the Rifle Brigade. He served with this unit at Bordon, Hampshire, and in Tipperary, Ireland, until October 1911, when he became adjutant of the Oxford University Contingent, Officers Training Corps. After the outbreak of the First World War in August 1914 Wilson was appointed brigade major of the newly-formed 48th Brigade, on 15 October 1914. In the following December he celebrated his promotion to acting major by marrying Hester Wykeham, of Tythrop Hall, near Buckingham.

Wilson became a substantive major on 15 September 1915 and served on the Western Front with his brigade from December 1915 to June 1916. He was then appointed a General Staff officer, grade 2, in the 41st Division, with which he served in the battle of the Somme (1 July–18 November 1916). He was awarded the DSO in January 1917. During the third battle of Ypres (31 July–6 November 1917), he was a GSO 2 at the headquarters of XIX Corps, before becoming GSO 1 of the New Zealand Division, with promotion to temporary lieutenant colonel on 28 October 1917. Wilson spent the rest of the First World War with this formation and was promoted to brevet lieutenant colonel on 1 January 1919. During the war he was mentioned in despatches three times.

Wilson joined the first post-war course at the Staff College, Camberley, in 1919. In August 1920, after qualifying as a trained staff officer, he was given command of a company of gentlemen cadets (at that time a General Staff appointment) at the Royal Military College, Sandhurst. Wilson became second in command of the 2nd Battalion, the Rifle Brigade, at Aldershot, in August 1923. He joined the 1st Battalion, the Rifle Brigade, on the North-West Frontier of India in January 1927, as commanding officer, with promotion to substantive lieutenant colonel on 15 June 1927. He returned to the Staff College in June 1930 as a chief instructor and GSO 1, where he was promoted to substantive colonel from 1 January 1923, by virtue of his earlier brevet as lieutenant colonel. On completing his tenure of this appointment in 1933, Wilson spent nine months on the half-pay list, before being promoted to temporary brigadier in command of the 6th Infantry Brigade at Blackdown, Camberley. Wilson was promoted to major general on 30 April 1935 and again went on to half-pay. He rejoined the full-pay list in August 1937, on appointment as GOC 2nd Division.

In June 1939 Wilson was appointed GOC-in-C British Troops in Egypt. He was promoted to lieutenant general, with seniority from 26 June 1938 and thus superseded his contemporary, Alan Brooke [112], by one day. He was appointed colonel commandant of the 2nd Battalion, the Rifle Brigade, in October 1939 and retained this post until September 1951. On the outbreak of the Second World War in September 1939, his command was renamed the Army of the Nile. In 1940 he was awarded the KCB. Sir Henry Maitland Wilson was not directly engaged in the operations conducted against the Italians in Libya by Sir Archibald Wavell [111], C-in-C, Middle East. At the beginning of February 1941 he was appointed British Military Governor of the captured Italian colony of Cyrenaica (north-eastern Libya). A few weeks later, he was given command of the British expedition sent to support the Greeks in their resistance to an Italian invasion, but the intervention of German troops, beginning on 6 April 1941, turned the tide against the Allied cause. He completed the evacuation of his troops on 29 April 1941 and returned to Cairo.

Wilson was then made GOC-in-C British Troops in Palestine and Transjordan, with promotion to general on 6 May 1941. Troops from his command entered the former British mandate of Iraq in May 1941, occupied Baghdad and restored a government friendly to the British. In a brief campaign lasting from 9 June to 12 July 1941, Wilson's troops also took control of the French mandates of Syria and Lebanon, previously controlled by the German-dominated Vichy government. Winston Churchill, the British Prime Minister, urged the new C-in-C Middle East, Sir Claude Auchinleck [116], to give Wilson command of the British army in the Western Desert. Auchinleck disregarded Churchill's views and appointed Sir Alan Cunningham, a younger general, who had defeated the Italians in East Africa. Cunningham's own defeat by the Germans and their Italian allies caused Churchill again to recommend Wilson, but Auchinleck once more refused to appoint him. In December 1941 Wilson's command was renamed the Ninth Army. Further defeats suffered by the Eighth Army in the Western Desert brought him to Sinai in July 1942, to prepare defences against a possible German march through Egypt. In August 1942, Wilson was appointed GOC-in-C Tenth Army, with the task of holding Iran and Iraq against the threat of a German advance from the Caucasus to the oilfields of the (Persian) Gulf. After the Russian victory at Stalingrad, this threat receded and in February 1943 Wilson returned to Egypt to become C-in-C, Middle East. Wilson's main tasks were the administrative support for the Eighth Army's campaign in Tunisia and the subsequent Allied invasion of Sicily. In September 1943, prompted and encouraged by Churchill, he launched a British invasion of the Dodecanese islands. The Allied Chiefs of Staff withheld the amphibious resources needed for this operation and Wilson was defeated with heavy casualties.

In January 1944 Wilson succeeded General Dwight D Eisenhower as Supreme Allied Commander in the Mediterranean and became responsible for controlling the campaigns in Southern France and Italy and supporting the partisan operations in Yugoslavia and Greece. In October 1944 he made a point of returning in person to Athens, from where he had been driven out three and a half years earlier. Wilson established a reputation for getting on well with his American allies and, on the death of Sir John Dill [109], was appointed to succeed him as head of the British Joint Chiefs of Staff Mission in Washington. He was promoted to field marshal on 29 December 1944, prior to taking up this post in January 1945. Wilson maintained the special relationship that Dill had fostered between the British and United States Army Chiefs of Staff and attended the Yalta and Potsdam conferences, as well as taking part in the strategic plans associated with the development of nuclear weapons. He was created Baron Wilson of Libya and Stowlangtoft on 12 March 1946 and remained in Washington until May 1947, when his post was abolished. Lord Wilson then returned to the UK after an absence of eight years. He held no further active commands, but in 1947 became a very popular and respected president of the Army Cadet Force

Association. He retired to Chilton, Buckinghamshire, where he died on 31 December 1964. He was buried in his native parish of St George's, Stowlangtoft, Suffolk and was succeeded as 2nd baron by his only son.

WOLSELEY
Sir GARNET JOSEPH, 1st Viscount Wolseley, KP, GCB, OM, GCMG, VD (1833–1913) [67]

Garnet Wolseley was born in County Dublin on 4 June 1833, the eldest son of a major in the British Army. Major Wolseley's early death left his widow and their seven children in straitened circumstances and the young Garnet Wolseley worked for a time in a Dublin survey office, before obtaining a commission as an ensign in the 12th Foot on 12 March 1852. Brought up by a mother who taught him to defer to Divine Providence, Wolseley took a fatalistic approach to the chances of personal survival in battle and later advised young officers that, if they wished to rise in their profession, they should begin by trying to get themselves killed. He transferred to the 80th Foot to take part in the Second Burma War and was at Kyaukazin (Myah-Tun's stockade, 19 March 1853), where he was wounded and left with a permanent limp. Wolseley was promoted to lieutenant on 16 May 1853 and joined the 90th Light Infantry at Dublin. He went with the 90th to the Crimean War and became a captain on 26 January 1855. On the basis of his experience of surveying, he led construction parties in the siege-works at Sebastopol, where he was badly wounded, losing the sight of one eye, on 30 August 1855.

Wolseley remained in the Crimea, where he served as a staff officer until the end of the war in 1856. He was then sent with the 90th Light Infantry to the Second China War, but was landed in India, following the outbreak of the Indian Mutiny in May 1857. Wolseley was at the relief of Lucknow (14–19 November 1857) and the subsequent defence of the Alambagh, prior to obtaining an appointment on the staff in February 1858. He was promoted to brevet major on 24 March 1858 and to brevet lieutenant colonel on 26 April 1859. Wolseley then joined the campaign in China, where he was at the storming of the Taku forts (21 August 1860) and the occupation of Peking (Beijing). During 1861–65 he served on the staff in Canada, from where he paid close attention to the American Civil War and visited the Confederate generals Robert E. Lee and "Stonewall" Jackson. Wolseley was promoted to colonel on 5 June 1865, and in the same year married Louisa Erskine, his "dearest Snipe". A lady of determined and strong character, she encouraged and supported him in his ambitions, just as his mother had done earlier in his career. Wolseley became a major general on 6 March 1868. In 1869 he published his *Soldier's Pocket Book*, a wide-ranging treatise in which he set out the strong views he had formed on the importance of staff duties and on the need for the Army to occupy itself in peace solely with training for war.

Wolseley's first independent command came in 1869 when he returned to Canada to lead the Red River Expedition against the Métis under Louis Riel. There was little fighting, as Riel fled to the USA on the approach of the government troops. Nevertheless, by moving his 1,200 men through 600 miles of wild territory, from Lake Superior to Fort Garry, in thirty-nine days, Wolseley achieved a logistical triumph. He was awarded the KCMG and in 1871 became assistant adjutant general at the War Office, where he enthusiastically supported the army reforms then being introduced. Sir Garnet Wolseley was given administrative and military charge of the Gold Coast (later Ghana) in October 1873, at the beginning of the Second Ashanti War. The powerful Ashanti (Asante) kingdom had defeated the British on previous occasions and was well-defended by its climate and terrain. This time, in a campaign lasting only four weeks, Wolseley defeated the Ashanti ruler, Kofi Karikari, at Amoafu (21 January 1874) and occupied Kumasi, the Ashanti capital. The British casualties totalled eighteen killed, 185 wounded and fifty-five died of fever. This success made Wolseley's name. He became known as Britain's "only general" and was the inspiration for the polymath "model of a modern major-general" in Gilbert and Sullivan's *Pirates of Penzance*. The phrase "all Sir Garnet" entered the language as a synonym for efficiency.

Wolseley was promoted to lieutenant general on 25 March 1878. He was appointed as the British High Commissioner and military commander in Cyprus, when this became a British protectorate after the Anglo-Turkish agreement of June 1878. In February 1879, he was sent to Natal as Governor and C-in-C, to restore British prestige after the Zulu victory at Isandhlawana (22 January 1879). Lord Chelmsford, the previous C-in-C, Natal, refused to await his arrival and defeated the Zulus at Ulundi (4 July 1879), so that Wolseley had little to do but hunt down the Zulu king and break up his kingdom into petty states. In 1880 Wolseley was appointed to the Council of India, to give the Secretary of State for India expert military advice on ways of reforming the Indian Army. In practice he achieved little in the face of determined opposition from Sir Henry Norman [72] and other members of the Indian military establishment, though he succeeded in securing several posts in India for members of "the Wolseley Ring". This group consisted mostly of officers who had been trained at the Staff College (which Wolseley himself never attended, but enthusiastically supported) and had subsequently served under his command. Wolseley was Quartermaster General from 1880 to 1882 and pressed on with reforms, despite the objections of the Duke of Cambridge [45], Commander-in-Chief of the Army, who regarded Wolseley as a pushy upstart. Wolseley, for his part, despised Cambridge for going home from the Crimea on medical grounds and resented him for achieving command not through professional merit, but through his royal birth.

Wolseley again went on active service in 1882, in command of the British army sent to suppress the nationalist regime in Egypt led by Urbi (Arabi) Pasha. Once more he achieved a quick victory, by winning the decisive battle of Tel-el-Kebir (13 September 1882) in a risky night attack. He was created Baron Wolseley, of Cairo and of Wolseley, with promotion to general on 18 November 1882. He returned to the War Office, where he remained as Adjutant General until 1890, apart from a brief absence to command the Gordon Relief Expedition of 1884–85. In this, his final campaign, Wolseley's star deserted him. Hampered by Cabinet indecision and by the poor performance of those members of his "Ring" to whom he had given the subordinate commands, Wolseley ended his fighting career with his only failure. From 1890 to 1895 he was C-in-C, Ireland, with promotion to field marshal on 26 May 1894. He then achieved his ambition by becoming Commander-in-Chief of the Army. His own pressure for reform, however, had played a part in the weakening of this office to such an extent that he found himself, as he put it, "the fifth wheel on the coach". He was appointed colonel-in-chief of the Dublin-based Royal Irish Regiment and became colonel of the Royal Horse Guards in March 1895.

As C-in-C, Wolseley secured increases in the Army's establishment and acquired large tracts of Salisbury Plain for use as training areas. He was not on good terms with Lord Lansdowne, the parsimonious Secretary of State for War, and regarded him as a personal and official enemy. The "battle of the Rings" (the rivalry between Wolseley and Lord Roberts [68] and their respective favourites) led Lansdowne to wish that British generals would fight the enemy as well as they fought each other. Personal relations between Wolseley and Roberts were courteous enough, but Wolseley considered that Roberts, having spent his entire career in India, knew nothing about the British Army at home. In 1897 Wolseley suffered some kind of a stroke, which left him, in his own words, "an extinct volcano". He remained in office during the first part of the South African War and supervised the rapid mobilization and movement of a fully-equipped army corps to the theatre of operations.

The poor performance of the British Army at the beginning of this war revealed serious weaknesses among the generals and especially among the staff, whose training had become one of Wolseley's obsessions. Aware that his mental and physical faculties were in decline, he resigned from office in November 1900 and was advanced in the peerage to become Viscount Wolseley. He died on 25 March 1913 at Mentone, on the French Riviera, and was buried in St Paul's Cathedral. Wolseley had no male heirs and his viscountcy, by special remainder, was inherited by his only daughter.

Wolseley saw active service in four continents, ranging from conventional and colonial campaigns as a junior officer to commands as a general in forest, jungle, and desert warfare. He was, in his day, the British Army's most famous and successful general. His impatience, quick temper, conviction that he was always right, and confidence in his own powers of judgement made him disliked by those with whom he did not agree, but proved valuable qualities both in war and in the battle for promotion.

WOOD
Sir HENRY EVELYN, VC, GCB, GCMG (1838–1919) [74]

Evelyn Wood, the youngest son of a baronet, the Reverend Sir John Wood, was born at Cressing, Essex, on 9 February 1838. After running away from Marlborough College in response to an unjust beating, he joined the Royal Navy in 1852 as a midshipman. During the Crimean War he served with the Naval Brigade at Inkerman (5 November 1854) and in the siege of Sebastopol, where he was wounded at the Redan (18 June 1855). Invalided home, he left the Navy and became a cornet in the 13th Light Dragoons on 1 September 1855, with promotion to lieutenant on 1 February 1856. Wood returned to the Crimean theatre, but only reached as far as the British base at Scutari, where in January 1857 he became so seriously ill that he was scarcely recognized by his mother when she subsequently arrived to nurse him. On recovering, he considered joining the French Foreign Legion, but, with the outbreak of the Indian Mutiny in May 1857, transferred to the 17th Lancers for service in this campaign. Wood began inauspiciously, when he tried to ride a giraffe in the menagerie of a friendly Indian prince and was severely trampled. He joined the campaign in Central India under Sir John Michel [60], where he served with various Indian cavalry units in several minor engagements, including combats at Sindhara (19 October 1859) and Kurai (25 October 1859), for which he was awarded the

Victoria Cross. In December 1859 he joined the 2nd Central India Horse, a localized unit primarily intended for the suppression of banditry in that area. He commanded this regiment until November 1860, when he was invalided back to England.

Wood became a captain in the 17th Lancers on 16 April 1861 and was promoted to brevet major on 19 August 1862. He then passed the entrance examination for the new Staff College, Camberley. At this time, the regulations did not permit two officers from the same regiment to join the same course. As another officer of the 17th Lancers had gained higher marks, Wood therefore transferred first to the 73rd Foot and next to the 17th Foot, so that he could take up a place. He passed out in 1864 and in the same year married the Honourable Mary Southwell, sister of the 4th Viscount Southwell, who had been his friend and comrade in India. Southwell, who had known nothing of this romance, opposed the marriage because his was a Roman Catholic family, and Wood, though not of strong religious views, declined to leave the Church of England. The viscount's fear that a mixed marriage would lead to unhappiness proved unfounded and, in due course, the couple raised a family of six children. Seeing little prospect of gaining a staff appointment, Wood studied law and was admitted a barrister at the Middle Temple.

Wood purchased his majority in the 90th Light Infantry in 1871, in one of the last transactions before the purchase system was abolished. He became a brevet lieutenant colonel on 19 January 1873. During the Ashanti War, in the Gold Coast (later Ghana), Wood served under Sir Garnet Wolseley [67] and commanded a flank at Amoafu (21 January 1874), where he was wounded. He was promoted to brevet colonel on 1 April 1874, with appointment as superintendent of garrison instruction at Aldershot. In 1878 he went to Natal with the 90th Light Infantry and took part in the last of the Kaffir Wars, where he was at Tutu Bush (May 1878). During the opening phase of the Zulu War, he commanded No 4 Column. The British defeat at Isandhlawana (22 January 1879) obliged Wood, who had been operating successfully in his own sector, to retreat to a defended position at Khambula. Using his mounted troops, he maintained the initiative until meeting the Zulu victors of Isandhlawana at Inhlobana (28 March 1879), where his horse was shot under him and he was forced to retreat. Wood defeated a Zulu attack on Khambula (29 March 1879) and joined the main British force under Lord Chelmsford at Ulundi (4 July 1879).

Wood was awarded the KCB in 1879 and became a major general on 12 August 1881. After a brief spell commanding the Chatham garrison, Sir Evelyn Wood was gathered into the "Wolseley Ring" and, on the approach of the First Boer War, was appointed second-in-command to Sir George Colley, the Governor and C-in-C, Natal. He succeeded to the command after Colley's defeat and death at Majuba (27 February 1881), but lacked the resources to do more than stand on the defensive while the British Cabinet negotiated a peace settlement. After another period at Chatham (February–August 1882), he went as a brigade commander in Wolseley's expedition to Egypt. In December 1882 Wood was appointed as Sirdar (C-in-C) of the Egyptian Army. With a small group of British officers, including Francis Grenfell [77] and Herbert Kitchener [79], he began the reorganization of this Army on British lines. After the Gordon Relief Expedition of 1884–85, Wood resumed his career in the British Army. He served as GOC Eastern District from April 1886 until January 1889, when he became GOC Aldershot District. He was promoted lieutenant general on 1 April 1890.

Wood was Quartermaster General from 1893 to 1897, with promotion to general on 26 March 1895. He became Adjutant General in October 1897 and retained this post during the South African War until his retirement from active employment in October 1901. He became honorary colonel of the 14th Middlesex (Inns of Court) Rifle Volunteer Corps in November 1899 (an appointment for which his qualification as a barrister was very appropriate) and supported its reorganization in 1908 as a unit of the Officers Training Corps in the new Territorial Force. He was promoted to field marshal on 8 April 1903 and was appointed colonel of the Royal Horse Guards in November 1907. Sir Evelyn Wood died at Harlow, Essex, on 2 December 1919 and was buried at Epping.

WOODFORD
Sir ALEXANDER GEORGE, GCB, GCMG (1782–1870) [47]

Alexander Woodford, the elder son of John Woodford, a captain in the 1st Foot Guards and lieutenant colonel in the Army, was born at Welbeck Street, London, on 15 June 1782. His mother was the eldest daughter of the 3rd Duke of Gordon. His uncle was the Lord George Gordon who instigated the Gordon Riots of June 1780, during which Lieutenant Colonel John Woodford was called out with his troops to fire on the London mob. The young Woodford attended Winchester College and Dr Bonnycastle's military school at Woolwich, before being commissioned as an ensign in the 9th Foot on 6 December 1794. He became a lieutenant of the 22nd Foot on 15 July 1795, but was too young for regimental service and accordingly was placed on the half-pay list. In 1799 he rejoined the 9th Foot as a lieutenant. He took part in the expedition to the Helder in the autumn of that year and was at Alkmaar (19 September 1799), where he was wounded. Woodford was promoted to captain in the 9th Foot on 11 December 1799, prior to joining the Coldstream Guards as lieutenant in the regiment and captain in the Army on 20 December 1799. He served as an ADC in the British army in Sicily from 1803 until returning to London with promotion to captain in his regiment and lieutenant colonel in the Army on 8 March 1810. During the Peninsular War, Woodford was at the defence of Cadiz (March-April 1811); Ciudad Rodrigo (stormed 19 January 1812), where he commanded a battalion made up of the light companies of the Foot Guards); Badajoz (stormed 6 April 1812); Salamanca (22 July 1812) and Burgos (besieged unsuccessfully from 16 September–21 October 1812). Woodford commanded the 1st Battalion, Coldstream Guards at Vittoria (21 June 1813); San Sebastian (August 1813); the Nivelle (10 November 1813); the Nive (9–13 December 1813) and the siege of Bayonne (27 February–13 April 1814). He was promoted to colonel on 4 June 1814. During the Hundred Days campaign, Woodford was in command of the 2nd Battalion, Coldstream Guards, at Quatre Bras (16 June 1815), Waterloo (18 June 1815) and Cambrai (24 June 1815).

In 1820 Woodford married Charlotte Fraser, daughter of a British diplomat. They later had a son, who was killed in action during the Indian Mutiny. Woodford became a major general on 27 May 1825 and was lieutenant-governor and brigade commander at Malta from then until 1827. He was awarded the KCB in 1831 and commanded the British garrison in the Ionian Islands from 1832 to 1835. Sir Alexander Woodford then became lieutenant-governor of Gibraltar, where he was appointed Governor and C-in-C in 1836 and remained until his retirement from active employment in 1843. He was promoted to lieutenant general on 28 June 1838 and to general on 20 June 1842. He was colonel of the 40th Foot from April 1842 to December 1861, when he became colonel of the Scots Fusilier Guards (later the Scots Guards). Sir Alexander Woodford was promoted to field marshal on 1 January 1868 and later became Governor of the Royal Hospital, Chelsea, in August 1898. He died there on 26 August 1870 and was buried at Kensal Green, London.

YORK
HRH DUKE OF, see **FREDERICK AUGUSTUS [15]**

YORKE
Sir CHARLES, GCB (1790–1880) [56]

Charles Yorke, the son of a colonel in the British Army, was born on 7 December 1790. He was commissioned as an ensign in the 35th Foot on 22 January 1808 and was promoted to lieutenant on 18 February 1808. Shortly afterwards, he transferred to the 52nd Light Infantry, and served with this regiment in the Peninsular War at Vimiero (21 August 1808); Fuentes d'Onoro (3–5 May 1811); Ciudad Rodrigo (8–19 January 1812); Badajoz (6 April 1812), where he was wounded; Salamanca (22 July 1812); Vittoria (21 June 1813); the Pyrenees (July 1813); the Nivelle (10 October 1813); the Nive (December 1813) and Orthez (27 February 1814), where he was again wounded. Yorke was promoted to captain on 24 December 1813. During the Hundred Days campaign he was at Waterloo (18 June 1815) as an aide-de-camp in Major General Adam's brigade, of which the 52nd Light Infantry formed part.

Yorke went onto the half-pay list on 25 February 1816. He returned to full pay on 7 August 1817, when he joined the 13th Foot, and exchanged to the 52nd Light Infantry in July 1818. He went back to the half-pay list as a major, unattached, on 9 June 1825, from which he was appointed as an inspecting officer of Militia, with promotion to lieutenant colonel on 30 November 1826. He was promoted to colonel on full pay on 23 November 1841. Between 1842 and 1850, Yorke served on the staff, first in Cork and then in Manchester. He was sent to South Africa as deputy commander of the British forces in the Kaffir War of 1850–1853 with promotion to major general on 11 November 1851, but arrived too late to take part in the main campaign. Yorke was given responsibility for rear area security and for providing logistic support to the troops operating in the Transkei, where the movement of supplies was made difficult by the wild terrain. After returning to the United Kingdom he was appointed Military Secretary in May 1854 and remained in this post until retiring from active employment in June 1860. He became colonel of the 33rd Foot in February 1855, was awarded the KCB in February 1856 and was promoted to lieutenant general on 13 February 1859. Sir Charles Yorke became colonel of the 2nd Battalion, the Rifle Brigade (the Prince Consort's Own), on 1 April 1863 and a general on 5 September 1865. He was promoted to field marshal on 2 June 1877, so becoming the last British veteran of the Napoleonic wars to reach this rank. Yorke died in South Street, Mayfair, on 20 November 1880 and was buried at Kensal Green cemetery.

YOSHIHITO
HIM Emperor of Japan, KG (1879–1926) [87]

The future Emperor Yoshihito, the third son of the Emperor Mutsuhito and an imperial concubine, was born on 21 August 1879. He was designated Crown Prince after the death of his two elder brothers and succeeded to the Japanese throne on 30 July 1912. He had been the first Crown Prince of Japan to receive a Western form of education and, in 1908, the first to leave the home islands, when he visited Korea, two years before it became a Japanese protectorate. Yoshihito named his royal era *Taisho* or "Great Justice" but played little part in politics. His reign began with a constitutional crisis, after the War Minister (in the Japanese constitution, a serving military officer) resigned in protest at the Cabinet's refusal to fund two extra divisions. When the Imperial Army refused to nominate a successor, the government was unable to continue in office. Yoshihito appointed a trusted aide, the former general Katsuro Taro, as his new Prime Minister. Katsuro solved the problem by ordering the Imperial Navy to provide a War Minister, an action that was widely regarded as an abuse of the Emperor's prerogative. This in turn led to the appointment of a new Cabinet, made up of politicians who deferred to Yoshihito's divine status, but in other respects treated him as a constitutional rather than an absolute monarch.

On the outbreak of the First World War in August 1914, Japan honoured her treaty of alliance with the British and joined the Entente Powers. Japanese warships escorted British troopships from India and Australia, while Japanese troops captured the German possessions in China and the Pacific. British gratitude was expressed by the appointment of Yoshihito as a field marshal on 1 January 1918. In November 1921, when the ill-health from which he had suffered throughout his life began to affect the Emperor's mental faculties, Crown Prince Hirohito [99], his son and heir, was declared Regent. Yoshihito was placed under medical confinement in a royal palace, where he died on 25 December 1925.

YPRES
EARL OF, see **FRENCH, Sir JOHN, [83]**

Table 1

THE FIELD MARSHALS' SENIORITY LIST

<u>Note</u> Throughout this work, numerals in **bold** within square brackets refer to the position of field marshals in this list.

Name and title.	*Date of promotion*
1. Hamilton, George, 1st Earl of Orkney, KT (1666–1737)	*12 Jan 1736*
2. Campbell, John, 2nd Duke of Argyll and Duke of Greenwich, KG, KT (1673–1743)	*14 Jan 1736*
3. Boyle, Richard, 2nd Viscount Shannon (1674–1740)	*2 July 1739*
4. De la Rochefoucauld, Francis, Marquis de Montandre (1672–1739)	*2 July 1739*
5. Dalrymple, John, 2nd Earl of Stair, KT (1678–1743)	*18 Mar 1742*
6. Temple, Sir Richard, 3rd Baronet, 1st Viscount Cobham (1669–1749)	*14 Dec 1742*
7. Wade, George (1673–1748)	*14 Dec 1742*
8. Rich, Sir Robert, 4th Baronet (1685–1768)	*28 Nov 1757*
9. Molesworth, Richard, 3rd Viscount Molesworth (1680–1758)	*29 Nov 1757*
10. Ligonier, Sir John, 1st Earl Ligonier, KB (1680–1770)	*30 Nov 1757*
11. O'Hara, James, 2nd Baron Tyrawley and 1st Baron Kilmaine (1690–1773)	*1 Jun 1763*
12. Conway, the Honourable Henry (1721–1794)	*12 Oct 1793*
13. William, HRH 1st Duke of Gloucester and Edinburgh, KG (1743–1805)	*12 Oct 1793*
14. Howard, Sir George, KB (1720–1796)	*12 Oct 1793*

15.	Frederick, HRH Duke of York and Albany, KG, GCB, GCH (1763–1827)	*10 Feb 1795*
16.	Campbell, John, 5th Duke of Argyll (1723–1806)	*30 Jul 1796*
17.	Amherst, Sir Jeffery, 1st Baron Amherst, KB (1717–1797)	*30 Jul 1796*
18.	Griffin, Sir John, 4th Baron Howard de Walden and 1st Baron Braybrooke, KB (1719–1797)	*30 Jul 1796*
19.	Hodgson, Studholme (1708–1798)	*30 Jul 1796*
20.	Townshend, George, 1st Marquess Townshend (1724–1807)	*30 Jul 1796*
21.	Cavendish, Lord Frederick (1729–1803)	*30 Jul 1796*
22.	Lennox, Charles, 3rd Duke of Richmond and Lennox, KG (1735–1806)	*30 Jul 1796*
23.	Edward, HRH Duke of Kent and Strathearn, KG, KT, KP, GCB, GCH (1767–1820)	*5 Sep 1805*
24.	Wellesley, Sir Arthur, 1st Duke of Wellington, KG, GCB, GCH (1769–1852)	*21 Jun 1813*
25.	Ernest I, HM King of Hanover, HRH Duke of Cumberland, KG, KP, GCB, GCH (1771–1851)	*6 Nov 1813*
26.	Adolphus, HRH 1st Duke of Cambridge, KG, GCB, GCMG, GCH (1774–1850)	*26 Nov 1813*
27.	William, HRH 2nd Duke of Gloucester and Edinburgh, KG, GCB, GCH (1776–1834)	*24 May 1816*
28.	Leopold I, HM King of the Belgians, HSH Prince of Saxe-Coburg-Gotha, KG, GCB, GCH (1790–1865)	*24 May 1816*
29.	Moore, Charles, 1st Marquess of Drogheda, KP (1730–1821)	*19 Jul 1821*
30.	Harcourt, William, 3rd Earl Harcourt, GCB (1743–1830)	*19 Jul 1821*
31.	Clarke, Sir Alured, GCB (1745–1832)	*22 Jul 1830*
32.	Hulse, Sir Samuel, GCH (1747–1832)	*22 Jul 1830*
33.	Albert, HSH Prince of Saxe-Coburg-Gotha, HRH Prince Consort, KG, KT, KP, GCB, GCMG, KSI (1819–1861)	*8 Feb 1840*
34.	William II, HM King of the Netherlands, GCB (1792–1849)	*28 Jul 1845*
35.	Nugent, Sir George, 1st Baronet, GCB (1757–1849)	*9 Nov 1846*
36.	Grosvenor, Thomas (1764–1851)	*9 Nov 1846*
37.	Paget, Lord Henry, 1st Marquess of Anglesey, KG, GCB, GCH (1768–1854)	*9 Nov 1846*

38.	Somerset, Lord Fitzroy, 1st Baron Raglan, GCB (1788–1855)	5 Nov 1854
39.	Cotton, Sir Stapleton, 6th Baronet, 1st Viscount Combermere, GCB, GCH, KSI (1773–1865)	2 Oct 1855
40.	Byng, Sir John, 1st Earl of Strafford, GCB, GCH (1772–1860)	2 Oct 1855
41.	Hardinge, Sir Henry, 1st Viscount Hardinge, GCB (1785–1856)	2 Oct 1855
42.	Colborne, Sir John, 1st Baron Seaton, GCB, GCMG, GCH (1776–1863)	1 Apr 1860
43.	Blakeney, Sir Edward, GCB, GCH (1778–1868)	9 Nov 1862
44.	Gough, Sir Hugh, 1st Viscount Gough, KP, GCB, GCSI (1779–1869)	9 Nov 1862
45.	George, HRH 2nd Duke of Cambridge, KG, KT, KP, GCB, GCSI, GCMG, GCIE, GCVO (1819–1904)	9 Nov 1862
46.	Campbell, Sir Colin, 1st Baron Clyde, GCB, KSI (1792–1863)	9 Nov 1862
47.	Woodford, Sir Alexander, GCB, GCMG (1782–1870)	1 Jan 1868
48.	Gomm, Sir William, GCB (1784–1875)	1 Jan 1868
49.	Ross, Sir Hew, GCB (1779–1868)	1 Jan 1868
50.	Burgoyne, Sir John, 1st Baronet, GCB (1782–1871)	1 Jan 1868
51.	Pollock, Sir George, 1st Baronet, GCB, GCSI (1786–1872)	24 May 1870
52.	Fitzgerald, Sir John, GCB (c.1785–1877)	29 May 1875
53.	Hay, George, 8th Marquess of Tweeddale, KT, GCB (1787–1876)	29 May 1875
54.	Edward VII, HM King of Great Britain and Ireland (1841–1910)	29 May 1875
55.	Rowan, Sir William, GCB (1789–1879)	2 Jun 1877
56.	Yorke, Sir Charles, GCB (1790–1880)	2 Jun 1877
57.	Rose, Sir Hugh, 1st Baron Strathnairn, GCB, GCSI (1801–1885)	2 Jun 1877
58.	Napier, Sir Robert, 1st Baron Napier of Magdala, GCB, GCSI (1810–1890)	1 Jan 1883
59.	Grant, Sir Patrick, GCB, GCMG (1804–1895)	24 Jun 1883
60.	Michel, Sir John, GCB (1804–1886)	27 Mar 1886
61.	Dacres, Sir Richard, GCB (1799–1886)	27 Mar 1886
62.	Paulet, Lord William, GCB (1804–1893)	10 July 1886
63.	Bingham, Charles, 3rd Earl of Lucan, GCB (1800–1888)	21 June 1887

64. Simmons, Sir Lintorn, GCB, GCMG
    (1821–1903)   *21 May 1890*
65. Haines, Sir Frederick, GCB, GCSI, CIE
    (1818–1909)   *21 May 1890*
66. Stewart, Sir Donald, 1st Baronet, GCB,
    GCSI, CIE (1824–1900)   *26 May 1894*
67. Wolseley, Sir Garnet, 1st Viscount Wolseley,
    KP, GCB, OM, GCMG, VD (1833–1913)   *26 May 1894*
68. Roberts, Sir Frederick, 1st Earl Roberts,
    VC, KG, KP, GCB, OM, GCSI, GCIE, VD
    (1832–1914)   *25 May 1895*
69. Edward, HRH Prince of Saxe-Weimar, KP,
    GCB, GCVO (1823–1902)   *22 Jun 1897*
70. Chamberlain, Sir Neville, GCB, GCSI
    (1820–1902)   *25 Apr 1900*
71. William II, HM German Emperor and King
    of Prussia, KG, GCVO (1859–1941)   *27 Jan 1901*
72. Norman, Sir Henry Wylie, GCB, GCMG, CIE
    (1826–1904)   *26 Jun 1902*
73. Arthur, HRH Duke of Connaught and Strathearn,
    KG, KT, KP, GCB, GCSI, GCMG, GCIE,
    GCVO, GBE, VD, TD (1850–1942)   *26 Jun 1902*
74. Wood, Sir Evelyn, VC, GCB, GCMG (1838–1919) *8 Apr 1903*
75. White, Sir George, VC, GCB, OM, GCSI
    GCMG, GCIE, GCVO (1835–1912)   *8 Apr 1903*
76. Francis Joseph, HIM Emperor of Austria and
    King of Hungary, KG (1830–1916)   *1 Sep 1903*
77. Grenfell, Sir Francis, 1st Baron Grenfell, GCB,
    GCMG (1841–1925)   *11 April 1908*
78. Brownlow, Sir Charles, GCB (1831–1916)   *20 Jun 1908*
79. Kitchener, Sir Herbert, 1st Earl, KG, KP, GCB,
    OM, GCSI, GCMG, GCIE (1850–1916)   *10 Sep 1909*
80. George V, HM King of Great Britain and Ireland
    (1865–1936)   *7 May 1910*
81. Methuen, Paul, 3rd Baron Methuen, GCB,
    GCMG, GCVO (1845–1932)   *19 Jun 1911*
82. Nicholson, Sir William, 1st Baron Nicholson,
    GCB (1845–1918)   *19 Jun 1911*
83. French, Sir John, 1st Earl of Ypres, KP, GCB,
    OM, GCVO, KCMG (1852–1925)   *3 Jun 1913*
84. Nicholas II, HM Emperor of Russia, KG
    (1868–1918)   *1 Jan 1916*

85.	Haig, Sir Douglas, 1st Earl Haig, GCB, OM, GCVO, KCIE (1861–1928)	*1 Jan 1917*
86.	Egerton, Sir Charles, GCB, DSO (1848–1921)	*16 Mar 1917*
87.	Yoshihito, HIM Emperor of Japan, KG (1879–1926)	*1 Jan 1918*
88.	Foch, Ferdinand, Marshal of France, GCB, OM (1851–1929)	*19 Jul 1919*
89.	Plumer, Sir Herbert, 1st Viscount Plumer, GCB, GCMG, GCVO, GBE (1857–1932)	*31 Jul 1919*
90.	Allenby, Sir Edward, 1st Viscount Allenby, GCB, GCMG, GCVO (1861–1936)	*31 Jul 1919*
91.	Wilson, Sir Henry, 1st Baronet, GCB, DSO (1864–1922)	*31 Jul 1919*
92.	Robertson, Sir William, 1st Baronet, GCB, GCMG, GCVO, DSO (1860–1933)	*29 Mar 1920*
93.	Barrett, Sir Arthur, GCB, GCSI, KCVO (1857–1926)	*12 April 1921*
94.	Albert I, HM King of the Belgians, KG, GCB (1875–1934)	*4 Jul 1921*
95.	Birdwood, Sir William, 1st Baron Birdwood, GCB, GCSI, GCMG, GCVO, CIE, DSO (1865–1951)	*20 Mar 1925*
96.	Jacob, Sir Claud, GCB, GCSI, KCMG (1863–1948)	*30 Nov 1926*
97.	Milne, Sir George, 1st Baron Milne, GCB, GCMG, DSO (1866–1948)	*30 Jan 1928*
98.	Alfonso XIII, HM King of Spain, KG, GCVO (1886–1941)	*3 Jun 1928*
99.	Hirohito, HIM Emperor of Japan, KG, GCB, GCVO (1901–1989)	*26 Jun 1928*
100.	Byng, Sir Julian, 1st Viscount Byng, GCB, GCMG, MVO (1862–1935)	*17 Jul 1932*
101.	Lambart, Sir Frederick, 10th Earl of Cavan, KP, GCB, GCMG, GCVO, GBE (1865–1946)	*31 Oct 1932*
102.	Chetwode, Sir Philip, 1st Baron Chetwode, GCB, OM, GCSI, KCMG, DSO (1869–1950)	*13 Feb 1933*
103.	Montgomery-Massingberd, Sir Archibald, GCB, GCVO, KCMG (1871–1947)	*7 Jun 1935*
104.	Edward VIII, HM King of Great Britain and Ireland, Duke of Windsor (1894–1972)	*21 Jan 1936*
105.	Deverell, Sir Cyril, GCB, KBE (1874–1947)	*15 May 1936*

106. George VI, HM King of Great Britain and Ireland (1895–1952)	*12 Dec 1936*
107. Ironside, Sir Edmund, 1st Baron Ironside, GCB, CMG, DSO (1880–1959)	*20 Jul 1940*
108. Smuts, Jan, OM, CH, DTD (1870–1950)	*24 May 1941*
109. Dill, Sir John, GCB, CMG, DSO (1881–1944)	*18 Nov 1941*
110. Vereker, John, 6th Viscount Gort VC, GCB, CBE, DSO, MVO, MC (1886–1946)	*1 Jan 1943*
111. Wavell, Sir Archibald, 1st Earl Wavell, GCB, GCSI, GCIE, CMG, MC (1883–1950)	*· 1 Jan 1943*
112. Brooke, Sir Alan, 1st Viscount Alanbrooke, KG, GCB, OM, GCMG, GCVO (1883–1963)	*1 Jan 1944*
113. Alexander, Sir Harold, 1st Earl Alexander of Tunis, KG, GCB, OM, GCMG, CSI, DSO, MC (1891–1969)	*4 Jun 1944*
114. Montgomery, Sir Bernard, 1st Viscount Montgomery, KG, GCB, DSO (1887–1976)	*1 Sep 1944*
115. Wilson, Sir Henry Maitland, 1st Baron Wilson of Libya, GCB, GBE, DSO (1881–1964)	*29 Dec 1944*
116. Auchinleck, Sir Claude, GCB, GCIE, CSI, DSO, OBE (1884–1981)	*1 Jun 1946*
117. Slim, Sir William, 1st Viscount Slim, KG, GCB, GCMG, GCVO, GBE, DSO, MC (1891–1970)	*4 Jan 1948*
118. Blamey, Sir Thomas, GBE, KCB, CMG, DSO (1884–1951) *(Australian Military Forces)*	*1 Jan 1950*
119. Philip, HRH Duke of Edinburgh, KG, KT, OM, GBE (1921-)	*15 Jan 1953*
120. Harding, Sir John, 1st Baron Harding of Petherton, GCB, CBE, DSO, MC (1896–1989)	*21 Jul 1953*
121. Henry, HRH Duke of Gloucester, KG, KT, KP, GCB, GCMG, GCVO (1900–1974)	*31 Mar 1955*
122. Templer, Sir Gerald, KG, GCB, GCMG, KBE, DSO (1898–1979)	*27 Nov 1956*
123. Festing, Sir Francis, GCB, KBE, DSO (1902–1976)	*1 Sep 1960*
124. Mahendra Bir Bikram Shah Deva, HM King of Nepal (1921–1972)	*17 Oct 1962*
125. Haile Selassie, HIM Emperor of Ethiopia, KG, GCB, GCMG (1892–1975)	*20 Jan 1965*
126. Hull, Sir Richard, KG, GCB, DSO (1907–1989)	*8 Feb 1965*
127. Cassels, Sir James, GCB, KBE, DSO (1907–1996)	*29 Feb 1968*

128. Baker, Sir Geoffrey, GCB, CMG, CBE, MC
(1912–1980)   *31 Jan 1971*

129. Carver, Sir Michael, Baron Carver, GCB,
CBE, DSO, MC (1915-2001)   *18 Jul 1973*

130. Gibbs, Sir Roland, GCB, CBE, DSO, MC
(1921–2004)   *13 Jul.1979*

131. Birenda Bir Bikram Shah Deva, HM King of
Nepal (1945–2001) *(honorary rank)*   *18 Nov 1980*

132. Bramall, Sir Edwin, Baron Bramall, KG,
GCB, OBE, MC (1923–)   *1 Aug 1982*

133. Stanier, Sir John, GCB, MBE (1925-   )   *10 Jul 1985*

134. Bagnall, Sir Nigel, GCB, CVO, MC (1927-   )   *9 Sep 1988*

135. Vincent, Sir Richard, Baron Vincent, GBE,
KCB, DSO (1931-)   *2 Apr 1991*

136. Chapple, Sir John, GCB, CBE (1931-   )   *14 Feb 1992*

137. Edward, HRH Duke of Kent, KG, GCMG,
GCVO (1935-   )   *11 Jun 1993*

138. Inge, Sir Peter, Baron Inge, KG, GCB (1935-   ) *15 Mar 1994*

Table 2

THE FIELD MARSHALS' REGIMENTS AND CORPS

The regiments and corps listed in this table are those existing in the regular British Army at the date of publication, in which (or, in the case of regiments formed by amalgamation, in the ancestors of which) the field marshals served. The previous regimental numbers of cavalry forming part of the Royal Armoured Corps, and of the regiments of Foot from which the regular battalions of the Infantry of the Line are descended, are shown in brackets after the present day titles. Colonels (or colonels commandant) and colonels-in-chief appointed without previous service in the regiment or corps (or in one of its ancestors) are indicated by *italics* and _underlining_ respectively. Militia, Volunteer, or Territorial service is not taken into account in this table. The field marshals are listed under the names by which they were known at the end of their careers.

THE LIFE GUARDS

2nd Duke of Argyll [2]; Viscount Shannon [3]; *Lord Tyrawley* [11]; *Lord Amherst* [17]; *Viscount Combermere* [39]; *Lord Seaton* [42]; *Marquess of Tweeddale* [53]; _Edward VII_ [54]; Earl of Lucan [63]; *Prince Edward of Saxe-Weimar* [69]; *Lord Grenfell* [77]; _George V_ [80]; *Viscount Allenby* [90]; _Edward VIII (Duke of Windsor)_ [104]; _George VI_ [106]; *Lord Harding of Petherton* [120]

THE BLUES AND ROYALS (ROYAL HORSE GUARDS AND 1st DRAGOONS)

2nd Duke of Argyll [2]; *Viscount Cobham* [6]; *Earl Ligonier* [10]; *Hon Henry Conway* [12]; *Duke of Richmond* [22]; *Duke of Wellington* [24]; *King Ernest I of Hanover* [25]; *Marquess of Anglesey* [37]; *Lord Raglan* [38]; *Viscount Gough* [44]; _Edward VII_ [54]; *Lord Strathnairn* [57]; *Sir Patrick Grant* [59]; *Viscount Wolseley* [67]; _William II, German Emperor_

[71]; *Sir Evelyn Wood* [74]; George V [80]; *Earl Haig* [85]; *Sir William Robertson* [92]; Edward VIII (Duke of Windsor) [104]; George VI [106]; *Sir Gerald Templer* [122]

ROYAL ARMOURED CORPS
Viscount Montgomery [114]; Sir Nigel Bagnall [134]; Sir Richard Hull [126]; Lord Carver [129]; Sir John Stanier [133]

1st THE QUEEN'S DRAGOON GUARDS (1st and 2nd Dragoon Guards)
2nd Duke of Argyll [2]; *Viscount Cobham* [6]; *Earl Ligonier* [10]; *Sir George Howard* [14]; *Marquess Townshend* [20]; Francis Joseph, Emperor of Austria [76]; George VI [106]

THE ROYAL SCOTS DRAGOON GUARDS (CARABINIERS AND GREYS) (3rd and 6th Dragoon Guards, 2nd Dragoons)
Viscount Shannon [3]; *Earl of Stair* [5]; *Sir Robert Rich* [8]; Viscount Combermere [39]; Emperor Nicholas II of Russia [84]; Sir William Robertson [92]; Lord Chetwode [102]; George V [106]; Edward, 2nd Duke of Kent [137]; Sir John Stanier [133]

THE ROYAL DRAGOON GUARDS (4th, 5th and 7th Dragoon Guards, 6th Dragoons)
Earl of Stair [5]; *Viscount Cobham* [6]; *Earl Ligonier* [10]; *Lord Tyrawley* [11]; *Hon Henry Conway* [12]; Lord Amherst [17]; *Studholme Hodgson* [19]; Marquess Townshend [20]; *Leopold I, King of the Belgians* [28]; Sir George Nugent [35]; Duke of Connaught [73]; Viscount Allenby [90]; Albert I, King of the Belgians [94]; Sir Nigel Bagnall [134]

THE QUEEN'S OWN HUSSARS (QUEEN'S OWN AND ROYAL IRISH) (3rd, 4th, 7th, 8th)
Viscount Cobham [6]; *Sir Robert Rich* [8]; *Lord Tyrawley* [11]; *Hon Henry Conway* [12]; *Sir George Howard* [14]; *Lord Howard de Walden* [18]; Marquess Townshend [20]; *Marquess of Anglesey* [37]; Lord Raglan [38]; *Viscount Combermere* [39]; Sir Edward Blakeney [43]; George, 2nd Duke of Cambridge [45]; Earl of Lucan [63]; Duke of Connaught [73]; Earl of Ypres [83]; Earl Haig [85]; *Viscount Byng* [100]; Duke of Edinburgh [119]; Sir John Stanier [133]

9th/12th ROYAL LANCERS (PRINCE OF WALES'S)
(9th, 12th)
Viscount Molesworth [9]; Marquess of Drogheda [29]; Duke of Wellington [24]; Lord Birdwood [95]; Edward VIII (Duke of Windsor) [104]

THE KING'S ROYAL HUSSARS (10th, 11th, 14th, 20th)
Viscount Cobham [6]; *Lord Tyrawley* [11]; *5th Duke of Argyll* [16]; *Studholme Hodgson* [19]; *Albert, Prince Consort* [33]; *Edward VII* [54]; George V [80]; Viscount Byng [100]; George VI [106]; Henry, Duke of Gloucester [121]

THE LIGHT DRAGOONS (13th, 15th, 18th, 19th)
Hon Henry Conway [12]; *Sir Robert Rich* [8]; Earl Harcourt [30]; *King Ernest I of Hanover* [25]; Sir Evelyn Wood [74]; Earl of Ypres [83]; Lord Chetwode [102]

THE QUEEN'S ROYAL LANCERS (5th, 16th, 17th, 21st)
Earl Harcourt [30]; Marquess of Anglesey [37]; Viscount Combermere [39]; George, 2nd Duke of Cambridge [45]; Earl of Lucan [63]; Sir Evelyn Wood [74]; Earl Haig [85]; Viscount Allenby [90]; Sir William Robertson [92]; King Alfonso XIII of Spain [98]; Sir Richard Hull [126]

ROYAL TANK REGIMENT
George V [80]; *Sir Archibald Montgomery-Massingberd* [103]; Edward VIII (Duke of Windsor) [104]; George VI [106]; *Viscount Montgomery* [114]; Lord Carver [129]

ROYAL REGIMENT OF ARTILLERY
John, 2nd Duke of Argyll [2]; *Earl Ligonier* [10]; *Marquess Townshend* [20]; *Duke of Richmond* [22]; *Duke of Wellington* [24]; *Marquess of Anglesey* [37]; *Viscount Hardinge* [41]; *Lord Raglan* [38]; George, 2nd Duke of Cambridge [45]; Sir Hew Ross [49]; Sir George Pollock [51]; Edward VII [54]; Sir Richard Dacres [61]; Earl Roberts [68]; Duke of Connaught [73]; George V [80]; Lord Milne [97]; Sir Archibald Montgomery-Massingberd [103]; Edward VIII (Duke of Windsor) [104]; George VI [106]; Lord Ironside [107]; Viscount Alanbrooke [112]; Sir Geoffrey Baker [128]; Lord Vincent [135]; Sir John Chapple [136]

CORPS OF ROYAL ENGINEERS

Duke of Wellington **[24]**; *Marquess of Anglesey* **[37]**; *Viscount Hardinge* **[41]**; *Lord Raglan* **[38]**; <u>*George, 2nd*</u> Duke of Cambridge **[45]**; Sir John Burgoyne **[50]**; Edward VII **[54]**; Lord Napier of Magdala **[58]**; Sir Lintorn Simmons **[64]**; Duke of Connaught **[73]**; Earl Kitchener **[79]**; <u>George V</u> **[80]**; Lord Nicholson **[82]**; <u>Edward VIII (Duke of Windsor)</u> **[104]**; <u>George VI</u> **[106]**

GRENADIER GUARDS

Sir Robert Rich **[8]**; *Earl Ligonier* **[10]**; Hon Henry Conway **[12]**; *William, 1st Duke of Gloucester and Edinburgh* **[13]**; Duke of York **[15]**; Lord Amherst **[17]**; Studholme Hodgson **[19]**; Marquess Townshend **[20]**; Lord Frederick Cavendish **[21]**; *Duke of Wellington* **[24]**; Earl Harcourt **[30]**; Sir Samuel Hulse **[32]**; *Albert, Prince Consort* **[33]**; Viscount Hardinge **[41]**; George, 2nd Duke of Cambridge **[45]**; Marquess of Tweeddale **[53]**; Edward VII **[54]**; Prince Edward of Saxe-Weimar **[69]**; *Duke of Connaught* **[73]**; <u>George V</u> **[80]**; Earl of Cavan **[101]**; Edward VIII (Duke of Windsor) **[104]**; <u>George VI</u> **[106]**; Viscount Gort **[110]**; *Duke of Edinburgh* **[119]**

COLDSTREAM GUARDS

Viscount Molesworth **[9]**; *Lord Tyrawley* **[11]**; Duke of York **[15]**; *Adolphus, 1st Duke of Cambridge* **[26]**; Sir George Nugent **[35]**; Lord Frederick Cavendish **[21]**; *Earl of Strafford* **[40]**; *Lord Clyde* **[46]**; Sir Alexander Woodford **[47]**; Sir William Gomm **[48]**; <u>Edward VII</u> **[54]**; <u>George V</u> **[80]**; <u>Edward VIII (Duke of Windsor)</u> **[104]**; <u>George VI</u> **[106]**

SCOTS GUARDS

Earl of Stair **[5]**; *William, 1st Duke of Gloucester and Edinburgh* **[13]**; *5th Duke of Argyll* **[16]**; Lord Howard de Walden **[18]**; William, 2nd Duke of Gloucester and Edinburgh **[27]**; *Albert, Prince Consort* **[33]**; Thomas Grosvenor **[36]**; Earl of Strafford **[40]**; *George, 2nd Duke of Cambridge* **[45]**; *Sir Alexander Woodford* **[47]**; <u>Edward VII</u> **[54]**; Earl of Lucan **[63]**; *Duke of Connaught* **[73]**; <u>George V</u> **[80]**; Lord Methuen **[81]**; <u>Edward VIII (Duke of Windsor)</u> **[104]**; *George VI* **[106]**; *Henry, Duke of Gloucester* **[121]**; *Edward, 2nd Duke of Kent* **[137]**

IRISH GUARDS

<u>Edward VII</u> **[54]**; *Earl Roberts* **[68]**; <u>George V</u> **[80]**; *Earl of Ypres* **[83]**; *Earl of Cavan* **[101]**; <u>Edward VIII (Duke of Windsor)</u> **[104]**; <u>George VI</u> **[106]**; Earl Alexander of Tunis **[113]**

WELSH GUARDS
George V [80]; *Edward VIII (Duke of Windsor)* [104]; George VI [106]; *Duke of Edinburgh* [119]

THE ROYAL SCOTS (THE ROYAL REGIMENT) (1st)
Earl of Orkney [1]; Viscount Molesworth [9]; *5th Duke of Argyll* [16]; *Duke of Kent* [23]; Viscount Hardinge [41]; *Sir Edward Blakeney* [43]

THE PRINCESS OF WALES'S ROYAL REGIMENT (THE QUEEN'S AND ROYAL HAMPSHIRE) (2nd, 3rd, 31st, 35th, 37th, 50th, 57th, 67th, 70th, 77th, 97th, 107th)
2nd Duke of Argyll [2]; Sir George Howard [14]; *Lord Amherst* [17]; *Lord Howard de Walden* [18]; *Studholme Hodgson* [19]; *Lord Frederick Cavendish* [21]; Earl Harcourt [30]; Sir Alured Clarke [31]; Sir George Nugent [35]; Viscount Hardinge [41]; George, 2nd Duke of Cambridge [45]; *Lord Clyde* [46]; Sir Charles Yorke [56]; Sir John Michel [60]; Prince Edward of Saxe-Weimar [69]; Sir Charles Egerton [86]; Edward VIII (Duke of Windsor) [104]; Sir Gerald Templer [122]

THE KING'S OWN ROYAL BORDER REGIMENT (4th, 34th, 55th)
Hon Henry Conway [12]; *Studholme Hodgson* [19]; *Lord Frederick Cavendish* [21]; Viscount Hardinge [41]; Edward VII [54]; Sir Frederick Haines [65]; George V [80]

THE ROYAL REGIMENT OF FUSILIERS (5th, 6th, 7th, 20th)
Earl of Orkney [1]; Viscount Cobham [6]; Lord Tyrawley [11]; *Studholme Hodgson* [19]; Marquess Townshend [20]; Duke of Richmond [22]; *Duke of Kent* [23]; *William, 2nd Duke of Gloucester and Edinburgh* [27]; Sir Alured Clarke [31]; Sir George Nugent [35]; Marquess of Anglesey [37]; Viscount Combermere [39]; Lord Seaton [42]; Sir Edward Blakeney [43]; *Sir John Fitzgerald* [52]; Sir John Michel [60]; Lord William Paulet [62]; Earl of Lucan [63]; George V [80]; Viscount Montgomery [114]; Viscount Slim [117]; *Sir Francis Festing* [123]; Edward, 2nd Duke of Kent [137]

THE KING'S REGIMENT (8th, 63rd, 96th)
Earl of Lucan [63]; Sir Frederick Haines [65]; George V [80]

THE ROYAL ANGLIAN REGIMENT (9th, 10th, 12th, 16th, 17th, 44th, 48th, 56th, 58th)

George Wade [7]; Earl Ligonier [10]; *Lord Tyrawley* [11]; *Hon Henry Conway* [12]; Duke of Wellington [24]; *Sir Samuel Hulse* [32]; Sir Edward Blakeney [43]; Lord Clyde [46]; Sir Alexander Woodford [47]; Sir William Gomm [48]; Edward VII [54]; Sir William Rowan [55]; Sir Frederick Haines [65]; Viscount Wolseley [67]; *Prince Edward of Saxe-Weimar* [69]; Sir Evelyn Wood [74]; Sir Alexander Woodford [47]; George V [80]; Sir Arthur Barrett [93]; *Earl of Cavan* [101]; George VI [106]

THE DEVONSHIRE AND DORSET REGIMENT (11th, 39th, 54th)

5th Duke of Argyll [16]; Sir Alured Clarke [31]; Sir George Nugent [35]; Edward, 2nd Duke of Kent [137]

THE LIGHT INFANTRY (13th, 32nd, 46th, 51st, 53rd, 68th, 85th, 105th, 106th)

William, 1st Duke of Gloucester and Edinburgh [13]; Sir Alured Clarke [31]; Sir George Nugent [35]; *Lord Raglan* [38]; *Sir William Gomm* [48]; Sir John Fitzgerald [52]; Sir Charles Yorke [56]; Lord William Paulet [62]; Edward VIII (Duke of Windsor) [104]; George VI [106]; Lord Harding of Petherton [120]

THE PRINCE OF WALES'S OWN REGIMENT OF YORKSHIRE (14th, 15th)

Lord Amherst [17]; Sir Cyril Deverell [105]; George VI [106]; *Viscount Slim* [117]

THE GREEN HOWARDS (ALEXANDRA, PRINCESS OF WALES'S OWN YORKSHIRE REGIMENT) (19th)

Sir Samuel Hulse [32]; *Sir William Rowan* [55]; Lord Strathnairn [57]; Sir Nigel Bagnall [134]; Lord Inge [138]

THE ROYAL HIGHLAND FUSILIERS (PRINCESS MARGARET'S OWN GLASGOW AND AYRSHIRE REGIMENT) (21st, 71st, 74th)

Lord Clyde [46]; Lord William Paulet [62]; Earl of Lucan [63]; Sir Frederick Haines [65]; Duke of Connaught [73]; Edward VIII (Duke of Windsor) [104]

THE CHESHIRE REGIMENT (22nd)
Viscount Gough [44]; Sir Alexander Woodford [47]

THE ROYAL WELCH FUSILIERS (23rd)
Marquess of Anglesey [37]; Viscount Combermere [39]; George V [80]; George VI [106]

THE ROYAL REGIMENT OF WALES (24th, 41st, 69th)
Sir George Howard [14]; Duke of Wellington [24]; Marquess of Tweeddale [53]; Edward VIII (Duke of Windsor) [104]

THE KING' S OWN SCOTTISH BORDERERS (25th)
Viscount Shannon [3]; *Earl Haig* [85]

THE ROYAL GLOUCESTERSHIRE, BERKSHIRE AND WILTSHIRE REGIMENT (28th, 49th, 61st, 62nd, 66th, 99th)
Marquess Townshend [20]; *Sir Samuel Hulse* [32]; Sir George Nugent [35]; Lord Seaton [42]; *Viscount Gough* [44]; *Sir John Fitzgerald* [52]; George VI [106]; Henry, Duke of Gloucester [121]

THE WORCESTERSHIRE AND SHERWOOD FORESTERS REGIMENT (29th, 36th, 45th, 95th)
Earl of Strafford [40]; *Lord Strathnairn* [57]; **Sir Claud Jacob [96]**

THE QUEEN'S LANCASHIRE REGIMENT (30th, 40th, 47th, 59th, 81st, 82nd)
Viscount Combermere [39]; Viscount Hardinge [41]; Sir Edward Blakeney [43]; *Sir Alexander Woodford* [47]; Marquess of Tweeddale [52]; Edward VIII (Duke of Windsor) [104]; Sir John Dill [108]; Sir Gerald Templer [122]; Sir Francis Festing [123]

THE DUKE OF WELLINGTON'S REGIMENT (WEST RIDING) (33rd, 76th)
George Wade [7]; *Lord Howard de Walden* [12]; Duke of Richmond [22]; Duke of Wellington [24]; Earl of Strafford [40]; *Sir Charles Yorke* [56]; Sir Charles Egerton [86]

THE STAFFORDSHIRE REGIMENT (THE PRINCE OF WALES'S) (38th, 64th, 80th, 98th)
Marquess Townshend [20]; Marquess of Anglesey [37]; Lord Clyde [46]; Sir John Michel [60]; Viscount Wolseley [67]

THE BLACK WATCH (ROYAL HIGHLAND REGIMENT) (42nd, 73rd)

5th Duke of Argyll [16]; Duke of Wellington [24]; *Marquess of Tweeddale* [52]; Sir Evelyn Wood [74]; George V [80]; Earl Wavell [111]

THE HIGHLANDERS (72nd, 75th, 78th, 79th, 92nd)

Viscount Gough [44]; Sir John Fitzgerald [52]; Edward VII [54]; Lord Strathnairn [57]; *Sir Patrick Grant* [59]; Sir George White [75]; George V [80]; Edward VIII (Duke of Windsor) [104]; George VI [106]; Duke of Edinburgh [119]; Henry, Duke of Gloucester [121]; Sir James Cassels [127]

THE ARGYLL AND SUTHERLAND HIGHLANDERS (PRINCESS LOUISE'S) (91st, 93rd)

Lord Clyde [46]; Lord Strathnairn [57]

THE ROYAL GREEN JACKETS (43rd, 52nd, 60th, the Rifle Brigade)

Duke of York [15]; Lord Amherst [17]; Duke of Wellington [24]; Adolphus, 1st Duke of Cambridge [26]; *Sir Alured Clarke* [31]; *Albert, Prince Consort* [33]; Lord Raglan [38]; Earl of Strafford [40]; Lord Seaton [42]; Sir Edward Blakeney [43]; Viscount Gough [44]; George, 2nd Duke of Cambridge [45]; Lord Clyde [46]; Sir John Fitzgerald [52]; Marquess of Tweeddale [53]; Edward VII [54]; Sir William Rowan [55]; Sir Charles Yorke [56]; Lord Grenfell [77]; Duke of Connaught [73]; George V [80]; Sir Henry Wilson [91]; George VI [106]; Lord Wilson [115]; Henry, Duke of Gloucester [121]; Sir Francis Festing [123]; Sir Roland Gibbs [130]; Lord Bramall [132]

THE ROYAL IRISH REGIMENT (27th, 83rd, 86th, 87th, 89th, 108th, Ulster Defence Regiment) *Note: The original Royal Irish Regiment (18th) was disbanded in 1922.*

Viscount Molesworth [9]; *Viscount Gough* [44]; *Sir John Michel* [60]; *Lord William Paulet* [62]; Sir George White [75]; George V [80]; *Sir Henry Wilson* [91]; *Sir Claude Auchinleck* [116]; Henry, Duke of Gloucester [121]; Sir Gerald Templer [122]

THE PARACHUTE REGIMENT

Sir John Dill [108]; *Viscount Montgomery* [114]; Sir Roland Gibbs [130]; Sir Nigel Bagnall [134]

THE ROYAL GURKHA RIFLES (2nd, 6th, 7th and 10th Gurkha Rifles)

Earl Kitchener **[79]**; Viscount Slim **[117]**; *Lord Harding of Petherton* **[120]**; *Sir Gerald Templer* **[122]**; *Lord Bramall* **[132]**; Sir John Chapple **[136]**

SPECIAL AIR SERVICE REGIMENT

Lord Bramall **[132]**

THE ROYAL LOGISTICS CORPS

Duke of Connaught **[73]**; *Lord Milne* **[97]**; George VI **[106]**; Henry, Duke of Gloucester **[121]**

CORPS OF ROYAL ELECTRICAL AND MECHANICAL ENGINEERS

Duke of Edinburgh **[119]**; *Lord Carver* **[129]**; *Lord Vincent* **[135]**

ROYAL ARMY MEDICAL CORPS

Duke of Connaught **[73]**

ADJUTANT GENERAL'S CORPS

Sir James Cassels **[127]**; *Sir Geoffrey Baker* **[128]**; *Lord Inge* **[138]**

INTELLIGENCE CORPS

Duke of Edinburgh **[119]**

ARMY PHYSICAL TRAINING CORPS

Viscount Montgomery **[114]**; *Sir James Cassels* **[127]**; *Sir Nigel Bagnall* **[134]**; *Lord Inge* **[138]**

Table 3

ARMS OR BRANCHES OF THE ARMY IN WHICH THE FIELD MARSHALS SERVED

Note *in several cases, future field marshals served in more than one arm or branch during the course of their career. In this table, the arm or branch shown is that in which the individual spent most of his regimental duty. Numerals in* **bold** *indicate the position of field marshals in their seniority list.*

BRITISH ARMY

CAVALRY

Household Cavalry	**3**	1
Cavalry of the Line	**9, 12, 17, 26, 29, 30, 37, 38, 39, 45, 63, 74, 83, 85, 90, 92, 100, 102, 121**	19
		Total Cavalry 20

ARMOUR

126, 129, 133, 137	Total Armour 4

ARTILLERY

49, 51, 61, 68, 97, 103, 107, 112, 128, 135	Total Artillery 10

ENGINEERS

50, 58, 64, 79, 82	Total Engineers 5

INFANTRY

Foot Guards	**8, 13, 15, 18, 19, 20, 21, 27, 32, 36,**	
	40, 47, 53, 69, 81, 101, 110, 113	18
Fusiliers	**11, 23, 31, 43, 122**	5
Scottish regiments		
of the Line	**1, 2, 5, 16, 57, 75, 111, 127**	8
Other regiments		
of the Line	**4, 6, 7, 10, 14, 22, 24, 35, 41, 44,**	
	46, 48, 60, 65, 89, 105, 109, 114, 134, 138	20
Rifle Corps and		
Light Infantry	**42, 52, 55, 56, 62, 67, 73, 77, 91,**	
	115, 120, 123, 130, 132	14
Gurkha Rifles	**136**	1

Total Infantry 66

Total British Army 105

INDIAN ARMY

Cavalry	**86, 95**	2
Indian Infantry	**59, 66, 70, 72, 78, 96, 116**	7
Gurkha Rifles	**93, 117**	2

Total Indian Army 11

BRITISH AND FOREIGN MONARCHS, ROYAL CONSORTS AND OFFICERS OF COMMONWEALTH OR ALLIED ARMIES

25, 28, 33, 34, 54, 71, 76, 80, 84, 87, 88, 94, 98, 99, 104, 106, 108, 118, 119, 124, 125, 131   22

Grand Total of Field Marshals 138

Table 4

SCHOOLS ATTENDED BY
THE FIELD MARSHALS

The names are those by which the field marshals were known at the end of their careers.

ABERDEEN GYMNASIUM	Lord Milne [97] Sir Donald Stewart [66]
ALDENHAM SCHOOL	Lord Vincent [135]
CHARTERHOUSE SCHOOL	Sir George Nugent [35] Sir Archibald Montgomery- Massingberd [103] Sir Richard Hull [126]
CHELTENHAM COLLEGE	Sir John Dill [108]
CLIFTON COLLEGE	Earl Haig [85] Lord Birdwood [95]
ST PHILIP'S SCHOOL, EDGBASTON	Viscount Slim [117]
ETON COLLEGE	Duke of Wellington [24] Sir John Burgoyne [50] Sir John Michel [60] Lord William Paulet [62] Earl Roberts [68] Lord Methuen [81] Viscount Plumer [89] Viscount Byng [100]

Earl of Cavan [101]
Lord Chetwode [102]
Lord Wilson [115]
Henry, Duke of Gloucester [121]
Sir Roland Gibbs [130]
Lord Bramall [132]
Edward, 2nd Duke of Kent [137]

GORDONSTOUN SCHOOL — Philip, Duke of Edinburgh [119]

ELIZABETH COLLEGE, GUERNSEY — Sir Lintorn Simmons [64]

HAILEYBURY AND I. S. COLLEGE — Viscount Allenby [90]
Sir John Chapple [136]

HARROW SCHOOL — Viscount Gort [110]
Earl Alexander of Tunis [113]

ILMINSTER GRAMMAR SCHOOL — Lord Harding of Petherton [120]

KING WILLIAM'S COLLEGE, ISLE OF MAN — Sir George White [75]

LEEDS GRAMMAR SCHOOL — Lord Nicholson [82]

ST PAUL'S SCHOOL, LONDON — Viscount Montgomery [114]

MARLBOROUGH COLLEGE — Sir Evelyn Wood [74]
Sir Henry Wilson [91]
Sir John Stanier [133]

MILTON ABBAS SCHOOL — Lord Grenfell [77]

COLLEGE DE ST CLEMENT, METZ — Ferdinand Foch [88]

RUGBY SCHOOL — Sir James Cassels [127]

SHERBORNE SCHOOL	Sir Claud Jacob [96]
VICTORIA COLLEGE, STELLENBOSCH	Jan Smuts [108]
TONBRIDGE SCHOOL	Lord Ironside [107]
WAGGA WAGGA PUBLIC SCHOOL	Sir Thomas Blamey [118]
WELLINGTON COLLEGE	Sir Claude Auchinleck [116]
	Sir Gerald Templer [122]
	Sir Geoffrey Baker [128]
	Sir Nigel Bagnall [134]
WESTMINSTER SCHOOL	Duke of Richmond [22]
	Thomas Grosvenor [36]
	Marquess of Anglesey [37]
	Lord Raglan [38]
	Viscount Combermere [39]
	Earl of Lucan [63]
WINCHESTER COLLEGE	Sir Alexander Woodford [47]
	Lord Seaton [42]
	Earl Wavell [111]
	Sir Francis Festing [123]
	Lord Carver [129]
WREKIN COLLEGE	Lord Inge [138]

Table 5

ESTABLISHMENTS ATTENDED BY THE FIELD MARSHALS AS MILITARY CADETS

ROYAL MILITARY ACADEMY, WOOLWICH
Sir George Nugent [35]
Sir Hew Ross [49]
Sir John Burgoyne [50]
Sir George Pollock [51]
Sir Richard Dacres [61]
Sir Lintorn Simmons [64]
Sir Neville Chamberlain [70]
Duke of Connaught [73]
Earl Kitchener [79]
Lord Nicholson [82]
Lord Milne [97]
Lord Ironside [107]
Viscount Alanbrooke [112]
Sir Geoffrey Baker [128]

ROYAL MILITARY COLLEGE, SANDHURST
Earl Roberts [68]
Prince Edward of Saxe-Weimar [69]
Sir George White [75]
Earl Haig [85]
Sir Charles Egerton [86]
Viscount Allenby [90]
Lord Birdwood [95]
Sir Claud Jacob [96]
Earl of Cavan [101]
Sir Archibald Montgomery-Massingberd [103]
Sir John Dill [108]

Lord Gort **[110]**
Earl Alexander **[113]**
Viscount Montgomery **[114]**
Lord Wilson **[115]**
Sir Claude Auchinleck **[116]**
Henry, Duke of Gloucester **[121]**
Sir Gerald Templer **[122]**
Sir James Cassells **[127]**
Lord Carver **[129]**
Sir Roland Gibbs **[130]**

ROYAL MILITARY ACADEMY SANDHURST
Edward, 2nd Duke of Kent **[137]**
Lord Inge **[138]**

EAST INDIA COMPANY'S MILITARY SEMINARY, ADDISCOMBE
Lord Napier of Magdala **[58]**
Earl Roberts **[68]**

OFFICER CADET TRAINING UNITS
Sir Roland Gibbs **[130]**
Lord Bramall **[132]**
Sir John Stanier **[133]**
Sir Nigel Bagnall **[134]**
Lord Vincent **[135]**
Sir John Chapple **[136]**
Lord Inge **[138]**

ECOLE MILITAIRE, ANGERS
Duke of Wellington **[24]**

ECOLE ROYALE MILITAIRE, BRUSSELS
Albert I, King of the Belgians **[94]**

ECOLE D'APPLICATION, FONTAINEBLEU
Ferdinand Foch **[88]**

ECOLE POLYTECHNIQUE, PARIS
Ferdinand Foch **[88]**

BIBLIOGRAPHY

REFERENCE PUBLICATIONS

Army Lists, published by authority, annually, half-yearly, quarterly or monthly, London, 1772–1998.

Burke's Peerage and Baronetage, London, 1886.

Debrett's Peerage and Baronetage, London, 1990.

Dictionary of National Biography, 77 vols., London, 1885–1990.

Hart's Army Lists, published annually, London, 1842–1914.

Who's Who, published annually, London, 1974–1987.

Boatner, Mark M., *Cassell's Biographical Dictionary of the American War of Independence 1763–1783*, London, 1973.

Dalton, Charles, *The Waterloo Roll Call* (reprint), London, 1971.

—— *English Army Lists and Commission Registers 1660–1694*, 3 vols., London, 1905.

Dupuy, Trevor N., Johnson, Curt, and Longard, David L, *The Encyclopaedia of Military Biography*, London, 1992.

Embree, A.T., *Encyclopaedia of Asian History*, 3 vols., New York, 1988.

Fletcher, C.R.L., and Walker, Emery, *Historical Portraits 1700–1850*, 2 vols., Oxford, 1919.

Herwig, H., and Heyman, N., *Biographical Dictionary of World War I*, London, 1982.

Keown-Boyd, Henry, *Soldiers of the Nile: A Biographical Dictionary of the British Officers of the Egyptian Army 1882–1925*, Bromyard, Herefordshire, 1996.

Lee, M. (ed.), *Chambers' British Biographies: The 20th Century*, Edinburgh 1993.

Leslie, N.B., *The Succession of Colonels of the British Army from 1660 to the present day*, Journal of the Society for Army Historical Research, Special Publication No. 11, London, 1974.

Mason, David, *Who's Who in World War II*, London, 1978.

Montgomery-Massingberd, H., *Burke's Royal Families of the World*, London, 1978.

Pope, Stephen, and Wheal, E-A., *The Macmillan Dictionary of The First World War*, London 1995.

Wheal, Elizabeth-Anne, and Pope, S., *The Macmillan Dictionary of The Second World War*, London, 1989.

Windsrow, Martin, and Mason, Francis K., *A Concise Dictionary of Military Biography*, London, 1975.

BIOGRAPHIES

Adington, Richard, *Wellington*, London, 1946.

Alice, Princess, Duchess of Gloucester, *The Memoirs of Princess Alice, Duchess of Gloucester*, London, 1983.

Anglesey, Marquess of, *One-Leg. The Life and Letters of Henry William Paget, 1st Marquess of Anglesey 1768–1854*, London, 1961.

Anon., *Memoir to Illustrate the Origins and Foundations of the Pollock Medal*, [Woolwich, 1875].

Arthur, George C.A., and Maurice, Frederick.B.,(ed), *The Letters of Lord and Lady Wolseley*, London, 1923.

Ash, Bernard, *The Lost Dictator. A Biography of Field Marshal Sir Henry Wilson, Bart.*, London, 1968.

Aston, George, *HRH the Duke of Connaught and Strathearn. A Life and Intimate Study*, London, 1929.

—— *The Biography of the late Marshal Foch*, London, 1929.

Barnett, Correlli, *The Desert Generals*, London, 1960.

Behr, Edward, *Hirohito: Behind the Myth*, New York, 1989.

Bennett, Daphne, *King without a Crown. Albert, Prince Consort of England 1819–1861*, London, 1977.

Benson, E.F., *King Edward VII. An Appreciation*, London, 1933.

Birdwood, William, (Field Marshal Lord) *Khaki and Gown. Autobiography of Field Marshal Lord Birdwood*, London, 1941.

Blake, Robert, *The private Papers of Douglas Haig 1914–1919*, London, 1952.

Bled, Jean-Paul, (tr., Bridgeman, T.), *Franz Joseph*, Oxford, 1992.

Bonham-Carter, Victor, *Soldier True. The Life and Times of Field Marshal Sir William Robertson, Bart. 1860–1933*, London, 1963.

Boraston, J.E. (ed.), *Sir Douglas Haig's Despatches, December 1915-April 1919* (2 vols.), London 1919, reprinted 1979.

Brett-James , Anthony, *Conversations with Montgomery*, London, 1984.

—— *Wellington at War 1794–1815*. London, 1961.

Brook-Shepherd, Gordon, *Uncle of Europe* [Edward VII], London, 1975.

Brown, W.D.E., "Field Marshal Sir Geoffrey Baker. A Personal Tribute" (Journal of the Royal Artillery, vol. CVII, no.2), September, 1980.

Buchan, Susan, *The Sword of State. Wellington after Waterloo*, London, 1928.

Burne, Alfred H., *The Noble Duke of York*, London, 1949.

Caldwell, C.E., *Field Marshal Sir Henry Wilson*, 2 vols., London, 1927.

Carver, Michael (Field Marshal Lord), *Out of Step. The Memoirs of Field Marshal Lord Carver*, London, 1969.

—— *Harding of Petherton. Field Marshal*, London, 1978.

Cassar, G.H., *Kitchener: Architect of Victory*, London, 1977.

Chalfont, Alan, *Montgomery of Alamein*, London, 1976.

Charteris, John, *Field Marshal Earl Haig*, London, 1929.

Clayton, Anthony, *Three Marshals of France, Leadership after Trauma*, London, 1992.

Cloake, John, *Templer: Tiger of Malaya. The Life of Field Marshal Sir Gerald Templer*, London, 1985.

Collier, Basil, *Brasshat* [life of Field Marshal Sir H.H.Wilson], London, 1961.

Collins, R.J., *Lord Wavell. A Military Biography 1883–1941*, London, 1948.

Colville, J.R., *Man of Valour. Field Marshal Lord Gort*, London, 1972.

Combermere, Countess of, and Knollys, W.W., *The Combermere Correspondence*, 2 vols., London, 1866.

Conmaerts, Emile, *Albert of Belgium, Defender of Right*, London, 1935.

Connell, John, *Wavell: Supreme Commander 1941–1943*, London, 1969.

—— *Auchinleck. A Biography of Field Marshal Sir Claude Auchinleck*, London, 1959.

Cooper, Duff, *Haig* (2 vols.), London, 1935–36.

Cowles, Virginia, *The Kaiser* [life of William II of Germany], London, 1963.

—— *The Last Tsar and Tsarina* [life of Nicholas II of Russia], London, 1977.

Dalton, Charles, "Francois de la Rochefoucauld, Marquis de Montandre". Proceedings of the Royal Artillery Institution, June 1896.

Danchev, Alex, *Very Special Relationship. Field Marshal Sir John Dill and the Anglo- American Alliance 1941–1944*, London, 1986.

Davidson, J., *Haig, Master of the Field*, London, 1953.

De Groot, G.J., *Douglas Haig 1861–1928*, London, 1988.

Dennis, P., and Preston, S., *Soldiers as Statesmen* [Lord Byng in Canada], London, 1976.

Dewar, George A.B., and Boraston, J.H., *Sir Douglas Haig's Command, December 19, 1915 to November 11, 1918* (2 vols.), London, 1922.

Donaldson, Frances, *Edward VIII*, London, 1974.

Duncan, G.S., *Douglas Haig as I knew him*, London, 1966.

Durand, Mortimer, *The Life of Field Marshal Sir George White VC*, 2 vols., London, 1915.

Elsmie, G.R., *Field Marshal Sir Donald Stewart. An account of his life, mainly in his own words*, London, 1903.

Evans, Geoffrey, *Slim as Military Commander*, London, 1969.

Fergusson, James, *Argyll in the '45*, London, 1951.

Forbes, Archibald, *Colin Campbell, Lord Clyde*, London, 1895.

Forrest, George W., *Life of Field Marshal Sir Neville Chamberlain*, London, 1909.

Frankland, Noble, *Prince Henry: Duke of Gloucester*, London, 1980.

Fraser, David, *Alanbrooke*, London, 1982.

Fulford, Roger, *Royal Dukes. The father and uncles of Queen Victoria*, London, 1933.

Gardner, Brian, *Allenby*, London, 1965.

Gash, Norman (ed.), *Wellington. Studies in the Military and Political Career of the First Duke of Wellington*, Manchester, 1990.

Glover, Michael, *Wellington as Military Commander*, London, 1968.

Graham, Evelyn, *The Life Story of King Alfonso XIII*, London, 1930.

Greenwood, Alexander, *Field Marshal Auchinleck, A Biography*, Pentland Press, 1990.

Griffith, Paddy G., *Wellington: Commander. The Iron Duke's Generalship*, Chichester, 1984.

Guedalla, Philip, *The Duke* [life of Wellington], London, 1940.

Haig, The Countess, *The Man I knew*, London, 1936.

Hamilton, Nigel, *Monty: The Making of a General, 1887–1942*, London, 1981.

—— *Monty: Master of the Battlefield, 1942–1944*, London, 1983.

—— *Monty: The Field Marshal, 1944–1976*, London, 1976.

—— *Monty: The Battles of Field Marshal Bernard Montgomery*, London, 1981.

Hannah, W.H., *"Bobs", Kipling's General. The Life of Field Marshal Earl Roberts of Kandahar VC*, London, 1972.

Hardinge, C., *Viscount Hardinge and the advance of British Dominion into the Punjab*, Oxford, 1900.

Harington, Charles, *Plumer of Messines*, London, 1935.

Harris, J.P., *Men, Ideas and Tanks. British Military thought and armoured forces 1903–1939*, [inc. brief studies of FMs Milne, Montgomery-

Massingberd and Deverell as Chiefs of the Imperial General Staff], Manchester, 1995.

Heald, Tim, *The Duke. A Portrait of Prince Philip*, London, 1990.

Heffer, Simon, *Power and Place. The Political Consequences of King Edward VII*, London, 1998.

Hetherington, John, *Blamey*, Melbourne, 1954.

Hibbert, Christopher, *Wellington: A Personal History*, London, 1997.

—— *The Destruction of Lord Raglan*, London, 1961.

—— *Edward VII. A Portrait*, London, 1976.

Hollis, Leslie, *The Captain General. A Life of Prince Philip, Duke of Edinburgh*, London, 1961.

Holmes, E. Richard, *The Little Field Marshal. Sir John French*, London, 1981.

Horner, David, *Blamey, Commander-in-Chief*, Canberra, (forthcoming publication).

Howarth, Patrick, *George VI. A New Biography*, London, 1987.

Howarth, T.E.B., *Monty at Close Quarters. Recollections of the man*, London, 1985.

Hughes, Matthew, *Allenby and British Policy in the Middle East 1917–1919*, London, 1999.

Ingham, Kenneth, *Jan Christian Smuts. The Conscience of a South African*, London, 1986.

Ironside, E. (ed.), *High Road to Command. The Diaries of Major-General Sir Edmund Ironside 1920–1922*, London, 1972.

Jackson, William, *Alexander of Tunis as Military Commander*, London, 1971.

James, David, *Lord Roberts*, London, 1954.

James, Lawrence, *Imperial Warrior. The Life and Times of Field Marshal Viscount Allenby 1861–1936*, London, 1993.

—— *The Iron Duke. A military biography of Wellington*, London, 1992.

James, Robert Rhodes, *Albert, Prince Consort. A Biography*, London, 1983.

—— *A Spirit Undaunted. The Political Role of George VI*, London, 1998.

Janetschek, O., (tr.Whitman,H.S.) *The Emperor Franz Joseph*, London, 1953.

Judd, Denis, *King George VI 1895–1952*, London, 1982.

—— *The Life and Times of George V*, London, 1973.

Keegan, John, (ed.), *Churchill's Generals*, London, 1991.

Kohut, Thomas A., *Wilhelm II and the Germans, a Study in Leadership*, Oxford, 1996.

Lee, Sidney, *King Edward VII. A Biography* (2 vols.), London, 1927.

Lee-Warner, William, *Memoirs of Field Marshal Sir Henry Wylie Norman*, London, 1908.

Lehman, Joseph E., *All Sir Garnet. A life of Field Marshal Lord Wolseley*, London,1964.

Lewin, Ronald, *Slim: The Standard Bearer*, London, 1976.

—— *Montgomery as Military Commander*, London, 1971.

—— *The Chief. Field Marshal Lord Wavell, Commander-in-Chief and Viceroy 1939 –1947*, London, 1980.

Liddell Hart, Basil, *Foch, The Man of Orleans*, London, 1931.

Lieven, Dominic, *Nicholas II: Emperor of all the Russias* [London, 1990].

Longford, Elizabeth (Countess of), *Wellington. The Years of the Sword*, London, 1972.

—— *Wellington. Pillar of State*, London, 1972.

Macleod, R., and Kelly, D., (ed.) *The Ironside Diaries 1937–1940*, London, 1962.

Macleod, R., "Field Marshal Lord Ironside, his life and times" (Journal of the Royal Artillery, vol. CVII, no.1, March 1980).

Magnus, Philip., *Kitchener, Portrait of an Imperialist*, London, 1958.

—— *King Edward the Seventh*, London, 1964.

Marcus, Harold G., *Haile Selassie. The Formative Years 1892–1936*, London, 1987.

Marshall-Cornwall, James, *Haig as Military Commander*, London, 1973.

Massie, Robert, *Nicholas and Alexandra* [life of Nicholas II of Russia], London, 1968.

Maurice, Frederick, and Arthur, George, *The Life of Lord Wolseley*, London, 1924.

Middlemas, Keith, *The Life and Times of George VI*, London, 1974.

—— *The Life and Times of Edward VII*, London, 1972.

Millin, Sarah Gertrude, *General Smuts*, London, 1936.

Milner, David, "The Lost Warrior. Field Marshal Sir William Rowan, GCB". Friends of the Waterloo Committee. Publication No.2, August 1998.

Montgomery, Bernard, (Field Marshal Viscount), *The Memoirs of Field Marshal the Viscount Montgomery of Alamein*, London, 1958.

—— *Normandy to the Baltic*, London,1947.

Montgomery, Brian, *A Field Marshal in the Family*, London, 1973.

Moore Smith, G.C., *The Life of John Colborne, Field Marshal Lord Seaton*, London, 1903.

Moorehead, Alan, *Montgomery. A Biography*, London, 1946.

Mosley, Leonard, *Haile Selassie. The Conquering Lion*, London, 1965.

—— *Hirohito. Emperor of Japan*, London, 1966.

Napier, H.D., *Field Marshal Lord Napier of Magdala*, London, 1927.

Negash, Askale, *Haile Selassie*, New York, 1989.

Nicol, Graham, *Uncle George. Field Marshal Lord Milne of Salonika and Rubislaw*, London, 1976.

Nicolson, Harold, *King George V. His Life and Reign*, London, 1952.

Nicolson, Nigel, *Alex. The Life of Field Marshal Earl Alexander of Tunis*, London, 1973.

North, John, (ed.), *The Alexander Memoirs 1940–1945*, London, 1962.

Parkinson, Roger, *The Auk. Auchinleck, Victor at Alamein*, London, 1977.

Petrie, Charles, *King Alfonso XIII and his age*, London, 1963.

Pilar of Bavaria, and Chapman-Huston, D., *Don Alfonso XIII. A Study in Monarchy*, London, 1931.

Pollock, John, *Kitchener: The Road to Omdurman*, London, 1998.

—— *Kitchener*, Vol.I, London 1998.

Powell, Geoffrey, *Plumer. The Soldier's General*, London, 1990.

Rait, R.S., *The Life and Campaigns of Hugh, 1st Viscount Gough, Field Marshal*, 2 vols., London, 1903.

—— *The Life of Sir Frederick Paul Haines*, London, 1911.

Recouly, Raymond, *Foch. His Character and Leadership*, London, 1920.

Roberts, Frederick Sleigh, *Forty-One Years in India* [memoirs of FM Lord Roberts], 2 vols., London, 1897.

Robertson, William (F.M. Sir), *From Private to Field Marshal*, London, 1921.

—— *Soldiers and Statesmen 1914–1918*, 2 vols., London, 1926.

Robson, Brian, (ed.), *Roberts in India. The Military Papers of Field Marshal Lord Roberts, 1876–1893*, London, 1993.

Rohl, John C.G., *Young Wilhelm. The Kaiser's Early Life 1859–1888*, Cambridge, 1998.

Royle, Trevor, *The Kitchener Enigma*, London, 1985.

St. Aubyn, Giles, *The Royal George. The life of HRH Prince George of Cambridge 1819–1904*, London, 1963.

Savage, Raymond, *Allenby of Armageddon*, London, 1925.

Secrett, T., *Twenty-Five Years with Earl Haig*, London, 1929.

Severns, Karen, *Hirohito*, New York, 1988.

Sheppard, Edgar, *George, Duke of Cambridge. A Memoir of his Private Life based on the journals and correspondence of His Royal Highness*, 2 vols., London, 1906.

Slim, Willam (FM Viscount), *Unofficial History*, London, 1959.

—— *Defeat into Victory*, London, 1956.

Stuart, Louisa, *Some Account of John, [5th] Duke of Argyll and his Family*, London, 1863.

Sweetman, John, *Raglan, from the Peninsula to the Crimea*, London, 1993.

Terraine, John, *Douglas Haig, The Educated Soldier*, London, 1963.

Thompson, R.W., *The Montgomery Legend*, London, 1967.

—— *Montgomery. The Field Marshal*, London, 1969.

Van Overstraeden, R., (trans. Savill, M.), *The War Diaries of Albert I, King of the Belgians*, London, 1954.

Verner, W., *The Military Life of HRH George, Duke of Cambridge*, 2 vols., London, 1905.

W. ("H.W") "Field Marshal Sir Archibald Montgomery-Massingberd". Journal of the Royal Artillery Institution, Vol. LXXV, No.1, January 1947.

Warner, Philip, *Auchinleck, the lonely soldier*, London, 1981.

—— *Field Marshal Earl Haig*, London, 1991.

Wavell, Archibald (Field Marshal Earl), *Allenby, Soldier and Statesman*, London, 1942.

Wellington, 2nd Duke of, (ed.), *The Despatches, Correspondence, and Memorials of Field Marshal Arthur, Duke of Wellington*, 13 vols., London, 1856–58.

Wheeler-Bennett, John W., *King George VI. His Life and Reign*, London, 1958.

Whitworth, Rex, *Field Marshal Lord Ligonier*, Oxford, 1958.

Wilkes, Lyall, *Festing- Field Marshal. A study of Front-Line Frankie*, Sussex, 1991.

—— (Moon, P., ed.) *The Viceroy's Journal*, Oxford, 1963.

Williams, Jeffery, *Byng of Vimy*, London, 1983.

Wilson, Henry Maitland (FM Lord Wilson), *Eight Years Overseas, 1939–1947*, London, 1948.

Wilson, Joan, *A Soldier's Wife. Wellington's Marriage*, London, 1987.

Wilson, Lawrence, *The Incredible Kaiser. A portrait of William II*, London, 1963.

Winter, Denis, *Haig's Command: A Reassessment*, London, 1991.

Wolseley, Garnet (FM Viscount), *The Story of a Soldier's Life*, 2 vols., London, 1903.

Wood, E., *Winnowed Memories* [memoirs of FM Sir Evelyn Wood], London, 1917.

—— *From Midshipman to Field Marshal*, 2 vols., London, 1906.

Woodham-Smith, Cecil, *The Reason Why* [Lord Lucan and Lord Cardigan in the Charge of the Light Brigade at Balaclava], London, 1953.

Woodward, David R., *The Military Correspondence of Field Marshal Sir William Robertson, Dec 1915-Feb 1918*, London, 1989.

Wright, M.M., *The Military Papers, 1940–48, of Field Marshal Sir Claude Auchinleck*, John Rylands University, 1988.

Yonge, Ian, "John Colborne- Officer and Gentleman", Association of Friends of the Waterloo Committee, Publication No.2, August 1998.

Ziegler, P.J. *King Edward VIII. The Official Biography*, London, 1990.

ARMY, DIVISIONAL AND REGIMENTAL HISTORIES

Almack, Edward, *The History of the Second Dragoons "Royal Scots Greys"*, London, 1908.

Askwith, W.H., *List of Officers of the Royal Artillery 1716–1899*, 4th ed., London, 1900.

Atkinson, C.T., *The Royal Hampshire Regiment*, vol. I, Glasgow, 1930.

—— *History of the Royal Dragoons 1661–1934*, Glasgow, [1935].

—— *The South Wales Borderers, 24th Foot, 1689–1937*, Cambridge, 1937.

Barclay, C.N., *History of the 16th/5th The Queen's Own Royal Lancers 1925 to 1961*, Aldershot, 1963.

Barrett, C.R.B., *The 7th (Queen's Own) Hussars*, 2 vols., London, 1914.

—— *The 85th King's Light Infantry*, London, 1913.

—— *History of the XIII Hussars*, 2 vols., Edinburgh, 1911.

Barrow, T.J., (ed.), *The Story of the Bedfordshire and Hertfordshire Regiment*, 2 vols., [Farnham], 1986.

Beckett, Ian F.W., *The Army and the Curragh Incident 1914*, London, 1986.

Blake, George, *Mountain and Flood. The History of the 52nd (Lowland) Division 1939–1945*, Glasgow, 1950.

Brereton, J.M., *A History of the 4th/7th Royal Dragoon Guards and their predecessors 1685–1980*, Catterick, 1982.

—— *The 7th Queen's Own Hussars*, London, 1975.

Bruce, Anthony, *The Purchase System in the British Army, 1660–1871*, London, 1980.

Buchan, John, *The History of the Royal Scots Fusiliers, 1678–1918*, London, 1925.

Burden, P.N., *History of the East Lancashire Regiment in the War, 1939–1945*, Manchester, 1953.

Callwell, C., and Headlam, J., *The History of the Royal Artillery from the Indian Mutiny to the Great War*, 2 vols., Woolwich, 1937.

Cannon, R., *Historical Records of the 1st or King's Regiment of Dragoon Guards*, London, 1837.

—— *Historical Records of the 6th Regiment of Dragoon Guards (The Carabiniers)*, London, 1836.

—— *Historical Records of the First or Royal Regiment of Foot*, London, 1847.

—— *Historical Records of the 15th or Yorkshire East Riding Regiment of Foot*, London, 1848.

—— *Historical Records of the 34th or the Cumberland Regiment of Foot*, London, 1844.

Chandler, David G. and Beckett, Ian F.W., (ed.), *The Oxford History of the British Army*, London, 1996.

Colenbrander, H.T., *Willem II. Koning der Nederlanden*, Amsterdam, 1938.

Cunliffe, Marcus, *The Royal Irish Fusiliers 1793–1950*, London, 1952.

—— *History of the Royal Warwickshire Regiment 1919–1955*, London, 1956.

Daniell, David Scott, *Cap of Honour. The Story of the Gloucestershire Regiment*, London, 1951.

Denman, T., *Ireland's Unknown Soldiers. The 16th (Irish) Division in the Great War 1914–1918*, London, 1992.

Duncan, Francis, *History of the Royal Regiment of Artillery*, 2nd ed., London, 1874.

Dunsterville, A., *History of the 20th (Duke of Cambridge's Own) Infantry (Brownlow's Punjabis)*, 2 vols., Devonport, 1909, and Frome, 1922.

Evans, Roger, *The Story of the Fifth Royal Inniskilling Dragoon Guards*, Aldershot, 1951.

Everett, Henry, *The History of the Somerset Light Infantry (Prince Albert's) 1685–1914*, London, 1934.

ffrench-Blake, R.L.V., *A History of the 17th/21st Lancers 1922–1959*, London, 1962.

Filmer-Bennett, John, *The Royal Inniskilling Fusiliers, a Record of the Regiment's Activities 1954–1968*, London, 1978.

Fortescue. The Hon. Sir John W., *A History of the British Army*, (13 vols), London, 1899–1930.

Fox, Frank, *The Royal Inniskilling Fusiliers in the Second World War*, Aldershot, 1951.

Fyler, A.E., *The History of the 50th or (The Queen's Own) Regiment*, London, 1893.

Gardyne, C.G., *The Life of a Regiment: The History of the Gordon Highlanders*, London, 1903.

Gibbs, H. R. K., *Historical Record of the 6th Gurkha Rifles 1919–1948*, Aldershot, 1955.

Graham, H., *History of the Sixteenth, The Queen's Light Dragoons (Lancers) 1759 to 1912*, London, 1912.

Graves, C., *The Royal Ulster Rifles* (vol. III of regimental history), pub. privately, 1948.

Gray, Jeffery, *The Commonwealth Armies and the Korean War*, Manchester, 1988.

Gretton, G.L., *The Campaigns and History of the Royal Irish Regiment from 1684 to 1902*, Edinburgh, 1911.

—— *The Royal Inniskilling Fusiliers, being the History of the Regiment from December 1688 to July 1914*, London, 1928.

Gurney, R., *History of the Northamptonshire Regiment 1742–1934*, Aldershot, 1935.

Hamilton, F.W., *The Origin and History of the First or Grenadier Guards*, 3 vols., London, 1874.

Hamilton, H.B., *Historical Record of the 14th (King's) Hussars 1715–1900*, London, 1901.

Harclerode, Peter, *"Go To It". The Illustrated History of the 6th Airborne Division*, London, 1990.

Hayden, F. A., *Historical Records of the 79th, Hindostan, Regiment*, Lichfield, 1908.

Headlam, C., *History of the Guards Division in the Great War 1915–1918*, London, 1924.

Higgins, R., *The Records of the King's Own Borderers or Old Edinburgh Regiment*, London, 1873.

Jackson, William, and Bramall, Edwin, (Field Marshal Lord), *The Chiefs. The Story of the United Kingdom Chiefs of Staff*, London, 1992.

Johnston, S.H.F., *The History of the Cameronians (Scottish Rifles)*, Aldershot, 1957.

Kingsford, C.L., *The Story of the Royal Warwickshire Regiment*, London, 1921.

—— *The Story of the Duke of Cambridge's Own (Middlesex Regiment)*, London, 1916.

Kipling, Rudyard, *The Irish Guards in the Great War* (2 vols.), London, 1923.

Knight, H.R., *Historical Records of the Buffs (East Kent Regiment) 3rd Foot*, London, 1905.

Leaske, J.C. and McCance, H.M., *The Regimental Records of The Royal Scots*, Dublin, 1915.

Lee, Albert, *The History of the Tenth Foot (The Lincolnshire Regiment)*, 2 vols., Aldershot and London, 1911.

—— *History of the Thirty-third Foot*, Norwich, 1922.

Leeke, William, *The History of Lord Seaton's Regiment (The 52nd Light Infantry) at Waterloo*, 2 vols, London, 1866.

Lloyd, F., and Russell, A., *First or Grenadier Guards in South Africa 1899–1902*, London, 1907.

Lomax, D.A., *A History of the Services of the 41st (The Welch) Regiment 1719–1895*, Devonport, 1899.

McCance, S., *History of the Royal Munster Fusiliers*, 2 vols., Aldershot, 1927.

McGregor, M., *Officers of the Durham Light Infantry 1758 to 1968*, [Esher, 1989].

Mackay, J.N., *History of 7th Duke of Edinburgh's Own Gurkha Rifles*, Edinburgh, 1962.

Mackinnon, D., *Origin and Services of the Coldstream Guards*, 2 vols., London, 1833.

Mann, Michael, *The Regimental History of 1st The Queen's Dragoon Guards*, Norwich, 1993.

Marden, T.O., *A Short History of the Sixth Division August 1914-March 1919*, London, 1920.

Maurice, F. B., *The 16th Foot. A History of the Bedfordshire and Hertfordshire Regiment*, London, 1931.

Merewether, J.W., and Smith, F., *The Indian Corps in France*, 2nd ed,. London, 1919.

Molesworth, George, *The History of the Somerset Light Infantry (Prince Albert's) 1919–1945*, Regimental Committee, Somerset Light Infantry, 1951.

Molloy, H., *History of the 5th Royal Gurkha Rifles (Frontier Force) 1858–1928*, Aldershot, 1929.

Moorsom, W.S., *Historical Record of the Fifty-Second Regiment (Oxfordshire Light Infantry) 1755–1858*, London, 1860.

Murray, Robert H., *The History of the VIII King's Royal Irish Hussars 1693–1927*, 2 vols., Cambridge, 1928.

Oatts, L.B., *Proud Heritage. The Story of the Highland Light Infantry*, 4 vols., Glasgow, 1952–1963.

—— *I Serve. Regimental History of the 3rd Carabiniers*, Norwich, 1966.

Oldfield, J.B., *The Green Howards in Malaya 1949–1952*, Aldershot, 1953.

Petre, F.L., *The History of the Norfolk Regiment*, 2 vols., Norwich, 1924.

Pomeroy, R.L., *The Story of a Regiment of Horse* [5th Dragoon Guards], 2 vols., London,1924.

Porter, W., *History of the Corps of Royal Engineers*, 2 vols., London, 1889.

Powell, Geoffrey, *The History of the Green Howards*, London, 1992.

Qureshi, M.I., *The First Punjabis. History of the First Punjab Regiment 1759–1956*, Aldershot, 1958.

Raikes, G.A., *Roll of the Officers of the York and Lancaster Regiment 1756–1884*, London, 1885.

Russell, A., *First or Grenadier Guards in South Africa 1899–1902*, London, 1907.

Salmond, J., *The History of the 51st Highland Division 1939–1945*, Edinburgh, 1953.

Sheppard, E.W., *The Ninth Queen's Royal Lancers 1715–1936*, Aldershot, 1936.

Singh, Rajendra, *The Grenadiers. Historical Record of the Regiment*. Nasirabad, 1962.

Smyth, B., *A History of the Lancashire Fusiliers*, 2 vols., London, 1903.

Sutherland, Douglas, *Tried and Valiant. The History of the Border Regiment (34th and 55th Regiments of Foot) 1702–1759*, London, 1972.

Sym, John, *Seaforth Highlanders*, Aldershot, 1962.

Verney, Peter, *The Micks, the story of the Irish Guards 1900 to 1970*, London, 1970.

Vibart, H. M., *Addiscombe. Its Heroes and Men of Note*, London, 1894.

Wake, Hereward, and Deedes, W.F. (ed.), *Swift and Bold. The Story of the King's Royal Rifle Corps in the Second World War 1939–1945*, Aldershot, 1949.

Walker, H.M., *A History of the Northumberland Fusiliers 1674–1912*, London, 1919.

Watkin, H., and Pragnell, W., *A Short History of the IV Queen's Own Hussars*, Meerut, 1925.

Watson, W.A., *King George's Own Central India Horse*, London, 1930.

Weaver, Lawrence, *The Story of the Royal Scots*, London, 1915.

Webb, E.A., *History of the 12th (The Suffolk) Regiment 1685–1913*, London, 1914.

Wheater, W., *Historical Record of the Seventh or Royal Regiment of Fusiliers*, Leeds, 1875.

Whitton, F.E., *The History of the Prince of Wales's Leinster Regiment*, 2 vols., Aldershot, 1924.

Willcox, W.T., *The Historical Records of the Fifth (Royal Irish) Lancers*, London, 1908.

Williams, G.T., *The Historical Records of the Eleventh Hussars, Prince Albert's Own*, London, 1908.

Wylly, H.C., *XVth (The King's) Hussars 1759 to 1913*, London, 1914.

—— *Neill's "Blue Caps"* [Madras Fusiliers; Royal Dublin Fusiliers], 3 vols., London, 1923.

Wyrall, E., *The East Yorkshire Regiment in the Great War 1914–1918*, London, 1928.

—— *The History of the Second Division 1914–1918*, 2 vols., London, 1921–1922.

INDEX

358

362

British Army (continued)
Devonshire and Dorset Regt, 114, 332
Dorset Yeomanry, 57
Dublin Fusiliers, Royal, 27
Duke of Cornwall's Light Infantry, 107, 111, 332
Duke of Cumberland's Sharpshooters, 117
Duke of Edinburgh's Royal Regt, 239, 333
Duke of Lancaster's Own Yeomanry, 107, 137, 140
Duke of Wellington's Regt, 35, 333, see also 33rd Foot
Duke of York's Greek Light Inf, 129–30
Durham Light Infantry, 237, 332
East Kent Regt, see Buffs
East Kent Yeomanry, Royal, 27
East Lancashire Regt, 103, 119, 333
East Yorkshire Regt, 101, 103, 140, 332
Electrical and Mechanical Engineers, Royal, 79, 239, 285, 335
Engineers, Royal, 7, 26, 61, 62, 111, 137, 140, 142, 143, 192, 194, 224, 225, 228, 230, 257, 330; East Anglian Divisional, 195; East Lancashire, 214; Glasgow Volunteer, 195; Gloucester Volunteer, 43; Special Reserve, 263
Essex Regt, 68, 332
Finsbury Rifles, 85, 167, 170
Fusiliers, Royal, (City of London Regt), 137, 214, 331, see also 7th Foot
Fusiliers, Royal Regiment of, 144, 331
Glider Pilot Regt, 59
Gloucestershire, Berkshire and Wiltshire Regt, Royal, 239, 333
Gloucestershire Regt, 176, 333
Gordon Highlanders, 107, 176, 296, 334
Green Howards, 35, 183, 184, 185, 332, see also 19th Foot
Green Jackets, Royal, 54, 56, 120, 145, 334 see also 2nd Green Jackets; 3rd Green Jackets
Grenadier Guards, 13, 27, 106, 108, 111, 114, 137, 140, 143, 197, 198, 239, 279, 280, 281, 283, 294, 330, see also 1st Foot Guards
Gurkha Rifles, Royal, 86, 335, see also 2nd Gurkha Rifles; 6th Gurkha Rifles; 7th Gurkha Rifles
Hampshire and Isle of Wight Militia Artillery, 27
Hampshire Regt, Royal, 28, 137, 331
Hertfordshire Regt, 198
Highland Light Infantry, 27, 28, 80, 332
Highlanders (Seaforth, Gordon and Cameron), 239, 334
Honourable Artillery Company, 13, 107, 111–12, 118, 137, 283
Horse Grenadier Guards, 25, 127, 153, 234, 245, 272
Horse Guards, Royal, (the Blues), 45, 72, 73, 94, 111, 118, 137, 140, 150, 151, 159,
200, 203, 237, 253, 255, 277, 294, 313, 316, 327, see also Blues and Royals
Horse Guards, Troops of, 25, 52, 72, 234, see also Life Guards
Inniskilling Dragoons, see 6th Dragoons; 5th Dragoon Guards (Royal Inniskilling)
Inniskilling Fusiliers, Royal, 29, 34, 176, 212, 334
Inns of Court Regt, 243, 316
Intelligence Corps, 239, 274, 275, 277, 335
Irish Fusiliers, Royal, 137, 149, 273, 274, 277, 334
Irish Guards, 14, 15, 17, 106, 111, 135, 137, 140, 198, 249, 250, 330
Irish Rangers, Royal, 176, 334
Irish Regt, Royal, see also 18th Foot, 122, 135, 304, 313
Irish Rifles, Royal, 208, 307, 334
Isle of Wight Rifles, Princess Beatrice's, 137
Kent Yeomanry, see 97 Field Bde RA; East Kent Yeomanry, Royal
King Edward's Horse (King's Colonials), 137
King's German Legion, 9
King's (Liverpool) Regt, 85, 111, 331
King's Own (Royal Lancaster) Regt, 107, 111, 331
King's Own Scottish Borderers, 159, 333
King's Royal Rifle Corps, 53, 54, 85, 137, 140, 143, 144, 145, 153, 334, see also 60th Rifles
King's Shropshire Light Infantry, 29, 332
Leicestershire Yeomanry, 140, 233
Leicestershire and Derbyshire Yeomanry, 239
Leinster Regt, 102, 103, 111
Life Guards, 23, 25, 41, 42, 52, 92, 96, 111, 115, 137, 140, 153, 170, 173, 327
Limerick Militia, 148
London Irish Rifles, 17, 26, 150, 277
London Regt, (8th), 107; (11th), 117; (14th), 159; (15th), 107, 111; (16th), 111; (18th), 28
London Rifle Brigade, (1st City of London Rifle Volunteer Corps), 143
London Scottish Rifles, 159
London Yeomanry, 1st County of, 195
Longford Militia, 304
Loyal (North Lancashire) Regt, 274
Machine Gun Corps, 167, 168
Manchester Regt, 137, 331
Middlesex Regt, 111, 143, 331
Middlesex Rifle Volunteer Corps, (14th), 316; (28th), 28, 150
Middlesex Rifles, Royal, 2nd (Edmonton) Militia, 64
Middlesex Yeomanry, 143
Military Police, Royal, 39, 82, 185, 335
Munster Fusiliers, Royal, 164
Norfolk Militia Artillery, 107
Norfolk Regt, (Royal), 107, 137, 140, 287, 332
Norfolk Yeomanry, 107, 137

Wade, George, 92, 202, **284–6**, 320, 332, 333
Walcheren (1809), 63, 69, 146, 154, 236, 257
Wales, Princes of, *see* Edward VII; Edward VIII; George IV
Walpole, Sir Robert, Prime Minister, 73, 92, 99, 272
Warburg (1760), 153, 180
Waterloo (1815), 6, 47, 63, 91, 95, 147, 200, 236, 256, 257, 267, 294, 298, 317, 318
Wavell, Sir Archibald, Earl Wavell, 16, 32, 33, 34, 50, **287–91**, 309, 325, 340
Wellesley, Sir Arthur, Duke of Wellington, 3, 6, 7, 13, 26, 61, 69, 75, 91, 146, 150, 172, 173, 236, 255, 267, 268, **291–5**, 297, 298, 321, 327, 329, 330, 332, 333, 334, 338, 342
Wellesley, Richard, Marquess Wellesley, 89, 292
Wellington College, 29, 35, 37, 273, 340
Wellington, Duke of *see* Wellesley, Sir Arthur
Western Desert campaigns (1940–43), 32–3, 76, 169, 216–17, 289, 310
Westminster School, 41, 94, 154, 199, 237, 267, 340
White, Sir George, 131, 156, **295–7**, 323, 334, 339, 341
White Plains (1776), 167
Whitewell, John, *see* Griffin, John
Wilkes, John, 74, 93
Willems (1794), 95, 117, 128, 182
William (Wilhelm) II, HM German Emperor, 4, 26, 27, 107, 133, 226, **299–301**, 323, 327
William (Willem) II, HM King of the Netherlands, Prince of Orange, 3, 91, 201, **297–8**, 321
William III, HM King, (William of Orange), 97, 99, 100, 165, 211, 245, 272
William IV, HM King, 3, 10, 90, 113, 114, 118, 183
William Augustus, HRH Duke of Cumberland, 82, 93, 179, 200, 203, 277, 278

William Frederick, HRH 2nd Duke of Gloucester and Edinburgh, **301–2**, 321, 330, 333
William Henry, HRH 1st Duke of Gloucester and Edinburgh, 3, 180, **302–3**, 320, 330, 332
Wilson, Sir Henry Hughes, 6, 22, 132, 158, 198, 250, 252, 288, **303–8**, 323, 334, 339
Wilson, Sir Henry Maitland, Lord Wilson, 50, 289, **303–8**, 325, 334, 339, 342
Winchester College, 75, 90, 118, 287, 291, 340
Windsor, HRH Duke of, *see* Edward VIII, HM King
Wingate, Maj Gen Orde, 162, 289, 290
Wolseley, Sir Garnet, Viscount Wolseley, 27, 130, 143, 152, 164, 192, 205, 228, 248, 296, **311–14**, 315, 316, 323, 327, 332, 333
Wood, Sir Evelyn, 7, 8, 152, 155, 192, **314–16**, 323, 328, 329, 332, 334, 339
Woodford, Sir Alexander, **316–17**, 322, 330, 332, 333, 340
Woolwich, *see* Royal Military Academy

York, Dukes of, *see* Frederick Augustus, HRH Duke of York and Albany; George V, HM King; George VI, HM King
Yorke, Sir Charles, **318**, 322, 331, 332, 333, 334
Yoshihito, HIM Emperor of Japan, 177, **319**, 323
Ypres, battles of; first (1914), 14, 21, 56, 66, 87, 133, 158, 186, 198, 209, 213; second (1915), 21, 101, 109, 242; third (1917), 14, 57, 101, 158, 186, 191, 198, 214, 242, 280, 308
Ypres, Earl of, *see* French, Sir John

Zand River, 20, 131, 209, 229, 249, 251
Zimbabwe, *see* Rhodesia
Zulu War, 152, 312, 315